SPORT GOVERNANCE AND POLICY DEVELOPMENT

An Ethical Approach to Managing Sport in the 21st Century

Thomas H. Sawyer
Indiana State University

Kimberly J. Bodey
Indiana State University

Lawrence W. Judge
Ball State University

Sagamore Publishing, L.L.C.
Champaign, Illinois

Publishers: Joseph J. Bannon/Peter Bannon
General Manager: Doug Sanders
Production Manager: Jose Hernandez
Interior Design: Michelle Dressen
Copy Editor: Susan Moyer
Cover Design: Meghan Rosselli
Cover Images: Image Copyright tm-media 2008
                    used under license from Shutterstock, Inc.

Library of Congress Catalog Card Number: 2001012345
ISBN 978-1-57167-536-1
Printed in the United States.   .

Sagamore Publishing, L.L.C.
804 North Neil Street
Champaign, IL 61820
www.sagamorepub.com

Dedication

This book is dedicated to Dr. Sawyer's grandchildren,
Grayson James Rosselli (2004) and Findlay Elise Sawyer (2005)
and Alexandra Alsip (1995).

This book is also dedicated to Dr. Bodey's father,
Christopher F. Bodey.

Dr Judge dedicates this book to his father, Dr. Ira Lee Judge. He was inspiring,
encouraging, and motivating to all of the lives he touched. He showed many aspiring
young students how to achieve their full potential through his feedback, insight,
guidance and countless number of hours he dedicated. It was through his inspiration
with the help of his assistant coach, my mother Joan that I embarked on my journey
into education.

Table of Contents

Preface vii
Foreword ix
Acknowledgments xi
Author Biographies xii

Part I   **Organizational Governance and Policy Development** 1
Chapter 1   Introduction to Sport Organizations and Governance 3
Thomas H. Sawyer and Kimberly J. Bodey, Indiana State University
Chapter 2   Planning Function 21
Thomas H. Sawyer, Indiana State University
Chapter 3   Policy Development in Sport 39
Kimberly J. Bodey, Indiana state University

Part II   **Ethical Decision Making and Professional Ethics** 61
Chapter 4   Foundations of Ethical Decision Making 63
Kimberly J. Bodey, Indiana State University
Chapter 5   Organizational Ethics 77
Kimberly J. Bodey, Indiana State University

Part III   **Sport Governance Organizations** 91
Chapter 6   Impact of Government on Athletic Associations 93
Thomas H. Sawyer, Indiana State University
Chapter 7   Youth Sport Governance 109
Thomas H. Sawyer, Indiana State University
Chapter 8   Interscholastic Sport Governance 127
Thomas H. Sawyer, Indiana State University
Chapter 9   Recreational Sport 149
Thomas H. Sawyer, Indiana State University
Chapter 10   Intercollegiate Sport Governance 165
Lawrence Judge, Ball State University
Chapter 11   Governance of Professional Sport 197
Thomas H. Sawyer, Indiana State University
Chapter 12   Motorsports Governance 223
Thomas H. Sawyer, Indiana state University
Chapter 13   Olympic Sport Governance 241
Lawrence W. Judge, Ball State University
Chapter 14   Paralympics Sport Governance 267
Thomas H. Sawyer, Indiana State University
Ronald Davis, Texas Christian University
Chapter 15   Special Olympics Governance 285
Thomas H. Sawyer, Indiana State University
Ronald Davis, Texas Christian University

Chapter 16   Senior Olympics/Senior Games Governance 297
             Nathan A. Schaumleffel, Indiana State University
Chapter 17   Community Sport Support Structures..309
             Thomas H. Sawyer, Indiana State University
Index 323

Preface

SPORT GOVERNANCE AND POL-ICY DEVELOPMENT: *An Ethical Approach to Managing Sport in the 21st Century* is designed for use in sport governance and policy development courses with upper-level undergraduate students or graduate students. It focuses on two NASPE/NASSM curriculum standards that are applicable to both the undergraduate and graduate level curriculum. These standards are as follows: Standard 5 (a) moral and ethical developmental theories, (b) teleological and deontological theories of ethics, (c) models of ethical analysis, (d) code of professional ethics, personal and management values, and (e) situational analysis; and Standard 11 includes (a) identification of governing bodies in amateur and professional sport, (b) organizational structure of a variety of governing bodies, (c) authority and functions of various governing bodies, (d) requirements for membership in governing bodies, sanctions and appeal processes utilized by governing bodies, and (e) influence of governmental bodies and sports commissions on sport governing bodies.

The premise behind this book, is as follows: After studying from this book the student should be familiar with (a) organization theory, leadership, and policy development, (b) sport organizations, their authority, organizational structure, and functions, and impact issues, and (c) ethical and moral issues related to sport governance in intrinsic and extrinsic dimensions, as well as developing a personal philosophy regarding social responsibility in sport governance settings.

This book focuses primarily on American sport organizations. It challenges students to integrate organization theory and behavior with leadership and governance to ensure sound policy development practices. It outlines where the power rests in an organization and how individual sport organizations fit into the greater sport industry.

This book is organized into three major sections including 17 chapters. The purpose of having these three sections is to establish a theoretical knowledge base related to governance, leadership, and policy development that future sport managers need to function within sport organizations, to explain how ethical and moral issues impart sport organizations and managers, and to present information relating to how sport organizations are organized and the impact issues sport managers struggle with on a regular basis.

Part I introduces the student to organizational governance and policy development in the world in general and specifically to the sport industry. Chapter 1 develops the foundation for organizational structure, theory, and behavior, management theory, and leadership. It is followed by a discussion of the planning function within organizations in Chapter 2. The section ends with Chapter 3, which reviews the policy-development process within an organization.

Part II opens the door to ethical decision making and professional ethics. Chapter 4 lays the foundation for ethical decision making. It is followed by Chapter 5, which describes a variety of professional ethics and codes of conduct.

Part III provides the student with a picture how sport is governed at various levels of amateur and professional organizations. Chapter 6 describes the influences of governmental bodies and sports commissions on sport governing bodies in the United States. The discussion is followed by a description of youth sport governance in Chapter 7. The authors, shed some light on how interscholastic sports are managed in Chapter 8. Chapter 9 contains a discussion relating the recreational sports in America from community programs to military and collegiate programs. Chapter 10 opens the

doors on how intercollegiate sports are governed from the junior colleges to the largest senior institutions of higher education. Following the intercollegiate discussion, the authors provide a description of governance in professional sports in Chapter 11. Then the authors describe the governance of motorsports in Chapter 12. Chapter 13 discussions highlight amateur sport involvement in the United States by outlining the governance of Olympic sports. This discussion is followed by a detailed description of Paralympic Sports in Chapter 14. The authors then describe the Special Olympic movement in America in Chapter 15. Chapter 16 sheds light on the Senior Olympic programs nationwide. Finally, Chapter 17 provides a discussion relating to community sport support structures, engaging the student in learning about and understanding what these not-for-profit entities do within a community to support and promote sport.

We hope that instructors and students will find this book to be useful and interesting in learning about governance, policy development, and ethical issues in sport organizations. It is a book designed to open the door to the big picture regarding sport governance. It should assist future sport managers to better understand their roles.

Foreword

In *Sport Governance and Policy Development*, Thomas H. Sawyer, Kimberly J. Bodey and Lawrence W. Judge successfully take on the challenge of analyzing the complexity of organizational governance and policy development across a broad spectrum of sport organizations and settings. The journey takes you full circle from topics of structure and leadership to the more detailed nuances of the sport industry. Not only do the authors develop these concepts for you, but they explore how leadership and policy development are impacted by ethical decision-making within an organization.

The book covers the entire continuum of sport from youth leagues to the professional. Sections are provided that differentiate amateur sport from professional leagues and tournaments.

Sport governance is examined from not only the United States (U.S.) perspective, but from an international point of view as well. Too many U.S. students know only of the National College Athletic Association (NCAA) and the U.S. professional leagues. There is a lot more to understand about sport governance and it is succinctly provided in this book. In addition, the authors discuss the impact of U.S. legislation and case law and delve into the intricacies of the international law and the Court of Arbitration for Sport.

Of particular significance given the globalization of sport is how well the authors cover the Olympic Movement. Their accurate and concise portrayal of this highly complex governance structure is spot-on. All tiers of international sport are presented from national governing bodies in individual sports, to the international federations and the International Olympic Committee itself.

Clearly the authors have engaged in the depth of research needed to facilitate an understanding of these important topics for today's sport manager. The book can serve as an excellent textbook for the novice sport management student as well as a seasoned veteran in the profession. Nowhere else in a single source will you find the information you need to navigate sport governance and policy. This work represents a must read for every sport management professional.

David K. Stotlar, Ed. D.
Director, School of Sport and Exercise Science
University of Northern Colorado

Acknowledgments

This book would not have been possible without the assistance of three professionals: Dr. Kimerly J. Bodey, Dr. Lawrence W. Judge, and Dr. Nathan A. Schaumleffel. These young professionals provided not only a number of key chapters in the book but provided very useful guidance in the development of the book. Further, Dr. Ronald Davis (Texas Christian University) for his valuable insight in the development of the chapters related to Special Olympics and Paralympics.

My partner in life as well as my love in my life (Kathleen) was of tremendous assistance in making the chapters read smoothly. She also is the resident English professional who made sure we were consistent in our use of the English language.

No book is complete without the hard work and dedication of the developmental editor, Dr. Robert "Bob" Barcelona, University of New Hampshire, Department of Recreation Management and Policy. Bob is a graduate of Indiana University. Dr. Barcelona spent many long hours reviewing each chapter. He made very good comments and challenged each author to consider other perceptions. Dr. Barcelona's work made this book more complete and very readable.

Further, I would be remiss for not acknowledging the excellent work done by the cover artist, layout editor, copy editor, and indexer. Finally, there would be no book without Dr. Joe Bannon, Sr., Acquisitions Editor, who decided to make this book possible when he recognized the value of such a book in the sport management field.

Dr. Bodey wishes to thank my mom, Susan M. Bodey, for loving and supporting me all these years. I appreciate her patience in my all-too-slow responses to telephone calls and emails and her willingness to take the "kids" for any length of time.

I would like to express my appreciation to Thomas H. Sawyer for his willingness to mentor young faculty. I aspire to be the professional he has envisioned.

I would also like to acknowledge my "Oak Lawn" friends. Though times do change, they, thankfully, do not!

Along my journey through life, I have learned from so many individuals. Dr. Judge would like to say thanks to each and every one of them, but this is an impossible task due to the countless number; I could fill this whole page with names. Special thanks to Dr. Tom Sawyer for not only being a great mentor, colleague and friend, but also for directing me into my new career as a college professor.

Author Biographies

Thomas H. Sawyer, Ed.D.

Thomas H. Sawyer is a 40-year veteran of higher education. He began as an instructor of health and physical education, has been a director of recreational sports, department head, department chair, associate athletic director, director of articulation and transfer, director of a college prison education program, executive director of regional education centers, and an interim dean of continuing education and is ending his career, by choice, as a full professor teaching sport management theory to undergraduate and graduate students.

He has written over 175 peer-reviewed articles for notable professional journals, made over 250 state, regional, national, and international presentations, and written 10 professional books and over 20 chapters in other publications.

Further, he has served as a state AHPERD president (Indiana), district vice president (Midwest), association president (AAALF), chaired numerous district and national committees, editor of the Indiana AHPERD journal and newsletter, chaired the JOPERD Editorial and Policy Boards, and is a member of the AAHPERD BOG.

Dr. Sawyer has also been active in the community serving as a volunteer for the American Red Cross in four communities in four different states since 1964. He has been a first aid, CPR, and water safety instructor (over 30 years), a chapter board member (off and on for 30 years), chapter chairperson (off and on for eight years), chair of a state consortium (three years), chair of numerous regional committees, and currently serves as chair of the Great Lakes Region, Service Area 5, Resource Council.

Finally, Dr. Sawyer has received numerous awards for his leadership and service to the American Red Cross, YMCA, a regional alcohol and drug consortium, Council on Facilities and Equipment, Indiana AHPERD, American Association for Active Lifestyles and Fitness, American Alliance for Health, Physical Education, Recreation, and Dance, and Indiana State University. Further, he has received Caleb Mills Outstanding Teaching Award from Indiana State University and the Howard Richardson's Outstanding Teacher/Scholar Award from the School of Health and Human Performance at Indiana State University.

Kimberly J. Bodey, Ed.D.

Kimberly J. Bodey is an assistant professor and sport management concentration coordinator in the Department of Recreation and Sport Management at Indiana State University. She earned an Ed.D. in Recreation with an emphasis in public policy and a MEd in Sport Management from the University of Arkansas. She holds a BS in Kinesiology from the University of Illinois. While on faculty at Indiana State, Dr. Bodey has taught graduate and undergraduate courses in administrative theory and management practice, organizational leadership and ethics, governance and policy development, research and evaluation, and sport law. She is also a member of the University Athletics Committee.

During the last five years, Dr. Bodey has worked closely with sport administrators and educators in Morocco and Cyprus. Funded by the U.S. State Department, the *Sport Management & Leadership Capacity Project* was a partnership between Indiana State University, La Federation Royale Marocaine de Football, Hassan II University-Mohammedia, and E'cole des Lioceaux de l'Atlas de Football. This training program intended to strengthen the administrative and managerial capacity of sport leaders in Morocco. Working in conjunction with the Global Center for Independent Studies (Limassol, Cyprus), Dr. Bodey has presented workshops on the Organization and Function of Sport Leagues and Research Methods in Sport Management. She has also taught graduate courses in Governance and Compliance, Evaluative Research, and Legal Aspects of International Sport Management.

Dr. Bodey has given more than 20 presentations in the United States and abroad. Her research interests include how governance structure impacts ethical decision making and practice in sport organizations. She has a particular interest in how policies are created and the way rules encourage and discourage fair play in intercollegiate and professional sport. Dr. Bodey has several publications in scholarly journals and academic textbooks related to risk management, organizational justice and legal authority, and jurisdiction in sport management.

Dr. Bodey is a member of the American Alliance of Health, Physical Education, Recreation and Dance, North American Society of Sport Management, National Recreation and Parks Association, Sport and Recreation Law Association, and the Indiana Association for Health, Physical Education, Recreation and Dance. Dr. Bodey also serves on the editorial board of the *International Journal of Sport Management* and *LARNet: The Cyber Journal of Applied Leisure & Recreation Research*.

Lawrence W. Judge, Ph.D.

Lawrence W. Judge is currently an assistant professor of Physical Education at Ball State University in Muncie, Indiana. Besides his teaching and research responsibilities, he serves as the undergraduate adviser for the Sports Administration program.

As both an associate head coach and head coach, Larry has a total of 18 years work experience coaching Division I track and field/cross country. In addition to field experience (training eight Olympians and 10 NCAA Champions and coaching over 100 All-Americans), Judge has firsthand knowledge of NCAA rules and current issues in amateur, intercollegiate, and professional athletics.

Widely recognized as the premiere throws coach in the USA, Larry Judge completed his collegiate coaching career with the University of Florida in 2005. Under Judge's direction, the Florida throws group has reached the pinnacle of the sport amassing unparalleled honors. In just four years at UF, Judge has tutored eight All-Americans, five Southeastern Conference Champions, two NCAA champions and three Olympians adding to an already impressive resume. Gator throwers have collected an astounding 34 All-American honors and 16 individual SEC titles, and six individual NCAA titles since Judge's arrival in Gainesville prior to the 2000-01 season. In 2005, Judge capped off a stellar career at the University of Florida with three athletes competing in the world championships in Helsinki. Judge served as an assistant coach for Trinidad and Tobago.

Dr. Judge has guided eight athletes in the last three Olympic Games. Judge served as the personal coach for Brad Snyder and Lisa Misipeka at the Olympic Games in Atlanta and guided Dawn Ellerbe to the 1996 U.S. Olympic Trials title in the hammer. Snyder put the shot for Canada and Misipeka competed in the same event for American Samoa. In 2000, five of his former athletes competed in the 2000 Olympic Games in Sydney. Judge served as the personal coach for Jesseca Cross and Dawn Ellerbe of the U.S. and Jason Gervais of Canada. Ellerbe was Judge's top finisher in the games, finishing seventh in the hammer throw with a distance of 219-1. In 2004 Judge served as an assistant coach for Trinidad and Tobago in Athens and watched as three of his Gators competed, Candice Scott for Trinidad and Tobago, Kim Barrett for Jamaica, and Erin Gilreath for the United States.

Larry's research area of emphasis over the last 15 years is the use of technology in coaching. He has worked on numerous research projects involving elite athletes with the United States Track and Field elite athlete program. In area of scholarship, Judge is a well-respected author and clinician. He has published approximately 30 articles on track and field technique, nutrition, and resistance training.

Judge is the USA Track & Field National Chairman for Coaches Education in the Throws and lectures throughout the USA at various camps and clinics, including USA Track & Field level II and Level III Coaching Education Schools. Aside from being a lead instructor for the USATF coaching programs, he is also a level II instructor for the International governing body of track and field coach's education program. In 2003, Larry conducted an IAAF level II throws school in San Juan, Puerto Rico and he recently conducted another school in December 2006. He helped develop, revise and update curriculum for the level I and level II USATF certification programs and wrote the complete throws manual for the level II course in 2006. In 1997, he administered an Olympic Solidarity Clinic in Pago Pago, American Samoa and in 1999, conducted a NCAA Y.E.S. clinic at the Indoor National Championships in Indianapolis.

A black belt in karate, Judge has impressive educational credentials, including a Master's Degree In Sport Management and Exercise Science, a Master's Degree in Public Administration, and a Ph.D. in Higher Education Administration.

PART I
_____

**Organizational Goverance and
Policy Development**

CHAPTER 1

Introduction to Sport Organizations and Governance

Governing bodies are an important part of the sport industry. Any given governing body is structured in a way to achieve its stated mission within the environment in which it works. There is inherent challenge in this process because the governing body must maintain a level of consistency and stability over time as well as be responsive to changes in the marketplace. Knowledge about how a governing body is organized will help the sport manager understand why the governing body operates in a particular manner and why some bodies are more effective than others.

Organizational theory is an area of study that seeks to understand the structure and design of organizations. Scholars analyze the "patterns" and "regularities" that emerge in order to better understand both their causes and consequences (Slack & Parent, 2006). The process of organizing is essentially the same for all types of organizations. Once the mission and goals have been formulated, sport managers must develop a systematic plan to bring together the necessary human and physical resources (Montana & Charnov, 2000). To a large extent, a sport governing body's ability to govern effectively is determined by its

structure, which in turn is impacted by the marketplace.

From the beginning, humankind has sought ways to make decisions for the group. That is, it looks for better ways to govern in order to resolve disputes, control disruptive behaviors, and achieve goals that advance the welfare of group and society as a whole. In this sense, sport governing bodies exist to make group decisions within a particular segment of the sport industry. When analyzing governance systems, the sport manager can study a governing body from two perspectives. From the micro approach, a governing body is itself an organization and is set up in a particular way to achieve goals. For instance, the internal workings of the Boys and Girls Clubs of America "home office" can be analyzed. From the macro approach, the governing body may be thought of as the tip of the iceberg. The governing body oversees all the individual organizations within its jurisdiction. In this case, how the home office interacts with all the community Boys and Girls clubs can be studied. The aim of this chapter is to introduce the sport industry and outline the component parts of a sport organization. Next, an overview of how governing bodies acquire legal authority and jurisdiction is presented. Finally, governance is defined and contrasted with management and leadership in sport management.

Learning Objectives

Upon completion of this chapter, the reader should be able to:

- Describe the sport industry.
- Define key terms, including organization, organizing, organizational context, organizational design, organizational structure, organizational chart, organizational behavior, and organizational culture.
- List and explain the structural elements of organizational design, including complexity, formalization, centralization, specialization, standardization, departmentalization, and size.
- Explain the relationship between mission, strategy, and structure.
- Discuss how governing bodies acquire legal authority and jurisdiction.
- Define governance and explain the component parts of good governance.
- Distinguish between governance, management, and leadership in sport organizations.
- Discuss why management is needed in an organization.
- Describe the differences between leaders and managers.
- Discuss the various types of leaders and outline the various types of leadership theories.

What is the Sport Industry?

An *industry* is any grouping of businesses that share a common method of generating revenue such as the "automobile industry", "cattle industry", or "fashion industry". Similarly, a "sport industry" exists that can be divided into a multitude of segments: youth sport, interscholastic sport, intercollegiate sport, Olympic sport, professional sport, sport manufacturing, sport retailing, sport consulting, sport marketing, sport merchandising, facility management, and others. Each segment is composed of a variety of individual organizations. For instance, consider participation in a single sport, such as track and field. There are a number of organizations to provide governance and input, including high schools, state high school athletic and activity associations, multisport (i.e., AAU), and single sport (i.e., USATF) governing bodies, collegiate athletic associations, collegiate recruiting services, sporting goods manufacturers and retailers, and sport media outlets (i.e., *Track & Field News*) to name only a few. Now, include all kinds of sports and all types of sport products and services across the various segments, and you can see the expansive nature of the sport industry.

Though difficult to measure, scholars agree the sport industry is growing at an exponential rate. Within the United States alone, the gross national sport product is projected to increase from $157 billion in 2005 to $236 billion by 2015. This tremendous growth is attributed to increased discretionary income, heightened awareness of the relationship between an active lifestyle and good health, and a greater number of opportunities for all to participate in sport. Some scholars have argued sport is an integral part of the entertainment industry. Whether sport is a freestanding industry or segment of the entertainment industry, it continues to expand as a global multibillion-dollar industry.

What is an Organization?

An *organization* is the entity that allows for a group of two or more people to work together more effectively than they might work alone in order to achieve goals. A governing body is an organization with five essential elements: social identity, involvement in sport industry, goal-directed focus, consciously structured activity system, and identifiable boundaries (Slack & Parent, 2006). In other words, a governing body is a discernable entity apart from its individual members that is set up in a way to achieve identified goals within a specific jurisdiction in the sport industry. The third section of this book will describe the governance system of various sport organizations (see Figure 1.1) and discusses present challenges and those that may be faced in the future.

Fundamentally, organizing involves analyzing, identifying, and defining the work to be performed. If this process is done properly, it will result in some logical ordering of work and a manner for individuals to cooperate efficiently and effectively to achieve objectives (Montana & Charnov, 2000). When thinking about organizing in relation to governing bodies, a sport manager should consider several factors. Unity of purpose is an agreement about the work to be performed. Division of labor entails how tasks are partitioned and what authority will be given to responsible individuals. Staffing requires decisions about the type, number, and experience of individuals who will complete the work. Finally, organizational framework is the structure that will allow for effective cooperation among individuals (e.g., chain of command, flow of information, etc.).

The organizational context refers to the "setting which influences the (governing body's) structural dimensions" (Daft, 2003, p. 17). Determinants, also known in the literature as contingencies or imperatives, which influence the organizational structure, include age, size, strategy, technology, and sociopolitical and economic factors found in the external environment. Organizational design is the pattern of structural elements in a governing body (i.e., complexity, formalization, etc.). The preferred design will depend largely on the stated mission as well as the organizational context. The organizational structure refers to how jobs are broken down and assigned to members, communication and reporting relationships among individuals, and the coordination and control mechanisms used within the governing body. According to Miller (1987), organizational structure is important to study because it "influences the flow of interaction and the context and nature of human interactions. It channels collaboration, specific modes of coordination, allocated power and responsibility, and prescribes levels of formality and complexity" (p. 7). In other words, the organizational structure shapes how sport managers interact with one another, how decisions are made and tasks completed, and whether the atmosphere feels casual and friendly or formal and reserved.

The visual representation of how a governing body is structured is referred to as the organization chart (see Figure 1.2). The organization chart may reflect many aspects, such as the levels of management, supervisory relationships, major subunits, division of work, and communication channels (Montana & Charnov, 2000). It should be noted the formal chart might not accurately reflect the important relationships that exist in governing bodies. In fact, these "informal" relationships may significantly influence what and how tasks are performed to achieve stated goals.

Organizational behavior and organizational culture

Daft (2007) defines organizational behavior as the study of how individuals and small groups function within the organization and the characteristics of the environment in which people work. Researchers who study organizational behavior are concerned with such issues as leadership traits

Sports Industry

Amateur Sports	Professional Sports	Sport Services
Youth Sports	National Basketball Association	Athletic Foundations
Basketball	Women's National Basketball Association	Arena and Stadium Operators
Baseball	Continental Basketball Association	Cable Sports
Bowling	United States Basketball League	Network Sports
Cheerleading	Major League Baseball	Race Tracks - Auto and Trucks
Field Hockey	Minor League Baseball	Race Tracks - Horses
Football	National Hockey League	Race Tracks - Greyhounds
Golf	National Football League - European	Sport Agency/Player/Coach Representations
Gymnastics	Arena Football League	Sport Media
LaCrosse	Major League Soccer	Sport Sponsorship Agencies
Soccer	Major Indoor Soccer League	Sport Event Agencies
Softball	National Hot Rod Association	Sport Marketing Agencies
Swimming	*Motor Sports:*	Sport Facility Management
Wrestling	NASCAR	Sport Commissions
Interscholastic Sports	IRL	Sport Fundraisers
High School Associations	F1	Sport Museums
Intercollegiate Sports	NSRA	Sport Libraries
Collegiate Conferences	Track and Field	Sport Hall of Fame
United States Olympic Committee	Beach Volleyball	Sport Architects
National Governing Bodies for Olympic Sports	Bench Tennis	Sports Facility Development Consultants
Special Olympics	*Golf:*	Sports Facility Concessions and Food
Paralympics	PGA	Sports Ticket Services
Senior Olympics	LPGA	
State Games	*Tennis:*	
Military Sports	APT	
Recreational Sports	WTA	
Campus Recreation	Professional Bowling Association	
Community Recreation	Professional Figure Skating	
	Professional Rodeo	

Figure 1.1
Categories of Sport Organizations

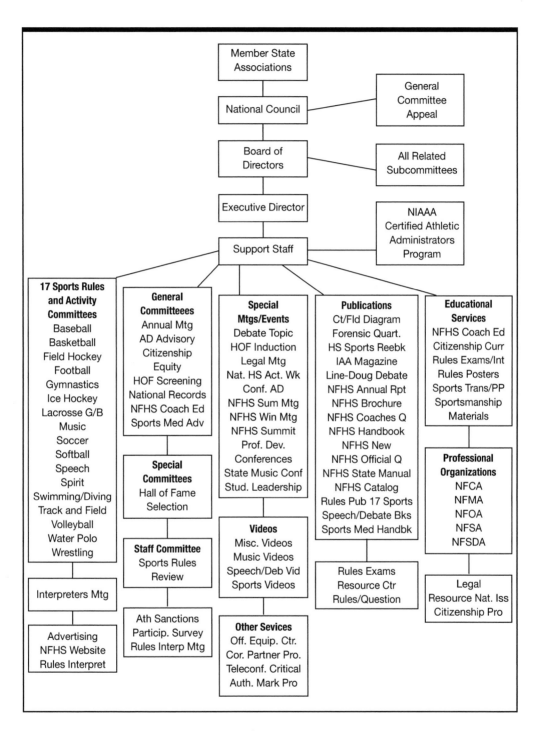

Figure 1.2
National Federation of State High School Associations (NFHS)

and styles, team building, job satisfaction, communication, and motivation. In the sport management literature, scholars have focused primarily on topics such as leadership traits and approaches, level of job satisfaction, and workplace motivations (Slack & Parent, 2006).

Organizational culture refers to the shared philosophies, values, beliefs, and behavior patterns that form the organization's core identity. As people interact with the governing body, they become familiar with the "manifestations" of the organizational culture. These manifestations may include the organization's formal rules and practices, dress norms, and co-worker stories as well as the informal codes of behavior, rituals, reward and promotion system, tasks, pay system, jargon, and jokes understood only by insiders. Sport managers, by their actions and non-actions, send signals about what they value. Regardless of what may be written in an organization's formal documents, how individuals behave in the workplace is a candid representation of the organizational culture.

Structural elements of organizational design

Organizational design refers to how structural elements are arranged to create the governing body. There are several structural elements to be considered, including complexity, formalization, centralization, specialization, standardization, departmentalization, and size. No two governing bodies are exactly the same, because the organizational design reflects the organization's mission and environment.

Complexity is the extent to which a sport organization is horizontally, vertically, or spatially (geographically) differentiated. Sport organizations are horizontally differentiated when work is broken down into narrowly defined tasks, when professionals or trained specialists are employed, and when the organization is departmen-

talized. Vertical differentiation refers to the number of levels in the organization and is represented by the "hierarchy of authority." A tall structure is characterized by (a) greater levels of hierarchy and (b) relatively narrow span of control. Conversely, a flat structure is characterized by (a) fewer levels of hierarchy and (b) relatively wide span of control. Spatial differentiation may be vertical or horizontal. Vertical spatial differentiation occurs when different levels of the organization are dispersed geographically. Horizontal spatial differentiation is when the different functions (or departments) of the organization take place in different locations (Slack & Parent, 2006).

As differentiation increases in an organization, so does the complexity. In other words, complexity increases when an organization has many departments, multiple levels of authority, and physical separation between members. Poor communication, coordination, and supervision are a few of the problems organizations face when they become too complex.

Formalization is a means to control the amount of discretion individuals or groups have when performing job functions (Slack & Parent, 2006). Written documents, such as job descriptions, codes of conduct, and policies and procedure manuals, direct and control staff member behavior (Daft, 2003). These documents complement the organizational chart by describing the tasks, responsibilities, and decision authority within a governing body. It should be mentioned, however, that formalization may not be the same across all hierarchical levels or departments with an organization.

Centralization is concerned with who makes decisions and at what level. Mitzberg (1979) writes, "When all power for decision making rests at a single point in the organization—ultimately in the hands of a single individual—we shall call the structure centralized; to the extent that the power is dispersed among many individuals we shall call the structure decentralized" (p. 181). Generally speaking, in a centralized governing body, decisions are made by a relatively small number of people at the top of the hierarchy. In a decentralized governing body, decisions are made by a greater number of people at lower levels in the organization.

Work *specialization* is the extent to which jobs are divided into separate activities. Another term for this is division of labor. For example, the production of one pair of Nike shoes involves 34 operations and approximately 170 workers. Some authors have argued that division of labor maximizes productivity by increasing workers' skills, saving time lost when changing tasks, and by creating laborsaving inventions and machinery (Daft, 2003).

One of the primary methods governing bodies use to coordinate interdependent tasks is *standardization*. As sport organizations have become more complex, new oversight systems that specify roles, plan work, and monitor activities have been introduced. Specifically, standardization refers to the extent to which work activities in different areas are performed in a uniform manner and the extent to which such uniformities are documented. Uniformity may be analyzed in terms of technical procedures, administrative procedures, workplace arrangements, equipment and tools, among others.

Another fundamental characteristic of organizational structure is *departmentalization*. The goal of departmentalization is to group people into manageable work units to achieve their objectives in the most efficient and effective manner possible (Montana & Charnov, 2000). This process involves placing individual positions within departments as well as locating entire departments within the overall organization (Daft, 2003).

According to the management literature, departments may be coordinated based on (a) *function* (i.e., similar skills, expertise, and resources used); (b) *product* (i.e., spe-

cialized knowledge about product or services); (c) *market* (i.e., specialized knowledge about clientele; (d) *division* (i.e., organizational outputs such as product or service for single customer); (e) *customer* (i.e., targets for organizational outputs); (f) *geographic area or territories* (i.e., physical location); and (g) *matrix* (i.e., multiple approaches to emphasize cross-functional teams).

Size is another important factor influencing the structure of an organization. There are a number of possible ways to measure size: total assets, market share, number of clients, number of employees, number of members, and net profits. While scholars debate the impact size has on structure, the majority of studies recognize the two concepts are related. As Daft (2003) writes, "The overall size of an organization has been shown in many research surveys to be closely associated with the type of structure adopted" (p. 10).

While not technically a structural element of organizational design, an important aspect of organizational structure is the distinction between line departments and staff departments. A line department performs activities most closely associated with the organization's mission or purpose. In a sport goods company, the line department makes and sells the product. Staff departments include those departments that provide specialized skills to support line departments. These departments have an advisory or auxiliary relationship with line departments. For example, ordinarily facility maintenance is considered a staff function in a sport goods manufacturing company. The organization is not in the business of providing maintenance. However, in an arena or stadium, facility maintenance is a critical operation. Poor maintenance may result in a decrease in attendance; thus, it is considered a line department function.

Structure follows strategy

As previously mentioned, no two governing bodies are exactly the same because the organizational design reflects the organization's mission and environment. To state this in a slightly different way, mission defines strategy and strategy defines structure within a particular environment. Every organization has a set of assumptions about its business type, products, and services offered to customers. It also has a declaration of intent, which is the mission statement, to guide its method of operation. For example, NASCAR aims to organize and promote stock car racing on an international level. Strategy converts the theory of business into performance. Thus, NASCAR has a strategic plan that outlines how it will conduct all business operations during the next three to five years to accomplish the mission. In order for the organization to achieve its strategy in an unpredictable environment, it must be structured in an appropriate way. Therefore, within the NASCAR organization, different departments, such as marketing and promotion, media relations, and technology and development, are set up to be responsible for aspects of the strategic plan. This specialization allows NASCAR to respond to changes in the environment. Since strategy is dynamic, changing in response to marketplace, it may require the sport agency be "reorganized" from time to time so that its structure supports the new strategy.

Decisions about structure come from an analysis of activities, decisions, and relations. Activities analysis considers what work has to be performed, what kinds of work belong together, and the emphasis each task should be given within the overall organization. Decisions analysis determines what decisions are needed to obtain the desired performance to achieve goals and at what level in the organization the decisions should be made. Relations analysis reviews with whom individuals in an organization must work and the nature of contribution to complete specific job tasks (Drucker, 1999). These analyses occur within the context of the larger environment. The general environment includes the legal, political, technological, economic, and social context that affect all organizations. The task environment includes external factors such as customers, competitors, and suppliers that interact directly with a specific organization. The internal environment includes internal factors such as mission statement, policies and procedures, and personnel over which the organization has a large degree of control.

Legal Authority and Jurisdiction

There are many different types of organizations that combine to create the sport industry. Businesses that provide sport products and services may be classified as being in the public, private (for-profit), and nonprofit sectors. These businesses take different legal forms: sole proprietorship, partnership, and corporation. Typically, governing bodies are a corporation. A corporation is any business entity recognized as distinct from the people who own it (i.e., not a sole proprietorship or partnership). To be classified as a corporation, a business must be incorporated according to the laws of a particular state, province or national government. This includes filing the requisite documents (e.g., articles of incorporation) and paying a fee. In some cases, these businesses are called associations, organizations, or limited liability companies. Business law (i.e., taxation, rights, restrictions, etc.) varies from state to state; therefore, the prospective corporation will file documents in a state whose laws are most favorable to its business interests. Once registered, the corporation has artificial "personhood" until such time as the corporation is dissolved. Hence, the corporation may exist beyond the lifetime of any of its agents.

Corporations can be either for-profit companies or nonprofit entities. In for-profit companies the "owners" are called stockholders or shareholders. In nonprofit entities, the owners are called members. Revenue generated that exceeds operating expenses is distributed to shareholders in a for-profit corporation. For instance, the NFL and its teams, such as the Indianapolis Colts, are registered as for-profit corporations. This revenue is reinvested in the organization in a nonprofit corporation. For example, Boys and Girls Clubs of America and its local chapters are registered as not-for-profit entities. Tax exempt nonprofit businesses are often called a "501(c)3 corporations" in reference to the section of the IRS Code that outlines tax exemptions. It may be of interest to know that the U.S. Congress is reviewing the NCAA's nonprofit status given the revenue the governing body generates and how it is distributed to member institutions.

The board of directors (sometimes called executive committee or management council) is responsible for governing the affairs of a corporation. The board's power is derived from the shareholders (or members) they represent and is articulated in the corporation's governing documents: articles of incorporation, constitution and bylaws, and shareholder (member) agreements. The articles of incorporation specify the nature of the corporation, such as the corporate name, purpose, registered office, authorized capitol, duration, and board of directors. Constitution and bylaws govern the routine internal affairs of the corporation (e.g., core principles and values, committee structure, meeting procedure, financial operations, etc.). Stakeholder (member) agreements can very depending on the history, size, and type of business the corporation seeks to operate. For instance, NCAA Division I institutions (members) elect the executive committee (board). As the governing body of intercollegiate athletics, the NCAA's governing documents (available at www.ncaa.org) specifies its authority and jurisdiction as well as membership requirements, sanctioning, and appeals processes.

Typically, the board delegates, either formally or informally, decision-making authority to elected officers to operate the corporation on a day-to-day basis (Colley, Doyle, Logan, & Stettinius, 2003). The number of officers, also known as senior management, depends on the organization and may include chief executive officer (CEO), chief financial officer (CFO), president, vice-presidents, secretary, and others. For example, Myles Brand is the president of the NCAA. Interestingly, there is a fine line between the board delegating enough and too much decision-making authority to senior management. When senior management develops agendas, collects information, and prepares background information without significant guidance from or reference to the board, there is a shift in control. The board may become a "rubber stamp" for decisions made elsewhere, or the board might fight back by blocking decisions put forth by senior management (Friedman & Phillips, 2004). In any event, the board is the legitimate "leader" in the corporation and must retain its ability to make decisions to guide the organization.

What is Governance?

Governance refers to how governing bodies are directed and controlled. The governance mechanism (e.g., formal documents, organizational structure) specifies how rights, authority, and responsibility are distributed among the participants in order to monitor performance and achieve goals. The test of effective governance is the degree to which any organization is achieving its stated purpose.

On a larger scale, governance describes methods a governing body uses to ensure its constituents follow established protocol. At the macro level, there is a loosely coupled organizational structure that oversees and maintains accountability. For instance, the International Olympic Committee oversees international sport federations (e.g., International Association of Athletics Federations), national sport governing bodies (e.g., USA Track & Field), national Olympic committees (e.g., United States Olympic Committee), and local Olympic organizing committees (e.g., Chicago 2016). A proper governance strategy implements a system to monitor and record what is happening within the governing body's jurisdiction, take steps to ensure compliance with established policies and procedures, and provides corrective action in the event rules have been misconstrued or ignored.

There is a dichotomy between a governing body's role as an advocate within the sport industry and its requirement to regulate members (Friedman & Phillips, 2004). In other words, the governing body must make decisions to promote sport, but in order to promote sport, the governing body must make decisions about what members can and cannot do. For example, Major League Baseball wants players to hit home runs. This is good for baseball because the result, among other things, is increased attendance, media coverage, and merchandise sales. As such, Major League Baseball allows cities to build ballparks with varying dimensions (within certain limits) to make it easier for ballplayers to hit home runs. Similarly, Major League Baseball does not allow ballplayers to use performance-enhancing substances to increase home run production. Thus, to advocate for a sport in the industry, governing bodies must regulate its members' behavior.

There is no perfect organizational structure associated with good governance. In fact, organizational structure can impede the work of governance as much as it works to promote it. The challenge is to design a governance structure capable of a proactive approach to determining mission, strategy, and policy and be responsive to the external and internal environment as well as the needs and aspirations of members (Friedman & Phillips, 2004).

What is good governance?

Good governance has eight characteristics: participatory, responsive, equitable and inclusive, and consensus oriented. It is also transparent, accountable, effective and efficient, and follows the rule of law (UN-ESCAP, 2006). To facilitate participation, either direct or through legitimate representatives, members need to be informed and organized. Further, the governing body must be responsive, that is, to serve all members within a reasonable timeframe. To be equitable and inclusive, members must feel they have a stake in the governing body and have the opportunity to maintain, if not improve, their status. Since there are many viewpoints on how sport should be operated, mediation is needed to reach consensus on what is "good" for the sport and how it might be achieved.

Good governance also requires efficiency and effectiveness. This means processes must be developed to produce results that meet member needs in a way that makes good use of human and physical resources. When information is freely available and accessible to affected members, then the governing body is said to be transparent. Following the rule of law involves applying rules in an impartial manner during decision making and enforcement. In general, a governing body is accountable to those affected by its decisions or actions. Accountability cannot be enforced without transparency and rule of law.

Governance and Management: What's the Difference?

A governing body is an organization designed to achieve a specific mission. Governance is the means to coordinate and control the organization's actions and resources. Management involves translating the system of governance into performance. Both governance and management involve four functions: planning, organizing, leading (or directing), and controlling (POLC) human and physical resources to achieve organizational objectives. This is the same regardless of the type of industry, level within the industry, or sort of organization.

Management scholars (Mosley, Pietri, & Megginson, 1996; Rodenz, 2006; Williams, 2007) have defined the four managerial functions as follows:

Planning is the management function of choosing an organization's mission and objectives and then determining the courses of action needed to achieve them.

Organizing is the management function of determining resources and activities required to achieve the organization's objectives, combining these into a formal structure, assigning responsibility for them, and delegating authority to carry out assignments.

Leading (sometimes called directing) is the management function of influencing employees to accomplish objectives, which involves the leader's qualities, styles, and power as well as the leadership activities of communication, motivation, and discipline.

Controlling is the management function of devising ways of ensuring that planned performance is actually achieved.

In governance, the board of directors plan by outlining the mission statement and goals and a strategic plan to achieve them. The board organizes by structuring the organization to implement a specific strategy and delegating the authority and responsibility senior management needs to accomplish tasks. Leading (directing) comes in the form of guidance and support. Since the marketplace is constantly changing, the board must be prepared to provide input or change strategy when needed. Controlling is the means to ensure planned performance is achieved. The authority and jurisdiction to perform these functions come from the formal documents.

Management involves converting the system of governance into day-to-day operations. Senior management, working with the board, develops an operational plan to achieve the identified mission and goals within a specified time period. Using the organizational structure, senior management organizes by delegating specific responsibility and authority to staff members to carry out operations. Leading is the ability to influence others to work toward achieving personal and professional goals. Controlling is the documentation system to ensure tasks are completed according to policy in a timely fashion. The authority and jurisdiction to perform these functions comes from the board. In small organizations, the board and senior management are one and the same. In this case, senior management determines the governance system as well as the system to translate this into day-to-day operations.

Management—Why is it Needed by Organizations?

There are three key reasons why organizations need management: to establish objectives, to maintain balance among stakeholders, and to achieve efficiency and effectiveness. The initial task for management is to develop objectives for the organization. The objectives become the organizational energy currency. Once the objectives are established, the organization's human, financial, and physical resources attempt to accomplish them. Generally, top management establishes overall objectives for such areas as profitability, market share, growth, or new product development. Lower-level objectives are commonly determined by all of the employees.

In working to achieve objectives, managers need to maintain balance among the conflicting objectives of the stakeholders. The stakeholders are all those having a stake in the organization's success, including employees, owners, customers, government authorities, and creditors. Management holds in trust and must balance the interest of many different groups including community leaders, creditors, customers, employees, government needs and demands, public (consumer groups, environmentalists, and civil rights advocates) stockholders, suppliers, trade associations, and union leaders.

Further, management performs the function of stewardship on behalf of the owners who are seeking a satisfactory return on investment (ROI). The ROI may be profits (as in a business) or service (as in local, state, or federal governments). Finally, management must also consider the interests of its employees who seek good pay, safe and comfortable working conditions, fair and equitable treatment, the greatest possible job security, and more time off.

The last reason for management is achieving effectiveness and efficiency. The concept of effectiveness relates to the ability of management to set and achieve proper objectives. The other side of the management performance coin is efficiency. Efficiency is management's ability to get things done, achieving higher outputs relative to inputs. In the case of managing a sport retail store, this would include such resources as employees, food, and time. The store manager, who achieves the same sales volume with another store, while having only 15 percent of the payroll and inventory costs, would be considered more efficient in using resources.

Leadership

Attila the Hun, Napoleon, Marshall, Eisenhower, Patton, and Rommel believed that, under the right circumstances, every soldier in his army had the potential to be a general and lead the army in his absence. Whether you hold that belief or not, the plain fact is that "natural" leaders do not just happen, nor does anyone have a divine right to lead or rule.

You do indeed have a marshal's baton in your own knapsack. Recognizing your leadership potential is the first step toward leading others. The second is being able to manage yourself before trying to manage others. Finally, a third, as noted by Bennis (1989), is self-expression, and the key to self-expression is understanding one's self and the world, and the key to understanding is learning—from one's own life and experience.

Bennis based his bestseller *On Becoming a Leader* (1994) on the assumption that leaders are people who are able to express themselves fully. " . . . they know who they are, what their strengths and weaknesses are, and how to fully deploy their strengths and compensate for their weaknesses." Further, " . . . they know what they want, why they want it, and how to communicate what they want to others, in order to gain their cooperation and support" (p. 37).

Finally, Norman Lear's success was based on four very simple yet complex steps: (a) becoming self-expressive, (b) listening to the inner voice, (c) learning from the right mentors, and (d) giving oneself over to a guiding vision (Bennis, 1994).

Leadership and the Facility and Event Manager

Leadership has been defined by many and many continue to redefine it. For the purposes of this chapter, *leadership* will be defined as a set of qualities that causes people to follow. Leadership requires at least two parties; a leader and a follower. Many experts have argued over what exactly causes a group to follow one person and not another, but the decision to follow a leader seems to come down to few common traits (See Table 1.1).

Leaders have the ability to inspire people to go beyond what they think they are capable of doing, making it possible for a group to attain a goal that was previously thought unattainable. Leaders carry their followers along by (a) inspiring their trust, (b) acting consistently, and (c) motivating them by words and deeds.

Leadership boils down to a willingness to accept responsibility, and the ability to develop three skills that can be acquired through practice—elicit the cooperation of others, listen well, and place the needs of others above your own needs. When you properly put these skills together, people begin to turn to you when they need direction.

Responsibility and Accountability

Leadership begins with the willingness to embrace responsibility. You cannot be a leader if you are afraid of responsibility and accountability. With responsibility comes the concept of accountability. If you cannot answer yes to the following question, you are not ready to become a leader. Do you

Table 1.1
Ten Characteristics of a True Leader

The following are the 10 characteristics of a true leader:
- eager
- cheerful
- honest
- resourceful
- persuasive
- cooperative
- altruistic
- courageous
- supportive
- assertive

have enough confidence in yourself to accept responsibility for failure?

One of the realities about placing the needs of others above your own is that you cannot blame other people. If you are the type of person who looks outward for an excuse instead of inward for a reason, you will have a hard time earning the trust of others. An absence of trust makes eliciting their cooperation more difficult, which, in turn, makes it more difficult for you to lead, even if you have been given the title of leader.

On the other hand, the leader receives most of the accolades and rewards when things go well. No matter how hard your followers worked, no matter how modest you are, no matter how much you attempt to deflect credit to your entire team, yours is the name that people will remember. That is the great benefit of being the leader. Can you handle the limelight of success?

The Basic Ingredients of Leadership

Leaders come in every size, shape, and disposition. Yet they share some of the following ingredients (Bennis, 1994):

- guiding vision,
- passion,
- integrity (i.e., self-knowledge, candor, and maturity),
- trust (i.e., constancy, congruity, reliability, and integrity),
- curiosity, and
- daring.

Key Leadership Abilities

The trick to becoming a leader is to be able to elicit cooperation, to listen to the needs of others, and to put other people's needs ahead of your own with great consistency. After you decide that you can and want to embrace responsibility, leadership requires that you be able to do three things very well (also see Table 1.2):

- Elicit the cooperation of others. You must be able to get others to buy into your vision of the future and the right way to get there.
- Listen well. You have to be able to gather many kinds of information from others in order to lead; doing so requires that you hone your listening skills. The old adage, "listen and *hear* before you speak," is very important when dealing with people.
- Place the needs of others above your own needs. Leadership requires that you be willing to sacrifice for a greater good.

Characteristics of Leaders Coping with Change

There are 10 characteristics for coping with change and creating learning organizations (Bennis, 1994):

- leaders manage the dream,
- leaders embrace error,
- leaders encourage reflective backtalk,
- leaders encourage dissent,
- leaders possess the Nobel Factor (optimism, faith, and hope),
- leaders understand the Pygmalion effect in management (if you expect great things, your colleagues will give them

to you—stretch, don't strain and be realistic about expectations),
- leaders have what I think of as the Gretzky Factor (a certain "touch"),
- leaders see the long view,
- leaders understand stakeholder symmetry, and
- leaders create strategic alliances and partnerships.

Building Leadership Tools

John F. Kennedy once said, "Leadership and learning are indispensable to each other." Learning about the job, the employees, and yourself is very important to a leader and his/her leadership ability. There are a number of leadership traits that need to be developed by the leader. The remainder of this section will discuss these traits:

- Learning to use what you have. Intelligence is critical to leadership because synthesizing information is often necessary in order to create a vision.
- Responding to situations flexibly. Gathering new information and adjusting a response to a particular situation requires intelligence. Instead of responding in a knee-jerk way, an intelligent person responds flexibly based on circumstances and needs.
- Taking advantage of fortuitous circumstances. You not only have to be smart enough to adapt to new information with flexibility, but you also have to have the courage to seize opportunities when they present themselves.
- Making sense of ambiguous or contradictory messages. A good leader listens to all the information and then sorts through it. You test contradictory messages by asking for more information in order to find the truth.
- Ranking the importance of different elements.
- Finding similarities in apparently different situations. One of the normal

Table 1.2
Ten Ways to Master Leadership Skills

The following are the ten ways to master leadership skills:
- prepare
- volunteer
- keep an open mind
- give speeches
- develop discipline
- meet deadlines
- stay in touch
- listen
- cooperate
- do things for others

characteristics of intelligence is a talent for analogies. Analogous intelligence in leaders is the ability to draw on prior experience, no matter how tenuous the connection is, to find a similarity that you can use to solve a problem.

- Drawing distinctions between seemingly similar situations. You can find differences among situations just as often as you can find similarities and a good leader learns to recognize when A is not like B and emphasize the differences over what the two have in common.
- Putting concepts together in new ways. Along with analogies, one of the components of intelligence is the ability to synthesize new knowledge by putting together time-tested concepts in new ways.
- Coming up with novel ideas.

Leadership versus Management

Leadership is based on a person's ability to influence others to work toward achieving personal and organizational goals. Leadership is often defined as a process of influencing individual and group activities toward goal setting and achievement. However, management involves much more. While leadership is a part of management, management also includes performing the other functions—planning, organizing, and controlling. Keep in mind that effective managers must be effective leaders and the successful leader is one who succeeds in getting others to follow.

A leader is not a manager and a manager is not a leader. There are enormous differences between leaders and managers including:

Manager ↓	Leader ↓
Administers	Innovates
Copy	Original
Maintains	Develops
Focuses on systems & structure	Focuses on people
Short-range view	Long-range perspective
Relies on control	Inspires trust
Asks how and when	Asks what and why
Eye always on the bottom line	Eye on the horizon
Imitates	Originates
Accepts status quo	Challenges status quo
Classic good soldier	His own person
Does things right	Does the right thing
Wear square hats	Wear sombreros
Learn through training	Learn through education
Deductive	Inductive
Firm	Tentative
Static	Dynamic
Memorizing	Understanding
Facts	Ideas
Narrow	Broad
Surface	Deep
Direction	Initiative
Left brain	Whole brain
Common sense	Imagination
Rules	Risk
Rigid	Flexible
Reactive	Active

Types of Leaders

A leader has to work effectively with many people including superiors, peers, subordinates, and outside groups. However, the qualities of leadership are seen especially in a manger's relationship with subordinates (Mosley, Megginsen, & Pietri, 2005).

Leaders are often classified by their approach (i.e., autocratic, democratic or participative, or laissez-faire) or their orientation toward getting the job done (i.e., task- or production-oriented or people-oriented or employee-centered). These approaches have been defined by a variety of scholars (Mosley et al., 1996; Mosley et al., 2005; Rodenz, 2006; Williams, 2007) as follows:

Autocratic leaders are often called authoritarian leaders who make most decisions themselves instead of allowing their followers to participate in making them. They are also characterized as "pushers" or "drill instructors."

Democratic or participative leaders involve their followers in groups who are heavily involved in the decision process.

Laissez-faire leaders are often called free-rein leaders who are "loose" or permissive and let followers do what they wish.

Task-oriented or production-oriented leaders focus on getting the job done. They emphasize planning, scheduling, and processing work and they exercise close control of quality.

People-oriented or employee-centered leaders focus on the welfare and feelings of followers, have confidence in themselves, and have a strong need to develop and empower their team members.

Leadership Theories

There are six key leadership theories that all future managers need to be aware of as they develop their leadership skills. These theories are behavioral, contingency-situational, servant-leaders, traitist, transactional leaders, and transformational leaders. These theories are defined below:

Behavioral theories are a group of theories of leadership that emphasize favorable treatment of employees rather than their output or performance. The leading theories in this area are McGregor's theory X and Y, Ouchi's theory Z, Likert's four management systems, and Blake and Mouton's management grid.

Theory X suggests that workers dislike work and must be coerced, controlled, and directed in order to achieve company objectives.

Theory Y indicates that workers accept work as natural, seek responsibility, and will exercise self-direction and self-control to achieve company objectives.

Theory Z is a theory of leadership that emphasizes long-range planning, consensus decision making, and strong mutual worker-employer loyalty.

Leadership grid® is a leadership model that focuses on task (production) and employee (people) orientations of managers as well as combinations of concerns between the two extremes.

Contingency-situational theories are leadership theories (i.e., Tannenbaum and Schmidt's leadership continuum, and Hersey and Blanchard's life-cycle theory) prescribing that the style to be used is contingent on such factors as the situation, the people, the tasks, the organization, and other environmental variables.

Leadership continuum is a range of behavior associated with leadership styles from democratic to authoritarian.

Life-cycle theory is a theory that the leader's style should reflect the maturity level of employees and that draws heavily on previous leadership research.

Servant-leaders are leaders who serve the people he leads, which implies that they are an end in themselves rather than a means to an organizational purpose or bottom line. The servant leader **devotes him-/herself to serving the needs of organization members,** focuses on meeting the needs of those they lead, develops employees to bring out the best in them, coaches others and encourages their self-expression, facilitates personal growth in all who work with them, and listens and builds a sense of community. Servant leaders are felt to be effective because the needs of followers are so looked after that they reach their full potential and hence perform at their best.

Traitist theories are theories of leadership that claim leaders possess certain traits or characteristics (i.e., supervisory ability, need for occupational achievement, intelligence, decisiveness, self-assurance, and initiative) that cause them to rise above their followers.

Transactional leaders are leaders who identify desired performance standards, recognize what types of rewards employees want, and take actions that make receiving these rewards contingent upon achieving performance standards.

Transformational leaders are leaders who provide charismatic leadership, individualized consideration, and intellectual stimulation.

Summary

Sport is a global, rapidly growing industry. The sport industry is composed of organizations that are involved in sport. A large number of different types of organizations make up the sport industry, including amateur sports, professional sports, sporting goods manufacturers, sport goods retailers, public assembly facilities, sport management consultants, sport agencies, etc. Whether it is a freestanding industry or segment of the entertainment industry, sport is a multibillion-dollar business.

Governing bodies are an important part of the sport industry. Any given governing body is structured in a way to achieve its stated mission within the environment in which it works. The aim of this chapter was to introduce the sport industry and outline the component parts of a sport organization. An organization is when two or more people interact to achieve a common goal. Every organization is impacted by the general, task, and internal environments. Organization behavior is the study of individuals and small groups within the organization and the characteristics of the environment in which the people work. Organizational culture refers to the shared philosophies, values, beliefs, and behavior patterns that form the organization's core identity. Organizational theory is the study of the design and structure of organizations. The structural elements of organizational design

include complexity, formalization, centralization, specialization, standardization, departmentalization, and size. Governing bodies acquire legal authority and jurisdiction through its governing documents.

Management involves four functions: planning, organizing, leading, and controlling. Management is important because it establishes objectives for the organization, maintains a balance among stockholders, and achieves efficiency and effectiveness within the organization. Managers implement the plans and leaders develop and sell the plans. There are three generally accepted approaches to leadership—autocratic, democratic or participative, or laissez-faire. Some would say there is a fourth approach known as orientation toward completing a task—task- or production-oriented, or people-oriented or employee centered. There are six key leadership theories that all managers need to understand including behavioral theories (i.e., theory X, theory Y, theory Z, and leadership grid), contingency-situational theories (i.e., leadership continuum and life-cycle theory), servant-leaders, traitist theories, transactional leaders, and transformational leaders.

References

Colley, J. L., Doyle, J. L., Logan, G. W., & Stettinius, W. (2003). *Corporate governance*. New York: McGraw-Hill.

Daft, R. L. (2003). *Management* (6th ed.). Cincinnati, OH: South-Western.

Daft, R. L. (2007). *Organizational theory and design* (9th ed.). Cincinnati, OH: South-Western.

Drucker, P. F. (1999). *Management challenges for the 21st century*. New York: HarperCollins Publishers.

Friedman, A., & Phillips, M. (2004). Balancing strategy and accountability: A model for the governance of professional associations. *Nonprofit Management and Leadership, 15*(2), 187-204.

Miller, G. A. (1987). Meta-analysis and the culture of free hypothesis. *Organization Studies, 4*, 309-325.

Mitzberg, H. (1979). *The structuring of organizations*. Englewood Cliffs, NJ: Prentice Hall.

Montana, P. J., & Charnov, B. H. (2000). *Management* (3rd ed.). Hauppauge, NY: Barron's Educational Series.

Mosley, D. C., Megginson, L. C., & Pietri, P. H. (2005). *Supervisory management: The art of inspiring, empowering, and developing* (6th ed.). Cincinnati, OH: South-Western.

Mosley, D. C., Pietri, P. H., & Megginson, L. C. (1996). *Management: Leadership in action* (5th ed.). New York: HarperCollins Publishers.

Rodenz, E. (2006). *Management fundamentals.* Cincinnati, OH: South-Western.

Slack, T., & Parent, M. M. (2006). *Understanding sport organizations: The application of organization theory* (2nd ed.). Champaign, IL: Human Kinetics.

United Nationals Economic and Social Commission for Asia and the Pacific. (2006). *What is good governance?* Retrieved September 1, 2006, from http://www.unescap.org/pdd/prs projectactivities /ongoing/gg/governance.asp

Williams, C. (2007). *Management* (4th ed.). Cincinnati, OH: South-Western

NOTES

CHAPTER 2

Planning Function

Planning is the process of determining the organization's goals and objectives and selecting a course of action to accomplish them within the environment inside and outside the organization (Daft, 2001). Its primary purpose is to offset future uncertainties by reducing the risk surrounding the organization's operations. It requires the organization to review its internal accomplishments (strengths) and challenges (weaknesses) and external opportunities and threats (Daft, 2007). During this process, the organization will develop a SWOT chart. A SWOT chart is a four-panel diagram, which depicts internal strengths and weakness across the top two panels, and external opportunities and threats across the lower two panels. It identifies connections within the organization as well as externally that will allow the organization to become strategically competitive in the future (See Figure 2.1).

Planning is essential for facility and event managers. The planning process is best facilitated by the use of brainstorming. Finally, participation by large numbers of stack holders initially increases overall acceptance of the final plan.

Learning Objectives

After reading this chapter the student should be able to:

- Describe the planning process,
- Understand the importance of the planning process,
- Identify the different type of plans that might exist in a typical enterprise,
- Recount the importance of strategic planning,
- Assess an enterprise's strengths and weaknesses,
- Recognize the ten biggest pitfalls to successful planning,
- Recount the characteristics of a goal and objective, and
- List some benefits of objectives.

Brainstorming

Brainstorming, developed by Alexander F. Osborn (1888-1966), involves forming a group of six to eight members who are presented a problem and asked to identify as many potential solutions as possible.

The session usually lasts from 30 minutes to an hour. At least two days before a session, group members are given a one-page summary of the problem they are to consider (Hussey, 1991; Rodenz, 2006; Sawyer, 2005). There are four rules of brainstorming: (a) Criticism is prohibited—Judgment of ideas must be withheld until all ideas have been generated. (b) "Freewheeling" is welcome—The wilder and further out the idea the better. It is easier to "tame down" than to "think up" ideas. (c) Quantity is wanted—The greater the number of ideas, the greater the likelihood of an outstanding solution. (d) Combination and improvement are sought—In addition to contributing ideas of their own, members are encouraged to suggest how the ideas of others can be improved or how two or more ideas can be combined into still another idea.

Business leaders all over the world have used brainstorming techniques to solve problems for many years. Traditional brainstorming is time consuming but a very valuable team-building process. If you only have a short period of time to loosen up a group and get everyone talking about solutions to a problem or inventing new initiatives, the answer is "fun and games" brainstorming. (Ensman, 1999; Williams, 2007).

Ensman's (1999) humorous, slightly offbeat techniques can be used to stimulate out-of-the-box thinking and discussion. They can be used to overcome marketing obstacles and productivity problems. They can help identify ways to enhance customer service, lower costs, improve an organization's image, and position an organization's operations for the future. Here are a few examples of "fun and games" brainstorming activities:

- Castles in the sand—The participants physically build a solution to the problem using blocks, putty, sand, or other materials.
- Communication gaps—Seat the participants in a circle. Whisper some variation of your current business problem into the ear of the first person sitting on the right in the circle. Ask that individual to repeat what was heard to the next person and so on until the message comes back around full circle. By that time, it will have changed—and the group may have a new perspective on the situation.
- Detective work—Appoint members of the group as detectives and charge them with solving the crime at hand. Group members must conduct an investigation, seek clues having a bearing on the problem, identify suspect causes of the problem, and, eventually, pose a resolution of the case.
- Make it worse—Invite members of the group to imagine all the possible ways they could make the solution worse. In stark contrast to this humorous exercise, prospective solutions will probably abound.
- Playmates—Invite participants to bring a partner not connected to the group along to the brainstorming session and become part of the proceedings. Or, invite members of the group to select imaginary playmates such as historical figures, celebrities, or competitors and conduct imaginary discussions about the issues at hand with these individuals.
- Pretend—Invite the members of the group to portray the customers, employees, or vendors involved with the issue at hand. Then let these characters address the issue in their own words.

Conducting a Needs Assessment Survey

The success of a facility or event thrives on its ability to fulfill the needs of the consumer. Many facility and event managers administer needs assessment surveys to gauge client and/or community needs. Needs assessment surveys can help pinpoint what consumers want and do not want. They can be used to evaluate services or to predict if patrons will use new programs. The most difficult aspect of coordinating a needs assessment survey is determining what information is needed to plan for the future of your facility or event (Busser, 1999).

Busser (1999) offers the following tips when structuring survey questions:

Collecting Data

A needs assessment can collect eight major categories of information (Busser, 1999). Consider these categories of data collection to determine the information that will be needed: demographic data, user participation patterns or current levels of use, attitudes of employees, barriers to participation, predictions of future participation, appraisal of existing facilities and programs, health hazard appraisal, and areas of improvement.

Demographic data—This includes all relevant information regarding the demographics of consumers. Demographic data includes age, gender, marital status, residential location, number of family members living at home, number and ages of children, work shift, and job classification. Demographic data is useful in constructing a profile of the needs for particular groups of users or participants. For example, single users or participants may be interested in fitness activities, while others with children may desire family programs. Use this information to focus your program development on the needs of that particular audience.

User participation patterns or current levels of use—This category assesses the frequency of participation in existing programs and services. These data are useful in determining participation trends, i.e., examining if existing programs and services are under or over utilized given the allocated resources

and tracking changes in participation from year to year. Additionally, this information is valuable when you are faced with the need to purchase additional equipment or to justify requests for new facilities. Registration data is often used to construct participation trends. However, the patterns of facility and equipment use usually are not contained in registration data.

Attitudes of the consumer—It is essential to identify the attitudes and beliefs of consumers regarding the prominent aspects of program plans. Attitudes are the consumers' feelings related to the importance of various issues or services. Consider addressing consumers' attitudes such as the value they place on family programs, childcare, eldercare, and the opportunity to socialize with fellow users (Busser, 1999). The determination of these attitudes may be beneficial in setting objectives and establishing priorities for the facility or event.

Barriers to participation—Busser (1999) suggests the barriers to participation are the constraints that consumers perceive as preventing their participation in programs or services. One significant barrier to participation revolves around consumers' lack of awareness or knowledge that a program or service exists. Other potential barriers include work schedules, family responsibilities, lack of interest, and lack of convenience. If these and similar perceived barriers to participation are explored in a needs assessment, the programmer can resolve those issues that may prevent consumers from participating in programs and services. In turn the effectiveness of the facility or event is increased.

Predictions of future participation—If the provider is more concerned with long-term planning, ask the respondents to project their future needs. This is a very useful category of need identification when considering equipment purchases, constructing new facilities, or deliberating contractual arrangements to supplement the existing services and programs.

Appraisal of existing facilities and programs—Give the consumers the opportunity to rate the quality of existing facilities, services, and programs. Use the feedback and evaluation data to prove the need for appropriate changes. In addition, this information provides insight into the current level of consumer satisfaction with the association.

Health hazard appraisal—Health hazard appraisals are standardized instruments used to evaluate the current health status of consumers and to estimate the presence of potential risk factors that are predictors for disease. Risk factors include smoking, stress, family history of disease, high blood pressure, high cholesterol, and poor nutrition. The health hazard appraisal evaluates a respondent's risks compared to national statistics on the causes of death, the consumer's medical history and lifestyle. Comparisons are then made with others in the same age and gender group. Use the results of the appraisal to explain specific recommendations to an client or consumer. Results can also indicate potential areas for the development of services and programs.

Areas for improvement—This component of a needs assessment provides employees with the opportunity to share suggestions or issues related to the association and its programs, services, facilities, policies, and procedures. This willingness to go to the employees for their opinions fosters a dialogue, which indicates a commitment on the part of the association to resolve problems and to provide quality programs (Busser, 1999).

Collecting Data on Needs

Once the facility or event manager has determined the kind of information he or she would like to uncover from the needs assessment, the next step is to collect the data. There are many research methods available to collect data on needs. Using research methods to conduct a needs assessment requires specific knowledge and skills in order to ensure that the data collected is valid and reliable. The validity of a needs assessment refers to the degree to which the information collected accurately portrays the needs of consumers. For example, a needs assessment that focuses only on satisfaction with special events is not a valid assessment of overall satisfaction with the facility and should not be used as such.

Reliability is concerned with the consistency of the data. Consistency indicates that the information obtained through the assessment truly represents the employees' perspective and is not influenced by outside factors. For example, a needs assessment that asks for overall program satisfaction may obtain different responses if conducted in the summer versus the winter, especially if there is a strong summer activities program and no activities provided in the winter. If the planner wants to determine comprehensive levels of satisfaction, the reliability of this assessment is doubtful. While several methods of data collection are appropriate for needs assessment, we will focus on the survey (Busser, 1999).

Surveys

Surveys provide the greatest opportunity to solicit consumer input and to generalize the findings from a smaller group of consumers to the community as a whole. Surveys require expertise from knowledgeable individuals to implement successfully. Consider consulting the local and state Chamber of Commerce or a market research firm. There are five steps in the survey process: (a) an operational definition of the purpose of the survey, (b) the design and pre-testing of data-collection instruments (i.e., the questionnaire or the interview guide), (c) the selection of a community sample, (d) the data collection, and (e) an analysis of the data (Busser, 1999; Rodenz, 2006; Sawyer, 2005; Williams, 2007).

The design of the survey includes the development of the specific questions to be answered by consumers and decisions concerning the form of the questions (e.g., multiple choice, fill in the blank). At this stage, determine the directions for completing the survey, the procedures for carrying out the survey, and the method of returning completed questionnaires. Pre-testing the data-collection instrument is essential to uncovering and eliminating any difficulties that may exist in the data-collection procedure. Pre-tests are mini-surveys you can conduct with a small group of employees by administering to them the questionnaire and asking them to identify any difficulties in understanding directions, questions, or the type of information solicited (Busser, 1999; Sawyer, 2005).

Sampling is the use of particular procedures that allow you to generalize the findings of a representative small group of consumers to the whole corporate workforce. By selecting employees through a random process (e.g., selecting every tenth person from a random listing of consumers), the results of the assessment are likely to be representative of the needs of all consumers, even though all consumers were not surveyed (Busser, 1999; Sawyer, 2005).

In collecting the data from consumers, it is important that the cover letter of the questionnaire explains the purpose of the survey and indicates that this information is confidential. It is the ethical responsibility of those individuals conducting the survey to ensure anonymity for respondents. After sending the questionnaire to consumers, follow up with phone calls, memos, or other methods to continue to solicit the return of surveys. To be considered sufficiently representative, at least 35 percent of the surveys must be completed and returned. Try offering incentives to increase the return rate. For example, the organization could offer consumers a discount on programs or purchases in the pro shop for complet-

ing and returning the survey (Busser, 1999; Rodenz, 2006).

Once the provider has collected and tabulated the data, it can be analyzed. The frequencies and percentages of responses to particular questions may reveal significantly desirable information. The data should be carefully analyzed to answer the questions and purpose of the survey. These results, then, become the basis for decision making regarding the needs of consumers, programs, and services.

Developing a Needs Assessment Report

Compile a needs assessment report and present it to management. The most appropriate method of sharing this report is to compile tables, graphs, and statistics in a manner that is easily understood. Provide a comprehensive report to management and an executive summary to interested consumers. The report should consist of the following components (Busser, 1999):

+ Title page
+ Executive summary (i.e., a short introductory summary of the entire report to allow the reader a quick overview of the report prior to reading the entire report.)
+ Introduction to the needs assessment study; purpose
+ Overview of methods and procedures
+ Results
+ Conclusions and recommendations

The Steps in the Planning Process

There are six steps in the planning process including establishing identifying relationships, objectives, developing premises, decision making, implementing a course of action, and evaluating the results (Sawyer, 2005; Williams, 2007; Wright, 1994).

Step 1: Identifying Internal and External Connections and Relationships

The initial step in the planning process is identifying internal strengths (accomplishments) and weaknesses (challenges), and external opportunities and threats (concerns). This information is placed into a SWOT analysis chart, which will assist in the identification of connections and relationships relating to the organization's internal and external environment.

Step 2: Establishing Objectives

The next step in the planning process is the establishment of organization objectives. An objective is a quantitative statement that assists the organization in determining if it is fulfilling its goals. An objective always contains quantifiable measures such as numbers, percentages, or dollar values. Objectives are tied directly to achieving specific goals. A goal is defined as a broad statement, qualitative in nature, which provides general direction for an organization (see Figure 2.2 for examples). Objectives are an essential starting point as they provide direction for all other managerial activities. Objectives are generally based on perceived opportunities that exist in an organization's surrounding environment.

Step 3: Developing Premises

Once organizational objectives have been established, developing premises about the future environment in which they are to be accomplished is essential. This basically involves forecasting events or conditions likely to influence the attainment of objectives.

The best way to identify items under each category is through using traditional brainstorming with the organization's employees and others outside the organization. The external opportunities category relates to those unique favorable circumstances that the organization might be able to take advantage of in the future. The external threat category refers to those circumstances that might be harmful to the organization if not carefully understood.

Figure 2.1
A Connections SWOT Chart

```
┌─────────────────────────────────────────────────────────────┐
│     ┌───────────────────────────────────────────┐            │
│     │   Goal # 1 Increase Annual Attendance      │            │
│     └───────────────────┬───────────────────────┘            │
│   ┌───────────────────────────────────────────────────────┐  │
│   │ • Objective # 1 Increase season ticket sales by 15    │  │
│   │   percent                                             │  │
│   │ • Objective # 2 Increase group sales to not-for-profit│  │
│   │   entities by 10 percent                              │  │
│   │ • Objective # 3 Increase the number of party suites   │  │
│   │   by five                                             │  │
│   └───────────────────────────────────────────────────────┘  │
│        ┌───────────────────────────────────────────┐         │
│        │   Goal # 2 Increase Advertising Sales      │         │
│        └───────────────────────────────────────────┘         │
│   ┌───────────────────────────────────────────────────────┐  │
│   │ • Objective # 1 Increase available advertising space  │  │
│   │   by 10 percent                                       │  │
│   │ • Objective # 2 Increase advertising by 10 percent    │  │
│   │ • Objective # 3 Increase advertising in sponsorship   │  │
│   │   packages by five percent                            │  │
│   └───────────────────────────────────────────────────────┘  │
│       ┌───────────────────────────────────────────┐          │
│       │   Goal # 3 Increase Sponsorship Revenues   │          │
│       └───────────────────────────────────────────┘          │
│   ┌───────────────────────────────────────────────────────┐  │
│   │ • Objective # 1 Secure 10 new corporate sponsors      │  │
│   │ • Objective # 2 Increase the value of existing        │  │
│   │   sponsorships by five percent a year for the next    │  │
│   │   five years                                          │  │
│   │ • Objective # 3 Increase the revenue based services   │  │
│   │   available for each VIP suite                        │  │
│   └───────────────────────────────────────────────────────┘  │
└─────────────────────────────────────────────────────────────┘
```

Figure 2.2
Goals and Objectives

Step 4: Decision Making

After establishing objectives and developing premises, the next step is selecting the best course of action for accomplishing stated objectives from the possible alternatives. There are three phases of decision making: (a) available alternatives must be identified, (b) each alternative must be evaluated in light of the premises about the future and the external environment, and (c) the alternative with the highest estimated probability of success should be selected.

Step 5: Implementing a Course of Action

Once a plan of action has been adopted, it must be implemented. Plans alone are no guarantee of success. Managers must initiate activities that will translate these plans into action.

Step 6: Evaluating the Plan

Plans and their implementation must be constantly monitored and evaluated. All managers are responsible for the evaluation of planning outcomes. Comparison of actual results with those projected is necessary to refine plans.

Classification of Plans

Plans can be viewed from a number of different perspectives. From the viewpoint of application, plans can be classified in terms of functional areas (e.g., marketing plans, production plans, human resource management plans, financial plans). Plans may also be classified according to the period of time over which they are projected (e.g., short- or long-range) or with respect to their frequency of use (standing versus single-use). The nature of functional plans is evident by their descriptors (e.g., financial, marketing, strategic, etc.). However, further explanation is needed for period of time and frequency of use plans.

Short- and long-range plans are the most popular classification of plans. In practice, however, the terms short-range and long-range have no precise meaning, but rather express relative periods of time. These plans are interrelated in at least two respects. First, they compete for the allocation of resources. Consequently, there can be a dangerous tendency to sacrifice long-term results for short-term gains. Second, short-range plans should be compatible with long-range plans. It is usually difficult, if not impossible, for long-range plans to succeed unless short-range plans are accomplished. Thus, both are important in achieving an organization's objectives.

Short-term plans are often referred to as operational plans in many organizations; and long-term plans can be referred to as applied strategic plans. These terms will be used interchangeably throughout the remainder of the chapter.

There are three criteria most often used in determining the length of a plan: (a) how far into the future an organization's commitments extend, (b) how much uncertainty is associated with the future, and (c) how much lead time is required to ready a good or service for sale (Paley, 1991; Rodenz, 2006; Sawyer, 2005; Williams, 2007).

Planning by most effective organizations is often done on a "rolling" basis. This simply means those organizations that develop applied strategic plans for a five-year period and two-year operational plans are updating both plans on an annual basis. As the current year of a five- year plan closes, it is extended or rolled forward to include a new fifth year. This procedure allows an organization to revise its plans on the basis of new information and to maintain a degree of flexibility in its commitments. A gen-

eral guideline is to refrain from formalizing plans until a final commitment is absolutely necessary (Fogg, 1994; Sawyer 2005).

Standing plans are used on a recurring basis focusing on managerial situations that recur repeatedly. Standing plans include policies, procedures, and rules.

Policies are general statements that serve to guide decision making. They are plans in that they prescribe parameters within which certain decisions are to be made. Policies set limits, but they are subject to interpretation because they are broad guidelines. Table 2.1 provides examples of policies. Notice that each example is purposefully broad and only provides a general guideline subject to managerial discretion. However, each statement does prescribe parameters for decision making and, thus, sets limits to the actions of organization members.

A *procedure* is a series of related steps that are to be followed in an established order to achieve a given purpose. Procedures prescribe exactly what actions are to be taken in a specific situation. Procedures are similar to policies in that both are intended to influence certain decisions. They are different in that policies address themselves to single decisions while procedures address themselves to a sequence of related decisions. Table 2.2 shows how an organization might write procedures for processing a bill of sale.

Rules are different from policies and procedures in that they specify what personal conduct is required of an individual. Stated differently, rules are standing plans that either prescribe or prohibit action by specifying what an individual may or may not do in a given situation. Therefore, the statements "eye goggles must be worn", "no swimming alone", "no smoking", "no drinking on premises" are all examples of rules. Rules are usually accompanied by specifically stated penalties that vary according to the seriousness of the offense and number of previous violations. Unlike policies that guide, but do not eliminate discretion, rules

Table 2.1
Examples of Policies

Customer Service:	It is the policy of this organization to provide customers with the finest service possible within limits of sound financial principles. [Interpretation = What are the limits of sound finance?]
Employee Benefits:	It is the policy of this organization to provide its employees with acceptable working conditions and an adequate living wage. [Interpretation = What is acceptable and adequate?]
Promotion from Within:	It is the policy of this organization to promote qualified employees from within organization ranks whenever possible. [Interpretation = What is meant by qualified or feasible?]
Gifts from Suppliers or Vendors:	It is the policy of this organization that no employee shall accept any gift from any supplier or vendor unless it is of nominal value. [Interpretation = What is nominal?]

leave little room for interpretation. The only element of choice associated with a rule is whether it applies in a given situation. Of the three forms of standing plans discussed, rules are the simplest and most straightfor-

Table 2.2
Procedure for Processing a Bill of Sale

Step 1:	Prior to recording, all non-cash sales will be forwarded to the credit department for approval.
Step 2:	Following necessary credit approval, all bills of sale will be presented to production scheduling for an estimated product completion date.
Step 3:	Subsequent to production scheduling, all bills of sale will be delivered to the accounting department where they will be recorded.
Step 4:	Pursuant to their processing in the accounting department, all bills of sale will be filed with the shipping department within 24 hours.

ward. They are, without question, the narrowest in scope and application.

Single-use plans are specifically developed to implement courses of action that are relatively unique and are unlikely to be repeated. Three principal forms of single-use plans are budgets, programs, and projects.

A *budget* is a plan that deals with the future allocation and utilization of various resources to different activities over a given time period. Budgets are perhaps most frequently thought of in financial terms. However, they also are used to plan allocation and utilization of labor, raw materials, floor space, machine hours, and so on. A budget simply is a tool that managers use to translate future plans into numerical terms. Further, they are a method for controlling organization operations.

Programs are typically intended to accomplish a specific objective within a fixed time. Table 2.3 offers six guidelines for effective program development.

Projects are usually a subset or component part of a specific program. Accordingly, projects often share some of the same characteristics as the overall programs of which they are a part. Projects are less complex than

**Table 2.3
Guidelines for Effective Program
Development**

1. Divide the overall program into parts, each with clearly defined purpose.
2. Study the necessary sequence and relationships between the resulting parts.
3. Assign appropriate responsibility for each part to carefully selected individuals or groups.
4. Determine and allocate the resources necessary for the completion of each part.
5. Estimate the completion time required for each part.
6. Establish target dates for the completion of each part.

their supporting programs and are, by definition, narrower in scope. Table 2.4 summarizes the various standing and single-use plans.

Strategic planning

Strategic planning, unlike operational planning which focuses on more direct aspects of operating an organization, focuses on an organization's long-term relationship to its environment (Abraham, 2006; Hitt, Ireland, & Hoskisson, 2007; Wright, Pringle, Kroll, & Parnell, 1994). The strategic plan should be developed employing participatory involvement by all members of the organization and its clients. By focusing on an organization as a total system, strategic planning recognizes that all organizations face many uncontrollable elements within the environment. Competitors' actions, economic conditions, regulatory groups, labor unions, and changing customer preferences represent factors over which an organization achieves its objectives. Therefore, strategic planning concerns itself with shaping

**Table 2.4
Summary of Standing and Single-use Plans**

Type	Definition	Example
Policy	A general statement that guides decision making.	"Preference will be given to hiring employees with disabilities.
Procedure	A series of related steps that are to be followed in an established order to achieve a given purpose.	Filing for travel expenses reimbursement.
Rule	A statement that either prescribes prohibits action by specifying what an individual may or may not do in a specific situation.	"No eating at work stations."
Single-Use Plans Budget	A plan that deals with the future allocations and utilization of various resources to different enterprise activities over a given time.	Allocation and utilization of machine hours.
Program	A plan typically intended to accomplish a specific objective within fixed time.	Membership Recruitment Program.
Project	A subset or component part of a specific program.	Telemarketing project.

an organization so it can accomplish its goals. A strategic plan attempts to answer such questions as:

- What is the organization's business and what should it be?
- What business should the organization be in five years from now? 10 years?
- Who are the organization's customers and who should they be?
- Should the organization try to grow in this business or grow primarily in other businesses? (Abraham, 2006; Antoniou, 1994; Hitt, Ireland, & Hoskisson, 2007)

Objectives

Objectives are those ends that an organization seeks to achieve by its existence and operation. There are two essential characteristics of an objective: (a) objectives are predetermined and (b) objectives describe *future* desired results toward which *present* efforts are directed. According to Drucker and others (Abraham, 2006; Drucker, 1988; Hitt, Ireland, & Hoskisson, 2007), there are eight *key result areas* in which all organizations should establish objectives including market share, innovation, productivity, physical and financial resources, profitability, manager performance and development, worker performance and attitude, and social responsibilities.

There are two ways to establish objectives. The first is the entrepreneurial method. Entrepreneurs (i.e., top managers or stack holders) establish the objectives in the entrepreneurial method. An organization's objectives are defined as the entrepreneur's objectives. The entrepreneur insures that employees' actions are consistent with these objectives by paying them—salaries, bonuses, or pensions—to support the goals.

The second method is the consensual method. In this method, the objectives of an organization are established by the general consent of those concerned. Organization members share in setting the objectives thus eliminating conflict by identifying common or consensual goals.

The Planning Premise

Once organizational objectives have been established, developing planning premises about the future environment in which they are to be accomplished is essential (Abraham, 2006; Hamel and Prahalad, 1994; Hoffman, 1993; Sawyer, 2005). Unfolding environmental conditions almost invariably influence enterprise objectives, forcing modifications in both current and anticipated activities. Premises, which attempt to describe what the future will be like, provide a framework for identifying, evaluating, and selecting a course of action for accomplishing organizational objectives.

The applied strategic plan is composed of a situational analysis, highlights, introduction, vision statement(s), value(s), mission statement, internal environment, external environment, connections, major action plans, action priorities, monitoring and evaluating, and review, approval, and commitment (Abraham, 2006; Goodstein, 1993; Hitt, Ireland, & Hoskisson, 2007; Sawyer, 2005). The *situational analysis* has five sections including a description of the geographical location and pertinent demographics (e.g., population, economic indicators, industry, average income, etc.), a description of the organization, a SWOT summary, an overview of major strategies and plans, and organization progress since last review.

The *highlight* section describes major challenges, customer/client needs, and major accomplishments. The *introduction* provides the reader with a brief description of the planning process and the people involved in the process. The *vision statement* describes the dream of the future for the organization. The *values* section describes that which is desirable or worthy of esteem by the organization (e.g., fostering a we care image with our clients). The *mission statement* is a statement outlining the purpose and mission of the organization. The *internal environment* is composed of a description of the organization's strengths (accomplishments) and weaknesses (challenges) and the *external environment* consists of a description of the organization's external opportunities and threats (concerns). After the internal and external environments have been analyzed, a series of *connections* are established based on the relationships found in the analysis. From the connections, a series of *major action plans* are established. The actions plans are then translated into *major action priorities*. These major action priorities are the foundation for the one- or two-year operational plan. The applied strategic plan must have established *monitoring and evaluating* procedures in place to assure the proper implementation of the plan. Finally, there must be *review, approval, and commitment* steps established for the final acceptance of the plan.

The operational plan includes the following components: major action priorities, problem, project summary, priority issue(s), background, vision of success, goals and objectives of the plan, and action plans (strategies, objectives, baseline data, and action steps).

Each major action priority will have a specific *problem(s)* that will be resolved at the completion of the project. The *project summary* describes briefly the project that will be undertaken by the organization. Each project will have one or more *priority issues* to be tackled during the project. Each major action priority will have a section that outlines the historical significance of the issue(s) relating to the action priority. This section is called *background*. The authors of the operational plan will describe a *vision of success* for each major action priority. Each major action priority will have one or more *goals* and a series of *objectives* for each goal.

Each major action priority has an *action plan*. The action plan can have one or more *strategies*, which can have one or more *objectives*. Each action plan has *baseline data* to be used to compare what was with what is. This comparison over the years will establish progress. For each action plan, there will be a series of *action steps*. Each action step will outline the *resources* to be used to complete the step, who's *responsible* for the completion of each step, and when the project will *start* and *complete*.

What Are the Pitfalls of Planning?

Strategic planning is a process requiring great skill. It can be frustrating and require a great deal of time. An inability to predict the future can create anxiety and feelings of inadequacy. The ten biggest pitfalls to successful planning include:

- Top management assumes that it can delegate its planning function, and thus not become directly involved.
- Top management becomes so involved in current problems that it spends insufficient time on planning, and consequently planning becomes discredited at lower levels.
- Top management fails to clearly define and develop organizational goals as a basis for formulating long-range goals.
- Top management fails to adequately involve major line managers in the planning process.
- Top management is unsuccessful in using plans as a standard for assessing managerial performance.

Table 2.5
Tips for Writing Plans

The following are a few tips that may assist the organization planner in preparing the applied strategic or operational plans:

- Include a table of contents describing the overall content and organization of the plan, including page numbers.
- Format the plan consistently using the same style for sections, subsections, headings, and subheadings, etc., with a consistent use of numbers or letters for headings.
- Number all pages. Number the pages consecutively.
- Spell out and define all acronyms so that readers unfamiliar with the organization's programs and operations will understand the plan.
- Write clearly and concisely, with short declarative sentences and active verbs.
- Order the plan elements, provide cross-references when necessary, and develop a topic or subject index so that a reader can follow major ideas, themes, throughout the document.
- Make all references to other documents, plans, or reports clear and specific enough to allow a reader to easily find the item or section referenced.
- Include in an appendix any information that is not critical to understanding the plan but that provides useful background or context.
- Structure the plan in a way that will permit sections to be excerpted and distributed to specific audiences and that will permit changes, edits, or updates without revising the whole plan.
- Test the understandability of the document by having it reviewed by individuals who were not directly involved in its development.
- On each section, type its computer file name (to speed retrieval in the future). In addition, during the draft process, include date/time code (to keep track of the most up-to-date revision). During the draft process, it helps to also hand-write the draft (revision) number in the corner as each revision is printed or establishing a watermark (Draft Document 1).

- Top management falls short in creating a congenial and supportive climate for planning.
- Top management assumes that comprehensive planning is something separate from other aspects of the management process.
- Top management creates a planning program that lacks flexibility and simplicity and fails to encourage creativity.
- Top management fails to review and evaluate long-range plans that have been developed by department and division heads.
- Top management makes intuitive decisions that conflict with formal plans (Nolan, 1993; Poirier, 1996; Sawyer, 2005).

Effective Delegation in the Planning Process

Do any of these statements sound familiar? "If you want something done right—do it yourself!" "It will take me more time to explain it to you than if I do it myself!" "It is easier and faster for me to do it, so I will do it!"

One of the traps a manager falls into is PERFECTIONISM (i.e., feeling as though he/she is the only person who can work with a special supplier, handle a ticklish situation, or create the promotional materials for a program). A manager is much more effective if he teaches others how to do various tasks and then supervises their efforts. It is impossible to do everything equally as well when one is spread too thin. Finally, there are five common reasons why managers fail to delegate. They are: (a) Nobody does it better, (b) Guilt, (c) Insecurity, (d) Lack of trust, and (e) Takes time (Sawyer, 2005).

Effective delegation requires that the delegator: (a) state a clear objective, (b) determine guidelines for the project, (c) set any limitations or constraints, (d) grant the person the authority to carry out the assignment, (e) set the deadline for its completion, and (f) decide the best means for the person to provide the manager with regular progress reports (e.g., oral or written: weekly, monthly, semi-annually, or annually) (Sawyer, 2005). Further, the manager can employ any one of seven levels of delegation: (a) Decide and take action; you need not check back with me. (b) Decide and take action; but, let me know what you did. (c) Decide and let me know your decision, then take action unless I say not to. (d) Decide and then let me know your decision but wait for my go ahead, (e) Decide what you would do but tell me your alternatives with the pros and cons of each, (f) Look into this problem and give me the facts. I will decide. (g) Wait to be told (Sawyer, 2005).

Planning Teams . . . Friend or Foe?

If a planning team is formed the right way, it can accelerate the planning process, reduce the time to complete a plan, and reduce operating costs, but if it is done incorrectly, just the opposite can happen. There are a number of wrong reasons for initiating a team approach to planning, including (a) a belief that teams will produce better results automatically, (b) it is the popular thing to do, (c) we have downsized and have fewer managers, and (d) we have downsized and have fewer employees (Wilbur, 1999).

However, there are a number of right reasons to consider utilizing teams, including (a) an organizational belief in creating an environment where people can give their best, (b) an increase in the flexibility of the organization, and (c) an organization's structure is already suited to a team approach.

There are two categories of teams—performance and problem solving. *Performance teams* are structured around work processes (e.g., financial development, community and media relations, programming, etc.). The members are employees who have been hired to do the work. It is a permanent structure of the organization and operates on a daily basis. Participation on the team is mandatory. The team establishes its mission, identifies key performance indicators, measures and monitors performance, solves problems, removes barriers to performance, and holds itself accountable for high levels of performance. Further, the team is empowered to change work processes and has decision-making authority within boundaries. Finally, the team requires training in identifying customers, performance measurement, and work process evaluation, and team leadership, problem solving, group dynamics, and coaching.

The *problem-solving team* is structured around expertise in problem areas such as emergency management, financial development, risk management, and more. Its members are hand selected for their expertise in the problem area. The problem-solving team has a temporary structure that is disbanded after the problem is solved. It represents extra work for those assigned, as such participation is often voluntary. The team is provided a mandate outlining the problem to be solved. It uses a systematic approach to problem solving. Further, the team makes recommendations for change and has no decision-making authority. Finally, the team requires training in complex problem solving.

Transforming a group of people into a team requires the following:

- Management that values individual initiative and high levels of employee participation versus maintaining the status quo.
- Employees who are eager to learn and welcome the opportunity for training.
- Employees who have a "we can solve anything" attitude.
- Accountability is based on process and results.
- Performance management systems are aligned with and support teams.
- Management is willing to walk the talk.
- Strong team values are established.

Sample team values include: (a) perform with enthusiasm, (b) share time, resources, and ideas with each other, (c) consult together to achieve unity of thought and action, (d) listen to each other, encourage, clarify points of view, ask questions and support other coworkers' opinions, (e) encourage continuous improvement in work and in learning, (f) perform tasks right the first time, (g) not initiating or receiving gossip, (h) encourage using appropriate channels to express disagreement/concern, work through problems and look for win-win solutions, and (i) attach problems aggressively and support people.

In Chart 2.1, Wilbur (1999) describes common team problems and how to solve them.

Summary

The need for planning stems from the fact that virtually all organizations operate in a changing environment. The uncertainty resulting from environmental change makes planning a necessity in all but the simplest circumstances. This chapter has identified the phases of the planning process, commented on the importance of planning, examined the scope and application of different types of enterprise plans, introduced the concept of strategic planning and discussed pitfalls in planning.

The planning process is composed of five repetitive and interactive phases that must be considered simultaneously. During each phase, an organization should look ahead and back to determine how other phases affect implementation at a particular time. The five phases of the planning process are: (a) establishing goals and objectives, (b) developing premises, (c) decision making, (d) implementing a course of action, and (e) evaluating results.

Planning is important for at least four basic reasons: (a) it helps enterprises succeed, (b) it provides direction and a sense of purpose, (c) it helps managers cope with change, and (d) it contributes to the perfor-

Chart 2.1
Common Team Problems and How to Solve Them

Problem	Solution
Too much time spent in meetings	One hour a week set aside for a meeting
Too much responsibility, no authority	Clarify boundaries and level of authority
Lack of direction	Management sets clear direction
Over/under empowerment	Empowerment tied to competency level
Unclear purpose	Clarify mission and performance objectives
Lack of training	Provide necessary training
Withdrawal of management support	Build team structure to sustain itself

mance of other managerial functions. Plans can be classified in terms of (a) functional areas (i.e., marketing plans, production plans, personnel plans, financial plans, and so forth), (b) period of time (i.e., short- versus long-range), and (c) frequency of use (i.e., standing versus single-use). Strategic planning is important because it serves to define an enterprise's overall character, mission, and direction.

The assessment of an enterprise's strengths and weaknesses involves considering a range of factors related to a specific industry and the positioning of a company within the industry.

Objectives are predetermined and stated in advance and describe future desired results toward which present efforts are directed. Objectives serve as: (a) guidelines for action, (b) constraints, (c) a source of legitimacy, (d) standards of performance, and (e) a source of motion.

References

Abraham, S. C. (2006). *Strategic planning: A guide for competitive success.* Cincinnati: South Western.

Antoniou, P. H. (1994). *Competitiveness through strategic success.* Oxford, OH: Planning Forum.

Bannon, J. J. (1978). *Leisure resources: It's comprehensive planning.* Englewood Cliffs, NJ: Prentice-Hall.

Busser, J. A. (1999). Conducting a needs assessment survey. *ESM Magazine, 42*(9), 28-31.

Daft, R. L. (2007). *Organizational theory and design.* (9th ed.). Cincinnati: South Western.

Daft, R. L. (2001). *Essentials of organizational theory and design.* (2nd ed.). Cincinnati: South Western.

Ensman, R. G., Jr. (1999). Fun and games: Solving problems with playful brainstorming techniques. *Employee Services Management, 42*(2), 9-10.

Fogg, D. C. (1994). *Team-based strategic planning: A complete guide to structuring, facilitating, and implementing the process.* New York: American Management Association.

Girdano, D. A. (1986). *Occupational health promotion: A practical guide to program development.* New York: Macmillian.

Goodstein, L. D., Nolan, T. M., & Pfeiffer, W. J. (1993). *Applied strategic planning: A comprehensive guide.* New York: McGraw-Hill.

Hamel, G., & Prahalad, C. K. (1994). *Competing for the future.* Boston: Harvard Business School Press.

Hitt, M. A., Ireland, R. D., & Hoskisson, R. E. (2007). *Strategic management: Concepts and cases.* Cincinnati: South Western.

Hoffman, A. N., & O'Neill, H. M. (1993). *The strategic management casebook and skill builder.* Minneapolis/St. Paul: West Publishing.

Hussey, D. E. (1991). *Introducing corporate planning: Guide to strategic management.* New York: Pergamon Press.

Nolan, T. M. (1993). *Plan or die: 10 keys to organizational success.* San Diego: Pfeiffer & Co.

Paley, N. (1991). *The strategic marketing planner.* New York: AMACOM.

Poirier, C. C. (1996). *Avoiding the pitfalls of total quality.* Milwaukee, WI: ASQC Quality Press.

Pollar, O. (1997). Effective delegation. *Employee Services Management, 40*(9), 13-16.

Rodenz, E. (2006). *Management fundamentals.* Cincinnati: South Western.

Sawyer, T. H. (2005). *Facility design and management for health, physical activity, recreation, and sports facility development.* (11th ed.). Champaign, IL: Sagamore Publishing.

Wilbur, R. A. (1999). Teams ... friend or foe? *Employee Services Management, 42*(5), 9-11.

Williams, C. (2007). *Management* (4th ed.). Cincinnati: South Western.

Wright, P. L., Pringle, C. D., Kroll, M. J., & Parnell, J. A. (1994). *Strategic management: Text and cases.* Boston: Allyn and Bacon.

York, R. O. (1982). *Human service planning.* Chapel Hill, NC: The University of North Carolina Press.

NOTES

CHAPTER 3

Policy Development in Sport

Sport is a colossal undertaking in the global arena. For any given sport, there is likely to be local, national, and international governing bodies responsible for creating and implementing policy. Policies should not be thought of as merely outputs from a governing body. Rather, polices are living, breathing entities (Anderson, 2006). These entities shape and are shaped by the political and social conditions within the governing body as well as the external environment.

As a result, the contemporary sport manager must have a sound understanding of how policies are created and used, and an appreciation for the scope, complexity, diversity, and vast number of policies created on an annual basis. In this chapter, policy making will be discussed in relation to sport governing bodies. This is a macro approach where decisions impact the functioning of sport business on a large scale. From this perspective, policies that are enacted impact a sizeable number of people, with differing goals, spread across a large geographic area over a relatively long period of time. Understanding policy development will allow the sport manager to influence decisions in his or her favor.

Learning Objectives

Upon completion of this chapter, the reader should be able to:

- Discuss policy making as a form of applied problem solving.
- Recognize why sport managers study public policy.
- Describe what makes public policy public.
- Distinguish between key terms such as policy domain, policy analysis, policy development, public policy, and policy statements.
- Distinguish between the various types of policy.
- Recognize the different participants in the policy process.
- Describe the elements of policy design.
- Discuss the stage model of policy development.

Public Policy as Applied Problem Solving

Sport problems are complex. For any given challenge, there is a myriad of cause-

and-effect relationships that can be fraught with confusion, contradiction, and consternation. Further, the political environment and value system of those involved add to issue complexity. Nonetheless, managers must use problem-solving techniques to find practical solutions in the sport environment. Public policy is a type of applied problem solving. Simply put, problem solving is the ability to generate new answers (Arnold, Heyne, & Busser, 2005). A basic model may include five stages: problem recognition, proposal of solution, choice of solution, implementing solution, and monitoring results. Similarly, the policy process involves strategically thinking about the causes and cures of problems. The stage model of the policy cycle includes agenda setting, policy formation, decision making, policy implementation, and policy evaluation. As shown in Figure 1, there is a degree of "sameness" between these models.

The environment directs and limits what policy makers can effectively do. Therefore, sport managers should be aware of the ever-changing political culture as well as the relevant socioeconomic conditions that impact how problems are resolved. Political culture includes values, beliefs, and attitudes about what governing bodies should try to do, how they should operate, and their relationships with members. Both social and economic conditions limit the type and extent of oversight a governing body can provide. For example, consider drug testing and penalties in professional sport. What are the prevailing social values, beliefs, and attitudes about recreational or performance-enhancing drug use? Do the major leagues have a responsibility or obligation to monitor athletes', trainers', or coaches' behavior in this area? To what extent can and should they "police" participants? Do we assume guilt until proven innocent or vice versa? What are the rights, implied or contracted, of participants? What are the social and financial costs? Does constant and unremitting oversight fit with national imperatives such as freedom or self-determination? The answers to these questions set parameters for how the specific governing body should approach and manage the problem.

When trying to solve problems, sport managers have different perspectives on what is "right", what "should" be done, or what is "good" policy. As such, value systems and moral philosophies are an inherent part of the policy process because they are an inherent part of the policy maker.

Applied Problem Solving	*Stages in Policy Cycle*
1. Problem recognition	Agenda setting
2. Proposal of solution	Policy formation
3. Choice of solution	Decision making
4. Putting solution into effect	Policy implementation
5. Monitoring results	Policy evaluation

Figure 3.1
Comparing Models

Moreover, sport managers have different outcome goals. The process of merging conflicting positions into acceptable outcomes (Gerston, 2004) relies on input from many social sciences. For instance, when generating and evaluating the merits of alternatives related to drug testing and penalties, the policy maker should consult with sport specialists trained in biochemistry, economics, history, law, philosophy, psychology, sociology, and other disciplines. This facilitates a more comprehensive understanding of the cause-effect relationships that created the problem and increases the likelihood of identifying an appropriate solution.

Why Do Sport Managers Study Public Policy?

Sport managers study policy to understand the process in order to effect change in the sport environment. Ultimately, it is about practicality. Sport managers need to know enough about the "game" to be players at the table. Being in the game provides an opportunity to give voice to the preferred problem definition and, more importantly, to advocate for policy options that benefit the organization. Alternatives may be crafted in ways to either maximize resources and benefits or minimize costs and burdens. By understanding the process, sport managers (as policy actors) can advocate for their preferred alternative to solve problems.

You may recall reading *The Little Prince* by Niccolo Machiavelli in your high school literature class. Machiavelli argued if we understand political action and plan to achieve our goals, we are better prepared to seize the opportunities when they become apparent. The sport environment is constantly evolving. It is essential to be prepared, because sport managers may not know when the chance to effect change will occur.

What Makes Public Policy Public?

In the broadest sense, public policy is public because it affects a variety of people in a way different from private decisions. This is why governing body policies are often so controversial, frustrating, and, at the same time, important. We can describe "public" in terms of interest, large number of people, and outside force (Birkland, 2001).

Sport managers often argue for their preferred policy in the name of *public interest*. In other words, an individual advocates for what he or she believes to be "good for everyone." However, what is "good for everyone" depends a great deal on who is doing the defining. Each individual or stakeholder group is going to have a particular viewpoint or ideology, and there are multiple and overlapping publics at the local, national, and international levels. For example, the International Olympic Committee (IOC) has a corporate sponsorship policy. Specifically, The Olympic Partner (TOP) program arranges agreements with multinational corporations to provide direct support, sponsor services, or expertise for staging the Games. Stakeholders argue business operations of some corporate sponsors are not aligned with the Olympic movement and, therefore, should not be included in the program. In this case, "what is good for everyone" is to select only those corporations who fully comply with the IOC mission. Others may argue; what is "good for everyone" is to select corporate sponsors best able to provide the support, services, and expertise needed at the Games.

Public policy also affects a *large number of people* at any given time. However, many of the people affected by any given sport policy do not have a voice in the process because they lack awareness about the issue or institutionalized barriers, such as closed meetings, limit their access to the debate.

Still other stakeholders have their voices "captured" by agencies that claim to advocate on their behalf. For instance, the U.S. Olympic Committee (USOC) is authorized by the U.S. Congress to oversee Olympic competition. The USOC has sole authority to "select" the Olympic delegation; however, it allows each sport national governing body to submit a roster of participants. The U.S. Congress, as the governing entity overseeing the USOC, may order the USOC not to submit the delegation to the IOC as part of political maneuvers. Athletes may not be aware that Congress can authorize a boycott or, at any given time, is considering such a decision. Further, individual athletes do not have a mechanism to speak directly to Congress. National governing bodies may argue sport and politics should be separate; however, athletes may not necessarily agree with or support statements made by the national governing body on their behalf.

Finally, public policy may be seen as an *outside force* impacting the way individuals go about their daily lives. By nature, individuals are inclined to be against policies they perceive as interfering or having a negative impact on their day-to-day activities. For example, as part of the Olympic Games, an athletes' village is constructed to enhance solidarity. Individual delegations are allowed to determine if and when athletes must report to the village. Some athletes may be opposed to this policy, believing it is their right to choose a residence most conducive to peak athletic performance.

Key Terms and Definitions

The creation of policy is a dynamic process. Events, actors, and political institutions combine and conflict in a wide array of unpredictable ways. To engage in the study of sport policy, a manager must have knowledge of terms and be able to relate those definitions to the literature. In this section, several terms are presented including policy domain, policy analysis, policy development, public policy, and policy statements.

Policy Domain

There are several different perspectives from which a sport manager may begin the policy-development process (Page, 2002; VanderZwaag, 1998). This is the policy domain, and it may be characterized in five different ways. First, policy allows a governing body to *take a stand on an issue*. A key point to remember is the issue must be a legitimate area of debate or within the jurisdiction of the organization. For example, Olympic athletes using performance-enhancing substances impacts how the Olympics Games are perceived by a worldwide audience. The IOC, as the governing body of the Games, is within its jurisdiction to make policy to deter the use of banned substances. However, it would be inappropriate for the IOC to establish a policy prohibiting coaches and athletes enrolled in NCAA member institutions from gambling on intercollegiate sport events.

Second, policy allows a governing body to *make progress toward solving a problem or eliminating an obstacle*. The policy provides direction for dealing with similar situations in a consistent manner over time. For example, the IOC has a policy that specifies the information to be included in a bid proposal and a timeline for site selection to host the Olympic Games. The bidding process is the same regardless of which cities are involved or whether it is the summer or winter games.

Third, a policy may be established to *facilitate consistent decision making*. Policies provide sport managers (decision makers) with limits, alternatives, and general guidelines. For instance, the NCAA has policies to manage institutions found guilty of violating association rules. The severity of the assigned penalty corresponds with the type and frequency of infractions found in the case; however, the method of discovery, due process, and determining penalties is consistent across all cases.

Next, polices may be designed to *set parameters*. Behavior is channeled to pursue an objective or by a system of control. For example, the NCAA has a policy stating student-athletes and coaches shall not engage in countable athletically related activities outside the institution's declared playing season. In this case, the NCAA controls athlete and coach behavior in order to create a level playing field by limiting opportunities to practice.

Finally, policies are established to provide a framework to *allow management to operate without constant intervention*. For instance, the NCAA has policies that detail facility or site specifications for regional and national championship events. As a result, sport managers may organize championships regardless of the location or type of sport without constant intervention from NCAA officials.

Policy Analysis and Policy Development

Policy analysis provides the information necessary for deciding upon, implementing, and evaluating different options. Dunn (2004, p. 2) writes policy analysis is "a process of multidisciplinary inquiry designed to create, critically assess, and communicate information that is useful in understanding and improving policies". Policy analysis requires the sport manager to (a) review the facts from multiple perspectives, (b) generate potential alternatives, (c) debate the merits of each alternative until the "best" solution emerges, (d) implement the policy, and (e) evaluate whether the desired outcome has been achieved. Discussing the feedback allows policy-makers to create "better" options in the future.

Often the terms "policy development" and "policy process" are used interchangeably in the literature. *Policy development* is

defined as the study of public problems and how they are acted on in governing bodies. This study is often difficult because it is hard to identify which governing body has jurisdiction of the issue. For instance, is the use of banned substances by Olympic track and field athletes a problem for USA Track and Field, the International Association of Athletics Federations, or the IOC to solve?

Others contend policy making is a process that involves the "search for, debate about, development of, application of, and evaluation of a given policy" (Gerston, 2004, p. 6). In either case, scholars agree policy making has a perpetual, dynamic, and evolutionary quality. Policy development is much like a revolving Ferris wheel at an amusement park. The wheel operates with a consistent pattern; it travels for a fixed period of time, stops, and proceeds again. While the wheel's movement is predictable, the entries, departures, and combinations of the passengers are not. Sometimes, the wheel is almost full; but at other times it is nearly empty. A few passengers may opt to ride the wheel for several turns while a single cycle will suffice for others. Public policy issues are the "passengers" who move off on the "wheels" of the governing body (Gerston, 2004). Some issues, such as the debate over minimum age for competition as a professional athlete, disappear quickly after their emergence. While others, like drug-testing standards and penalties, remain the subject of heated debate for a longer time.

Public Policy and Policy Statements

Throughout the literature there are many different definitions of public policy. Fundamentally, *public policy* is what results from the policy process. Public policy may be defined as political decisions for implementing programs to achieve societal goals (Cochran & Malone, 1995). For example, the NCAA specifies, "A basic purpose of this Association is to maintain intercollegiate athletics as an integral part of the educational program and the athlete as an integral part of the student body and, by so doing, retain a clear line of demarcation between intercollegiate athletics and professional sports" (2002, p. 1). The social goal is to promote educational attainment rather than use college athletics as a preparatory system for professional sport.

Public policy may also be defined as the sum of governing body activities, whether acting directly or indirectly through agents, to influence the lives of citizens (Peters, 1996). For example, the NCAA asserts, "It is the responsibility of each member institution to establish and maintain an environment that values cultural diversity and gender equity among its student-athletes and athletics department staff" (2002, p. 3). In this case, the NCAA promotes equity and diversity by requiring its agents, member institutions, to create environments to embrace these values.

A third way to define public policy is to say it is whatever governing bodies choose to do or not to do (Dye, 2002). For example, the NCAA outlines, "NCAA Championships are intended to provide national-championship competition among the best eligible student-athletes and teams at the conclusion of the respective sport seasons" (2002, p. 387). Here, the policy specifies what the NCAA will do: sponsor national championship events.

Finally, a sport manager may consider public policy as a stable, purposive course of action carried out by a designated "actor" to manage a problem (Anderson, 2006). For example, the NCAA manual states, "an institution shall not permit a student-athlete to represent it in intercollegiate athletics competition unless the student-athlete meets all applicable eligibility requirements, and the institution has certified the student-athlete's eligibility (2002, p. 125). The NCAA is requiring the actor (member institutions) to do something (certify eligibility) in an established manner.

Policy statements are then the formal expression of the policy itself (Anderson, 2006). These statements are typically organized into a code or manual. Governing bodies use multiple methods to facilitate access to policies. Frequently, constituents find policies published on the internet or from the governing body's home office.

Types of Policy

There are many ways to think about how decisions are made to solve problems. Classifying policy is useful because it facilitates understanding of how and why policies are shaped the way they are and why some groups fair better than others in the adoption and implementation of specific options. In this section, several categories will be reviewed, including (a) formal versus informal policy, (b) substantive versus procedural policy, (c) material versus symbolic policy, and (d) distributive, regulatory and re-distributive policy (Anderson, 2006; Birkland, 2001).

Formal versus Informal Policy

Formal policy outlines what a governing body is supposed to do. This type of policy prescribes what should happen to remedy a problem or achieve a goal. For example, the IOC has a formal policy specifying the Olympic Games be conducted in a manner compatible with the environment. As part of the bid process, host cities must specify how environmental damage will be mitigated. Further, the IOC has a commission to study and report on environmental concerns.

Informal policy, on the other hand, is what the governing body is actually doing. In this case, policy is descriptive in that it substantiates behavior. Continuing the example from above, the IOC informal policy may be the degree the environmental impact data is used to select the host city or the funding provided to support the Commission's work. If the environmental impact information were not considered by the selection committee or relatively little funding is given to the Commission, then the informal policy would contradict the formal policy.

Substantive versus Procedural Policy

Substantive policy involves what the governing body is going to do. This type of policy gives rights, spends money, prohibits, mandates, or in some other way says, "This is how it is going to be". For example, the USOC oversees the development of elite and emerging elite athletes in the United States. The substantive policy may be reflected in the annual budget that dictates the types of programs offered at each of the training centers, the manner in which facilities are maintained, and financial remuneration for athletes, coaches, and support staff.

Procedural policy dictates the process by which something is done. Procedural policies may affect the substance of a policy because, to some extent, how something is completed or who is taking action will impact what is done. Continuing the example above, the procedural policy specifies how the USOC will select and assign programs to specific training centers, the process by which the various facilities will be maintained or enhanced, and the specific pay scales and method for distributing funds to athletes, coaches, and support staff.

Material versus Symbolic Policy

Material policy provides "tangible resources or substantive power to their beneficiaries or impose real disadvantages on those who are adversely affected" (Anderson, 2006, p. 15). In other words, material policy is adopted because it provides "something". For example, the NCAA awards

exclusive broadcast rights for college football. The television network has discretion in selecting specific games and start times. Other networks may not broadcast these games but may choose to broadcast alternative contests. These alternative games tend to be less popular or have a more regional interest.

Symbolic policies provide no tangible advantages or disadvantages and, therefore, have little real impact on people. In this sense, symbolic policy is adopted for how it appears rather than what it does. For instance, the NCAA, in compliance with federal law, has a policy that minority applicants must be considered for administrative positions. In many cases, the job description is written such that minority applicants will fail to meet the minimum criteria for selection. Hence, the policy is symbolic, because while minorities are considered for the position, they do not have a legitimate chance in being awarded a position.

Generally speaking, policies are not entirely material or symbolic. Rather, material and symbolic should be considered at opposite ends of a continuum. Where a particular policy will fall on the continuum will be determined by the degree the policy is material or symbolic.

Distributive, Regulatory and Redistributive Policy

Distributive policy allocates services or benefits to a particular segment of the population. Distributive policies may provide benefits to relatively few recipients or to a considerable number of individuals. The beneficiaries do not compete with one another for benefits, and the costs are assessed to the entire population. For example, colleges and universities award athletic scholarships to student-athletes in various sports offered at the institution. Football players are not in competition with track and field athletes for scholarships; both are beneficiaries of university funding. The cost for scholarships is shared among the entire university population since awards take money away from other campus departments, tuition may be increased for students, or higher taxes may be collected from the general public to support public education.

Regulatory policy limits the individual or group's freedom (or discretion) to act in a particular way. Regulatory policy may dictate general rules of behavior; some actions are required while other actions are strictly prohibited, a minimum standard of quality is desired, and specific information must be provided. For instance, the IOC requires the recognized authority within a country to submit the Olympic delegation (e.g., USOC). Individual athletes may not represent themselves at the Olympics, only their country. Therefore, the IOC regulates who competes in the Games by specifying that athletes be members of a delegation created by the recognized agency.

Regulatory policy may be further divided into competitive regulatory and protective regulatory policy. Competitive regulatory policy is designed to "limit the provision of goods and services to one or a few designed deliverers." By limiting the provision of goods and services, the status of authorized deliverer is increased. For example, IOC awards the rights to use the Olympic logos to selected corporate sponsors (i.e., adidas). Protective regulatory policy aims to guard beneficiaries from the negative effect of private behavior. For instance, in the United States, athletic trainers and doctors must be licensed in order to practice sport medicine. This is to protect the athlete from physical and financial harm.

Re-distributive policy involves a shift in the allocation of power or money among individuals and groups. The governing body takes from those who are well off (haves) and give to the less well off (have-nots). The classic example of this is revenue sharing. A percentage of the revenue garnered from selected teams is re-distributed to other teams in a position to acquire less revenue. In the case of college football, teams that play in a bowl game give a portion of the proceeds to the conference who, in turn, re-distributes the funds to those teams not selected for participation. It is difficult to secure this type of policy because those in a position to lose power or wealth will strongly advocate against such a policy and may create barriers during the implementation process.

Participants in the Policy Process

Sport governance is a game. International, national, and local governing bodies write, approve, and interpret the rules of the game. This is sport policy. Individual constituents, as well as various interest groups, try to influence the writing of rules in their favor. Thus, part of the game itself involves the efforts by various players to modify the rules of the game (Colley, Doyle, Logan, & Stettinius, 2003), that is, to modify sport policy. Participants in the policy process can be examined in terms of the (a) basis for participation and (b) their classification as an official or unofficial actor.

Basis for Participation

The basis for participation in the policy process may be categorized as authority, expertise, and order (Colebatch, 2003). The *authority* in policy making depends on the governing body. It may be a single individual (e.g., Secretary-General) or a body of people (e.g., national council). The essential point is the individual or group is perceived as having a "legitimate" right to determine policy. Having *expertise* relevant to the problem is another reason for participation. It is likely needed information will be drawn from multiple fields of study rather than any one discipline. The key point is experts have knowledge needed to formulate policy.

Order is concerned with implementing policy in a stable and predictable manner. Sport administrators who implement policy play a significant role in the policy process because how a policy is implemented, to some extent, impacts the content of policy.

Official Actors and Unofficial Actors

Official actors are involved in the policy process because they are "authorized" by virtue of the position (e.g., member of a governing body). The governing body's charter, constitution, or mission statement specifies the official actors "duty" to act (Birkland, 2001). In a sense, they have legal authority or jurisdiction over the problem. Governing bodies are inclined to have members working in several functional areas: legislative, executive, judiciary, and administrative positions. Members of a governing body may act in one or more official capacities within the organization.

The *legislative* function involves the bulk of "governing". Legislative actors spend time analyzing information, receiving testimony, and generating and debating the merits of alternative solutions. Committee chairpersons wield significant power. Depending on the size of the committee (and power of individual members), cooperation and consensus building, necessary in the policy process, may be difficult to achieve. Further, policy problems often overlap. What one committee decides may not fit with the decision of another committee. The legislative function also includes supervision of policy implementation. For instance, IOC's Women in Sport Committee works to promote opportunities for women to participate as athletes and leaders in international sport. Recently, the IOC called for 10 percent of National Olympic Committee executive positions to be filled by women. However, current estimates indicate far fewer positions are actually held by women.

The effectiveness of a governing body depends on quality leadership. The executive position gains considerable media and public attention that may (or not) translate into support. However, because power is more highly concentrated, the executive has the ability to establish policies for more issues without worrying as much about building coalitions. For instance, Myles Brand, president of the NCAA, has strongly advocated for academic reforms and has been moderately successful tying scholarships and post season play to graduation rates.

Members who serve the *judicial* function attempt to review and interpret policy in terms of what is "fair" for all represented interests. The judicial actor will work to maintain the veracity of a policy. For example, the Court of Arbitration in Sport adjudicates disputes between athletes and the IOC or international sport federations.

The *administrative* function describes how the policies are enacted and is often characterized by a hierarchical structure, trained personnel, and specific rules and procedures. The amount of discretion used in the administration of policies will vary depending on the availability of resources and the degree of tolerance afforded by policy makers. For example, the NCAA Clearinghouse does not create regulations pertaining to core coursework requirements. However, the Clearinghouse does interpret whether School A's submission for Science III is appropriate to be counted as a "core" course to establish initial eligibility. Here, the Clearinghouse is given a tremendous amount of discretion in determining whether specific course content meets the established policy requirements.

Unofficial actors are involved in the policy process, not as a function of their professional duty but as a function of civic duty (Birkland, 2001). They participate because it is the right thing to do rather than because of explicit authority. They do not decide; rather, they provide information, exert pressure, and attempt to persuade (Anderson, 2006). Unofficial actors may include citizens, media, interest groups, issue networks, think tanks, and research organizations.

Birkland (2001) writes *citizens* are less inclined to participate in the process individually because of indifference, alienation, or a belief that others will take care of the problem. However, some citizens, through their intellectual activities or political activism, do contribute new ideas and directions to the policy process. For instance, Michael Jordan has voiced his perspective on the minimum age for professional basketball players to join the NBA.

The *media* contributes to the public debate by shaping how the problem is defined and by providing needed information. The media can expand issues from narrow groups to broader audiences; creating more pressure for change and influencing which alternatives are perceived as legitimate. For example, a series of articles published in *Sports Illustrated* pertaining to graduation rates for teams competing in the NCAA tournament may provide information and facilitate a national discussion of the issue.

Interest groups perform an important function because they express demands and present alternatives for policy action. They may also supply governing body members with needed information, often of a technical sort, concerning the nature and possible consequences of proposals. The amount of influence an interest group has depends on many factors, including membership size, resources, competition, leadership, social status, and acceptance by the governing body. For example, the Drake Group is a special interest group made up of college faculty and administrators. The group provides information related to academic reform issues in intercollegiate athletics.

Think tanks and *research groups* are independent agencies that report on policy issues, develop alternatives and proposals for managing problems, and evaluate the effectiveness and consequences of enacted policy. In some cases, the organization is going

to have particular ideological "leanings" that may influence how the problem is defined and the content of prescribed alternatives. It is important for the policy maker to be cognizant of these leanings. In other cases, the research organization may provide "expert but neutral" information. Often universities have research or policy centers in order to provide relevant information on various local, national, and international issues. For example, the Race & Gender Report Card is published by the Institute for Diversity and Ethics in Sport (located at the University of Central Florida) and provides information about coaching and administrative opportunities for minorities and women in amateur and professional sport.

Elements of Policy Design

The policy-design process requires both technical and political scrutiny. As the governing body member engages in the design of alternatives, several technical elements must be considered, including (a) policy goals, (b) causal models, (c) policy targets, and (d) policy instruments. Politics within the governing body influences the choices made for each element (Birkland, 2001).

Policy Goals

Policies allow a governing body to take a stand on an issue, make progress toward solving a problem or eliminating an obstacle, facilitate consistent decision making, set parameters, and allow managers to operate without constant intervention. The policy goal is the desired outcome. In other words, is the policy trying to eliminate a problem, alleviate a problem (but not eliminate), or manage the problem (keep from becoming worse)? For example, the IOC has a policy to randomly test Olympic athletes for performance enhancing drugs. This policy is attempting to eliminate a problem. Policies surrounding security around Olympic venues aim to manage a problem.

We can also look at policy goals in terms of equality, efficiency, security, and liberty (Stone, 2002). For instance, with respect to the IOC's drug-testing policy, the goal of the policy may be to treat everyone the same (i.e., equality), reduce the problem given available resources (i.e., efficiency), protect the health and welfare of all athletes and create a level playing field (i.e., security) or protect individual freedom to make decisions (i.e., liberty).

Sport problems are multifaceted and complex. There is often a great deal of ambiguity surrounding the problem and proposed alternatives. It is not uncommon to have competing, if not conflicting, goals within the given context. As in the example above, using policy to create a level playing field may reduce the individual's freedom to make behavioral decisions.

Causal Model

The causal model is a theory about what causes the problem and what intervention, that is, what policy response, would solve the problem (see Figure 2). Sport problems are complicated which, in turn, makes identifying the causal model a difficult task. Birkland (2001, p. 161) warns, "If one develops the wrong causal theory, no policy, no matter how well crafted, is likely to have a positive impact on the problem under consideration."

Further, how the model is portrayed influences the policy parameters. For example, the causal model may be described in terms of acceptability (e.g., level of tolerance), accountability (e.g., who must answer), liability (e.g., who is legally responsible), reliability (e.g., what is dependable or consistent), and responsibility (e.g., who or what is to blame). For example, if the problem of performance enhancing drug use by Olympic athletes is presented as the athletes attempting to gain an unfair advantage in order to secure lucrative corporate sponsorship deals post Games, the prescribed policy intervention will be different than if athletes are ingesting drugs unknowingly at the command of coaches or managers.

Policy Targets

Policy targets are the individuals or groups whose behavior is changed as a result of policy. Direct targets are first-order recipients of policy; their behavior is changed as a result of benefits received or directed action by the governing body. Indirect targets are second-order recipients of policy; their behavior is changed because the environment in which they act has changed. For example, the NCAA awards exclusive broadcasting rights for college football. The first-order recipients of policy are the networks (direct target). Their ability to televise specific games is influenced by whether or not they received the exclusive contract. Fans are indirect targets of the policy because viewing patterns adjust as a result of changes in when and where preferred games are televised. As second-order recipients of policy, fan behavior changes because their environment has changed.

X	(Policy Y)	Z
Problem Definition	Prescribed Intervention	Desired Outcome

Figure 2
Causal Model

Policy Instruments

In the simplest terms, a policy instrument is a way to modify behavior. Governing bodies use instruments to achieve a policy goal because instruments cause targets to do something they would not otherwise do. Depending on the intended behavior change, governing body members may select among several types of instruments.

Types of instruments. Sport governing bodies consider a variety of policy instruments when generating policy alternatives (Anderson, 2006). *Directive power* is pronouncements made by the governing body that carry the force of law. For example, the IOC requires member countries to comply with facets of the Olympic Movement. Failure to do so would risk being expelled from the IOC. *Services* are provisions or opportunities provided to constituents by the governing body. For instance, the IOC is responsible for regularly celebrating the Games and its Committees conduct research and publish information on sport practices. *Benefits* involve the transfer of money or other resources from governing body to constituents. For example, the IOC allows the Olympic Games to rotate to different sites. The benefit is the host city may promote the country's history, culture, and traditions as well as generate revenue. *Subsidies* are payments made by the governing body to ensure economic viability. For instance, International Sport Federations contribute developmental funds to promote sport advancement in many countries. Without these funds, substantially fewer opportunities to participate would exist. *Sanctions* are tangible payoffs used by the governing body to coerce constituents to behave in a certain manner. For example, the IOC prohibits countries with excessive civil rights violations from competing in the Olympic Games. Here, the IOC is manipulating member behavior by using participation as a tangible payoff. Failure to comply with the policy results in not being able to host or otherwise take part in the Games. *Licensing* involves limiting the provision of goods and services to authorized agents. For example, the IOC gives exclusive rights to use Olympic symbols and logos to corporate partners. The status of corporate sponsors is elevated in return for their contribution to staging the Games.

Selecting policy instruments. There are three factors to be considered when selecting a policy instrument: political feasibility, availability of resources, and behavioral assumptions of the targeted group. A policy tool must be selected for its "technical" merits (e.g., tool matches policy goal), but it must also generate sufficient political support for the policy to be adopted. To some extent, a tool is selected based on its popularity among members of the governing body. Given a particular problem, members may be more inclined to use sanctions rather than subsidies. Moreover, at any given time, there is a finite amount of resources available (e.g., time, money, human power). Governing body members may select one tool over another in order to efficiently achieve the goal. While one particular tool may be better because of the likelihood of success, it may not be selected because it consumes too many resources. Policy targets are the individuals or groups whose behavior the policy seeks to alter. A more or less coercive tool may be chosen based on the degree the targeted group is willing to modify behavior. A more coercive tool may be required if targets are resistant to change.

Levine, Peters, & Thompson (1990) outline nine characteristics of policy instruments to assist policy makers to determine the relative merit of different tools: *certainty* of the administrative process and compliance of targets, *timeliness* is the extent the tool works quickly, *less cost* is the relative expense of the tool, *efficiency* is the tool's ability to create maximum outputs for a given input, *effectiveness* is the degree the tool is likely to achieve its goal, *flexibility* is the ease with which the tool can be altered to match changing needs and circumstances, *visibility* is the degree a policy is more or less well known, *accountability* is the amount of implementer's responsibility for compliance, and *choice* is the degree that citizens are afforded decision making among options.

This is where policy study gets really messy. Tool characteristics change in relation to the context. Given a specific problem and desired outcome, tool A may provide greater flexibility and choice but is relatively expensive, while tool B has a high degree of certainty but takes a long time to implement and affords very little choice. If you change the problem and desired outcome, tool A may become timely and provides choice, while tool B may be visible and flexible.

In reality, many potential alternatives are developed using a variety of tools. These options are devised based on what may be the "best fit" given the specific problem. Once the policy goal, causal model, policy targets, and feasible policy instruments are determined, the members debate the relative merit of each option. The debate continues until the governing body members can agree that one alternative is the "best" solution to the problem.

Stage Model of Policy Development

Creating public policy is a dynamic process. Events, actors, and political institutions combine and conflict in a wide array of unpredictable ways. Yet, there is a method through which basic questions are raised, considered, and decided. Anderson (2006, p. 115) writes, "Problem identification, agenda setting, and policy formulation constitute the pre-decision segment of the policy process in that they do not involve formal decisions on what will become public policy. They are important because they help determine which issues will be considered, which will be given further examination, which will be abandoned."

The Stage Model presents the policy process as a cycle with five stages: (a) problem identification and agenda setting, (b) policy formation, (c) policy adoption, (d) policy implementation, and (e) policy evaluation (see Figure 3). While this might appear to be neat and clear in the abstract, in most cases, several of the stages are occurring at the same time with priority given to one or the other. Many governing bodies, for example, find themselves in the midst of agenda setting, formulating policy, adopting, implementing, and assessing all at the same time (Anderson, 2006).

Problem Identification and Agenda Setting

A problem involves a condition or situation that causes distress, dissatisfaction, or generates need for which some kind of corrective action is sought (O'Connor & Sabato, 1999). This may be done by those directly affected by the situation or by others acting on their behalf. At any given time, there are many conditions that disturb and distress people. All disturbing conditions do not automatically become problems. Some problems may be accepted as trivial, appropriate, inevitable, or beyond the control of the governing body. For example, during the last decade, it was widely believed athletes were tortured or otherwise abused in their home country for poor athletic performance. While disturbing, this problem is not necessarily within the jurisdiction of the international sport federation.

Distinguishing problems from conditions. For a condition to become a problem, there must be some standard that leads individuals to believe the condition should not be accepted. Further, the problem must be within the jurisdiction of the governing body. This is a dynamic process because conditions that, at one time, are

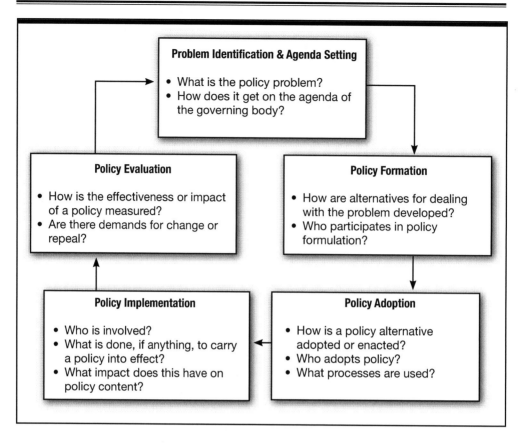

Figure 3.3
Stage Model of the Policy Cycle

accepted as appropriate or beyond the control of a governing body may at a later time be perceived within the reach and responsibility of the governing body. For instance, for many years, IOC members were invited to host cities and given gifts of great value in order to sway votes. Though not necessarily deemed "appropriate" in some cultures, this type of bribery was viewed as business as usual by the local organizing committee. In the U.S., scandals in recent years have heightened sensitivity to corporate misconduct. Revelations about bribery to secure the Salt Lake City Games resulted in demands for change in IOC policy related to, among other things, site-selection procedure, member travel, and accepting gifts.

Individuals face may problems on a daily basis; however, only those problems that move people to action become policy problems. Anderson (2006, p. 83) writes, "Conditions thus do not become policy problems unless they are defined as such, articulated, and then brought to the attention of (governing bodies)." This being said, matters may be defined as problems and relief sought by persons other than those directly affected. For example, following the Salt Lake City scandal, the U.S. Congress demanded the IOC take appropriate action to solve "problems" in the site-selection process. In a sense, Congress was acting on behalf of prospective host cities to increase fairness. Congress had suggested if the IOC did not comply, changes in the U.S. tax code would be authorized. Tax code changes would make corporate partnerships with the IOC less advantageous for American companies resulting in a decrease in available funding for the IOC.

Of course, there is the possibility that problems are defined differently by those directly affected than by others. Usually, there is not a single agreed-upon definition of a problem. Indeed, political struggle often occurs when defining the problem because how the problem is defined helps determine what sort of action is appropriate. For example, consider an interscholastic athlete who wishes to wear some sort of covering in line with religious doctrine (i.e., veil, yarmulke). High school federation rules generally require all athletes on a team to wear a prescribed uniform. Here the problem from the athlete's perspective is impingement on their freedom of expression. From the school's perspective, the problem is related to promoting player safety. The conflict inherent in problem definition is not easily resolved. Each stakeholder group will attempt to persuade the governing body to accept its definition (and proposed solutions) to the problem.

Causation is another important aspect of problem definition. To manage a problem, it is prudent to treat its causes rather than its symptoms. However, for many problems, the underlying causes are not easy to classify and measure. This process becomes exponentially more challenging as problems increase in magnitude and complexity. For instance, in a wide range of sports, on the field violence has amplified in recent years. While severe punishments have been directed at fans, athletes, and sport clubs in response to bad behavior, there has been little attempt to measure the underlying social or psychological causes for such violence in the sport arena.

Problems differ not only in terms of how they are defined but also in terms of their tractability. In other words, how easy are the problems to ameliorate or resolve? For example, there are a significant number of HIV positive athletes competing at an elite level. It is difficult to manage problems associated with the health and welfare of athletes or disease transmission when information about health status is kept confidential.

Problems that affect a large number of people or require widespread behavioral changes are more difficult to resolve. For instance, the health and safety of participants and spectators have always been an issue at large scale sporting events. Though greater attention has been given to security issues and concerns, new policies pertaining to venue access and search and seizure have met with mixed results. Further, tangible problems are more amendable to solutions than are intangible problems. For example, it is easier to change the number of events for women in the Olympic Games (tangible problem) than to manage sexism in sport (intangible problem).

Public policies themselves are frequently viewed as problems or causes of problems. For instance, the Gay Games is an international sport and cultural event held every four years. Cities around the world submit host bids to the Federation of Gay Games. United States law requires individuals to disclose health status (including HIV/AIDS) upon entering the country. This public policy may be interpreted as a problem, because some participants may not be allowed to attend if the Games are held in a U.S. city. Thus, enforcing this policy reduces the quality of the competition/ event, revenue generated from spectators (e.g., ticket sales, souvenirs), and reduced revenue generated by the city (e.g., hotels, meals, entertainment, etc.).

Gaining attention of policy makers. Only a small number of problems actually receive serious attention from policy makers. Simply put, an agenda is a set of problems to which policy makers believe they should be attentive. Agenda setting is "a dynamic process where problems and alternative solutions gain and lose public attention" (Birkland, 2001, p. 106). Before a policy decision can be made, members must determine if the problem is within the jurisdiction of the governing body and important enough to deal with at the present time.

Several factors impact whether a problem will be placed on the agenda (Anderson, 2006; Birkland, 2001; O'Connor & Sabato, 1999). *Political actors* (e.g., members, lobbyists, and interest groups) may demand a voice in the policy debate. Some issues draw the attention of the *media* and, consequently, gain agenda status. Similarly, there may be a peak in the *issue attention cycle* (e.g., playoff time) or *periods of activism* (e.g., human rights debate in an Olympic year). There may be *changes in the political environment.* This may include a shift in power among leaders as well as changes in national or international laws. A *triggering event* may occur that disturbs the routine environment (e.g., work stoppage). A change in agenda status may also occur as a result of a *random confluence of events* (i.e., terrorism).

Similarly, Anderson (2006) lists several tactics to keep an issue off the agenda. Leaders may *deny the problem exists* or argue *additional study* is needed. Further, the members may claim *burden* such as fixing the problem will cause other, more significant problems. The members may believe the problem should be *managed privately* or *outside governing body jurisdiction.* Finally, governing body members may set aside an issue as being too politically charged as a result of *interest group activity.*

It should be clear that all problems do not reach the agenda. Some problems, either because of size or scope, do not compel policy makers to act. To account for this inaction, the concept of non-decision is used. Bachrach and Baratz (1962, p. 44) define non-decision making as "a means by which demands for change in the existing allocation of benefits and privileges in the community can be suffocated before they are even voiced; or kept covert; or killed before they gain access to the relevant decision-making arena."

Policy Formation

Policy formation is the crafting of acceptable proposed courses of action to ameliorate or resolve problems. Formation is a process that has both political and technical components (Anderson, 2006; O'Connor & Sabato, 1999). Members of the governing body must decide what should be done, if anything, concerning a particular problem. This is the political component. The technical facet involves drafting specific language for policy. This is determined, in part, by choices in policy goal, causal model, policy targets, and policy instruments. The manner in which the policy is written may have a significant impact in its administration because the interpretation of vague policy may result in the distortion of legislative intent.

Various players in the policy process take part in policy formation. Members of the governing body, appointed officials or task force, advisory commissions or special study groups, interest groups (e.g., coaches association), and private citizens (e.g., athletes, coaches) may put forth alternatives. Advisory commissions are sometimes created to develop policy proposals as well as to help win support for the proposals. Often individuals asked to serve have a particular expertise or, perhaps more importantly, the political connections needed to advocate for alternatives. Interest groups play an important role in formulating policy because policy makers lack the resources needed to address the issue (i.e., data, staff, and time). Interests groups often have the technical knowledge to deal with complex problems.

This is not to say that more than one group cannot offer proposals. Often there are multiple proposals competing for acceptance. As a result, yet a new proposal is created. This new proposal outlines a compromised course of action and, in many cases, has a better chance of being adopted (Anderson, 2006).

In practice, it is very difficult to separate policy formation from policy adoption. In a sense, formulators are strategically thinking about the political and administrative feasibility of each alternative as it is being developed. Formulators will consider whether particular provisions should be included or excluded from a proposal in an attempt to enhance the likelihood of adoption and to facilitate efficient implementation.

Policy Adoption

In practice, policy formulation and policy adoption (decision) occur at approximately the same time. Formulators are strategically thinking about the feasibility of each alternative as it is being developed. A policy decision involves action by some official person or body to approve, modify, or reject a proposed alternative (Anderson, 2006). In reality, a policy decision is the culmination of a series of decisions made throughout the policy process.

Decision making can be studied as either an individual or collective process. In the first instance, the focus is on the criteria used by individuals in making choices. In the latter, the concern is with the process by which majorities are built or how broadbased approval is otherwise acquired. Of course, individual choices are usually made with some reference to what others involved in the decisional situation are likely to do.

Individual decision making. Individuals may be influenced by various factors when selecting among alternatives. Which factors predominate is often difficult to determine. Officials may reveal reasons for their decision in public statements. Interestingly,

these reasons may be those that were actually controlling the decision or they may be reasons thought to be more acceptable to constituents. Their actual basis for choice, in this case, if left unsaid.

When analyzing why governing body members select what to do or not to do, we often consider the broader social and political forces at work. However, this analysis would be incomplete if it did not consider how *values* are used to determine what is "good" or "bad", "desirable" or "undesirable". Further, personal, professional, and organizational values may be used to determine appropriate action in a situation. *Political affiliation* is an important decision-making criterion for many governing body members. Sometimes it is difficult to separate loyalty from other influences, such as leadership pressure, ideological commitments, and constituency interests.

When acting on behalf of *constituency interests,* the member of the governing body may operate as a delegate (e.g., carry out actual or perceived instructions), trustee (e.g., exercise best judgment), or some combination of both. In some cases, membership interests are clear and strongly held. There are times when constituent interests are clear and obvious, while at other times, the member is hard pressed to know what the people want. In this case, the representative must solicit input, trust political leadership, rely on personal values, or a combination of multiple techniques. *Public opinion* is viewpoints or perspectives on problems taken into consideration by officials. Public opinion may be gauged through written documents, public demonstrations, meeting with officials, or survey research. *Deference* is when a governing official seeks the judgment of others when charged with making a decision. When policy makers are unable to decide how to vote from their own analysis of an issue, deference to someone whose judgment they trust is a reasonable, rational, low-information strategy for making decisions. Often the "others" are hierarchical superiors such as executive officers and chairpersons, but this is not always the case, such as policy experts outside the governing body.

When governing body members are faced with making many decisions, guidelines are devised to simplify and regularize the individual's decision-making process. These rules of thumb tend to focus on the facts and pertinent relationships. While there is no standard set of *decision rules*, some common guidelines include *stare decisis* (i.e., let the decision stand) and *per se* (i.e., as such). The stare decisis decision rule involves making decisions based on past precedent in a similar situation. The per se decision rule is used when the course of action appears obvious such that further analysis would provide little helpful information. In sport governance, policy decisions tend to be of such size and importance that it becomes necessary to build a coalition of support. Often these decisions are of such magnitude that it is unlikely that any one member would make a decision without the expressed consent of other members within the governing body.

Collective decision making. Collective decision making is an integral part of sport governance. Collective decision making is a social, interactive process that may take the form of bargaining, command, and persuasion (Anderson, 2006). *Bargaining* is a process in which two or more persons in positions of power or authority adjust their at least partially inconsistent goals in order to formulate a course of action that is acceptable, but not necessarily ideal, for all the participants. In other words, bargaining is a give and take between individuals in an attempt to reach a mutually acceptable position. For bargaining to exist, bargainers must be willing to negotiate, have something to negotiate about, and possess some resource that the other wants or needs.

Bargaining can be explicit or implicit. Explicit bargaining exists when both sides state their agreements clearly to minimize the chance of confusion. Implicit bargaining exists when terms of the agreement are left vague or ambiguous. One member may agree to support the other on the basis of a pledge for "future cooperation". Common forms of bargaining include logrolling, side payments, and compromise. Logrolling exists when governing officials trade support for initiatives (e.g., trade votes). Side payments are rewards that are not related directly to the issue at hand (e.g., budget enhancements). Compromise involves the give and take between members where each is willing to give up something so as to come into agreement. In this sense, bargaining persists because getting part of what is wanted is better than none at all.

Command is the ability of those in superior positions to make decisions that are binding upon those within their span of control. Subordinates are ordered to act (decide) in a particular manner. This behavior is reinforced through the use of rewards or penalties.

Persuasion is the utilization of facts, data, and information; the skillful construction of arguments; and the use of reason and logic to convince another person of the wisdom or correctness of one's own position. The persuader seeks to build support for his preferred alternatives without having to modify his original position. The persuasion activities attempt to convince others of the proposition's merits, the benefits to be derived from the proposition, or a combination of the two. Accurate information, reason and logic, and effective arguments rather than manipulation, deception, and bullying are the instruments of persuasion. When there is a belief that bargaining is inappropriate or there is a lack of capacity to command, persuasion becomes the relied-upon method of collective decision making.

Use of power in the policy process. How power is used in the policy process is not well understood because power is dynamic, multidimensional, and derived from multiple sources. Moreover, power is thought to have multiple causes and effects, can be subtle, and is very difficult to measure. Nonetheless, power is an important aspect of policy discussion because it is necessary for collaboration. In a sense, power is a sort of "electricity" which drives the "motor" of human interaction.

Put simply, power is the ability to determine how resources will be used to accomplish identified goals. A detailed discussion about power relationships within a sport governing body is beyond the scope of this book. However, it should be mentioned that "players" within a sport organization will use their individual sources of power (e.g., coercive, referent, expert) and organizational sources of power (e.g., centrality, control over resources) (Slack & Parent, 2006) to increase the amount of power they possess and to maximize the desired benefits. These benefits may include keeping an undesirable topic off the agenda, crafting and adopting policy using preferred tools, and using implementation strategies to achieve the desired outcome.

Policy Implementation

Policy implementation refers to how policies are carried out. Much like the line between policy formation and adoption is blurred, the line between policy formation and implementation is not always clear. In should be remembered, the content of policy, and its impact on those affected, may be substantially modified, elaborated, or even negated during the implementation stage. On the surface, the act of implementing a policy may seem tedious and mundane, but in reality, the consequences may be quite profound.

Implementation techniques. Administrators may be authorized by the governing body to use a number of techniques to implement policies. These techniques can be categorized as authority, incentive, capacity, and hortatory depending on the behavioral assumptions of targets. In the following examples, the NCAA is the governing body and the member institutions are the administrators of policy.

Authoritative techniques rest on the notion that people's action must be directed or restrained by the governing body in order to prevent or eliminate activities that are unsafe or unfair. Administrators have the authority to issue rules, set standards, and monitor for compliance. Penalties for violations may be imposed. For example, the NCAA has a policy that limits the number of hours per week a student-athlete can participate in athletically related activities. The athletic director can require student-athletes to sign a form weekly to document hours of participation. The athletic director can also establish a series of progressive penalties for coaches if athletes are found to be exceeding stated limits.

Incentive techniques are based on the assumption that people act in their own best interest and must be provided with payoffs or financial inducements to get them to comply with policies. For instance, as part of reform efforts, the NCAA monitors the Academic Progress Rate (APR) of each team fielded by member institutions. The athletic director may institute a recognition program where coaches and athletic support staff share a cash bonus if teams meet APR standards so long as the bonus complies with NCAA compensation rules.

Capacity techniques provide people with information, education, training, or resources to enable them to undertake desired activities. The assumption underlying these techniques is that people have the incentive or desire to do what is right but lack the capacity to act accordingly. For example, member institutions may publish NCAA generated information about banned substances and testing procedures in student-athlete handbooks. This allows student-athletes to stay current on which medications are not permissible so to be in compliance with the NCAA policy.

Horatory techniques encourage people to comply with policy by appealing to their "better instincts" in an effort to get them to act in desired ways. In this instance, policy implementers assume people decide how to act based on their personal values and beliefs about what is right or wrong. For instance, the NCAA prohibits the use of tobacco products by athletes, coaches, administrators, and staff during practices and competitions. The athletic director is authorized to post signage to make game personnel aware of this policy. As part of this signage, visual images may be used which highlight the negative consequences of using tobacco products. These images attempt to persuade people to behave a particular way.

Whether or not administrators can effectively implement policy depends on which (and how many) techniques they are authorized to use. Successful implementation also depends on available resources, political support, clarity and specificity of the written policy, and the skill of the administrator. There is no easy formula that will guarantee successful policy implementation; in practice, many policies only partially achieve their goals (O'Connor & Sabato, 1999).

Implementation failure. Why do some policies not work as intended? Scholars argue policy can be appropriately formulated and adopted, but breakdowns may occur during the implementation stage. Van Vorn & Van Meter (1976) suggest three common barriers. First, implementers do not want to do what they are supposed to do (disposition). Second, implementers do not know what they are supposed to do (communication). And third, implementers are not able to do what they are supposed to do (capability). Bardach (2005) warns about "adverse implementation of outcomes." These types of barriers may include long delays between policy adoption and implementation, excessive costs, and policy complexities that leave administrators uncertain about benefits and requirements.

Another reason why implementation fails is because the policy captures an undeserving or unintended constituency. For example, suppose an athletic department instituted a policy where any coach guilty of negative recruiting would be suspended from practice for two weeks. The head basketball coach and three top assistants are found to have violated the policy. If an athletic director suspends the head coach and assistants, student-athletes are left without coaches. By enforcing the policy an undeserving constituency is captured. As a result, the athletic director may not implement the policy because student-athletes would be negatively affected. The policy does not achieve its goal to deter negative recruiting practices.

Policy Evaluation

Policy evaluation is the appraisal of the content, implementation, and outcomes of policy (Anderson, 2006). Evaluation is not merely the last stage; rather it occurs throughout the process. The anticipated consequences of various alternatives are an essential part of the policy debate, and these consequences must somehow be quantified and presented.

Policy makers make judgments about policy in many different, often subjective, ways. Sometimes decisions about effectiveness or necessity are based on anecdotal and fragmentary evidence. Other times, a policy is deemed "good" simply because it is politically popular. Alternatively, policy makers may approach evaluation by asking questions related to policy administration. Questions may include: What are the financial costs? Who receives benefits and in what amounts? Is there unnecessary overlap or duplication with other policies? Were legal standards and procedures followed?

This kind of evaluation may reveal the efficiency of a policy, but it provides little information of whether the policy effectively deals with the problem it was intended to solve. Therefore, it becomes necessary to implement carefully designed studies by qualified staff to measure the impact of policy and whether or not it achieved the specified goals (O'Connor & Sabato, 1999). Probably the most useful function of evaluation is in "debugging policy." Debugging, also known as policy monitoring, uses evaluation results to improve policy performance. This monitoring is best accomplished when data is routinely gathered and processed as a part of policy implementation.

Summary

Governing bodies are an integral and pervasive part of the sport industry. Knowledge of how a governing body is organized will assist the sport manager understand why the governing body operates in a particular manner. This chapter introduced policy making as a form of applied problem solving and outlined key terms and definitions, participants in the process, types of policies, and elements of policy design. Understanding the stage model of policy development will allow sport managers to be players in the game; specifically, to give voice to preferred problem definitions and advocate for solutions that benefit their organizations.

References

Anderson, J. E. (2006). *Public policymaking* (6th ed.). New York: Houghton Mifflin Company.

Arnold, M. L., Heyne, L. A., & Busser, J. A. (2005). *Problem solving: Tools and techniques for the park and recreation administrator*. Champaign, IL: Sagamore Publishing.

Birkland, T. A. (2001). *An introduction to policy process: Theories, concepts, and models of public policy making*. New York: M. E. Sharpe.

Bardach, E. (2005). *A practical guide to policy analysis: The eightfold path to more effective problem solving* (2nd ed.). Washington, D.C.: CQ Press.

Bachrach, P., & Baratz, M. (1962). The two faces of power. *American Political Science Review, 56*, 947-952.

Cochran, C. E., & Malone, E. F. (1995). *Public policy: Perspectives and choices*. New York: McGraw Hill.

Colebatch, H. K. (1998). *Policy*. Minneapolis, MN: University of Minnesota Press.

Colley, J. L., Doyle, J. L., Logan, G. W., & Stettinius, W. (2003). *Corporate governance*. New York: McGraw Hill.

Dunn, W. N. (2004). *Public policy analysis: An introduction* (3rd ed.). Upper Saddle River, NJ: Pearson-Prentice Hall.

Dye, T. R. (2002). *Understanding public policy* (10th ed.). Upper Saddle River, NJ: Pearson-Prentice Hall.

Gerston, L. N. (2004). *Public policy making: Process and principles* (2nd ed.). New York: M.E. Sharpe.

Levine, C. H., Peters, B. G., & Thompson, F. J. (1990). *Public administration: Challenges, choices and consequences*. Glenview, IL: Brown Higher Education.

National Collegiate Athletic Association Manual. (2002). *National Collegiate Athletic Association manual* (Division 1). Indianapolis, IN: Author.

O'Connor, R. W., & Sabato, L. (1999). *Agendas, alternatives, and public policies* (2nd ed.). New York: Harper Collins.

Page, S. B. (2002). *Establishing a system of policies and procedures*. Westerville, OH: Process Improvement Publishing.

Peters, B. G. (1996). *American public policy: Promise and performance* (5th ed.) Chappaqua, New York: Seven Bridges Press.

Slack, T., & Parent, M. M. (2006). *Understanding sport organizations: The application of organization theory*. Champaign, IL: Human Kinetics.

Stone, D. (2002). *Policy paradox: The art of political decision making* (Rev. ed.). New York: W. W. Noron & Company.

Vanderzwaag, H. J. (1998). *Policy development in sport management* (2nd ed.). Westport, CT: Praeger.

Van Horn, C. E., & Van Meter, D. S. (1976). The implementation of intergovernmental policy. In C. O. Jones, & R. D. Thomas (Eds.), *Public policy making in a federal system*. Beverly Hills, CA: Sage Publications.

NOTES

PART II

Ethical Decision Making and Professional Ethics

CHAPTER 4

Foundations of Ethical Decision Making

Sport plays a significant role in the lives of millions of people throughout the world. On any given day sport business managers make millions of decisions. These decisions affect men and women who actively participate in sport as well as those who are relatively uninvolved. This is because sport has a tremendous impact on language, thought, and culture.

A regular decision involves a choice among two or more alternatives. An ethical decision has an additional connotative of what "should" be done in a particular situation. "Should" statements come from individual values and moral philosophies as well as organizational values and mission statements. Most people consider what is "right" to be the action that betters the community, organization, and fellow human beings.

Many of the decisions a sport manager will make on a daily basis have an ethical component. Therefore, the aim of this chapter is to provide a foundation for understanding ethical decision making in the sport environment. In particular, this chapter seeks to generate awareness of how ethical issues are recognized and resolved.

This awareness allows the sport manager to be more ethical than he would otherwise be, and the sport environment will be a better place as a result of his or her decisions.

Learning Objectives

Upon completion of this chapter, the reader should be able to:

- Understand why it is important to study ethics.
- Define key terms, including beliefs, values, morals, ethics, ethical issue, ethical dilemma, and ethical conflict.
- Recognize models of ethical decision making in organizations.
- Discuss the foundations of ethical conflict.
- Understand ethical leadership principles, such as critical thinking and discovery, cultural differences, and common reasons why good people do bad things.
- Recognize and apply simple guidelines for ethical decision making.

Why Study Ethics?

One need only review a daily news source to see ethical wrongdoing is a growing concern. In recent years, politicians and high-ranking officials have been forced to resign in disgrace following various indiscretions. Accusations of falsified data have jeopardized funding for innovative medical therapies and undermined the trust in all scientific research. Sport superstars have been called to testify on what was seen or heard in locker rooms across the country.

Because of the frequency of the unethical behavior of our political and social leaders, it may be concluded that ethical transgressions are not random events but part of a larger cultural problem. In fact, the National Business Ethics Survey (2005), conducted by the Ethics Resource Center, found employees have observed misconduct in both large and small organizations across public, private, and nonprofit sectors. Problems such as deceptive advertising, defective products, employee theft, falsifying documents, and bribery are cited as evidence of declining ethical standards. The sport arena has been plagued with scandal as well. Professional baseball players have been accused of using performance-enhancing substances. Colleges and universities have been suspended from play for excessive rule violations. Youth sport has been permanently marked by tragically out of control parents.

Whether in sport, business, science, or politics, decisions are judged to be right or wrong, ethical or unethical. When decisions are socially determined as unethical, this judgment, whether correct or not, directly affects the organization's ability to achieve its mission (Ferrell, Fraedrich, & Ferrell, 2002). Therefore, it is important to understand ethical decision making in sport management. It is commonly believed that if a sport organization hires good people with strong values, then it will be an ethical organization. However, ethical issues that arise in the workplace are complex. The values learned from family, religion, and school may not be enough. As you will see, an individual's personal values and moral philosophies is only one component in the ethical decision-making process.

Key Terms and Definitions

People differ in their ethical judgments. Examples are found in all areas of sport management. Why do some people believe we should not keep score in youth sport contests while others believe it is okay? Why do some people believe it is ethical to pay college athletes while others believe it is wrong? Why do some people believe it is right to consider race, gender, and ethnicity when hiring coaches while others believe it is inappropriate? The answers to these questions are grounded in personal differences in beliefs, values, morals, and ethics.

Beliefs, Values, Morals and Ethics

Any idea held to be true is called a *belief*. A person's reasoning process involves using three types of beliefs: descriptive, evaluative, and prescriptive or proscriptive. Descriptive beliefs can be empirically measured and determined to be true or false. Evaluative beliefs involve some positive or negative judgment about a characteristic or object of the belief. Prescriptive and proscriptive beliefs reflect a decision about the desirability or undesirability of some action or means to an end (Shields & Bredemeier, 1995). For instance, imagine a sport manager has decided to organize a Senior Hockey League in the community. The sport manager must believe (a) planning a sport league fits with the agency's mission (descriptive belief), (b) giving seniors competitive sport opportunities is appropriate (evaluative belief), and (c) providing sport opportunities for various patron groups benefits the community (prescriptive belief).

A person's belief system, developed through interaction with parents, peers, mentors, educational material, and social institutions, can have a profound impact on how the sport manager lives his or her life. These influences determine an individual's most fundamental, or core, beliefs upon which intermediate and peripheral beliefs are built. As one moves away from central beliefs to less significant ones, there is a corresponding decrease in the influence beliefs have on the individual's manner of thinking. Another important consideration is how intensely a belief is held. Some beliefs are more vital to self-identity than others and, therefore, play a more critical role in the reasoning process (Rokeach, 1968). For instance, imagine growing up in a home where the father modeled personal integrity. He was fair, honest, and a man of his word. Now imagine the father was asked to take part in what might be perceived as unfair business practices. Rather than do so, the father resigned from the lucrative corporate position that resulted in months of financial hardship for his family. This personal experience may instill a core belief that integrity matters, and it is appropriate to act with integrity even if it creates other, perhaps substantial, problems in the short term. When making decisions, a sport manager with this core belief will seek alternatives that are consistent with maintaining personal integrity.

Green (1971) writes that humans have an amazing capacity to maintain a system of beliefs that are inconsistent with one another. This is because people can isolate one set of beliefs from another, often unconsciously. What someone determines to be "moral" behavior in one situation may be significantly different from the moral principles used to guide behavior in day-to-day life. This may occur even if there are clear or obvious contradictions. For example, consider a situation where an individual yells at an official during a close game between rival teams. Using profanity or other belittling words to harass the official may be considered the "right" thing to do in the competitive sport environment. However, the same individual may consider using profanity or criticizing people in authority positions highly inappropriate in the workplace or religious setting.

A sport manager's values are grounded in his or her belief system. According to Rokeach (1973, p. 5), a *value* "is an enduring belief that a specific mode of conduct or end-state of existence is personally or socially preferable to an opposite or converse mode of conduct or end-state of existence". In other words, a value is a judgment (e.g., preferable) that some way to behave (e.g., mode of conduct) or some achieved outcome (e.g., end-state of existence) is better than some other way to behave or some other achieved outcome. It is important to remember that while society, through its various institutions, attempts to sway the individual to appreciate certain ways of behaving or desired outcomes, the individual does not passively internalize these values. Rather the individual is an active participant, merging social norms with his or her unique history and experience to transform and adopt particular values.

A person may hold many types of values. For instance, there are aesthetic, cultural, economic, educational, political, and religious values. Moral values, or *morals*, are the fundamental baseline values that dictate appropriate behavior in a society (Solomon, 1992). In other words, moral values outline how each person should behave in order for society to function smoothly. For example, honesty, justice, fairness, responsibility, and respect are moral values. A non-moral value is charm. While a sport manager may act charming and desire to associate with others who have similar qualities, society would not breakdown if people no longer valued charm.

A *moral agent* organizes his values into a value system. These sets of values then form prescriptions (i.e., statements of what to do) and proscriptions (i.e., statements about what not to do) that guide daily life (Lennick & Keil, 2004). An essential component of a sport manager's personal and professional philosophy is a summary of his or her values.

Ethics is a term used to describe the study of morality. Ethics, sometimes called moral philosophy, is concerned with the kinds of morals and values an individual or society finds desirable or appropriate. Ethical theories provide a set of rules or principles that defines what is "right or wrong" and "good or bad" in a given situation (Daft, 2003; Northhouse, 2004). Ethical theories can be divided into three areas: meta-ethics, normative ethics, and applied ethics. Meta-ethics investigates where ethical principles come from and what they mean. Normative ethics focuses on determining a standard of behavior to regulate right and wrong conduct within a society. Applied ethics uses meta-ethics and normative ethics as a basis for examining controversial issues such as drug testing, gender equity, and fair play in sport.

Ethical Issues, Dilemmas and Conflicts

An *ethical issue* is a problem, situation, or opportunity that requires the individual to select among several actions that may be evaluated as right or wrong, good or bad, benefit or harm, propriety or impropriety, and ethical or unethical (Foster, 2003). Because a moral philosophy is made up of a complex system of principles, it is inevitable that at some point one or more principles will clash with one another. An *ethical dilemma* exists when the problem involves a choice between a strongly held principle and some non-ethical consideration. In other words, do the right thing but risk losing a friend, a job, opportunity for advance-

ment, etc. For example, perhaps the sport manager observed a colleague steal $100 from the gate receipts. The sport manager must decide whether to (a) report the colleague to management because of a strong belief in maintaining professional integrity or (b) keep silent because of the potential to lose a friend. The non-ethical consideration can be a powerful influence and may be important enough to justify selecting it rather than the ethical action.

An *ethical conflict* exists when the problem involves a choice between two or more strongly held principles. In some cases, the principles require opposite actions in the same situation. For instance, perhaps your colleague confesses that in order to pay overdue rent he stole $100 from gate receipts but promises to return the money at the next home game. The sport manager must decide whether to (a) report the colleague in order to maintain professional integrity or (b) not report the colleague because of a principle that trustworthiness is a key aspect of a person's character. In this case, following through with Ethical Action A: maintaining professional integrity by reporting a colleague for stealing results in a violation of Ethical Action B: upholding one's character by being trustworthy.

Sometimes an ethical conflict exists when strongly held principles require equally compelling, though not necessarily opposite, ethical actions. For example, suppose the sport manager firmly believes in protecting the health and well-being of participants and equality in the provision of programs and services. Due to an unforeseen budget cut, the sport manager must decide whether to (a) resurface the skate park or (b) provide childcare services in the community center. Here, both actions may be considered ethical actions, but following through with Ethical Action A: protecting the health and well-being of participants by resurfacing the skate park results in not being able to follow through with Ethical

Action B: providing equality in programs and services such as childcare at the community center. Solving ethical conflicts may require prioritizing or establishing a hierarchy of ethical principles. The key point to remember is that resolving ethical conflict has social implications that extend far beyond personal preferences.

Ethical Decision Making in Organizations

Ethical decision-making is the process in which a decision is found to be both morally and legally acceptable to the larger community (Jones, 1991). To be sure, ethical decision making does not occur in a vacuum. Rather the process is affected by both internal and external factors. To gain a better understand of these factors, three models are briefly described: (a) four component model, (b) person-situation interactionist model, and (c) Hunt and Vitell model.

Rest (1986) offered the *four component Model* to determined moral behavior: (a) moral sensitivity, (b) moral judgment, (c) moral motivation, and (d) moral character. Moral sensitivity involves being aware of different potential actions and how each action could affect other people. Moral judgment is an individual's ability to make a choice among the alternative actions. Moral motivation refers to the priority of moral values in competition with other personal values. For instance, the individual must determine whether to place doing the "right" thing above pursuing self-interest or protecting the organization. Moral behavior involves implementation of an action plan. A sport manager may be morally sensitive, make moral judgments, and place high value on moral values, but if the person succumbs to the pressure, then moral failure results.

Unlike previous approaches, Trevino's (1986) *Person-Situation Interactionist Model* recognizes the role of both individual and situational variables. Essentially, the sport manager responds to an ethical dilemma with "cognitions" (e.g., beliefs about what is right or wrong in a situation) that are determined by his or her stage of cognitive moral development. Individual moderators, such as locus of control, influence the likelihood an individual will act on his or her thoughts. Situational moderators are drawn from the immediate job context, organizational culture, and characteristics of work. Moral judgments, "cognitions" tempered by the individual and situational factors, influence whether ethical or unethical behavior occurs.

Hunt and Vitell model (1986) offer a multistage process of ethical decision making. Environmental factors and personal factors influence the perception of an ethical problem, alternatives, and consequences. In turn, these perceptions influence two sets of evaluations. The individual determines (a) the inherent rightness and wrongness of each alternative and (b) the probability and desirability of consequences for various important stakeholder groups. This process leads to ethical judgments. Ethical judgments affect intentions. Intentions, along with situational constraints, determine behavior.

While guidelines for individual ethical decision making are presented later in the chapter, the models presented here highlight the idea that ethical decision making in organizations is affected by a multitude of factors. If the manager is aware of these influences within the sport organization and larger environment, he or she can use the contextual information to generate politically and administratively feasible alternatives. As a result, a solution both morally and legally acceptable to the larger community is more likely to be found.

Foundations of Ethical Conflict

Ethical issues arise from conflict. Incongruity may exist among individuals' personal values and moral philosophies, the values and attitudes of the organizations in which they work, and those of the society in which they live. For example, in many western countries, it is widely recognized that people should not try to influence the outcome of a decision by providing gifts, personal payments, and special favors. However, bribery is recognized in many countries as an acceptable means of doing business. In fact, it is estimated that approximately $80 billion of paid "incentives" are used worldwide each year (Ferrell, Fraedrich, & Ferrell, 2002).

Classification of Ethical Issues

Broadly speaking, ethical issues in sport business can be placed in four categories: (a) issues related to conflict of interest, (b) issues of honesty and fairness, (c) issues in communications, and (d) issues pertaining to technology (Ferrell, Fraedrich, & Ferrell, 2002). A sport manager faces a conflict of interest when he or she must decide whether to advance personal interests, the organization's interests, or the interests of some outside entity. Suppose a head coach is paid a sum of money if his or her athletes wear a particular brand of shoe. There is circumstantial evidence to suggest the shoe contributes to a higher than average injury rate in the sport. The conflict is whether the coach should pursue personal interests (e.g., money) or organizational interests (e.g., healthy athletes).

Honesty and fairness pertain to the moral character of the sport manager. Honesty refers to an individual's truthfulness, integrity, and trustworthiness. Sport managers, at a minimum, are expected to follow applicable laws and regulations as well as not knowingly deceive or harm staff, patrons, or the larger community. Fairness involves the qualities of being just, equitable, and impartial. However, what is considered fair may be shaped by vested interests. That is, fair or ethical depends on whether the outcome matched expectations. For example, a home school student group has requested to use the gymnasium for one hour each week to fulfill a physical education requirement. Since local tax revenue supports the school, the principal may believe it fair to make reasonable accommodation to allow the group to use the facility. The basketball coach, who as a result must change scheduled practice times, may not think the decision is fair.

Communication involves the transmission of information and the sharing of meaning. All methods a sport manager uses to proactively deliver key messages to constituents fall within this category. For instance, consider a sport promotion that advertises "free admission" to an athletic contest between rival teams. However, upon arriving at the arena patrons discover they must disclose personal information on a marketing survey in order to qualify for a "free" ticket. Sport managers who use false or misleading communication strategies can undermine patrons' trust in an organization.

The final category of ethical issues involves the use of technology. In recent years, there have been tremendous gains in the development of sport equipment. In fact, advances in equipment have reduced the amount of skill and fitness necessary to play. However, the sport manager should realize that what appears to be good or helpful may result in some harm or undesirable consequences. For example, while advances in sport equipment may allow physically disabled players to compete with able-bodied players, the undesirable consequence is materials are costly and may only be available to wealthy participants.

Participant – Function Interaction

Ethical issues in sport business arise from the interaction between the participants and the functions of business. The participants are the owners/managers, employees/staff, and customers/patrons. The functions of business include finance, management, marketing, and accounting (Ferrell, Fraedrich, & Ferrell, 2002). For example, consider the owner-finance interaction. One aspect of finance is pricing. Suppose you are the owner of a business that provides a place to practice sport skills (i.e., batting cages, driving range, etc). How do you price the services? Does a discounted local tax rate impact pricing? Is it fair that money, which may be generated to support public park and recreation spaces, is not being collected in order to facilitate local business? Would price change if you knew 60 percent of community members live below the poverty line? Should everyone have an opportunity to play or only those who can afford to participate?

Another example involves the owner-management interaction. The agency's policy manual clearly states failure to collect payment for services will result in immediate termination. You discover a longtime employee and trusted member of the staff allowed children from low-income families to use the batting cages for free when no other paying customers were using the facility. What is the ethical thing to do in this situation? In each of these cases, the participants and the functions of business connect to create scenarios that have an ethical component.

Recognizing Ethical Issues

Sometimes ethical issues are difficult to recognize; other times they are not. The danger exists when managers act as if sport business is a game in which the rules of fair play do not apply. This is called moral callousness (Kretchmar, 1994). Common symptoms include rationalizing behavior with statements like, "Everyone is doing it." or "This behavior is not explicitly prohibited so it must be okay." When a sport manager assumes this position, he or she is willing to take unethical, and perhaps illegal, steps in order to achieve desired outcomes.

One way to develop moral sensitivity, or the ability to recognize ethical issues, is to discuss whether a specific behavior or decision has an ethical component with a trusted colleague. This conversation may include statements about how the colleague feels about the situation, whether they approve of the action, and whether they think it is customary behavior within the larger industry. Similarly, a sport manager may consult the code of conduct defined by professional organizations or sport industry. The organization's policy manual can shed light on the issue. A sport manager may also critically think about the various roles of people affected by the decision. This way the "cause-consequence" chains may be evaluated.

Principles of Ethical Leadership

If a sport manager waits until a conflict arises to begin thinking about how to make an ethical decision, he or she has waited too long. The sport business world is fast paced, and rarely will the sport manager have the luxury to sit and ponder the situation. Consequently, the individual must prepare for decision making before being confronted with difficult choices in the workplace (Browne, Giampetro-Meyer, & Williamson, 2004). In setting this foundation, the sport manager must engage in critical thinking and discovery, appreciate that cultural differences exist, and recognize common reasons why good people do bad things.

Critical Thinking and Discovery

Many authors have discussed the relationship between moral philosophy and leadership. In the literature, ethical leadership is described as occurring at multiple levels: (a) personal, (b) interpersonal, (c) managerial, and (d) organizational (Covey, 1991). At the *personal level*, a sport manager is aware of his or her value system and how it translates into moral action. Essentially, the sport manager must answer three questions: Who am I?, What do I stand for?, and What is my vision of the ideal world and how do I help create it? This process involves reasoning skills to identify and weigh relevant information. Prioritizing values is important because sport managers will face situations where they will be required to reconcile external pressure from the environment and internal pressure to act as a responsible, moral citizen (Browne, Giampetro-Meyer, & Williamson, 2004). Further, the sport manager should reflect on new experiences and insights because this allows the individual to adjust, and perhaps improve, his or her moral principles.

At the *interpersonal level*, the sport manager must recognize each person assumes many personal and professional roles, and each role has a particular interest. These interests may come into conflict, even within the same individual. Therefore, trust must be developed between the sport manager and his or her colleagues. Trust is the expectation that another will not, through words, actions, or decisions, act opportunistically (Robbins & Decenzo, 2004). The sport manager must consider the five dimensions of trust and its implications in the sport agency. He or she should ask such questions: Am I acting with integrity?, Do I have the technical or interpersonal skill to handle the situation?, Am I using good judgment consistently?, Where do I place my loyalty?, and Am I positioned to give or receive critical information or ideas?

Similar to the individual sport manager, the sport agency possesses values and value priorities. Browne, Giampetro-Meyer, & Williamson (2004) stated that in order to move toward a moral partnership, managers and staff will need to discuss a range of value issues. It is essential for the sport manager to listen with an open mind because people will differ in how they define specific values and there is more than one set of reasonable ethical positions. This dialogue allows for value conflicts to be identified and resolved.

At the *managerial and organizational levels*, the sport manager extends the interpersonal relationships in such a way to empower staff members to act in an ethical manner. Further, the sport manager will facilitate behaviors consistent with the organization's values (Covey, 1991).

This is an ongoing process summarized by five principles (Northhouse, 2004). Showing *respect* involves a sense of unconditional worth and value of individual differences. Sport managers show respect by listening, being empathic, giving credence to others ideas, and being tolerant of opposing viewpoints. *Service* involves prioritizing the welfare of others when selecting plans of action. Sport managers serve others by mentoring, empowering, and team-building behaviors. *Justice* involves treating others equitably. Sport managers treat everyone in a similar fashion and, when necessary, differential treatment should be justified by sound moral values. Clear and responsible rules for the distribution of work, resources, and rewards are shared with all co-workers. *Honesty* entails more than not deceiving. Sport managers must avoid misrepresentation and making promises they cannot fulfill. The challenge for the sport manager is to balance being open and candid with appropriate discretion. Dishonesty, even when used with good intentions, contributes to the breakdown of relationships. *Community* considers the needs of all persons involved. Sport managers must make decisions that contribute to the common good. By engaging in critical thinking and discovery, the sport manager develops his or her personal philosophy that serves as a core component of ethical decision making.

Cultural Differences

Certain standards of behavior are universally accepted in human societies (Trevino & Nelson, 2004). For example, the golden rule (i.e., Do unto others are you would have them do unto you) appears in teachings from every major religion. While this suggests some common ethical understanding exists across cultures, the world is a complicated place and perceptions vary. For instance, many people value honesty; however, the meaning of honesty may differ significantly depending on the particular culture. As mentioned previously, in collectivist cultures, with its emphasis on relationships and family, gift giving is seen as appropriate and necessary action. While in individualist cultures, gift giving is seen as an objectionable form of influence on decision making.

Given the international nature of modern sport, sport managers must be aware of how standards of behavior vary across the world. With regard to business practices, the United States, Canada, and Northern Europe are seen as being comparable given the cultural similarities. In Southern Europe, there are fewer comparable values and, therefore, greater ethical challenges. The greatest challenges exist in developing countries, particularly those with autocratic governments, because significant cultural and value differences exist (Trevino & Nelson, 2004). Sport managers who are involved in international business must stay informed about the changing legal and ethical landscapes in the countries in which they work.

Why Good People Do Bad Things

There are many reasons why good managers do bad things in sport business. In some cases, there is no intention to reach an unethical decision. The sport manager may not be aware or does not have the relevant information and time to make an appropriate decision. In other cases, the sport manager lacks sufficient capacity to reconcile multiple and diverse pressures. However, there is evidence to suggest individuals knowingly engage in "mental maneuvers" when faced with difficult decisions. The outcome of these decisions, in some cases, may result in unethical behavior.

Several barriers that undermine ethical decision making in the workplace are described in the literature. Kerns (2003) outlines five different "mind games". *Quickly simplifying and satisficing* involves oversimplifying the problem and then selecting the familiar and easily formulated alternative when making a decision. This quick and dirty process is likely to overlook key aspects of the ethical issue. In general, people want to be liked, but when the *need to be liked* interferes with business objectivity it becomes a problem, because the individual may ignore ethical transgressions. *Dilute and disguise* involves using euphemisms to reduce the anxiety associated with unethical behaviors. For example, a sport manager may not feel compelled to report a colleague for "inappropriately using agency resources" when, in fact, he or she is "stealing". *Making positive* occurs when the individual compares his or her behavior to more heinous behavior. Unethical behavior is made to appear ethical when it is compared to worse behavior. The *overconfident* sport manager discounts the perceptions of other people, preferring to consider only his or her own ideas about alternatives. As a result, the individual may be blind to the most appropriate ethical choice.

Werhane (2005) offers a slightly different system to classify mental traps in the workplace. It is *human nature* to make mistakes. However, when faced with similar ethical situations the sport manager cannot excuse repeated misjudgment. Pursuing one's *self-interest* is not necessarily bad, but when the interest supersedes law, fiduciary responsibility, and a sense of propriety, then the behavior becomes unacceptable. People deal with ethical issues differently, but *disregarding others* suggests the sport manager failed to realize ethical decisions involves more than personal preferences. At any given time, people simultaneously serve in *overlapping social, professional, cultural, and religious roles* with corresponding moral demands. This overlap may be problematic when role demands are confused, roles come in conflict with other roles, or demands come in conflict with social norms or sense of morality. *Inadequate training* can be overcome through in-service workshops where professional and institutional codes of ethics are discussed and sport managers have an opportunity to practice applying moral theories to case studies. *Compartmentalization* occurs when the individual separates social responsibilities. There is disconnect when behavior considered inappropriate in one area (e.g., lying to significant other) is permissible in another area (e.g., lying to supervisor).

Simple Guidelines to Ethical Behavior

Once ethical issues have been identified; sport managers must decide how to resolve them. In many cases, the right course of action is not altogether clear. The sport manager should remember that ethical decision making is less about finding the one and only "right" thing to do than it is about finding the "better" thing to do. This judgment is grounded in the individual's value system and moral philosophy. The following guidelines can assist the sport manager in ethical decision making. However, not all strategies apply in a given situation (Browne, Giampetro-Meyer, & Williamson, 2004; Lussier & Kimball, 2004; Russell, 2005).

Four-Way Test

This test asks sport managers to consider four simple questions: (a) Is it the truth?, (b) Is it fair to all concerned?, (c) Will it build goodwill and friendship?, and (d) Will it be beneficial to all concerned? If the sport manager can answer yes to each of these questions, he is probably making an ethical choice. For instance, the local humane society may propose an end-of-season *Soggy Doggy Day* at the local pool as a fundraising event. The pool manager must assess whether the activity (a) coincides with the agency's mission and policies, (b) is fair for pool users who are pet owners and non-pet owners, (c) builds community relations, and (d) benefits outweigh the associated activity costs.

Stakeholder Approach

Using this approach, the sport manager attempts to create a win-win situation so that all the relevant constituents benefit from a decision. It may be helpful for the sport manager to ask: Am I proud to tell others of this decision? If the answer is yes, the decision is probably ethical. If the answer is no, the decision may not be ethical. If the sport manager seems to be rationalizing the decision or is reluctant to speak to colleagues about the choice, the decision is probably not ethical. For example, the sport manager may want to recognize the exemplary customer service provided by season staff members. He or may devise a system where employees score "stars" which may be redeemed for a cash bonus at the end of the season.

Result Approach

This strategy suggests the sport manager consider a series of assessments. In end result ethics, the decision's action or outcome is evaluated against the expected consequences. Rules ethics considers relevant policies and procedures. Organizational values ethics requires the sport manager to consider the acknowledged written and unwritten agency rules. Personal conviction ethics is an assessment of how a decision corresponds with personal beliefs and principles. For example, consider a proposal to drop the men's swimming, wrestling, and golf programs from the athletic department in order to adequately fund other sport programs offered at the college. Using end results ethics, the sport manager judges whether the consequences (increased resources, enhanced quality) justify the decision (reduction in participation opportunities). Rules ethics determines the appropriate course of action based on conference or national governing body policies for cutting sport programs. When assessing organizational values, the sport manager determines whether eliminating sports fits the mission and purpose of the athletic department. Finally, the sport manager must ascertain whether he or she believes it is right to eliminate sport opportunities in the college setting for primarily one gender.

Golden Rule

There are many interpretations of the golden rule: (a) do to others as you want them to gratify you, (b) be considerate of others' feeling as you want them to be considerate of your feelings, (c) treat other as persons of rational dignity like yourself, (d) extend brotherly or sisterly love to others, as you would want them to do to you, (e) treat others according to moral insight, as you would have others treat you, and (f) do to others as God wants you to do to them (Wattles, 1987). Each of these suggests the sport manager must consider how actions impact others, those seen and unseen, because human beings matter. For instance, suppose a sport manager must reprimand an employee for repeatedly being late to work. He would do well to consider the golden rule when determining location and time for the meeting, verbal and nonverbal communication strategies, and remediation methods.

Public Disclosure Test

This approach requires the sport manager to select an alternative course of action and imagine what would happen if the action was made public. Considering how the public would react if actions were made transparent gives the sport manager insight he or she might otherwise miss because of the personal ties to alternative options and results. Suppose an athletic director witnessed a brawl among opposing college football players during a game. When considering sanctions for players and coaches, the athletic director may consider how the public would react if more or less severe penalties were imposed. Of course, this process assumes one can actually determine how the public would react as well as the social norms of the public itself. For example, hockey fans expect players will fight during the game. Fans may be outraged if officials imposed sanctions for what is considered a meaningful part of the game.

Universalization Test

This test asks the sport manager to contemplate whether the world would be a better place if the decision were copied on a large scale. In other words, what if everyone did it? Suppose credible evidence was brought to the league commissioner to suggest a coach is instructing athletes on how to "take out" opposing players. For any alternative, the commissioner must consider whether sport would be better if other commissioners selected the same course of action.

FILOP

Much like the previous guidelines, using the FILOP method requires the sport manager to consider a series of questions in order to develop a well-rounded perspective on an ethical problem. Using FILOP, the sport manager determines: What are the *f*acts shaping the dilemma?, How can the ethical *i*ssue be framed?, What *l*aws (or regulations) are relevant in the situation?, What are the potential options for consideration?, and How do principles shape behavior?

For instance, consider the operations manager of a minor league baseball facility. It has become apparent staff have been selling alcohol to minors at the ballpark. First, the sport manager must determine the *facts*. What is the extent of the problem? Who is involved? How long has the problem existed? Second, the *issue* must be identified. This assessment may be difficult because sport problems are complex with overlapping causes and effects. For instance, Do staff knowingly providing alcohol to underage patrons? Do staff know they are suppose to check identification? Do staff believe someone else is responsible for checking? Are patrons using false identification?

In terms of *laws and regulations*, clearly there is a legal liability associated with selling alcohol to minors, but the sport manager must also consider how operating policies and staff training may have contributed to the situation. Next, the sport manager must generate **options**. Should the involved staff members be fired, reprimanded, or moved to another position? Should the operating manual or staff training be reviewed? Should additional security personnel be assigned to games? Should the facility stop selling alcohol? Finally, the sport manager must consider his or her personal values and *principles*. The sport manager may value the health and well-being of fans and feel a need to protect them. On the other hand, he or she may strongly believe in the freedom of choice; therefore, a wide selection of concessions should be available at the facility. Perhaps the sport manager believes mistakes are part of human nature and ought to be overlooked, but preparation is important. Training and resources should be provided for staff members. Using the FILOP process, the sport manager has a better understanding of the ethical issue and potential courses of action. Alternative decisions emerge that may be judged more "right" or "wrong". The sport manager proceeds to select the "best" or "most ethical" decision based on the circumstances.

Cavanaugh's Model

It is important for an individual to anticipate the consequences of a decision or action. In fact, it is a social and moral responsibility. Therefore, the sport manager must develop his or her skills for envisioning and evaluating the potential for risk or harm to others as a result of behavior. Cavanaugh's (1990) model of ethical decision making offers a three-step process that takes into account the impact of decisions on others.

Step 1: Determine the facts of the situation. From this, alternative decisions for action are generated. Step 2: Determine whether each potential decision is acceptable according to three criteria. First, does the decision optimize benefits?, does the action fit with the organization's mission and goals?, and can it be enacted effectively and efficiently given the available resources? Second, does it respect the rights of those involved? Rights may include freedom of choice, freedom of conscience, free speech, truthfulness, privacy, and safety. Finally, is the decision fair? Fairness may be assessed in terms of treatment, administration of rules, distribution of work, resources, rewards, and due process.

Step 3: Determine whether the decision is ethical or unethical. If the sport manager decides the decision is acceptable according to the three criteria, then the action is ethical. If the sport manager decides the decision is not acceptable according to the three criteria, then the action is unethical. If the decision is unacceptable according to one or two criteria, then three overriding factors are considered: Is one criterion more important?, is the action freely taken?, and are undesirable effects outweighed or uncontrollable? If the sport manager determines there are overriding factors, then the decision is ethical. If there are no overriding factors, then the decision is unethical.

Consider again the scenario that involves staff selling alcohol to minors at the ballpark. The facts show two staff members knowingly sold alcohol to underage patrons on a limited basis. A potential decision is to reprimand the staff members involved and reassign the individuals to other duties at the ballpark. Is this an ethical decision? Determine *utility*: Does the action fit with the organization's mission and goals? and Can it be enacted effectively and efficiently given the available resources? Determine *rights*: Does it respect the rights of those involved? Determine *justice*: Is decision fair in terms of treatment, administration of rules, due process? Are there any overriding factors to be considered?

If the sport manager determines the decision is ethical, then the process is complete. If the decision is unethical, the sport manager selects an alternative decision and begins again. This process is repeated until an ethical decision is reached.

Summary

Those individuals who are admired as leaders are identified as being highly principled with strong beliefs (Pierce & Newstrom, 2002). Sport business is fast paced, and ethical decision making directly affects the organization's ability to achieve its mission. The sport manager must be prepared to make ethical decisions. This chapter introduced core concepts of ethical decision making including key terms, classifications, models and guidelines. The hope is sport managers will be able to recognize and resolve ethical issues faced in the sport environment.

References

Browne, M. N., Giampetro-Meyer, A., & Williamson, C. (2004). *Practical business ethics for the busy manager.* Upper Saddle River, NJ: Pearson Education.

Cavanaugh, G. (1990). *American business values* (3rd ed.). Englewood Cliffs, NJ: Prentice-Hall.

Covey, S. (1991). *Principled-centered leadership.* New York: Summit.

Daft, R. L. (2003). *Management* (6th ed.). Cincinnati, OH: South-Western.

Ethics Resource Center. (2005). *National business ethics survey.* Retrieved September 1, 2006, from http://www.ethics.org/research/nbes-2005.asp

Ferrell, O. C., Fraedrich, J., & Ferrell, L. (2002). *Business ethics: Ethical decision making and cases* (5th ed.). Boston: Houghton Mifflin Company.

Foster, G. D. (2005). Ethics: Time to revisit the basics. In J. E. Richardson (Ed.), *Business ethics* (17th ed.). (pp. 5-10). Dubuque, IA: McGraw-Hill.

Green, T. (1971). *The activities of teaching.* New York: McGraw-Hill.

Hunt, S. D., & Vitell, S. J. (2005). Personal moral codes and the Hunt-Vitell Theory of Ethics: Why do people's ethical judgment differ? In R. A. Peterson, & O. C. Ferrel (Eds.), *Business ethics: New challenges for business schools and corporate leaders.* (pp. 18-37). Armonk, NY: M.E. Sharpe.

Jones, T. M. (1991). Ethical decision making by individuals in organizations: An issue-contingent model. *Academy of Management Review, 16*(2), 366-395.

Kerns, C. D. (2005). Why good leaders do bad things. In J. E. Richardson (Ed.), *Business ethics* (17th ed.). (pp. 13-15). Dubuque, IA: McGraw-Hill.

Kretchmar, R. S. (1994). *Practical philosophy of sport.* Champaign, IL: Human Kinetics.

Lennick, D., & Keil, F. (2004). *Moral intelligence.* Upper Saddle River, NJ: Pearson Education.

Lussier, R. N., & Kimball, D. (2004). *Sport management: Principles, applications, skill development.* Cincinnati, OH: South-Western.

Northhouse, P. G. (2004). *Leadership: Theory and practice* (3rd ed.). Thousand Oaks, CA: Sage Publications.

Pierce, J. L., & Newstrom, J. W. (2002). *The manager's bookshelf: A mosaic of contemporary views* (6th ed.). Upper Saddle River, NJ: Prentice Hall.

Rest, J. R. (1986). *Moral development: Advances in research and theory.* New York: Praeger Publishing.

Robbins, S. P., & Decenzo, D. A. (2004). *Fundamentals of management: Essential concepts and applications* (4th ed.). Upper Saddle River, NJ: Pearson Education.

Rokeach, M. (1968). *Beliefs, attitudes and values*. San Francisco: Jossey-Bass.

Rokeach, M. (1973). *The nature of human values*. New York: Free Press.

Russell, R. V. (2005). *Leadership in recreation* (3rd ed.). New York: McGraw Hill.

Shields, D. L., & Bredemeier, B. J. (1994). *Character development and physical activity*. Champaign, IL: Human Kinetics.

Solomon, R. C. (1992). *Above the bottom line: An introduction to business ethics*. Forth Worth, TX: Harcourt Brace.

Trevino, L. K. (1986). Ethical decision making in organizations: A person-situation interactionist model. *Academy of Management Review, 11*(3), 601-617.

Trevino, L. K., & Nelson, K. A. (2004). *Managing business ethics: Straight talk about how to do it right* (3rd ed.). New York: John Wiley & Sons.

Wattles, J. (1987). Levels of meaning in the Golden Rule. *Journal of Religious Ethics, 15*, 106-129.

Werhane, P. H. (2005). Why good people do bad things: Challenges to business ethics and corporate leadership. In R. A. Peterson & O. C. Ferrel (Eds.), *Business ethics: New challenges for business schools and corporate leaders* (pp. 38-55). Armonk, NY: M.E. Sharpe.

NOTES

CHAPTER 5

Organizational Ethics

Ethical issues are as much an organizational issue as a personal one. Like an individual, organizations are expected to exhibit ethical behavior. Yet recent results from the National Business Ethics Survey are distressing. Results indicated 50 percent of employees observed at least one example of ethical misconduct in the workplace and 36 percent observed two or more instances of misconduct within the previous year. The most frequently cited types of observed misconduct include abusive or intimidating behavior toward employees; lying to employees, customers, vendors, and public; violations of safety regulations; and observed misreporting of time worked. These indiscretions exist despite the fact that 69 percent of employees reported their organization have an ethics training program, 65 percent indicated their organization has a place where employees can seek ethics advice, and 69 percent stated their supervisor assesses ethical conduct as part of his or her performance evaluation (Ethics Resource Center, 2005).

Concerns about unethical business practices such as repressive labor practices, unsafe products, abuse of the natural envi-ronment, widespread bribery, and immorality in the pursuit of money and power have been raised for more than a century. However, it was not until the 1960s that business owners and managers were called to address those issues (Lantos, 2001). Most recently, government leaders are accused of poor decision making, which led to mishandling of hurricane relief efforts, religious leaders are on trial for sexually abusing children, philanthropic organizations have spent contributors' funds irresponsibly, and Olympic figure skating judges admitted to fixing scores to secure medals. In each case, individual behavior occurred within a larger organizational context.

There is a growing need to examine ethical behavior in sport organizations. In this chapter, we will examine organizational ethics including several sources of influence that impact ethical decision making and behavior. Next, sport business' concern and obligation to make choices and take action to benefit the community, known as social responsibility, will be examined. Finally, three pillars of an ethical organization will be discussed.

Learning Objectives

Upon completion of this chapter, the reader should be able to:

- Understand why it is important to study organizational ethics.
- Define organizational ethics and recognize factors that influence ethical decision making in sport organizations in a global marketplace.
- Define social responsibility and how it is applied in sport management.
- Understand the three pillars of an ethical organization: ethical individuals, ethical leadership, and organizational structures and systems.

Organizational Ethics: Why Bother? Who Cares?

Most people agree individuals and organizations have responsibility to act in ethical ways. However, a sport organization is different from a person. It has to balance economic viability with the needs and desires of constituent groups and society. As a result, there are differences in the pressure placed on the sport organization. This influence may be discussed in terms of (a) social expectations, (b) decision making factors, and (c) personal preferences.

Social expectations

In order for society to function, social norms exist to govern the nature and operation of business. The community has an expectation that managers will properly implement ethical standards. This being said, the world is constantly changing. Sport business, like any other business, is impacted by social, political, and economic forces found in the external environment (Daft, 2003). Social forces are commonly held attitudes, ideas, and values that shape behavior. Political forces refer to power imbalances and legal institutions and how they impact people and organizations. Economic forces influence how, when, and to whom scarce resources are allocated.

In recent years, a serious problem, coined "basketbrawl", has existed in the National Basketball Association. Essentially, a bench clearing fight erupts as a result of excessive physical contact and verbal harassment. In this singular event, there are numerous social, political, and economic influences at play. Social influences may include team cohesion, player camaraderie, and the individual's need to protect teammates from physical harm as well as the idea that professional athletes are expected to be role models for youth. Political influences may be assessed in terms of the negative publicity and resulting public relations issues that occur after altercations as well as the legal ramifications of assault and battery charges. Economic influences may be characterized by player suspensions or fines incurred by the team. Another consideration is that fans have a choice in how they spend discretionary income and may select not to attend future games or purchase merchandise. Sport managers must be familiar with these forces and respond to changes in the environment in order to implement ethical standards of conduct to meet social expectations.

Decision making factors

Organizational ethical decision making is different from personal ethical decision making. An organization's ethics is not the same as the sum of its members' personal ethics. If it were, unethical behavior in organizations would be traced to a few "bad apples" that could be identified and removed (Trevino & Nelson, 2004). Rather, ethical decision making in an organization is influenced by a number of factors. To be sure, individual factors such as moral philosophy and moral development are important; but additional influences such as formal structure, organizational culture, ethical climate, influence of coworkers, and opportunity also impact the likelihood of ethical decision making. The sport manager should be aware the organization might inadvertently foster questionable behavior if it fails to properly monitor and manage these factors (Ferrell, 2005). For instance, the ticket office may not have a redundant system in place to record the sale of tickets and the deposit of revenue. This lack of checks and balances in departmental operations may foster inappropriate behavior among staff as well as inhibit efficient management.

Personal preferences

In the competitive marketplace, sport organizations are challenged to hire and retain the best workers. Evidence suggests people are more attracted to and more committed to ethical organizations. Moreover, federal and state legislation have made managers liable for the criminal activities of subordinates. Sport managers must be aware of organizational ethics because workers want and need guidance in order to define the boundaries of acceptable and unacceptable behavior in the workplace (Trevino & Nelson, 2004). Who cares about organizational ethics? The astute sport manager does because, like quality and leadership, organizational ethics make good business sense.

What Are Organizational Ethics?

Ethics are a code of moral values and principles that govern behavior. This code provides a basis for the individual to determine "right or wrong" and "good or bad." Like a person, an organization has values and guiding principles. These guiding principles are outlined in the sport business' mission, vision, and value statements. Organizational ethics are the standards used to determine how a sport business and its managers ought to behave in the workplace and larger social environment (Aldag & Stearns, 1991).

Organizational ethics can be understood in relation to three domains: codified law, ethical behavior, and free choice. Codified law and free choice exist on opposite ends of a continuum. Codified law is where standards are explicitly stated and enforced by the legal system. In a sense, lawmakers and judges have stated businesses must behave in a certain way. Obedience is to a legal standard. Free choice, on the other hand, is related to the discretion sport managers have to determine behavior. Obedience is to a personal standard. The law has no say in this area. Between these two areas is the ethical behavior domain. While this area does not have explicit laws, there are standards of

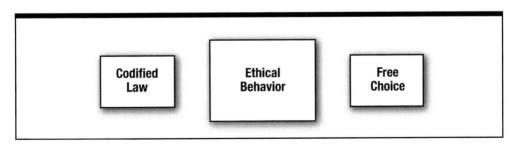

Figure 5.1
Three Domains of Organizational Ethics

conduct based on shared moral values and principles. In the ethical behavior domain, obedience is to known, yet unenforceable, norms and standards (Daft, 2003). For example, imagine a youth sport coach in a recreational league yelling and pointing at players on the field. While not against the law, there are norms and standards shared by the larger community that suggest this is inappropriate behavior when working with young athletes.

Sport managers get into trouble when they proceed as if only laws or free choice govern decisions. Hence, if an action is not illegal, it must be ethical. It is better to recognize a third domain exists, and serves a useful purpose in regulating behaviors both inside and outside the sport organization.

Framework of Organizational Ethics

For many years it was assumed that people make difficult decisions within an organization in the same way they resolve difficult issues in their personal lives. However, this is not the case. In sport organizations, few managers or staff members have the freedom to decide ethical issues apart from workplace pressures. Ferrell (2005) provides a framework to understand these pressures. The model indicates (a) ethical issue intensity, (b) individual factors, and (c) organizational factors collectively influence whether a person will make an ethical decision in the workplace.

Ethical issue intensity. Ethical issue intensity is defined as the perceived importance or relevance of a problem to an individual, work group, or organization. For example, lackluster ticket sales would be a serious issue to members of the sales department but much less important to staff in the facilities management department. Ethical issue intensity has a temporal component, which means the intensity will vary over time depending on the situation. Failing to meet projected ticket sales during the season would be perceived much differently

than failing to match projections during the off-season. Further, ethical issue intensity is influenced by the sport manager's values, needs, and perceptions as well as the pressure placed on the decision-maker. For instance, intensity will vary if the new marketing strategy is thought to have failed versus the perception that poor weather has negatively impacted ticket sales. Research suggests perceived importance of ethical issues can be modified through positive and negative incentives. In other words, rewards and punishments, codes of conduct, and organizational values may be used to influence ethical issue intensity (Robin, Reidenbach, & Forrest, 1996).

Individual factors. Individual factors such as moral philosophy and moral development are important in the evaluation and resolution of ethical issues. Moral philosophy represents the code people use to determine "right or wrong" and "good or bad". These principles are learned through a process of socialization from family members, social groups, religion and formal education. No single, universal moral philosophy for resolving workplace issues exists. Interestingly, research suggests people apply different moral philosophies in different situations; and depending on the situation, people may even change their value structure or moral philosophy when making decisions (Fraedrich & Ferrell, 1992).

Kohlberg (1971) suggested different people make different decisions when confronted with similar ethical situations because they are at different stages of development in their moral reasoning. This may be why people change their view on "what is right" across contexts. For instance, the sales department manager may consider falsifying the monthly ticket sales report. The same person may believe it is highly unethical to falsify his tax return. Kohlberg also argued people may change their moral beliefs and behavior as they gain education and experience in resolving conflicts. In the case of the sales manager, with education and experience, his moral reasoning may evolve such that individual recognizes it is inappropriate to falsify documents in either situation. This recognition would promote a corresponding change in behavior. See Chapter 4: Foundations of Ethical Decision making for more information on ethical decision making from the individual's perspective.

Organizational factors. There are several organizational factors that influence ethical decision making: formal structure, organizational culture, ethical climate, influence of coworkers, and opportunity. The *formal structure* specifies the manner in which employees are positioned within the organization. The size and scope of ethical issues faced by an individual will vary depending on his or her position. The more formal the structure, the more likely the organization will have detailed policies and procedures to define boundaries of appropriate behavior across situations.

Organizational culture is defined as a set of values, beliefs, goals, norms, and ways to solve problems shared by members (Ferrell, Fraedrich, & Ferrell, 2002). Research has shown social networks in the workplace play an important role in transmitting values, guiding decision making, and shaping behavior (Ferrell, 2005). Overtime it is believed an organization evolves such that it has a mind and a will of its own. Individuals are restricted in their ability to apply personal ethics to management systems and decision making. Moreover, decisions in the workplace are typically made in conjunction with coworkers, supervisors, and subordinates. These interactions are influenced by the organization's culture. While most organizational cultures reinforce ethics, some organizations create a culture that supports unethical decisions.

For instance, imagine if the organizational culture found in a sport team's ticket office supported an "anything-goes"

mentality toward sales. This might be reflected in the pressure tactics a sport manager uses with staff, reward systems that do not take into account unscrupulous behaviors, and inappropriate business operation techniques (e.g., high quota with severe deadlines). This environment may create a culture that supports unethical decisions because those who are successful will be retained while those who are not successful will be dismissed. If those who are retained are of the mind that unscrupulous behavior is appropriate they may transmit these norms and ways to solve problems to new employees.

A significant element of the organizational culture is the *ethical climate*. Whereas an agency's culture conveys the "ideals" to guide a wide range of behaviors, the ethical climate can be thought of as the character or conscience of the organization (Ferrell, Fraedrich, & Ferrell, 2002). On an organization-wide scale, the perception of "right" or "wrong" is reflected in the ethical climate (DeGeorge, 1987). The more ethical the climate is perceived to be, the less likely that members will engage in decision making that will result in unethical behavior (Ferrell, Fraedrich, & Ferrell, 2002).

Supervisors and coworkers provide information and advice; both formally and informally, on a daily basis to assist the sport manager in completing job tasks. Superiors can have a negative effect, either directly or indirectly, on ethical behavior by either setting a bad example or failing to supervise appropriately. In some cases, the supervisor may look the other way because he does not have to deal with the conflict or other risks associated with handling misconduct (Ferrell, Fraedrich, & Ferrell, 2002).

Other coworker issues that may influence ethical behavior include obedience to authority, groupthink, and job stress. In organizations that emphasize respect for superiors, sport managers may feel they are expected to unquestionably follow a supervisor's instructions even when the instructions conflict with the individual's personal values. Groupthink exists when a sport manager goes along with group decisions even they run counter to one's own value system. Indeed, there is evidence that peer coworkers can change a person's original value system. This value change can be either temporary or permanent and is more likely to occur is when the coworker is a supervisor and the employee is new to the organization (Ferrell, 2005). Role stress results from strain, conflict, or lack of agreement on job-related tasks. Sport managers in a role-stress situation are more likely to make decisions that result in unethical behavior (Ferrell, Fraedrich, & Ferrell, 2002).

Opportunity describes the conditions that permit or limit ethical behavior. Opportunity is typically discussed in terms of a sport manager's immediate work situation (e.g., where they work, with whom they work, nature of work) which may provide rewards or fail to erect barriers. Rewards may include bonuses and promotion, recognition, or simply a good feeling. Failing to erect barriers exists when there is no consequence associated with "bad" behavior. The absence of punishment contributes to unethical behavior because it allows the individual to engage in such activities without fear of reprisal.

Ethical decision making is a dynamic process in the modern sport organization. There are no hard and fast rules. Rather the sport manager must consider the unique aspects of the situation. Depending on the ethical issue intensity, individual factors and organizational factors, many potential decisions exist that may lead to either ethical or unethical behavior.

Organizational Ethics in a Global Marketplace

The modern sport manager should understand organizational ethics because it is an important component of ethical leadership. Moreover, the impact of globalization has increased ethical issue intensity. Sport managers working abroad or with international representatives need to have an openness and sensitivity to other belief systems as well as a maturity to work out the differences (Ferrell, 2005). Situations may exist where it is not appropriate to impose ethical standards from one's home country, and similarly, it is not appropriate to adopt local customs. For example, in Japan, gift giving is a natural part of business interaction. However, in the United States, giving expensive gifts is seen as an inappropriate means to influence decision making. In this case, the sport manager is caught between two belief systems. The individual risks behavior perceived as inappropriate by either providing a gift or not providing a gift.

Donaldson (1996) offers three guiding principles for handling these types of situations. First the sport manager must understand his or her core values which determine the absolute moral threshold for all decisions. Second, the sport manager must show respect for local traditions. Finally, the sport manager must critically think about the specific context. The decisions related to a particular business activity depend a great deal on who is involved, to what extent, for what reasons, and what are the expected outcomes.

In recent years, there has been tremendous interest in the development of global standards for ethical business conduct. This may benefit sport managers by providing a "guidebook" for negotiating the difficult terrain of international ethics. The Global Compact (2006) is an example of such a guidebook. It is a ten-principle declaration of global ethical principles in the areas of human rights, labor standards, environment, and anti-corruption.

Social Responsibility

Social responsibility, corporate accountability, social accounting, compliance, reputation management, and corporate citizenship are but a few terms used to describe the array of rights, responsibilities, and roles of business organizations (Thorne, Ferrell, & Ferrell, 2003). While there is no universal agreement on what is required, expected, or desired, it is clear the practice of "giving back" to the community is commonplace among sport businesses. For instance, a sport agency may request patrons exchange a non-perishable food item for reduced admission to a game or purchase a fun run T-shirt knowing a portion of the profit will be donated to a preferred charity.

Social responsibility reflects a sport business' concern and obligation to make choices and take actions that will contribute to the welfare of society as well as the organization (Aldag & Stearns, 1991). It refers to the duty to nurture, protect, enhance and promote the well-being of various groups such as employees, shareholders, patrons, and the community at large (Jones, 2004). While this may seem straightforward in the abstract, social responsibility can be a difficult concept to understand, because different people have different beliefs about what actions improve social welfare. For instance, consider a situation in which the price of a professional sport team ticket includes a $2 fee that will be redistributed to the professional team's charitable organizations. Some fans may believe this is socially responsible behavior. Others may believe the responsible behavior is to allow more fans to attend the game via lower ticket prices. For many issues it may be difficult to pinpoint what social action is the "right" or "good" thing to do. Continuing the example above, some fans may say contributing to any charitable organization is "good", while others may argue it is "right" to contribute to local charitable organizations so the money benefits the surrounding community.

Corporate Social Responsibility

In the literature, corporate social responsibility is defined as "a commitment to improve community well-being through discretionary business practices and contributions of corporate resources" (Kotler & Lee, 2005, p. 3). The term "discretionary" is a key element of the definition because it refers to the voluntary commitment a business makes when selecting a strategic course of action to fulfill its economic, legal, ethical, and philanthropic responsibilities to stakeholders. "Community well-being" is interpreted to include both human conditions and environmental issues. While social responsibility is often discussed in relation to corporations, it is important to remember that many types of businesses, including sole proprietorships and partnerships, engage in community initiatives. Support may take many forms, including cash contributions, grants, paid advertising, publicity, promotional sponsorships, technical expertise, in-kind contributions (i.e., printing services, computer equipment), employee volunteers, and access to distribution channels (Kotler & Lee, 2005). According to Business for Social Responsibility (2006), there are several bottom-line benefits of incorporating socially responsible practices into business operations. Socially responsible businesses report increased sales and market share; strengthened brand positioning; enhanced corporate image and clout; increased ability to attract, motivate, and retain employees; decreased operating costs; and increased appeal to investors and analysts.

A framework for analyzing social responsibility is often displayed as a pyramid. Beginning with the base, there are four criteria for total corporate social responsibility: economic responsibility, legal responsibility, ethical responsibility and philanthropic responsibility. Scholars suggest business managers typically cope with several responsibilities at the same time, and a business' ethical and philanthropic responsibilities

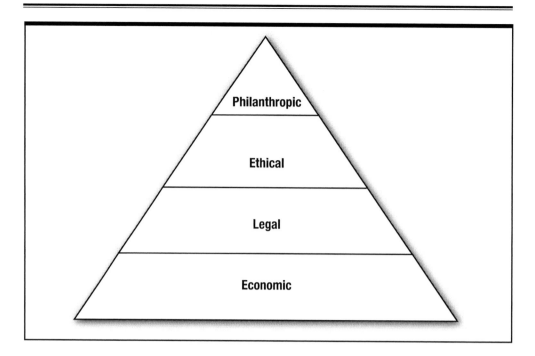

Figure 5.2
Framework for Analyzing Social Responsibility

are increasingly considered as important as economic and legal ones (Daft, 2003).

The basic building block is economic responsibility. The sport organization has a responsibility to be economically viable in order to generate a return on investment for owners, create jobs for the community, and contribute goods and services to the economy. Legal responsibility compels the business to obey laws and regulations that outline responsible business conduct. Essentially, these are the ground rules derived from what is deemed to be collectively "important." Society enforces its expectations through the legal system. Sport businesses are also expected to be ethical. At its most fundamental level, this is the obligation to do what is just, fair, and right as well as to avoid or minimize harm to constituents. Finally, philanthropic responsibility promotes human welfare and goodwill. This involves contributing financial and human resources to "give back" to the community so the quality of life can be enhanced and sustained

(Thorne, Ferrell, & Ferrell, 2003).

Organizing for Social Response

Prior to the 1990s, decisions about which social issues to support were based on the ongoing pressure to "do good to look good." A common practice was for businesses to contribute a fixed percentage of revenue or pretax earnings on an annual basis. In recent years, decision making reflects a desire to "do well while doing good." This means businesses select a limited number of strategic areas to focus on which (a) fit the agency's values, (b) support business goals, (c) are related to core products or core markets, (d) build a desired brand identity, and (e) are issues the community, patrons, and staff members care about (Kotler & Lee, 2005).

Prior to engaging in new or different social initiatives, a sport organization should consider conducting a social audit. This is a detailed examination of an organization's external programs and services. The purpose of the audit is to document program and service impact in the community, recognize areas of need, and identify new initiatives that may be pursued.

Once an organization has decided to engage in social action, it must develop an appropriate plan of action (Aldag & Stearns, 1991). The specific details will depend on the sport industry, size, and visibility of the organization, importance of the social issue, environmental characteristics, among other things. Much like other goals, social goals must be specific and measurable. Specific goals enhance credibility, increase the likelihood of success, and make evaluation of outcomes more feasible.

Managing Ethics & Social Responsibility

The challenge of ensuring ethical behavior may seem overwhelming. Sport business, like other industries, has had its share of ethical "missteps" and resultant public criticism in recent years. Perhaps now more than ever, managers are concerned with improving the ethical climate and social responsiveness of their organization (Daft, 2003). This involves finding ways to promote ethical behavior so that individuals resist the temptation to engage in unethical behavior or promote personal and organizational interests at the expense of social welfare is a challenge sport managers cannot afford to ignore. While there is no universally accepted approach for dealing with organizational ethics, sport managers must take active steps to make sure the sport business and its members stay on an ethical footing. This process begins by instituting the three pillars of an ethical organization: (a) ethical individuals, (b) ethical leadership, and (c) organizational structures and systems (Trevino, Hartman, & Brown, 2000).

Ethical Individuals

Fundamentally, ethical organizations are composed of ethical individuals. These individuals possess core values such as honesty and integrity as well as the capacity to identify and resolve ethical issues. Through education and experience they aspire to develop their moral reasoning. Sport managers are trusted because they act in ways consistent with the organization's mission and goals, show respect for others, and make decisions which benefit the organization as well as the larger community (Trevino, Hartman, & Brown, 2000).

With respect to ethical conduct, the sport manager has a two fold responsibility: make ethical decisions and create a climate that fosters ethical conduct on the part of coworkers. In order to do this, the sport manager must develop a personal strategy for making ethical decisions as well as develop a plan to promote the likelihood of ethical conduct among colleagues (Hitt, 1990).

Ethical Leadership

Ethical leadership deters unethical behavior. The ethical orientation of the sport manager is a fundamental aspect of promoting ethical behavior among staff members. Leadership skills are not enough, rather these skills must be coupled with integrity and ethical behavior. While these characteristics alone do not make an effective leader, these traits are important because they help the sport manager formulate a vision and transform that vision into reality (Carlson & Perrewe, 1995).

Since personal values direct human behavior, it is paramount for sport managers to convert identified organizational values into behavioral standards in the workplace (Zablow, 2006). The manager must then demonstrate these behaviors, showing patrons and staff members that ethical behavior is an inherent part of the day-to-day business operations. These standards of behavior must be communicated and upheld through reward systems or swift discipline. In addition, leaders must ensure that staff members know they can ask for clarification of policies or report possible wrong doing without fear of retaliation (Trevino, Hartman, & Brown, 2000).

Organizational Structures and Systems

The final aspect of an ethical organization is the structure and systems used to shape values and promote ethical behavior throughout the organization. The degree to which various structures and systems are well defined and implemented depends on the particular characteristics of the organization. Two common means to manage organizational ethics include (a) codes and (b) ethical structures.

Codes

Establishing organizational standards of conduct may encourage ethical behavior. These standards of conduct may take the form of a code of ethics or conduct of conduct. A *code of ethics* is a formal statement of an organization's values and concern for social issues. This code communicates what the agency "stands for." A *code of conduct* is a statement of behaviors that are expected and those that will not be tolerated (Daft, 2003). A code of conduct must be specific enough to be reasonably capable of preventing misconduct. General codes that propose "do no harm" or "be fair and honest" are not enough. The organization must provide enough direction so that the individual may avoid the risks typically associated with a particular sport business (Ferrell, Fraedrich, & Ferrell, 2002).

A code of conduct establishes important ground rules to enable staff members to respond responsibly and consistently throughout the organization. The code may outline fundamental decision making rules, guidelines, and procedures that staff can apply like a roadmap when dealing with ethical dilemmas faced on a daily basis. Incorporating a code of conduct allows the agency to create a cohesive culture of doing the right thing for the right reasons. Perhaps more importantly, implementing and enforcing an effective code of conduct will improve staff members' self-esteem and morale, making them happier and more productive, which in turn will enhance the organization's reputation and image among patrons and the community at large (Barth, 2003).

NSCA Code of Ethics

1. Strength and conditioning professionals should not practice nor condone discrimination.

2. Strength and conditioning professionals should not condone, engage in illegal behavior or defend unsportsmanlike conduct or practices.

3. Strength and conditioning professionals should refrain from using techniques and practices in which repeated acts of negligence would result in injury to an individual.

4. Strength and conditioning professionals should use care to be truthful and not misleading when stating their education, training, experience, and involvement of NSCA and shall not misrepresent or misuse their affiliation with the NSCA for unwarranted favors – monetary or otherwise.

Figure 5.3
Example of Code of Ethics

State of New Jersey | **Model of Athletic Code of Conduct**

The following model code of conduct is promulgated in accordance with the provisions of P.L. 2002, Chapter 74.

Preamble:
Interscholastic and youth sports programs play an important role in promoting the physical, social and emotional development of children. It is therefore essential for parents, coaches and officials to encourage youth athletes to embrace the values of good sportsmanship. Moreover, adults involved in youth sports events should be models of good sportsmanship and should lead by example by demonstrating fairness, respect and self-control.

In therefore pledge to be responsible for my words and actions while attending, coaching, officiating or participating in a youth sports event and shall conform my behavior to the following code of conduct:

1. I will not engage in unsportsmanlike conduct with any coach, parent, player, participant, official or any other attendee.
2. I will not encourage my child, or any other person, to engage in unsportsmanlike conduct with any coach, parent, player, participant, official or any other attendee.
3. I will not engage in any behavior which would endanger the health, safety or well-being of any coach, parent, player, participant, official or any other attendee.
4. I will not encourage my child, or any other person, to engage in any behavior which would endanger the health, safety, or well-being of any coach, parent, player, participant, official or any other attendee.
5. I will not use drugs or alcohol while at a youth sports event and will not attend, coach, officiate or participate in a youth sports event while under the influence of drugs or alcohol.
6. I will not permit my child, or encourage any other person, to use drugs or alcohol at a youth sports event and will not permit my child, or encourage any other person, to attend, coach, officiate or participate in a youth sports event while under the influence of drugs or alcohol.
7. I will not engage in the use of profanity.
8. I will not encourage my child, or any other person, to engage in the use of profanity.
9. I will treat any coach, parent, player, participant, official or any other attendee with respect regardless of race, creed, color, national origin, sex, sexual orientation or ability.
10. I will encourage my child to treat any coach, parent, player, participant, official or any other attendee with respect regardless of race, creed, color, national origin, sex, sexual orientation or ability.
11. I will not engage in verbal or physical threats or abuse aimed at any coach, parent, player, participant, official or any other attendee.
12. I will not encourage my child, or any other person, to engage in verbal or physical threats or abuse aimed at any coach, parent, player, participant, official or any other attendee.
13. I will not initiate a fight or scuffle with any coach, parent, player, participant, official or any other attendee.
14. I will not encourage my child, or any other person, to initiate a fight or scuffle with any coach, parent, player, participant, official or any other attendee.

I hereby agree that if I fail to conform my conduct to the foregoing while attending, coaching, officiating or participating in a youth sports event I will be subject to disciplinary action, including but not limited to the following in any order or combination.

1. Verbal warning issued by a league, organization or school official.
2. Written warning issued by a league, organization or school official.
3. Suspension or immediate ejection from a youth sports event issued by a league, organization or school official who is authorized to issue such suspension or ejection by a school board or youth sports organization.
4. Suspension from multiple youth sports events issued by a league, organization or school official who is authorized to issue such suspension by a school board or youth sports organization.
5. Season suspension or multiple season suspension issued by a school board or youth sports organization.

Figure 5.4
Example of Code of Conduct

While many sport organizations have codes in place, few positively affect staff behavior because they have not been properly adopted, implemented, enforced (Barth, 2003). Simply having a written code of conduct is not enough. It takes a real, ongoing organizational commitment to emphasize the critical importance of ethical behavior, modeled by top administrators, to achieve effective results and tangible benefits.

Ethical Structures

Ethical structures represent the various mechanisms a sport organization may undertake to facilitate ethical behavior. Large-scale sport operations, like other businesses, will typically have a *chief ethics officer* or *ethics committee* to oversee organizational ethics. This individual or group will oversee all aspects of ethics and legal compliance, including establishing and communicating standards, preparing informational or training materials, assuming responsibility for handling problems, and advising senior administrators on the ethical aspects of decisions. Large agencies are also likely to have a counselor available to assist staff members with difficult ethical issues or a hotline to allow employees to report questionable behavior as well as seek guidance concerning ethical dilemmas. In smaller organizations, a sport manager at the supervisory or administrative level will be assigned these responsibilities on a part-time basis (Daft, 2003).

Ethics training assists the sport manager to translate codes of ethics and value statements into everyday work behavior as well as recognize common ethical dilemmas in the sport industry. Unless a well-developed set of ethical practices and procedures are in place and understood, all staff are open to temptation. Education and experience prepares the sport manager to better answer the question "what is right?" in a given situation. Moreover, ethics training should

be ongoing. Beyond new employee orientation, policies and procedures should be communicated routinely through management meetings, email messages, regular training or help sessions, and as a part of the policy manual.

Summary

Sport organizations desire to hire and retain the best workers. Research suggests employees are more attracted to and more committed to ethical organizations. Interestingly enough, graduating seniors at more than 100 colleges and universities now sign or recite the "graduation pledge" in which they promise to "take into account the social and environmental consequences of any job" they consider. They also pledge to "try to improve those aspects of any organizations" where they work (*Business Week*, 2002).

This chapter provided an overview of organizational ethics including its relationship to codified law and free choice. Sport managers should be familiar with Ferrell's (2005) framework for understanding organizational ethics. Sport business' concern and obligation to make choices and take action to benefit the community, known as social responsibility, was also examined. Finally, three pillars to facilitate an ethical organization were reviewed. According to *Business Week* (2002), prospective employers are very interested in ethics minded graduates, with concerns that go beyond simply making a living.

References

Aldag, R. J., & Stearns, T. M. (1991). *Management* (2nd ed.). Cincinnati, OH: South-Western.

Barth, S. R. (2003). *Corporate ethics: The business code of conduct for ethical employees.* Boston: Aspatore Publishing.

Business for Social Responsibility. (n.d.). Retrieved September 1, 2006, from http://www.bsr.org/CSRResources

Carlson, D. S., & Perrewe, P. L. (1995). Institutionalization of organizational ethics through transformational leadership. *Journal of Business Ethics, 14(10)*, 829-837.

Daft, R. L. (2003). *Management* (6th ed.). Cincinnati, OH: South-Western.

DeGeorge, R. T. (1987). The stature of business ethics: Past and future. *Journal of Business Ethics, 6*, 201-211.

Donaldson, T. (1996). Values in tension: Ethics away from home. *Harvard Business Review*, 9/10, 48-62.

Ethics Resource Center. (2005). *National business ethics survey*. Retrieved September 1, 2006, from http://www.ethics.org/research/nbes-2005.asp

Ferrell, O. C. (2005). A framework for understanding organizational ethics. In R.A. Peterson, & O.C. Ferrel (Eds.), *Business ethics: New challenges for business schools and corporate leaders* (p. 3-17.) Armonk, NY: M.E. Sharpe.

Ferrell, O. C., Fraedrich, J., & Ferrell, L. (2002). *Business ethics: Ethical decision making and cases* (5th ed.). Boston: Houghton Mifflin Company.

Fraedrich, J. P., & Ferrell, O. C. (1992). Cognitive consistency of marketing managers in ethical situations. *Journal of the Academy of Marketing Science*, 20, 245-252.

Get a job, save the planet. (2002, May 6). *Business Week*, (p. 10).

Hitt, W. D. (1990). *Ethics and leadership: Theory into practice*. Columbus, OH: Battelle Press.

Jones, G. R. (2004). *Organizational theory, design, and change: Text and cases* (4th ed.). Upper Saddle River, NJ: Pearson-Prentice Hall.

Kohlberg, L. (1971). Stages of moral development as a basis for moral education. In C. M. Beck, B. S. Crittenden, & E. V. Sullivan (Eds.), *Moral education: Interdisciplinary approaches* (pp. 23-92). New York: Newman.

Kotler, P., & Lee, N. (2005). *Corporate social responsibility: Doing the most good for your company and your cause*. Hoboken, NJ: John Wiley & Sons.

Lantos, G. P. (2001). The boundaries of strategic corporate social responsibility. *Journal of Consumer Marketing, 18(7)*, 595-630.

National Strength and Conditioning Association. (2006). *Code of ethics*. Retrieved September 1, 2006, from http://www.nsca.com/Publications/posstatements.shtml

Robin, D. P., Reidenbach, R. E., & Forrest, P. J. (1996). The perceived importance of ethical issue as an influence on the ethical decision making of ad managers. *Journal of Business Research*, 35, 17-28.

State of New Jersey. (2006). *Model athletic code of conduct*. Retrieved September 1, 2006, from http://nj.gov/lps/model_athletic_code.pdf

Thorne, D., Ferrell, O. C., & Ferrell, L. (2003). *Business and society: A strategic approach to corporate citizenship*. Boston: Houghton Mifflin.

Trevino, L. K., Hartman, L. P., & Brown, M. (2000). Moral person and moral manager. *California Business Review, 42(4)*, 128-142.

Trevino, L. K., & Nelson, K. A. (2004). *Managing business ethics: Straight talk about how to do it right* (3rd ed.). Hoboken, NJ: John Wiley & Sons.

United Nations Global Compact. (2006). *The ten principles*. Retrieved September 1, 2006, from http://www.unglobalcompact.org/AboutTheGC/TheTenPrinciples/index.html

Zablow, R. J. (2006). Creating and sustaining an ethical workplace. *Risk Management*, 53(9), 26-30.

NOTES

PART III

Sport Governance Organizations

CHAPTER 6

Impact of Government on Athletic Associations

The organizations that govern amateur athletics are collectively referred to as athletic associations in this chapter. These athletic associations include (a) high school and college athletic associations, (b) high school and college conferences, (c) national and international governing bodies (e.g., United States Olympic Committee, International Olympic Committee), (d) youth sport governing bodies (e.g., Amateur Athletic Union, American Softball Association, Little League, and many more), (e) state games, (f) senior games or Olympics, and (g) disabled athlete organizations (e.g., Deaflympics, Paralympics, and Special Olympics. Most of these associations are organized as nonprofit entities with a constitution and bylaws.

The constitution and bylaws are generally drafted by the members of the association and can be modified only by a vote of the members and/or their representatives. These associations are generally governed by an executive committee, board of directors, chief operating officer, various other officers, and representatives from the members of the association. The association generally develops rules and regulations (e.g., minimum standards and requirements for eligibility and participation) to govern the sporting activities under its control.

The validity of association rules, under the U.S. Constitution, has historically come under frequent scrutiny. A key component in deciding such cases is whether or not the association is considered a private or a public institution in the eyes of the court. Further, these associations are impacted, beyond the Constitution, by specific laws including agency law, Amateur Sports Act of 1978 (revised in 1998), antitrust law, business laws, contract law (i.e., coaches contracts, scholarships, broadcasting contracts, endorsement contracts, sponsorship contracts), disability laws, discrimination legislation, drug-testing requirements, employee legislation (i.e., workers compensation) gambling, intellectual property rights, labor law, and television and broadcasting legislation.

Learning Objectives

Upon completion of this chapter, the reader should be able to:

+ Understand the impact of government upon the sporting industry.

- ♦ Discuss the impact of the Constitution and various federal and state statutes on the sport industry.
- ♦ Describe the impact of sport authorities, commissions, congresses, councils, or foundations on the sport industry.

Common Sport Delivery Sectors

There are three common sectors of sport delivery methods including commercial, nonprofit, and public. The commercial sector is composed of for-profit organizations, such as professional sport leagues and teams and motorsport race tracks and racing teams. These organizations are in business to generate a profit for its owners, investors, and in some cases stockholders. While the nonprofit organizations are concerned about the bottom line, their main function is to provide participation opportunities, services, and products for amateur athletes and their families. Finally, the public sector is responsible for providing, at a minimal cost, recreational sport opportunities for the taxpayers in a given jurisdiction.

Government Impact

All athletic associations are subject to fundamental legal principles. Although they are private and voluntary in nature, government through the legal system nevertheless scrutinizes them. The courts generally have two reasons to question these associations: (a) large numbers of public institutions form the membership of these association and (b) the opinion that these organizations are performing a traditional governmental or public function. The following sections will outline the impact of government upon amateur and professional sports in the United States:

Agency Law

As amateur and professional sports have grown into a billion-dollar industry since the 1980s, the role of the player agent has blossomed significantly within the world of sports. The prominence of agents within sports has paralleled the booming economic growth in the sport industry. With millions of dollars on the line in many player contracts, the need for competent representation has increased considerably. In addition to representing players, agents may handle representation for coaches, managers, and administrators.

The professional leagues require certification of player agents. Many states have passed legislation to deal with problems that may arise with the athlete agents. The federal government passed the Uniform Athlete Agent Act in 2000. Many states have adopted this legislation for the format of state legislation. There are three elements of an agency relationship: consent to represent, acting on behalf of a principal, and an agent is subject to the control of the principal. The principal is required to compensate for services rendered, reimburse appropriate expenses, and indemnify (protect) the agent.

Amateur Sports Act

The Amateur Sports Act (1978) was passed to recognize and coordinate amateur athletics in the United States and to encourage and strengthen participation of U.S. amateurs in international competition. The law focuses on two primary areas: (a) the relationship between athletes eligible for international amateur competition and the ruling bodies that govern these competitions and (b) the relationship between the ruling bodies themselves. This act establishes the United States Olympic Committee (USOC) as the principal mechanism for attaining these goals. The Amateur Sports Act creates a governing structure for the

SIDEBAR

A sports agent is a person who procures and negotiates employment and endorsement deals for an athlete. In turn the agent receives a commission that is usually between five and ten percent of the contract, although this figure varies. In addition, the agent often handles public relations matters for his or her client. In some large sport agencies such as IMG, Octagon, and Wasserman Media Group (WMG), agents deal with all aspects of an athlete's finances, from investment to filing taxes.

Famous sports agents are:
- Scott Boras: baseball agent whose clients include Carlos Beltrán, Barry Bonds, Alex Rodriguez, and others.
- Bill Duffy: basketball agent whose clients include Carmelo Anthony, Yao Ming, and Steve Nash
- David Falk: basketball agent whose clients are/have been Juwan Howard, Michael Jordan, Glen Rice.
- Mark McCormack: the main creator of the modern sports agency industry. First client was Arnold Palmer. Founded International Management Group.
- Rob Pelinka: basketball agent and former basketball player at University of Michigan, whose clients are Kobe Bryant and Carlos Boozer.
- Drew Rosenhaus: football agent, quickly becoming notorious for signing high profile athletes and making high demands. High-profile clients include Anquan Boldin, Plaxico Burress, Terrell Owens, Warren Sapp, and Santana Moss. Often represents players from his alma matter, the University of Miami. The real life inspiration for the character of Bob Sugar in the film *Jerry Maguire*.
- Matt Sosnick and Paul Cobbe: baseball agents who are partners. Their most notable client is Dontrelle Willis. Matt Sosnick is subject of the book *Licensed To Deal* by Jerry Crasnick.
- Leigh Steinberg: football agent, sports business pioneer. His clients include Steve Young, Troy Aikman, Warren Moon and Ben Roethlisberger.
- Paul Stretford: disgraced English football agent, represented Wayne Rooney, lied during a court case and was subsequently charged with misconduct.

USOC by empowering it to select one National Governing Body for each Olympic or Pan-American sport.

In 1998, the Amateur Sports Act was amended (commonly known as the [Ted] Stevens Amendment, Senator from Alaska). The changes include (a) the USOC incorporates athletes with disabilities into the governance structure by requiring the USOC to serve as the national Paralympic representative to the International Paralympic Committee, (b) requirement that athletic representatives, elected by fellow athletes, make up at least 20 percent of the membership and voting power of all USOC legislative bodies, (c) requirement

of a USOC report, issued every four years, that shall contain data on the participation of women, racial and ethnic minorities, and disabled athletes, (d) new language that prevents issuance of injunctive relief against the USOC in any suit concerning the "right to participate" by an athlete within 21 days of the beginning of the respective Olympic Games, and (e) the creation of an "athlete ombudsman" to provide free, independent advice to athletes about the Amateur Sports Act, the USOC bylaws and regulations, and the rules of the NGBs with respect to the resolution of any right to compete dispute.

It should be noted here that state governments or the federal government of the

United States have little or no day-to-day involvement in sport delivery or its governance, unlike other nations (e.g., China, former Soviet block countries, Russia, North Korea, and others) where sport is embedded in the government bureaucracy.

Antitrust Issues

Since the 1970s, antitrust legislation (i.e., Sherman Act, 1890; Clayton Act, 1914) has played an important role in influencing the business of the major professional sports leagues in North America (i.e., MLB, NBA, NFL, NHL, professional golf, and tennis). For years, professional sports leagues believed that they were protected from antitrust challenges under the broad antitrust immunity afforded professional baseball. However, players and their unions have challenged restrictive player rules (e.g., the draft, the reserve system, the commissioner's powers, and free agent compensation systems) since the end of the 1960s. Further, new competing leagues (e.g.,

American Football League in competition with the NFL) have challenged established leagues' monopoly power and owners have challenged league rules restricting expansion and relocation of franchises (e.g., Baltimore Colts to Indianapolis).

Antitrust litigation has played an important role at the intercollegiate level as well. Member universities, coaches, athletes, and shoe companies have all brought suit against the NCAA in order to recover damages resulting from the NCAA's perceived monopoly power. With varying degrees of success, these plaintiffs have used antitrust theory against the NCAA for its restrictions regarding issues such as broadcasting, coach's earnings, athlete eligibility, and commercialism.

Business Law

Running any type of business, whether it is sports related or not, requires understanding a number of important legal issues. The issues impacting sport organizations

SIDEBAR

Following the USFL's second season, its owners decided to file a lawsuit against the National Football League for violation of the Sherman Antitrust Act. The league sought actual damages of $567 million dollars which, when trebled, would amount to more than $1.7 billion.

Chief among the USFL's arguments was that the NFL, which had contracts with ABC, NBC and CBS, had pressured the networks to not televise the USFL in the fall. The league also claimed that the NFL had followed the practices outlined in the Porter Presentation, a package compiled by a Harvard professor to show the NFL how to conquer its new competitor. In particular, the USFL maintained that the NFL had conspired to harm the Oakland Invaders and New Jersey Generals.

The trial, which lasted 48 days, produced more than 7,100 pages of transcripts and thousands of pages of exhibits. Among those testifying were Pete Rozelle, USFL commissioner Harry Usher, Howard Cosell, Mike Davis, Donald Trump and a litany of television executives. Additionally, team owners from both leagues, including the late owner of the Tampa Bay Bandits, John Bassett, via videotape, were called to testify.

On July 29, 1986, the United States Football League won the battle but lost its war against the National Football League. After five days of deliberation, the jury that heard the USFL's case against the NFL found the older league guilty of monopolizing professional football and of using predatory tactics but awarded the USFL just $1 in damages. The fact that the antitrust award was trebled to $3 was of little solace to the struggling owners of the eight remaining USFL teams.

While the jury found that the NFL had willfully acquired and maintained a monopolization of professional football, it ruled against the rest of the USFL's claims. It did not find that the NFL controlled or attempted to control the television market. The vital claims were those based on television revenues, and those were the ones that the jury did not accept.

The jury felt that the USFL had abandoned its original plan to patiently build fan support while containing costs and had instead pursued a merger strategy. Moreover, the announced move to the fall also caused the abandonment of major markets and led to further fan skepticism. In essence, the jury ruled that although the USFL was harmed by the NFL's monopolization of pro football, most of the upstart league's problems were the result of its own mismanagement. Statements reflecting jury confusion were subsequently ignored.

On August 4, 1986, the USFL decided to suspend operations for the upcoming season. The league released most of its remaining players to look for employment in the NFL or Canadian Football League shortly thereafter. The league would not play another game.

The USFL's request for a new trial on damages was rejected, and subsequent appeals were unsuccessful. The league was able to win its court costs back, but this amounted to just $6-10 million (http://www.oursportscentral.com/usfl/trial.php).

and figures most often include taxes (i.e., player income tax liabilities state and federal, business income taxes, and tax implications of unrelated business income), and employee/employer relationships (i.e., equal pay, employment discrimination, age discrimination, and sexual harassment litigation).

Other aspects of business law that impact sport organizations include:

(a) Business structures – sole proprietorships, partnerships, and corporations,
(b) Not-for-profit organizations,
(c) Scholarships,
(d) Charitable contributions,
(e) Professional sport franchise tax issues,

(f) Depreciation issues,
(g) Gender discrimination, and
(h) Racial discrimination.

Constitutional Issues

There are a number of constitutional issues impacting both amateur and professional athletes. The issues include due process (i.e., the right to address grievances against oneself), equal protection (i.e., discrimination), freedom of expression (i.e., length of hair), protected interest or right (i.e., the right to participate in sports), right to privacy (i.e., blood or urine testing for drugs and the Buckley Amendment, which protects student-athlete's privacy), search and seizure (i.e., probable cause to search), and separation of church and state (i.e., locker room and pregame prayer).

The Family Educational Rights and Privacy Act of 1974 (sometimes called the Buckley Amendment) regulates the release and review of student-athletes' records. The NCAA and other third parties can be restricted and sometimes prevented from access to or publication of certain types of student-athlete information. The Buckley Amendment was designed to enhance comprehensive civil rights protections with two objectives in mind: (a) to assure parents of students, and students themselves, if they are attending an institution of post-secondary education or are 18 years old, access to their education records, and (b) to protect the students' right to privacy by restricting the transferability and disclosure of information in their records without prior consent.

The basic rights of the Buckley Amendment allow students to challenge any information in their education record that they or their parents believe to be inaccurate, misleading, or in violation of the student's rights. Further, the Buckley Amendment protects the right to prevent personally identifiable information from being disclosed, with some exceptions, in the absence of prior written consent of the student or parent. Finally, as a general rule, information concerning student-athletes should not be disclosed unless the student has completed and signed a consent-disclosure statement form.

The U.S. Supreme Court ruled that prayer does not belong in public schools, even if students initiate and lead the prayers. The court ruled 6-3 in a Texas case that public schools cannot allow student-led prayer before high school football games, a decision that reinforces the wall between church and state erected by the First Amendment.

The ruling came in *Santa Fe Independent School District* v. *Jane Doe*, a case involving the Sante Fe Independent School District in Galveston, Texas, which allowed student-initiated and student-led prayer to be broadcast over the public address system before high school football games. The central question was whether allowing prayer violates the First Amendment's establishment clause, which states that Congress shall make no law respecting an establishment of religion.

"We recognize the important role that public worship plays in many communities, as well as the sincere desire to include public prayer as a part of various occasions so as to mark those occasions' significance," Justice John Paul Stevens wrote for the majority. "But such religious activity in public schools, as elsewhere, must comport with the First Amendment," he added.

The School District Policy

Two students and their mothers filed suit in 1995 and were joined by the American Civil Liberties Union. The students, one Mormon and one Catholic, and their mothers were not named in court papers. The 4,000-student southern Texas school district, until 1995, had a policy in which students elected student council chaplains to deliver prayers over the public address system before the start of high school football games.

While the lower courts were considering the legal challenge, the school district adopted a new policy under which student-led prayer was permitted but not mandated. Students were asked to vote on whether to allow prayer and to vote again to select the person to deliver them. A lower court retooled that policy to allow only non-sectarian, non-proselytizing prayer. An appeals court found the modified policy constitutionally invalid. The nation's highest court agreed with the appeals court (http://archives.cnn.com/2000/LAW/06/19/scotus.schoolprayer.01index.html).

Contract Issues

Contract law underlies the daily activities of all facets of every athletic organization. Contracts (i.e., broadcast contracts, coaches contracts, player contracts, schedule contracts, sponsorships, officials contracts, etc.) are formed in order to document formal agreements and are referred to if the terms of such agreements come into dispute. A dispute may involve parties such as television networks, athletes, coaches, teachers, mascots, vendors, halftime show entertainers, secretaries, insurance companies, season ticket holders, and on and on.

Disability Issues

In sports, the line between lawful refusal to modify existing requirements and illegally discriminating against disabled persons is more than likely to be interpreted by the courts in the future. This is evidenced by the 2001 U.S. Supreme Court decision to require the PGA to permit Casey Martin, a disabled golfer, to use a golf cart in competition. In 1973, the Rehabilitation Act was enacted to provide individuals with disabilities the opportunity to participate in physical education and athletic programs without being discriminated against due to

SIDEBAR

The NBA Salary Cap is the limit to the total amount of money that NBA teams are allowed to pay their players. While this seems simple enough in concept, the salary cap is in actuality extremely complex, and contains many obscure rules and loopholes. The amount that is actually the "cap" varies on a year-to-year basis, and is calculated as a percentage of the League's revenue from the previous season; for instance, in 2004-05, the NBA's salary cap was approximately $44 million (U.S.) per team, while in 2005-06 it was $49.5 million. The NBA has a salary cap to keep teams in larger markets (with more revenue) from buying all of the top players and extending their advantage over smaller-market franchises.

The Collective Bargaining Agreement, or "CBA," is the contract between the NBA (the commissioner and the 30 team owners) and the NBA Players' Association that dictates the rules of player contracts, trades, revenue distribution, the NBA Draft, and the salary cap, among other things. In June 2005, the NBA's 1999 CBA expired, meaning the League and the players' union had to negotiate a new agreement; in light of the fiasco that was the 2004-05 NHL lockout, the two sides quickly came to an agreement, and ratified a new CBA in July 2005. The new agreement will expire following the 2010-11 season, but the League has the option to extend it through the 2011-12 season if they wish. If so, the League must exercise its option to extend the agreement by December 15, 2010 (http://www.nba/com).

Little changed in terms of the salary cap between the 1999 and 2005 versions of the CBA. In exchange for agreeing to the controversial player age minimum, the players will receive a slightly higher percentage of the League's revenues over the course of the new agreement. Additionally, the League's maximum salary decreased slightly in comparison to the 1999 CBA.

their disability. Two years later, in 1975, the Education for all Handicapped Children Act was passed, followed by other acts, including Individuals with Disabilities Education Act (IDEA) (1990), Amateur Sports Act (1978, amended in 1998)(paralympic athletes), and, most recently, the Americans with Disabilities Act (1990), which establishes the concept of "reasonable accommodation" as a standard for modification, adaptation, or access issues that often arise in discussions regarding disabled athletes. Yet, even with these bills passed, disabled athletes still face a number of obstacles to participate in athletics. In an attempt to protect and shield themselves from liability, as well as to protect the athletes, a number of athletic organizations (e.g., state high school activity or athletic associations, National Collegiate Athletic Association, National Association for Intercollegiate Athletics, and National Junior College Athletic Association) have developed policies to accommodate the disabled athletes and at the same time prohibit athletes with certain medical conditions or disabilities from participating in athletics or other extracurricular activities. Finally, many of these organizations have developed policies to guarantee equal access for participation opportunities for disabled athletes.

Discrimination Issues

Gender discrimination has been a highly litigated topic since 1970. In 1972, the Education Amendments were passed. These Amendments included Title IX, which prohibits gender discrimination and provides women with an important legal option to fight gender discrimination. Title IX has had the greatest impact in attacking gender discrimination in athletics in interscholastic and intercollegiate sports programs.

Civil rights laws have historically been a powerful mechanism for effecting social change in the United States. They represent a national commitment to end discrimination and establish a mandate to bring the excluded into the mainstream. These laws ensure the federal government delivers on the Constitution's promise of equal opportunity so that every individual has the right to develop his or her talents.

Title IX of the Education Amendments of 1972 bolsters this national agenda and prohibits sex discrimination in federally assisted education programs. Modeled on Title VI of the Civil Rights Act of 1964 prohibiting race, color, and national origin discrimination, it was followed by three other pieces of civil rights legislation: Section 504 of the Rehabilitation Act of 1973 prohibiting disability discrimination; the Age Discrimination Act of 1975; and Title II of the Americans with Disabilities Act of 1990 prohibiting disability discrimination by public entities.

Title IX legislation states: "No person in the United States shall, on the basis of sex, be excluded from participation in, be denied the benefits of, or be subjected to discrimination under any education program or activity receiving federal financial assistance" (20 U.S.C. Section 1681).

Twenty-five years after the passage of Title IX, we recognize and celebrate the profound changes this legislation has helped bring about in American education and the resulting improvements in the educational and related job opportunities for millions of young Americans. While no definitive study has been done on the full impact of Title IX, numerous government reports suggest that Title IX has made a positive difference in the lives of many Americans.

Substantial progress has been made, for example, in overcoming the education gap that existed between men and women in completing four years of college. In 1971, 18 percent of female high school graduates were completing at least four years of college compared to 26 percent of their male peers. Today, that education gap no longer exists. Women now make up the majority of students in America's colleges and universities in addition to making up the majority of those receiving master's degrees. Women are also entering business and law schools in record numbers. Indeed, the United States stands alone and is a world leader in opening the doors of higher education to women (http://www.ed.gov/pubs/titleIX/parts.html).

Title IX prohibits institutions that receive federal funding from practicing gender discrimination in educational programs or activities. Because almost all schools receive federal funds, Title IX applies to nearly everyone. The Office for Civil Rights in the U.S. Department of Education is charged with enforcing the civil rights and regulations in education, extending protection to

- about 51.7 million elementary and secondary school students;

- about 14.4 million college and university students;
- almost 15,000 school districts;
- more than 3,600 colleges and universities;
- more than 5,000 proprietary schools;
- thousands of libraries, museums, vocational rehabilitation agencies, and correctional facilities (http://www/ed.gov/pubs/titleIX/parts.html).

Drug Testing

A substance abuse policy, when perceived as excessively lenient or strict, can create a variety of issues for sports governing bodies to address. Organizations might enact a substance abuse policy for several reasons: (a) the concern for the health and/or safety of the participants, (b) the concern that a player's substance abuse might affect a team's chances of winning, (c) to gain

SIDEBAR

In a story that has grabbed national headlines, the University of Colorado (CU) is facing Title IX lawsuits brought by three female students who claim they were sexually assaulted during an off-campus football recruiting party. School law experts are debating whether the plaintiffs' success at trial would extend the scope of Title IX. Specifically, they are addressing Title IX's requirement that school officials must have "actual notice" or "actual knowledge" of the harasser's conduct before the school can be held liable for its failure to act to prevent further harassment. Until now, successful Title IX suits have involved the failure of school administrators to act to prevent further harassment by a single employee or student after being put on notice that the person is engaging in sexual harassment. The twist in the current suits is that they allege that CU failed to prevent the further use of alcohol and sex as recruiting tools by the football program even after the school received a complaint in 1997 of an alleged sexual assault during a football-recruiting weekend. Legal experts disagree over the implications for Title IX case law if the plaintiffs are successful. National School Boards Association staff attorney Tom Hutton suggests the suits' allegations could alter the judicial concept of "actual notice," setting a potentially troublesome precedent for schools. "If we go to the point where the overall environment is alleged to be actual notice," he said, "... that would be different from the pattern we're used to, which is that there's an individual (perpetrator) of harassment that the school needs to be aware of." However, Kim Hult, attorney for one of the plaintiffs, believes that existing federal law has already addressed the issue raised in her client's suit. Ms. Hult said, "This is close enough, if not identical, to case law that's already out there that there is a very good basis, as a legal matter, for saying that the actual-notice requirement is easily met" (http://www.nsba.org/site/doc_cosa.asp?TRACKID=&DID=332258&CID=448).

confidence of the public, and (d) to level the playing field when athletes use performance-enhancing drugs. However, organizations do not possess unilateral power to implement drug policy that it believes is optimal. The organizations are limited by existing laws and court precedents and are sometimes limited by terms of a collective bargaining agreement (in the case of professional sports leagues). Finally, to ensure that athletic competitions are fair and equitable, as well as to protect the health and safety of the athletes, athletic organizations at all levels have implemented drug-testing programs.

Illegal Gambling

The problems associated with illegal gambling and the influence it may exert on sporting events are of special concern for athletic administrators and others because gambling affects the integrity of the games, the games themselves, and the public confidence in athletes and sports. Over the years, gambling on intercollegiate athletics has steadily increased, most notably with the significant amount of money (in the millions of dollars) that is currently being wagered on the NCAA men's Division I basketball tournament. Finally, the success of the professional sports industry hinges on maintaining a high level of integrity so that the viewing public has no doubt about the outcome of the event. If people were to believe that there was a connection between the teams and the players and organized gambling, the integrity of the game could be damaged.

Intellectual Property Rights

The kind of property that results from mental labor is called intellectual property.

Intellectual property rights focuses on Lanham Act of 1964 or trademark law (i.e., names, logos, and symbols), ambush marketing (i.e., intentional efforts of a company to ambush a competitor's official association with a sports entity), licensing agreements, copyright law, and patent law. It is important to understand that organizations and players have a property interest in their name and likeness. Whether it is the trademarked logo of a favorite sports team, the copyrighted broadcast of a sporting event,

SIDEBAR

Collegiate Gambling Scandals

Arizona State, 1997: Two players plead guilty to point shaving; the inquiry, dating back to games in 1994, shows that 15 of 22 fraternities turned up in records of illegal gambling ring on campus.

Boston College, 1996: Thirteen football players are suspended for gambling on games; two players are found to have bet against their own team.

Maryland, 1995: Five athletes, including the starting quarterback on the football team, are suspended for gambling on sports.

Northwestern, 1994: Two players, one a starting tailback on the football team and the other a starting guard on the basketball team, are suspended for betting on college games.

Bryant College, 1992: Five basketball players, who had built up $54,000 in gambling debts, are suspended and a former player and student was arrested and charged with bookmaking.

Maine, 1992: Thirteen baseball players and six football players are suspended for gambling on games.

Florida, 1989: Four football players, including star-QB-to-be Shane Matthews, then a redshirt freshman, are suspended for betting on football games.

or the patent of the sporting equipment used during the game, intellectual property is an important and ever-increasing legal issue in the sports industry. The legal system provides certain rights and protections for owners of property. Rights and protections for owners of intellectual property are based on federal, patent, trademark, and copyright laws and state trade secret laws.

Labor Law

The difference between interscholastic or intercollegiate athletes and professional athletes is that professional athletes are considered by the courts to be employees whereas the courts have determined high school and college athletes to be primarily students. Therefore, as employees, professional athletes are covered under state and federal labor laws. High school and colle-

giate athletes do not have the protection of the labor laws; instead, they are protected by school, conference, and association rules. Further, constitutional laws and applicable athletics-related legislation also protect these athletes.

Nevertheless, high school and collegiate athletic administrators need not deal with players insofar as labor law; they often must deal with unionized employees, from secretaries to grounds crew to coaches. Consequently, it is beneficial for these administrators to understand the rights and expectations that labor law bestows upon employers and employees.

Television and Broadcasting Rights

All sport entities potentially have a valuable property right in the accounts and descriptions of their games and events,

---

SIDEBAR

The *New York Times* reports that Major League Baseball claims to own the commercial use of baseball statistics. If MLB prevails, unlicensed commercial fantasy-baseball operations would have to cease operation. Says the *Times*:

"The dispute is between a company in St. Louis that operates fantasy sports leagues over the Internet and the Internet arm of Major League Baseball, which says that anyone using players' names and performance statistics to operate a fantasy league commercially must purchase a license. The St. Louis company counters that it does not need a license because the players are public figures whose statistics are in the public domain.... The case is scheduled for jury trial in United States District Court in St. Louis beginning September 5, 2005. CBC and Major League Baseball Advanced Media filed motions for summary judgment that the court could rule on in July."

MLB already licenses operations that use player photos and team logos. But according to the *Times*:

"Major League Baseball Advanced Media, which runs its own array of fantasy games on the league's portal, MLB.com, has decreased its number of licensees from dozens in 2004 to 19 last season to seven in 2006, focusing on large multimedia outlets like CBS SportsLine and cutting out many of the four-figure licenses that had covered smaller operators' use of only names and statistics. CBC, which had a license from 1995 to 2004, filed suit to confirm that it has the right to use those limited materials freely."

Interestingly, baseball once took a different position:

"When several major leaguers from the 1940s and 50s sued Major League Baseball over use of their names and statistics in materials like promotional videos and game programs, baseball argued that such use was protected by the First Amendment."

(http://www.againstmonopoly.org/index.php?limit=&chuck0&topic=Is%20IP%20Property).

whether these activities are broadcast on radio, television, cable television, and/or the Internet. Copyright law and sports intersect whenever a sports organization broadcasts one of its games. The descriptions and accounts of these games are copyrightable work and the team may be entitled to royalty fees if the game is rebroadcast. Antitrust law and sports broadcasting meet when a sports organization (i.e., MLB, NBA, NFL, or the NCAA) attempts to negotiate broadcasting contracts on behalf of its member teams. While this is allowed on the professional level as a result of the Sports Broadcast Act of 1961, the pooling of broadcast rights on the intercollegiate level has been the cause of litigation that has reached the Supreme Court. Finally, a holder of property rights will enter into contracts with many different organizations (i.e., networks, advertisers, and cable companies) when broadcasting a sports contest.

Workers' Compensation

Workers' compensation is a statutorily created method for providing cash benefits and medical care to employees and their dependents when employees suffer personal injuries or death in the course of employment. The purpose of the benefits is to provide employees and their dependents with greater protection than afforded by the common law remedy of a suit for damages. Each state has its own workers' compensation act that provides a system of monetary payments for the loss of earning capacity to an employee. The primary reason for passage of workers' compensation statutes was to eliminate the inadequacies of the common law remedies that resulted from the injured party having to show that the employer was negligent.

Sport Authorities, Commissions, Congresses, Corporations, Councils, and Foundations Impact

These organizations have been formed to assist in the development of the sport industry in various areas throughout the United States. Generally, they assist in driving sports business in a geographical area (i.e., Atlanta, Detroit, Colorado Springs, Greater Cincinnati, Indianapolis, Miami, Philadelphia, New York, etc.) and have become an expert in determining local and statewide economic impact from the various sporting events. Further, these organizations are often governed by a volunteer board of trustees whose members come from a variety of fields that influence or are influenced by sports. The key to suc-

cess of these organizations is the strong relationship and involvement they have with statewide business leaders, facility owners, chambers of commerce, convention and visitor bureaus, and other organizations.

These organizations (a) serve as the chief link between amateur sports groups and other groups, (b) match events and sponsors with local facilities, accommodations, and businesses, (c) help amateur sports groups secure corporate sponsorships to help offset event expenses, (d) develop a bank of volunteers from which event organizers can draw, (e) arrange special events for participants, (f) build relationships to provide media coverage, (g) measure and provide event economic impact reports for the community, and (h) provide opportunity for local youth to participate in clinics and events (see Chapter 17 for greater details).

Stadium and Arena Financing Issues

Over the last few decades, the number of U.S. metropolitan areas large enough to host a franchise from one of the four major professional sports leagues has soared. Even as Major League Baseball, Major League Soccer, the National Football League, the National Basketball Association, and the National Hockey League have expanded to include more franchises, demand by metropolitan areas continues to exceed supply. As a result, metropolitan areas have been forced to compete with each other to retain and attract franchises.

Large public expenditures on the construction of new sports facilities have been the main form of this competition. Sports arenas and stadiums are extremely expensive. A new football or baseball stadium cost is approximately $325 million. A new basketball or hockey arena costs approximately $200 million. The public's share of these costs has averaged $200 million and $100 million respectively. During the 1990s, more than $6 billion in public funds was spent on construction of sports arenas and stadiums. Almost $8 billion has already been allocated toward new facilities scheduled to open prior to 2010.

The large public spending on sports facilities has been controversial. Usually, these costly projects are justified by claims that hosting a sports franchise spurs local economic development by creating numerous new jobs and boosting local tax revenue. However, independent economic studies suggest that taxpayers may not be receiving such a good deal. In seeking to quantify the job creation and tax revenue benefits produced by a sports franchise, these studies overwhelmingly find that the benefits are significantly less than the outlay of public funds.

Finally, does this mean that public funding of sports franchises is not justified? Perhaps not. An important element missing in the debate is the impact of a sports franchise on a metropolitan area's quality of life. While difficult to measure, the contribution of a sports franchise to quality of life may exceed more traditional job creation and tax revenue benefits. If so, when quality-of-life benefits are included in the calculation, public spending may not appear to be such a bad investment for some metropolitan areas.

Summary

The validity of association rules, under the U.S. Constitution, has historically come under frequent scrutiny. A key component in deciding such cases is whether or not the association is considered a private or a public institution in the eyes of the court. Further, these associations are impacted, beyond the Constitution, by specific laws including agency law, Amateur Sports Act of 1978 (Stevens Amendments 1998), antitrust law, business laws, contract law (i.e., coaches contracts, scholarships, broadcasting contracts, endorsement contracts, sponsorship contracts), disability laws, discrimination legislation, drug testing requirements, employee legislation (i.e., workers compensation) gambling, intellectual property rights, labor law, and television and broadcasting legislation.

Sport authorities, commissions, congresses, corporations, councils, and foundations have been formed to assist in the development of the sport industry in various areas throughout the United States. Generally, they assist in driving sports business in a geographical area (i.e., Atlanta, Detroit, Colorado Springs, Greater Cincinnati, Indianapolis, Miami, Philadelphia, New York, etc.) and have become an expert in determining local and statewide economic impact from the various sporting events. Further, these organizations are often governed by a volunteer board of trustees whose members come from a variety of fields that influence or are influenced by sports. The key to success of these organizations is the strong relationship and involvement they have with statewide business leaders, facility owners, chambers of commerce, convention and visitor bureaus, and other organizations.

Finally, over the last few decades, the number of U.S. metropolitan areas large enough to host a franchise from one of the four major professional sports leagues has soared. Even as Major League Baseball, Major League Soccer, the National Football League, the National Basketball Association, and the National Hockey League have expanded to include more franchises, demand by metropolitan areas continues to exceed supply. As a result, metropolitan areas have been forced to compete with each other to retain and attract franchises.

References

Age Discrimination Act (1975).

Amateur Sports Act (1978; Stevens Amendments, 1998).

Americans with Disabilities Act (1990).

Athlete Agent Laws (in over 30 states).

Civil Rights Act (1964) Title VI.

Civil Rights Restoration Act (1987).

Clayton Act (1914).

Copyright Act (1976).

Copyright Royalty Tribunal Reform Act (1993).

Curt Flood Act (1998).

Education Amendments (1972) of the Civil Rights Act. (1964) Title IX.

Education for all Handicapped Children Act (1975) http://archives.cnn.com/2000/LAW/06/19 scotus.schoolprayer.01index.html. (2006).

Family Educational Rights and Privacy Act of 1974 (Buckley Amendment).

http://www.againstmonopoly.org/index.php?limit=&chuck0&topic=Is%20IP%20Property. (2006).

http://www.ed.gov/pubs/titleIX/parts.html (2006).

http://www.nba.com. (2006).

http://www.nsba.org/site/doc_cosa.asp?TRACKID=&DID=332258&CID=448. (2006).

http://www.oursportscentral.com/usfl/trial.php (2006).

http://query.nytimes.com/gst/fullpage.html?res=9505E46173BF93BA25755COA964948260 (2006).

http://www.sportslawnews.com/archive/jargon/ljsportsbroadcastingact.htm. (2006).

Individuals with Disabilities Education Act (1990).

Lanham Act (1946).

National Labor Relations Act (Wagner Act, 1935).

Norris-LaGuardia Act (1932).

Patent Law.

Rehabilitation Act (1973). Section 504.

Sherman Act (1890).

Sport Broadcast Act (1961).

Taft-Hartley Act (1947).

Restatement of Contracts (1932; 1981).

Uniform Athlete Agent Act (2002).

Uniform Commercial Code (U.C.C.).

NOTES

CHAPTER 7

Youth Sport Governance

There has been an enormous increase in community-sponsored or private/commercial youth sports programs in America (e.g., baseball, basketball, bowling, golf, gymnastics, field hockey, football, ice hockey, lacrosse, soccer, softball, swimming, tennis, volleyball, and more). The objectives of most youth sports programs are to provide participants with an opportunity to learn culturally relevant sport skills and to develop attitudes and values about authority, competition, cooperation, discipline, social relationships, sportsmanship, and teamwork. However, there are private/commercial programs (i.e., sport academies), and some nonprofits that are significantly designed as career training or pre-Olympic programs.

There are a number of concerns in organized youth sports. One is that the intrusion of adults into the play of youngsters may negate the value of play for young participants. Another is that intense training and competition for prolonged periods of time may cause acute or chronic injury, boredom, and burn out. Further, the overemphasis on winning in some youth programs threatens to overshadow the expressive, self-fulfilling potential of sports participation. Finally, the

dramatic increase in privatization of youth sports at the same time the public sector is reducing its presence in the sport arena.

Learning Objectives

Upon completion this chapter, the reader should be able to:

- Identify youth sport governing bodies.
- Discuss the governance process commonly found within youth sport organizations.
- Identify and discuss the various issues surrounding youth sports in America.

Identification of Youth Sport Governing Bodies

Community youth sport programs (i.e., non-school programs) in America are organized by more than 25 organizations and by thousands of local and regional sports organizations (see Table 7.1). The National Council on Youth Sports estimates that the total number of participants is over 50 million or approximately 65 percent of Ameri-

Table 7.1
Youth Sport Organizations

All-American Soap Box Derby – www.aasbd.org
Amateur Athletic Union – www.aausports.org
Amateur Softball Association – www.softball.org
American Amateur Baseball Congress –www.aabc.org
American Legion Baseball – www.legion.org
American Youth Football – www.americanyouthfootball.com
Babe Ruth Baseball – www.baberuthleague.org
Black American Softball Association – www.basasofttball.com
Boys and Girls Clubs of America – www.bgca.org
Catholic Youth Organization – www.ny-archdiocese.org
Dixie Boys Baseball – www.dixie.org
Institute for the Study of Youth Sports – www.mus.edu/ysi
Kids Sports Network – www.ksnusa.org
Little League Baseball – www.littleleague.org
Milwaukee Youth Sports Authority – www.milwaukeeyouthsports.org
National Alliance for youth Sports – www.nays.org
National Association for Competitive Soccer Clubs – www.usclubsoccer.com
National Council of Youth Sports – ww.ncys.org
National Youth Sports Corporation – www.nyscorp.org
National Youth Sports Safety Foundation – www.nyssf.org
North American Youth Sport Institute – www.naysi.com
Oregon Sports Authority – www.oregonsports.org
Pony Baseball and Softball – www.pony.org
Pope Warner Football – www.popwarnerfootball.org
T-Ball USA Association – www.teeballusa.org
United States Amateur Boxing – www.usaboxing.com
United States Bowling Congress – www.bowl.com
United States Diving – www.usdivning.com
United States Judo – www.usjudo.com
United States Soccer Federation – www.ussoccer.com
United States Tennis Association – www.usta.com
United States Youth Volleyball League – www.volleyball.org/usyvl/
USA Field Hockey - www.usfieldhockey.com
USA Football – www.usafootball.com
USA Softball –www.usasoftball.com
USA Swimming - www.usaswimming.org
USA Track and Field – www.usaf.org
USA Youth Sports – www.usayouthsports.com
USA Wrestling – www.themat.com
US Association of Independent Gymnastics Clubs – www.usagic.com
US Lacrosse – www.uslacrosse.org
US Figure Skating Association – www.usfigureskating.org
US Speedskating – www.usspeedskating.com
US Ski and Snowboard – www.usskiteam.com
US Youth Soccer Association – www.usyouthsoccer.org
YMCA of the USA Youth Sports – www.ymca.net
Youth Basketball of America – www.yboa.org
Youth Lacrosse USA – www.youthlacorsseUSA.org

can youth under the age of 17 participate in at least one organized sport (http://www.ncys.org). As sports for children and adolescents have expanded and diversified, a wide variety of commercial and non-commercial sponsors have emerged. The types of agencies that sponsor or support youth sport in the United States are quite varied, and an example of each is shown in Table 7.2.

Little League baseball is the largest of the youth sport organizations with 25,000 leagues in 105 countries and more than 3 million youngsters engaged in Little League annually (http://www.littleleague.org). However, in terms of participants, soccer and softball have been growing faster than any other youth team sports since 1990. More than 5,000 Boys/Girls Clubs, YMCAs, and YWCAs provide some 16 million boys and girls the opportunity to participate in organized sports. The Junior Olympics Sports Program sponsors over 2,000 local, state, regional, and national events in 21 different sports (http://www.aausports.org).

The programs are becoming more elaborate and are enlisting younger and younger participants each year. There is a well or-

ganized outlet in the public and/or private sector for almost every child who has an interest in playing sports. Children can begin in age-group gymnastics and swimming programs at age two or younger; figure skating, football, ice hockey, soccer, T-ball, wrestling, and a half-dozen other sports begin at age four.

As the number of youth sports programs expands, so do the varying structural arrangements that support them. There are basically two types of programs available to youth in America. One emphasizes participation and carefully regulates the type and extent of stress placed on the participants, such as travel teams and elite clubs. The other options available are programs that find adults impacting enormously on the play of youngsters, such as sport academies. In many of these programs, the purpose is simply to train children to become champions. Accounts of the lives of the prodigies at these academies or clubs clearly demonstrate that their only goal in sports, or at least of their parents and coaches, is to become a professional or Olympic-level athlete. Yet, despite variations in youth sports forms and functions, advocates of youth

Table 7.2
Organizations That Impact and/or Organize Youth Sports

Type of Organization	Example of Specific Organization
National youth sport organization	Little League Baseball
National youth agency	Boys/Girls Clubs of America
National governing body	U.S. Gymnastics
National service organization	American Legion Baseball
National religious organization	Catholic Youth Organization
National youth sport advocate	National Alliance for Youth Sports
National youth sport institute	North American Youth Sport Inst.
National youth sports program	National Youth Sports Corporation
National youth sport safety organization	National Youth Sports Safety Foundation
Regional youth sport group	Soccer Association of America
State youth sport research organization	Inst. for the Study of Youth Sports
Local service club	Riley Lions Club
Municipal recreation department	Indianapolis Parks and Recreation
Private sports club	Terre Haute Gymnastics Club

sports programs claim they provide a means for the development of such personal-social attributes as self-discipline, cooperativeness, achievement motivation, courage, persistence, and so forth.

Governance

Regardless of the size of a youth sport organization, there needs to be a formal organizational structure, description of the role and function of the organization, a clear origin of its authority to administer a youth sport, requirements for membership in the organization, an outline regarding sanctions, and an appeals process for violations of the organization's bylaws, policies, and rules. The value of establishing an organization lies in the fact it is ready to function if called to do so. The organization can assist in policy making and other such matters as communication, financing, licensing, marketing, developing membership, regulating, sanctioning, scheduling, developing sponsorships, training paid staff and volunteers, and much more. There are six basic components of governance. These components consist of (a) organizational structure, (b) function, (c) authority, (d) requirements for membership, (e) sanctions and appeals process and (f) funding. The best way to illustrate governance of a youth sport organization is to feature such an organization throughout this chapter. The youth sport organization chosen to be illustrative of youth sport governance is the Amateur Athletic Union (AAU) (http://www.aausports.org).

Organizational Structure

The majority of the youth sport organizations are advocates for positive and safe sports and activities for children. They have been organized into corporations (generally limited liability corporations or LLCs) within a state. Most are non-profit 501(c)3 organizations. They offer programs and services for everyone involved in a specific youth sport. These programs and services include officials, parents, professional administrators, volunteer administrators, volunteer coaches, and youth athletes. The goal of these organizations is to make sports and activities safe and positive by providing programs and services that add value to a specific youth sport.

Chart 7.1 illustrates the organizational structure for the AAU. Each youth sport organization has a similar type of organizational structure. This structure delegates authority and responsibility in an organized fashion to a number of professional (or volunteer) administrators.

Function

The function of youth sport organizations is primarily to regulate the sport so that all players have an opportunity to experience a fair and level playing field. Further, the organizations are responsible for providing programs including coach training and certification, official training and certification, administrative training, and special programs (i.e., programs for players with disabilities, programs to prepare athletes for college, economically disadvantaged fundraising programs, and player/volunteer protection programs that protect kids and volunteers). Finally, all organizations provide important services for its members including developing useful training publications for players, parents, coaches, and officials, national office support (i.e., coach and official training, league history files, resource library, computer database of all players and volunteers, free software, liability insurance programs for players, coaches and officials, national accounting programs to assist with finances, legal assistance, media assistance, fundraising assistance, and sponsorship and licensing assistance), and supplies (i.e., patches, pins, manuals, coach and official instructional materials, merchandise with logos, posters, flyers, and more).

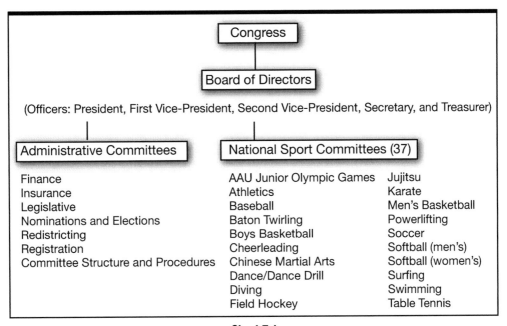

Chart 7.1
Amateur Athletic Union
Organizational Structure (simplified)

One of the major functions for a youth sport organization is to establish not only rules and regulations for participating in a sport but to develop and disseminate national policies of the organization. These policies generally relate to the following areas: membership policies (e.g., background checks, felony or other misconduct convictions, indemnification/assumption of risk, sexual misconduct, sport agents, waiver/release, etc.), release of club/membership data, financial policies, intellectual property policies, management of emergency situations, event policies, business practices, and more.

Authority

Nonprofits and private/commercial youth sport organizations gain their authority from a number of governance documents including articles of incorporation, constitution, and bylaws. The article of incorporation is a legal document required by the state in order to form a legal corporation in a state. Most nonprofits and private/commercial youth sport organizations form as either a simple corporation or a limited liability corporation (LLC), which limits the corporation's exposure to liability.

The AAU has established national policies in the following areas: membership policy (e.g., agreement and consent, binding arbitration, indemnification/assumption of risk, administrative remedies, sexual misconduct, felony and misconduct convictions, misrepresentation, sport agents, agency, waiver/release/authorization to use, background checks, etc.), release of club/membership data – mail list policy, financial policies (e.g., purchasing guidelines, solicitation of funds, sport committee finances, AAU credit policy, etc.), media/websites/spokespersons/logo policies, defense policy, management of emergency situations, business practices, sanction/event policies, event policies, sport committee policies, judicial procedures, and re-districting procedures (http://www.aausports.org).

The limited liability corporation form was introduced relatively recently to the United States with a statute having been considered (but not adopted) in Alaska in 1975 and the first statute adopted in Wyoming in 1978. An LLC provides limited personal liability to owners of its equity interest, similar to a corporation and a limited liability partnership, and in contrast to the personal liability for the debts and obligations of the business that are borne in the general partnership or sole proprietorship. A variant of the LLC available in some jurisdictions, typically limited to licensed professionals such as lawyers, physicians, or engineers, is the professional limited liability corporation (denoted by "P.L.L.C." or "PLLC"). All states permit an LLC to be organized with a single member.

Basically, an LLC allows for the flexibility of a sole proprietorship or partnership structure within the framework of limited liability, such as that granted to corporations. An advantage of an LLC over a limited partnership is that the formalities required for creating and registering LLCs are much simpler than the requirements most states place on forming and operating corporations; most LLCs will, however, choose to adopt an Operating Agreement or Limited Liability Corporation Agreement to provide for the governance of the organization and such agreement is generally more complex than a corporation's bylaws.

The constitution of an organization is the document, which contains its own basic rules relating principally to itself as an organization. It defines the primary characteristics of the organization and prescribes how the organization functions. Further, it includes all rules that the organization considers so important that they (a) cannot be changed without previous notice to the members and the vote of s specified large majority (such as two-thirds vote), and (b) cannot be suspended. Typically, there are ten articles found in a constitution:

(a) name of the organization, (b) its object, (c) members, (d) officers, (e) meetings, (f) executive board, (g) committees, (h) parliamentary authority, and (i) amendment, and (j) dissolution.

The following is the table of contents for the AAU constitution: Article I: Governance of the Union - (a) Adoption and Amendments, (b) Membership, (c) Congress, (d) Board of Directors, (e) Officers, and (f) Committees; Article II: Governance of the Districts - (a) Adoption, (b) Charter, (c) Name, Territory, Jurisdiction, (d) Objectives, (e) Management, and (f) Dissolution; Article III: Judiciary of the AAU – (a) Judicial Bodies, (b) Authority, and (c) Procedures (http://www.aausports.org).

Bylaws serve as the fundamental instrument establishing or conforming to the corporate charter. The bylaws mirror the constitution but provide much greater detail regarding the management of the organization. However, the constitution is much more difficult to amend then bylaws.

The bylaws for the AAU consist of the following: (a) Official Emblem, Seal, National Office, (b) Fiscal and Legal, (c) Sanctions, (d) Membership, (e) Dues, Fees, Reports, and Remittances, (f) Eligibility, (g) Competition, (h) Districts and Chartering, (i) Meetings, Notices, Voting, (j) Composition of Board of Directors, (k) National Councils, and (l) Miscellaneous (http://www.aausports.org).

Finally, youth sport programs operated by municipal or county government gain their authority from the government entity that houses the programs. The government entity most often is a department of recreation or parks and recreation. The programs are governed by a board and administered by a governmental administrator.

Requirements of Membership

Many youth sport organizations have

specific requirements for membership. In order to become a member (i.e., ability, age, gender, etc.), he must apply for membership. Once accepted into the organization, he must pay dues and applicable fees and, in some rare cases, an initiation fee. All members must follow the rules and pay annual dues to maintain membership in the organization. A number of the youth sport organizations have different levels of membership including individual (i.e., coach, official, parent, player, etc.) and team or club membership. All team members must be individual members and the team must register as an official team within that specific national organization as well. Finally, all prospective members must submit an application and appropriate fees to the national or district office. Once the application is reviewed and meets all requirements, it is approved and the applicant becomes a member.

Sanctions and Appeal Process

When an organization sanctions an event, it is providing authoritative permission or approval for the specific event. It further lends its support or encouragement for the event. However, it could be the organization penalizing an individual or team for noncompliance specified by the rules of the organization. Therefore, a sanction can be a penalty that acts to ensure compliance or conformity to the organizations rules or policies.

The AAU uses the sanctioning process, like many other national youth organizations, to provide permission for a member team or district or regional to organize a specific tournament. The sanctioning process is the written approval of the AAU for the conduct of the activity. Events that are sanctioned by the AAU are categorized as one of the following: practice, preliminary, inter-district, invitational, league, demonstration or clinic, physically challenged event, multisport/sports festivals, district championships, national AAU events, and national sport committee events (http://www/aausports.org).

However, the AAU has established a judicial body to deal with enforcement of its Constitution, bylaws, and national policies. It is common to find a similar process within other youth sport organizations. The

---

The AAU has the following membership requirements as found in the 2006 bylaws: Bylaw 4: Membership

4.1 Individual Membership. Membership is required of all persons who participate in the AAU in the following capacities:

Athletes	Coaches
District Officers	District Committee Chairs and Members
National Committee Chairs	National Committee members
Board of Directors	Members of Congress
National Officers	

4.2 Club and Individual Membership Applications. Applications for club and individual membership must be completed and submitted with the yearly membership fee. All club and individual memberships expire on August 31st of the membership year.

4.2.1 Review and Approval. Clubs and individuals memberships are effective immediately upon receipt of the application and fees by the AAU, subject to the right of the registrar to review the application. Within 15 days of the receipt of the application, the registrar may reject an application within fifteen (15) days. The decision of the registrar to reject an application is subject to the appeal process established by Article III of the Constitution (http://www.aausports.org).

judicial bodies enforce the provisions of the established policies and rules of the organization and afford due process by means of reasonable notice and opportunity for a hearing as to matters in which they hold an interest. Some organizations, like the AAU, have a national board of review, which is the body that makes the initial decision regarding a violation of a policy or rule of the organization and a board of appeals, which reviews any decision made by the board of review.

As indicated above, youth sport organizations must have an appeals body to review any decision made by a review group or commissioner/executive director. This requirement ensures the individuals due process rights as guaranteed by the U.S. Constitution. Whenever an organization removes an individual's right to membership or participation, the organization must allow the individual to appeal the decision that compromises his rights. The appeals body may review any decision made by the review group or commissioner/executive director. The appeals body may vacate, modify, sustain, or remand any decision of the review group or commissioner/executive director in which the appellant (formerly the defendant) sustains one or more of the following bases of appeal: (a) misapplication or misinterpretation of the organization's policies or rules, (b) newly discovered evidence, (c) findings of fact contrary to the evidence presented, or (d) excessive penalties. The review group can also assess costs and expenses against an unsuccessful party.

Funding

Generally youth sport programs are supported by participant fees, donations, fundraising activities, and sponsorships. Nonprofit youth agencies (e.g., Boys and Girls Clubs, YMCAs, YWCAs, and Family YMCAs) access membership fees and nonmembership fees for participants in youth sport programs. Other nonprofit youth sport associations (e.g. Little League Baseball, local softball or soccer associations or gymnastics clubs) also access participants either season or weekly fees in order to participate on the various teams.

Donations are an integral revenue source for youth sports programs. These are actively solicited by youth sport organizations on a regular basis. Campaigns for donations are planned for each new season. The organizations also participate in numerous special event fundraising activities throughout the season. Some agencies receive United Way Funding for youth sport programs as well.

Since the early nineties sponsorships have become a regular revenue source for youth sport programs. For example, team uniforms are purchased by local businesses or corporations and advertisement is placed on the uniforms. Further, sponsorships are sought to support facilities, scoreboards, and equipment. Often on baseball and softball outfield fences advertisements are seen representing the various sponsors for the program.

Youth Sport Issues

Coakley (2004) and Eitzen and Sage (2003) suggests that when, how, and to what end children play sports is an issue that concerns families, neighborhoods, communities, and even national and international organizations. Since the early 1970s, the research of sociologists and others has had a major impact on how people think about youth sports, especially sports emphasizing competition (Donnelly, 1993). Today, many parents, coaches, and program administrators are much more aware of the questions and issues that they must consider when evaluating organized youth sport programs (Coakley, 2004). The issues most frequently focused upon include adult intrusion in youth sports, burnout in youth sports, coaching education, disabled youth, elite youth athletes, kids and sports, privatization of youth sports, public youth sport programs – what do they want, risk of injury, sport specialization, sportsmanship, and "overemphasis on winning", and more. These issues will be discussed in the remaining pages of this chapter.

Adult Intrusion in Youth Sports

Coakley (2004) and Eitzen and Sage (2003) and many others are in agreement that one of the major problems of youth sports is the intrusion of adults into the sports life of youngsters. The rationale behind the organization of youth sports programs is admirable. They are to provide (a) boys and girls with structure for their sports, (b) opportunities for wide participation, (c) proper equipment for their safety, (d) coaches to teach them fundamental skills and strategies of the game, (e) officials who control the sport experience during competition, and (f) proper facilities for practice and competition. However, many parents and coaches live vicariously through the youngsters, living out their unfulfilled sports dreams through the children, making considerable emotional and, often, financial investments in the young athletes (Coakley, 2004; Eitzen & Sage, 2003). The parents and coaches, therefore, expect a payoff in sport achievement by way of victories and championships. If children succeed, the parents and coaches interpret this as their own personal achievement. But if they fail, these same parents and coaches feel disappointment, frustration, and failure and sometimes embarrassment because their child did not succeed. The stress applied to children because of this emotional attachment by the parents and coaches is not healthy or desirable. Yet parents and coaches often do not recognize what they are doing to the children. Finally, for parents and coaches whose aspirations are national rankings, a professional sport career, or Olympic-level status for the youngsters involved, youth sports are not play and games, they are a way of life (see elite youth athletes).

Should the governance structure reflect on this issue in terms of policy development and enforcement?

Burnout in Youth Sports

Buzby (1997), Coakley (2004), Eitzen and Sage (2003), and others indicate the best aspect of youth sports today is that kids have the opportunity to play organized sports when they are three years old. They can play multiple sports in one season. They can play one sport year-round, indoors and out. There are summer camps for every sport with a schedule to fit every child's needs. Conversely, the best aspect of youth sports today may also be the most troubling aspect.

Youth sports participation patterns are changing. In the 70s and 80s, kids played soccer or football in the fall, basketball or wrestling in the winter, and baseball or softball in the spring. The lucky (and wealthier) youth went to a summer camp for one week, while the rest spent the summer at local pools and playgrounds (Buzby, 1997).

Today, youth can play just about any sport they want year-round. There are fall baseball leagues, summer basketball leagues, indoor golf ranges and tennis courts, indoor and outdoor soccer fields and roller hockey rinks, and opportunities to play every other sport that can be imagined.

How much is too much? Sometimes youth do not want to disappoint mom or dad and will not admit they are tired of playing sports. Once in a while, it is a good idea for the parent to decide for the youth that it is time to take a season off. Unlike years ago, if you skip the fall soccer league, you can usually join an indoor team before Thanksgiving so it will not be an entire year before he can play again. How youth react to the break will also give the parent some indication as to whether it is a good idea to cut back next year.

Youth sports are great for youth. Those in governance positions should take steps to make sure youth do not become burned out. Well-balanced sports participation can be an important part of a youth's social, emotional, and physical well-being. Is it true the longer youth play sports, the better? Is it true the more fun youth are having, the longer they will play?

Statistics gathered by various non-profits, private, and governmental groups indicated that nearly 80 percent of youth dropout of sports altogether before they reach 18 and nearly 35 percent of the youth participating in a sport dropout annually. The top five reasons youth dropout of sports include (a) it is no longer fun, (b) it is boring, (c) too much emphasis is placed on winning, (d) poor coaching, and (f) no longer interested.

Coaching Education (see Chapter 8 for further details)

The vast majority of youth coaches are well-meaning moms and dads who have little or no formal instruction in the developmental or educational aspects of teaching/coaching. Many have some sport experiences as a kid; but, more often than not, they have had no sport experiences in the sport they are coaching. There is universal agreement that most youth sports coaches are ill equipped for their role. However, without them, millions of boys and girls would not have the opportunity to participate in organized sports. This is one of the fundamental weaknesses of youth sports as well as a major liability and safety issue for youth sport participants.

It was recognized by the National Association for Sport and Physical Education (NASPE) during the 70s that coaching education programs needed to be developed for youth coaches. The key leaders in this project were Rainer Martens (Human Kinetics Publishing Company Kinetics) and Vern Seefedlt (Youth Sports Institute,

Michigan State University). Since the development of the first coaching education program (American Coaching Education Program, 1976), there have been numerous other programs developed and implemented across the United States. Most national youth sport organizations have now developed their own coaching education programs. Existing programs in the United States and other countries provide coaches with information on how to (a) deal with young people responsively and safely, (b) be more effective in organizing their practices and teaching skills to young people, (c) provide sport first aid efficiently and effectively, (d) deal with parents, (e) develop appropriate conditioning and nutrition programs, (f) display desirable coaching behaviors, and (g) manage risk.

The major issue surrounding coaching education is what should be the end result of the education process. Should the programs ultimately foster a "techoscience approach"? Or should the programs develop an overall understanding of young people as human beings? Or should the programs produce "humanistic" coaches who are sports efficiency experts? The ideal coach will be able to provide young people with opportunities to become autonomous and responsible decision makers who can control their lives and to teach young people the appropriate sport skills and strategies for a specific sport. At this point, most coaching education programs have contributed to responsible coaching in youth sport programs. But will that be true in the future?

Disabled Youth

Participation in sports by children with disabilities is important for several reasons. The most important reason to promote youth sports is the personal benefits to participants such as health, physical fitness, skill development, self-concept, friends, and fun. Another important

SIDEBAR

Case Study .... Northeast Passage Program, University of New Hampshire (http://www.nepassage.org)

The mission of NORTHEAST PASSAGE is to create an environment where individuals with disabilities can recreate with the same freedom of choice, quality of life, and independence as their non-disabled peers. This is accomplished by developing, delivering, and evaluating innovative barrier-free recreation and health promotion programs. The guiding principles for the project are promoting client independence through education and problem solving, creating opportunities, and collaborating with others to create a strong network of accessible recreation.

The Northeast Passage (NEP) was founded in 1990 as a private, non-profit organization. In March of 2000, after years of successful collaboration, NEP officially merged with the University of New Hampshire as the service branch of the Recreation Management and Policy Department within the School of Health and Human Services.

NEP's philosophy is to listen carefully to consumers needs, think creatively to solve problems, attend to details, work as a team and explore the possibilities!

The NEP has a number of programs for its clients, including TREK, sports and recreation programs, Paralympics academy, and PATH.

TREK is designed to (a) work with parents, students, administrators, physical education, special education or classroom teachers, as well as other related service providers, (b) to ensure equal opportunity for students with physical and developmental disabilities, and (c) facilitate the inclusion of students into the curriculum (including phys. ed.), sports, after school programs, or summer programs through the use of adaptive equipment, direct instruction, and a focus on social awareness, students can upgrade their skills to a level where inclusive participation in recreation-based activities is successful.

The **Sports and Recreation** program offers a spectrum of service from entry-level instruction, to ongoing recreation and competitive sports. This program provides the appropriate level of support and challenge for clients of all abilities. NEP offers ongoing programs in nine sports of particular interest to people living in New England. In addition to the nine developed sports programs, Northeast Passage offers one Explore Clinic per year in a new and different activity. While these activities do not develop into ongoing programs for NEP they serve as a resource to explore the many different options for recreation and sport available to individuals with disabilities, their friends and families. Explore Clinics offer experienced instructors, equipment and information on how to pursue the activity following the clinic. In the past we have offered clinics in fencing, remote control planes, yoga, and many others.

The **Paralympic Academy** is an exploratory, daylong event for kids with physical disabilities and their parents to learn about the options available to them for participation in sports and athletics on a competitive level. Newly disabled and first time participants are welcome and encouraged to attend. The U.S. Paralympics is a division of the United States Olympic Committee (USOC) and is different and separate from Special Olympics.

This event is an introduction to Paralympic sports and is geared toward youth with physical disabilities, ages 8-21 and their families. The Academy will focus on the winter sports of sled hockey, cross country skiing, alpine skiing, and quad rugby. Throughout the day there will be introductory sport clinics, opportunities to see and try adaptive sports equipment, discussion forums for athletes and family members, and a question and answer time with current and former Paralympic athletes.

PATH (Promoting Access, Transition & Health) provides one-to-one consulting to individuals with disabilities empowering them to return to active healthy lives.

continued

Case Study …. Northeast Passage Program, University of New Hampshire (continued)

NEP, through its Health Promotion Program now offers seven primary services to its clients based on assessed need.

- **Wellness Education Series** - including risk management for prevention of most common secondary conditions, nutrition, stress management, selfadvocacy
- **Fitness Program** – direct strength and wellness programming.
- Functional Skill Development - development of advanced functional skills including transfers, self-direction, and wheelchair mobility.
- **Community Re-Integration in Home Community** - exploring home community, identifying accessible restaurants, stores, attractions, and places of business.
- **Resource & Network Development** - learning the process for tracking down resources including support agencies, accessibility guidelines, adapted recreation programs, adapted equipment resources, low interest loans, transportation etc.
- **Individual and Family Recreation Skill Development** - identifying recreation activities of interest and redeveloping the skills to participate independently.
- **Peer Advisor Program** – establishing a network of peer contacts.

reason is the development of elite athletes for international competitions such as the Paralympic Games and Deaflympics.

Youth with disabilities and their families are frequently frustrated in their attempts to locate physical activity and sport programs. Also, many teachers, coaches, recreation leaders, and physicians simply do not know where to refer the child with a disability who is interested in sports. Disability sports organizations are often restricted from disseminating information to children in schools because of confidentiality concerns about disability status.

Where can youth with disabilities (and their parents and teachers) learn about opportunities to participate in sports? How can parents facilitate sports participation by their children? What is the role of physical education teachers and youth sport coaches in introducing the students with disabilities to disability sports? What is the role of physicians and therapists at hospitals and rehabilitation centers in promoting disability sports? Which school sport programs should be accessible to students with disabilities? Should schools offer disability-specific sports programs in addition to Special Olympics? What can sports organizations do to attract children with disabilities?

Elite Youth Athletes

We have all seen and heard about the young elite figure skaters, golfers, gymnasts, speed skaters, skiing, ski jumping, soccer, swimmers, tennis players, and wrestlers who are being groomed for professional careers and Olympic-level status in sport academies whose costs range from $1,200 to over $100,000. These young athletes do not have normal childhood lives or normal school attendance. At first, the sports career and school may coexist peacefully, but when young athletes must practice six to eight hours per day, travel to distant cities and countries to participate in competition, and perhaps move from one region of the country to another to work with a notable coach, normal educational routines are disrupted.

The education disruption might be solved through the use of tutoring, but this leads to a fundamental question related to these practices used to develop upper-middle-class elite youth athletes: Is sport involvement so important during the developmental years that children must lose the normal experiences of childhood? To the very, very few who are successful, it may be justified. But for the vast majority of young athletes who endure this lifestyle and are not successful, a childhood may be lost for nothing.

Kids and Sports – What Do They Want?

Why do children want to play organized sports? What are their goals, hopes, and aspirations? Each child has his own specific answers to these questions. Understanding their reasons for wanting to play sports is a critical first step toward helping children to have the best possible experiences in sport. Articles in magazines and newspapers, as well as some coaching textbooks, often suggest that socialization is a major value of participating in youth sports. Certainly, learning to work together in a group and striving to achieve group goals are potentially important outcomes.

Learning about and practicing sportsmanship also is a worthwhile goal as is understanding how to deal with success and failure - winning and losing. Is this what the kids expect to get out of playing organized sports? Actually, NO! Numerous research studies completed in the last 20 years have asked youth sport participants why they decided to participate in organized sports. Although there is some variation in the ranked order of the reasons that children cite, depending on the particular sport they are playing, the top reasons are very consistent. Children expect to have fun, learn skills, develop fitness, and participate because they enjoy competition. Socialization-related reasons typically are near the bottom of the list, with sportsmanship somewhere in the middle. Winning and receiving individual awards (medals, trophies, etc.) also do not appear among the top reasons. What is the bottom line? Do children want an opportunity to participate in competitive sports? Or do they want to develop the skills and fitness that will allow them to play effectively? Or do they want to have fun doing it? Or do they want it all?

Privatization of Youth Sports

Privatization is a trend in youth sports. As cities and counties slowly reduce their youth sport programming, the private/commercial sport organizations are stepping in to fill the void. These programs depend on fund-raising, participation fees, and corporate sponsorships. They offer many of the same kinds of sport opportunities that have existed in public programs. However, these programs are expensive and tend to attract children from middle- and upper-middle income families. Even when there is a willingness to waive fees or seek funds for scholarships for children from low-income families, few participate.

The dilemma youth sports face is how to engage the low-income and single-parent families' children in sports. This is a growing concern across the United States. If a solution is not found, there will be a whole generation of children who do not have youth sport opportunities. This will produce the economic and ethnic inequalities that exist in the larger society in youth sports. This is a dangerous trend for youth sports.

The National Alliance for Youth Sports (NAYS, http://www.nays.org) has developed recommendations for communities regarding youth sports. These recommendations were developed through the National Summit in Raising Community Standards in Children's Sports, examining the violent and abusive behavior plaguing youth sports. This is one solution to the concern raised above.

Public Youth Sport Programs

Public youth sport programs are open to all with an emphasis on youth development and sport skill development. The cost of the public programs in the past has been generally low and in many areas, they were free. These programs emphasize open participation and fun and are not programs that place an emphasis on progressive skill development and competitive success. The latter programs are known as "performance principle" programs. The issue with public youth sport programs is the fact that the majority of the participants are minority children from low-income and single-parent families who cannot afford the more expensive and exclusive private/commercial programs. Privatized programs of all types are increasingly characterized by racial and ethnic segregation and exclusion. In many communities across the United States where this happens, it accentuates differences between the haves and have-nots and between people from different racial and ethnic groups (Coakley, 2004).

Often administrators of public programs do not have the resources to provide what a private program can for its student-athletes. As organized sports have become more popular, there has been a decline in the number of publicly supported programs with free and open participation policies. When local governments face budget crises, various social services, including youth sports, often are cut back or eliminated. Therefore, the dilemma for the administrator is to decide whether to increase fees to balance the budget and compete with the private programs or remain status quo or terminate the program forcing the parents of physically skilled children to seek other means to provide for the talented children.

Risk of Injury

Most sports are safe. Yet, sports are full of risk and potential injury.

Even when sport safety is emphasized, injuries happen. Daily living has risks, and the potential for injury is present all the time. Growing up is full of risks, but children need to understand and accept risk.

There are a number of safety issues that need to be understood when working with youth in sport activities. These safety issues include, but are not limited to the following: (a) improper fitting equipment in contact sports (i.e., helmets and pads in football, ice hockey, lacrosse, catching gear in baseball and softball, and shin guards in soccer), (b) unsafe playing fields or courts, (c) accelerated training regimens, (d) intensity of training regimens, (e) mismatching opponents (i.e., failing to take into consideration age, experience, gender, height, skill level, and weight), (f) background checks for coaches, and (g) overuse injuries.

Sport Specialization

Years ago, it was common for a young athletes to participate in at least three sports. They would play field hockey, football, soccer, or volleyball in the fall, basketball, swimming, or wrestling in the winter, and baseball, golf, softball, tennis, or track in the spring. The current emphasis upon sport performance in youth sport programs has also encouraged sport specialization by parents and coaches. Soccer is a great example of how sport specialization is encouraged by the various national organizations. The children play outdoor soccer in the fall, go inside for indoor soccer during the winter, return to the outside for spring soccer, and attend either sport camps or clinics during the summer. Children who specialize in one sport do not have the opportunity to learn additional sport skills found in other sports. Specialization has its advantages, but it also denies the children of a well-rounded sport experience.

Private/commercial sport programs often encourage, for economic reasons mainly, exclusive attention to a single sport. This practice is in the interest of program organizers to capture year-round commitments for membership, which pay salaries, rent or mortgages, and other operating expenses. Therefore, the organizer or owners encourage year-round commitments and participation and justify their encouragement in terms of the performance principle. This principle suggests that meeting performance goals and moving up to higher levels of competition requires a year-round commitment to a particular sport. Is this a good trend for youth sports?

What if families had an opportunity to join a year-round sport club that encourage youth to participate in at least three different sports annually? Wouldn't this type of sport diversity be better for children, developing them into a well-rounded athlete? Isn't society in general asking everyone to be more diverse in our everyday lives? The trend toward sport specialization in youth sports is a dangerous trend.

Sportsmanship

Everyone involved in sports seems to talk about sportsmanship and how important it is in youth sports. But what is sportsmanship? Many sport psychologists describe sportsmanship as the qualities and behaviors of athletes who treat their opponents with fairness and who can take a defeat without complaining and take a victory without gloating. This description should apply not just to opponents but also to teammates. As an athlete and a member of a team, youth should expect to be treated fairly by coaches and teammates, and youth should treat them fairly, too. Administrators, coaches, and parents must remember that everyone has different backgrounds and experience in sports. Youth may have played the particular sport for a couple of years but probably have teammates who are new to the sport. In order for the team to be successful, coaches should encourage these newer or less skilled youth so they can improve themselves and help the team. Making fun of them or giving them a

hard time when they make mistakes is poor sportsmanship. More experienced youth should remember that they were just like them not too long ago. How did they feel when teammates made fun of them? Probably not very good. Good teams are teams where everyone works together to help each other. Cooperation within a team is very important.

This same attitude should apply to opponents, too. All too often we watch professional athletes and think that the way they behave during games is the right way to act. Unfortunately, that is not always true. Youth should really think about what they do and say during a game. Youth should let their skills do the talking. Trash talking has become very common in sports. Many people feel that it is just a part of sports; but other people feel that it does not belong in sports at all! What do you think?

Sport administrators, coaches, and parents are the role models when it comes to sportsmanship. When adults fail to portray or model good sportsmanship (or citizenship), they teach the youth that it is acceptable to be poor sports. Sport administrators need to stop unsportsmanlike conduct swiftly. The sports administrator needs to teach and model good sportsmanship.

Parents and Sportsmanship

Pick up a sports page and you get a stark picture of the world of competitive sports-corporate sponsorship, fierce competition, and a win-at-any-cost mentality. For decades, recreational youth sports has been the beacon of hope for maintaining the purity of sport, where unsportsmanlike conduct has been the rare exception. And yet, even at a level where 20 million youngsters play in leagues throughout the USA, the signs of a decline in sportsmanship are evident: talking trash, challenging officials, refusing to shake hands with the opponent after the game, making excuses after every loss - and that's just the parents!

Often we reveal our true selves through sports. And like it or not, our kids are watching us and looking to us as role models of good sportsmanship.

Youth sports are supposedly an avenue to teach values to kids, such as teamwork, hard work and practice, handling and learning from mistakes, developing confidence, and winning and losing gracefully. Most parents are conscientious about their parenting role. And yet it constantly amazes many what some parents "reveal" about their character when it comes to their behavior in youth sports. Burnett (1996, p. 27) provides the following examples of parents in action:

- A team of eight- and nine-year-olds lost a baseball game in the last inning after the right fielder dropped a fly ball. One of the dads on the losing team said, loud enough for the coach and right fielder to hear, "We would have won if the coach would have played that kid in the middle of the game. Everybody knows he can't catch the ball. Why did the coach put him out there with everything on the line?
- The mother of a girls basketball team that won 51-19 in a tournament for 11- to 12-year-olds, in full earshot of the parents of the losing team, "I guess that team has never seen a real full-court press before. I can't believe their coach didn't teach them how to beat a press. Oh, well, maybe it taught them not to come to this level of a tournament until they're ready!"
- While baseball umpiring for a game of 10-year-old boys, a parent observed a small group of parents from the home team berating a boy at the plate from the visiting team who had gone hitless his first two times at bat. As he came to bat the third time, the parents yelled to their pitcher, "Here's an automatic out! He swings like a girl! He's

afraid up there! Blow it by him!" The batter lowered his head. He struck out a third time for the third out. As the pitcher came off the mound, the same group of parents shouted, "If they had more players like that kid, you'd have a no-hitter."

Why do parents lose it at youth league games? Coakley (2004) and Eitzen and Sage (2003) and others feel that parents get too wrapped up in the competition because they are living vicariously through their children. Other experts feel that parents might be filled with unrealistic expectations, hoping their child will be the next superstar. Consequently, they place too much emphasis on making sure their kid "wins" or "has a great game" or "looks good" (Burnett, 1996).

Is Winning the Only Thing?

No! But, there are a large number of folks who think it is. Everyone wants to win. Yet, any time two teams or youth are facing each other in a game or contest, someone will lose (unless it's a tie). Youth lose in small ways, like in a game of checkers; but they also might face losing in bigger ways, like when their team loses a championship game.

Losing is disappointing so it is not surprising that kids do not like it. Adults do not like it either but everyone can learn to control how they react to a loss. In other words, what should you do when you lose?

Teaching kids to lose is the first step in developing strong youth sport programs; but, teaching the attitude that winning is the first and only reason to compete in sports will be the beginning of the end for successful sport programs.

Summary

There has been an enormous increase in community-sponsored or private/commercial youth sports programs in America (e.g., baseball, basketball, bowling, golf, gymnastics, field hockey, football, ice hockey, lacrosse, soccer, softball, swimming, tennis, volleyball, and more). The objectives of most youth sports programs are to provide participants with an opportunity to learn culturally relevant sport skills and to develop attitudes and values about authority, competition, cooperation, discipline, social relationships, sportsmanship, and teamwork. However, there are private/commercial programs (i.e., sport academies) that are blatantly designed as career training or pre Olympic programs.

The issues most frequently focused upon include adult intrusion in youth sports, burnout in youth sports, coaching education, public youth sport programs, privatization of youth sports, disabled youth, elite youth athletes, kids and sports – what do they want, risk of injury, sport specialization, sportsmanship, and winning is the only thing, and more.

References

Amateur Athletic Union. http://www.aausports.org. (2006).

Burnett, D.J. (1996) Parents and sportsmanship. http://www.djburnett.com/. (2006).

Buzby, J. (1997). Preventing burnout in youth sports. http://www.youth-sports.com/getpage. cfm?file=/fundamentools.html&userid=21. (2006).

Coakley, J. (2004). *Sport in society: Issues and controversies.* (8th ed). Boston: Irwin-McGraw Hill.

Donnelly, P. (1993). Problems associated with youth involvement in big-performance sports. In B.A. Cahill, & A.J. Pearl (Eds.), *Intensive participation in children's sports.* (pp. 95-126). Champaign, IL: Human Kinetics.

Eitzen, D.S., & Sage, G.H. (2003) *Sociology of North American sport* (7th ed). Boston: McGraw-Hill.

Little League International. http://www.littleleague. org. (2006).

National Alliance for Youth Sports, http://www. nays.org. (2006).

Northwest Passage Project, http://www.nep.org. (2006).

 NOTES

CHAPTER 8

Interscholastic Sport Governance

High school athletics are considered a significant phase of the secondary school educational program. Coaches, athletic directors, and school administrators proclaim the educational values of their athletic programs with pride. However, school officials cannot take credit for the introduction of these activities into the school program. In fact, students themselves initiated them. Athletic contests were started by groups of students as social events in the colleges following the Civil War. Athletic clubs were formed patterned after independent athletic clubs to which many of the elite in society belonged during that era. Imitating their older brothers and friends, high school students began to form athletic associations around 1900. They elected their own managers, scheduled their own games, and played any teams available. As the interest in competition grew, it was not uncommon for persons outside the school to be recruited to play on the teams. Disputes and brawls occasionally occurred.

The interscholastic athletic program, originally an unwanted outsider and later a tolerated extracurricular activity, has now come to gain its rightful place in the overall secondary curriculum. The program provides opportunities and experiences that make a contribution to the general growth and development of individual students and that help create a healthy climate in the educational institution and its supporting community.

Learning Objectives

Upon completion this chapter, the reader should be able to:

+ Identify the various interscholastic governing bodies.
+ Understand the governance structure, function, authority, requirements for membership, and sanctions and appeal processes for the various interscholastic governing bodies.
+ Discuss various impact issues, such as: amateurism, cheating, deviance and violence, eligibility, equity, funding, pressure to win, school prayer, specialization, and substance abuse.

Evolution of High School Sports

There are four stages in the evolution of interscholastic sports. The stages include the following periods—opposition, toleration, recognition and capitalization, and exploitation (Keller & Forsythe, 1984). During the period of opposition, schools did not sponsor high school sports, yet the team representing the student athletic associations eventually came to be identified with their schools and began to embarrass them. School officials found themselves forced to take positions on the recruiting of outsiders to play on the teams, controversies that arose, and volunteer coaching by individuals who had no training as teachers and whose tactics were questionable. As enthusiasm developed for athletic contests among students and the community and the realization that they would be continued outside the schools' jurisdiction if outlawed the majority of school administrators came to the conclusion that the only feasible alternative would be to assume control over them, thereby inaugurating the period of tolerance.

The period of tolerance brought steps to make these athletic games more respectable. Faculty members were appointed to chaperone the teams. Schools began to adopt controls to prevent abuse, including requiring athletes to be bona fide students, creating student-athlete eligibility rules, and developing standards for coaches who had to be members of the faculty.

The next period of evolution schools began to recognize that some desirable educational outcomes could result from properly planned and administered interschool athletic contests. This motivated principals and coaches to formulate specific educational objectives for the interscholastic program. After the standards were adopted to guide the athletic programs, many schools began to capitalize on the educational values of athletic activities and to consider them as an integral part of the total secondary school program.

When a school activity reaches a certain point of popularity, it enters the fourth period, during which attempts are made to exploit the program. As non-school organizations and individuals recognized the attractiveness of interscholastic games, they began to promote events involving high school athletes and the interscholastic athletic program. The primary interests of these promoters were generally in gaining recognition, advertising, and raising funds. However, the collective efforts of high school activity associations at the state and national levels have been effective in eliminating much of this type of exploitation of high school athletes and school athletic programs (e.g., corporate sponsors seeking individual or team endorsements, corporations seeking exclusive use of sport equipment (i.e., Nike shoe and uniform contracts), agents contracting to provide services, and more).

Placed in its proper perspective, and organized and administered as part of a total school program, competitive sports serve as a laboratory for teaching special skills and developing desirable habits and attitudes. Interschool competition affords the superior student in the field of physical activities the opportunity to work toward a high level of achievement and to compete with his peers in other schools (Martens, 2006; Sawyer, 2006; Seefeldt, 1998).

The Value of Interscholastic Sports

An interscholastic sports program should be designed to develop such characteristics as: loyalty to purpose, respect for discipline, capacity to lead and direct, respect of rules and authority, ability to act effectively under stress, respect for others, capacity for self-discipline in the interest of accomplishment, ability to develop as an individual as well as a team member, determination to overcome obstacles, understanding that sportsmanship is the golden rule of practice, enduring relationships with teammates, and ability to develop good health habits, strength, and body vigor.

There are eight common arguments for interscholastic sports in the United States including: (a) involving students in extracurricular school activities, (b) linking extracurricular activities to academics, (c) developing occupational skills such as establishing responsibility, building achievement orientation, and acquiring teamwork skills, (d) providing opportunities for developing physical fitness, (e) stimulating interest in physical activities among all students in the school, (f) generating spirit and unity necessary to maintain the school as a viable organization, (g) promoting parental, alumni, and community support for all school programs, and (h) providing students opportunities to develop and display skills in activities valued in the society of large (Coakley, 2003).

In order to provide a balanced perspective, it is necessary to outline the arguments against interscholastic sports. There are eight common arguments against interscholastic sports including: (a) distracts the attention of students from academic activities, (b) relegates most students to the role of spectator, (c) causes too many serious injuries to active participants, (d) deprives educational programs of resources, facilities, staff, and community support, (e) applies excessive pressure on student-athletes, (f) focuses the attention of students on a power and performance orientation, (g) perpetuates dependence and conformity, and (h) creates a superficial and transitory spirit in the school (Coakley, 2003).

Interscholastic Sport Governing Bodies

Interscholastic sport governing bodies include conferences or leagues, state high school athletic associations, and the National Federation of State High School Associations (NFHS). Local conferences or leagues are formed to enhance scheduling, provide conference or league championship competition, and implement useful policies and procedures.

Types of State Associations

Although state athletic and activities associations function similarly in most respects, they fall into three general classifications in regard to administrative control. The great majority are voluntary associations through which their member schools cooperatively regulate interschool contests and activities. The second type is affiliated with a state education department. A third consists of those administered through institutions of higher learning.

Voluntary state associations. The most numerous state associations fall into this category. Membership is voluntary but is usually dependent upon member schools meeting specified requirements regarding the financial support of the school, its plan of organization, the status of its coaches, and the payment of annual dues. Usually such organizations limit their competition to member schools. In most states, membership is open to public secondary schools accredited by state departments of education. Some states also allow private and parochial schools to join, provided they meet the standards for membership. These organizations are not-for-profit educational corporations who are tax exempted 501(c)3 entities. Board members are elected by schools of different sizes and some have ex-officio members from legislative bodies or departments of education. Many state associations are responsible for speech, debate, theatre, music, and spirit programs. Some are responsible for only grades 9-12 (Indiana) while others coordinate activities for grades 6-12 (Texas).

The state associations in this category include Alabama, Alaska, Arizona, Arkansas, California, Colorado, District of Columbia, Florida, Georgia, Hawaii, Idaho, Illinois, Indiana, Iowa, Kentucky, Louisiana, Maine, Maryland, Minnesota, Missouri, Montana, Nebraska, Nevada, New Jersey, New Mexico, North Dakota, Ohio, Oklahoma, Pennsylvania, South Dakota, Tennessee, Utah, Washington, West Virginia, Wisconsin, and Wyoming.

State associations affiliated with state departments of education. The following states are affiliated with state departments of education: Connecticut, Delaware, Kansas, Massachusetts, Michigan, Mississippi, New Hampshire, New York, North Carolina, Rhode Island, and Vermont. These associations have direct links (i.e., communication, committee appointments, etc.) with the state departments of education but are not governed by the state.

University-directed state associations. The following state associations are university-directed: South Carolina (University of South Carolina), Texas (University of Texas), and Virginia (University of Virginia). These organizations are housed in colleges or schools of education on a university campus. The universities do not govern them. They are free-standing organizations with boards and bylaws.

Advantages of joining a state association. The advantages of belonging to the state association are: (a) eligibility for participation in state championship athletic events, (b) enforcement of regulations for the conduct of athletics, (c) sponsorship of a classification plan for athletic competition (i.e., a

state might have four classifications based on size of school population including 1-A, 2-A, 3-A, and 4-A), (d) certification and assignment of athletic officials, (e) enforcement of athletic standards (i.e., eligibility, transfer, and academic standards), (f) published bulletins and newsletters, (g) enforcement of sportsmanship, and (h) a final authority for the resolution of questions, controversies, and appeals. Finally, member schools have some obligations to the association, which include compliance with all regulations of the association, cooperation, support, and loyalty.

The National Federation of State High School Associations

By 1920 state high school associations had been formed in 29 states. They proved to be both desirable and necessary in keeping interscholastic athletics in perspective within the total school program and in making them educationally worthwhile. With the formation of the original Midwest Federation of State High School Athletic Associations in 1920, there came into being the first cooperative effort of state associations to control high school athletics. The original organization of five states (Illinois, Indiana, Iowa, Michigan, and Wisconsin) was the forerunner of the National Federation of State High School Associations (NFHS). In 1970, the word "athletics" was dropped from the name to expand the responsibilities to include non-athletic activities. The NFHS has six territorial sections within the United States.

The National Federation has two primary services, namely, controlling interstate competition and preventing exploitation of high school athletes and interscholastic athletics by promoters of athletic events to which high school teams and individuals athletes are invited. Other services include the National Federation Press, national interscholastic records, rules writing, audiovisual aids, athletic experimental studies, athletic insurance, athletic safety and protection, professional interscholastic athletic organizations, rules interpretation meetings, sports participation surveys, National Federation awards, award of merit, National High School Hall of Fame, National High School activities week, and legal aid pact.

The NFHS has six professional organizations under its umbrella, including the National Federation of Interscholastic Athletic Coaches (NFICA), National Association of Interscholastic Officials Association (NFIOA), spirit association, speech, debate, and theatre association, music association, and National Interscholastic Athletic Administrators Association (NIAAA).

National Interscholastic Athletic Administrator Association. The NIAAA (http://www.niaaa.org) promotes the professional growth and image of interscholastic athletic administrators. It promotes the development and prestige of state athletic administrators organizations, which will contribute, in cooperation with their state high school associations, to the interscholastic athletic program of each state. Further, it provides an efficient system for exchange of ideas between the National Federation of State High School Associations and state athletic administrators organizations as well as individual athletic administrators. Finally, it strives to preserve the educational nature of interscholastic athletics and the place of these programs in the curricula of schools.

Governance

Wong (2003, p. 26) suggests, "the power and authority in high school athletics are in the individual state organizations, which determine the rules and regulations for the sport programs and schools within that state." There are six basic components of governance. These components consist of (a) organizational structure, (b) func-

tion, (c) authority, (d) requirements for membership, (e) sanctions and appeals process and (f) funding. The best way to illustrate each of these components as they relate to an interscholastic governing body is to use a state high school athletic association as an example.

Organizational Structure

Most state high school athletic associations have the following organizational structure: Board of Directors (elected by the membership), executive committee as established by the by-laws, commissioner, an associate commissioner, and assistant commissioners (see Indiana organizational chart in Figure 8.1). The NFHS has a board of directors (elected by the membership), executive committee, executive director (appointed by the board), and directors (see Figure 8.2 for an organizational chart for the NFHS).

Function

The function or purpose of a state high school association are stated in their constitutions, which illustrate why these organizations were founded and what they are expected to accomplish.

In general, the function of state high school athletic associations is to encourage, regulate, and give direction to wholesome amateur interschool athletic competition between schools that are members of the association. All such interschool athletic competition shall be subservient to and complementary to the academic or curricular functions of the member schools. The primary purposes including to: (a) assure that the program of interschool athletic competition remains steadfast to the principles of wholesome amateur athletics and subservient to its primary academic or curricular functions of education of the member schools, the association shall cooperate with agencies vitally concerned with the health and educational welfare of second-

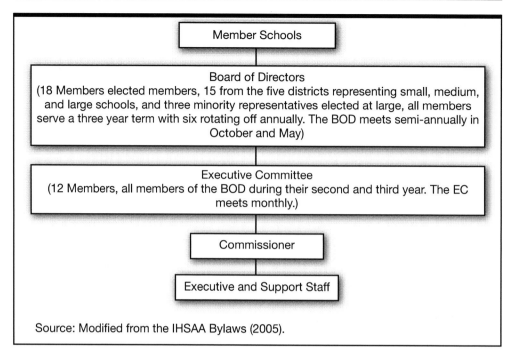

Figure 8.1
Organizational Chart for the Indiana High School Athletic Association (IHSAA)

ary school students, (b) furnish protection against exploitation of members schools of their students, determine qualifications of individual contestants, coaches, and officials, and (c) provide written communications to established standards for eligibility, competition and sportsmanship.

Typically, there are objectives of both athletic and activity types appearing as follows:

1. To foster and develop amateur athletics among the secondary schools of the state (New Jersey State Interscholastic Athletic Association).

2. To equalize athletic opportunities by standardizing rules of eligibility for individuals and by classifying the competitive purposes of the institutions which are members of the association (Indiana High School Athletic Association).

3. To promote uniformity in the arrangement and control of contests (Montana High School Association).

4. To protect the mutual interests of the members of the association through the cultivation of ideals of clean sport in their relation to the development of character (Missouri State High School Activities Association).

5. To ensure that interscholastic activities shall supplement the curricular program of the school to provide opportunities for youth to acquire worthwhile knowledge, skills, and emotional patterns (Washington Interscholastic Activities Association).

6. To foster a cooperative spirit and good sportsmanship on the part of school representatives, school patrons, and students (Illinois High School Association).

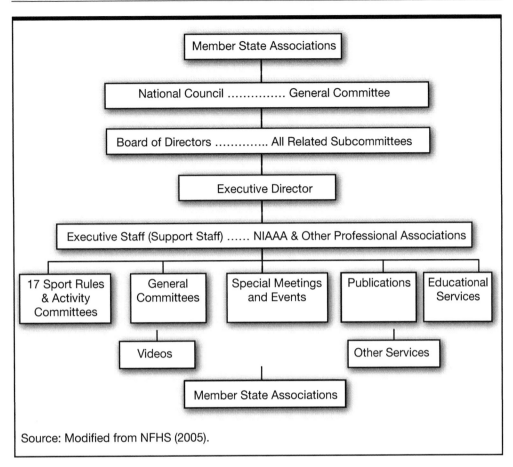

Figure 8.2
Organization Chart for the National Federation of State High School Associations (NFHS)

The mission of the National Federation of State High School Associations (NFHS; http://www.nfhs.org) is to serve its members and its related professional groups by providing leadership and national coordination for the administration of interscholastic activities, which will enhance the educational experiences of high school students and reduce risks of their participation.

The NFHS function is to: (a) promote participation and sportsmanship, and (b) develop good citizens through interscholastic activities, which provide equitable opportunities, positive recognition, and learning experiences to students while maximizing the achievement of educational goals.

Authority

The principals of the secondary schools or state departments of education establish the authority for state high school athletic associations. These voluntary associations are charged to plan, organize, and regulate a wholesome amateur program of interschool athletic competition in which school members of such association would participate. The NFHS gains its authority from the 50 member state associations plus the District of Columbia.

Requirements for Membership

All memberships are voluntary. Full membership in a state high school athletic association shall be open to all public, private, parochial, boarding, and institutional high schools of the state offering and maintaining two or more years of high school work, provided they meet the requirements of the association and also subscribe to its rules and regulations. For a school to be eligible for membership, it must have full accreditation from the state department of education or be fully accredited by a regional accrediting agency (i.e., North Central Association, Council on Accreditation and School Improvement, Southern Association of Colleges and Schools, and others).

Members of the NFHS include all 50 state high school athletic associations and the District of Columbia, and over 30 affiliate members. The affiliate members include all the Canadian provinces and a variety of state music associations. It is a not-for-profit organization located in Indianapolis, Indiana.

Sanctions and Appeals Process

Each state high school athletic association has established a sanction and appeals process. Commonly, the board of directors establishes the sanctions. The commissioners or executive directors implement the sanctions. Commissioners' or executive directors' decisions can be appealed to either the board of directors or executive committees. In some states, the decision of the board of directors or executive committees can be appealed to a state appointed appeals committee, such as in Indiana.

The NFHS does not sanction high schools but rather sanctions events between states or a foreign country. The NFHS requires sanctioning of the following events: (a) any interstate event involving two or more schools which is co-sponsored by or titled in the name of an organization outside the school community (e.g., AAU), (b) events in non-bordering states if five or more states are involved, (c) events in non-bordering states if more than eight schools

are involved, and (d) any event involving two or more schools that involves a team from a foreign country.

Funding

The major source of revenue for the NFHS is sales of publications. These publications include rule books (revised annually for all sports), miscellaneous sport items (e.g., tournament guides, facilities design materials, etc.), sport guides, handbooks, officials' interpretation books, debate and speech books, etc. In addition, the organization earns funds from membership dues, meetings and conferences, royalties, and contracts for injury insurance.

The major source of revenue for a state high school association is tournament revenue. The greatest source of tournament revenue is derived from football and boys basketball. However, girls basketball is beginning to show a dramatic increase. In addition, the state associations' generate revenue from membership dues, tournament fees, ball contracts (i.e., selection of tournament balls), sponsorships, and sale of publications.

High school athletic programs' key revenue source is gate receipts. In addition, in some states high schools have begun charging athletes for the privilege to participate in sports. Other sources of revenue includes concessions, merchandise sales, parking fees, advertising, and sponsorships. In general a very small amount is allocated from the general fund or taxpayer sources. The two exceptions are coaches salaries (paid through the teacher contract and negotiated by the teacher bargaining unit) and transportation, which generally is included in the transportation fund, often a separate tax.

Interscholastic Policy Areas

High school athletic associations have the responsibility of developing policy for the operation of interscholastic sports within a state. The policy areas most often focused upon are as follows: (a) membership in the association, (b) corporation/ association districts, (c) classes of schools and competition, (d) roles of the board, executive committee, commissioner, and executive staff, (e) eligibility, (f) age, (g) amateurism, (h) coaches, (i) conduct, character, and discipline, (i) intrastate and interstate contests, (j) game and official contracts, (k) officials, (l) enrollment and attendance, (m) academic standing/scholarship, (n) eligibility and transfer, (o) undue influence, and (p) specific policies for each sport over and above the NFHS established rules.

Interscholastic Athletic Issues

There are a number of important interscholastic athletic issues that impact sports on this level. They include issues such as amateurism, cheating, deviance and violence, eligibility (i.e., academic, age, red shirting, and transfer rules), equity (i.e., gender and home-schoolers), funding, pressure to win, school prayer, specialization, sportsmanship, and substance abuse.

Amateurism

Only an amateur student-athlete is eligible for interscholastic athletic participation in a particular sport. A student-athlete loses amateur status and shall not be eligible for interscholastic competition in a particular sport if he:

- Is paid (in any form) or accepts the promise of pay for participation in an athletic contest.
- Accepts a benefit other than of a symbolic nature, directly or indirectly, for athletic participation in that sport.
- Signs a contract or verbally commits

with an agent or a professional sports organization.

- Requests that his name be placed on a draft list or otherwise agree to negotiate with a professional sports organization.
- Uses his athletic skill directly or indirectly for pay in any form (TV commercials, skills demonstrations).
- Participates in athletic activities, tryouts, auditions, practices, and games held or sponsored by professional athletic organizations, clubs, or their representatives during the contest season.
- Participates on an amateur sports team and receives, directly or indirectly, any salary, incentive payment, award, gratuity, educational expenses, or expense allowances (other than playing apparel, equipment, actual and necessary travel, and room and board expenses for practice and games).
- Failure to return player equipment or uniforms issued by a school or nonschool team when the season for that sport concluded, or when the student's continued participation on such team concluded.

To avoid the risk of jeopardizing his current or future eligibility, a student-athlete should always check with the athletic director for compliance and/or his coach prior to participating in any contest in which awards or prizes are to be given and/or before beginning any employment related to his or her sport or sport skills.

Cheating

Cheating often involves a violation of the rules to gain an unfair advantage over an opponent. The types of cheating depend on the sport and the creativity of the participants. Clearly, cheating is antithetical to educational values and should have no place in educational programs (Eitzen & Sage, 2003).

There are coaches under pressure to win at all costs who use illegal techniques that are difficult to detect, (e.g., holding or tripping by the offensive linemen in football, touching the lower half of a basketball player when shooting, faking being fouled, faking an injury to gain an extra time out, or not going to the huddle and standing near the sidelines). Further, coaches sometimes break the spirit of a rule, if not the rule itself. For example, teams may not have organized practices before a certain date, yet coaches insist on players practicing, with captains in charge or coaches at a distance yelling orders.

As long as pressure to win is a reality, there will be cheating by coaches, parents, and student-athletes. High school athletic administrators need to emphasize the importance of honesty and integrity within athletics. It is a characteristic that student-athletes should learn while participating in sports. Winning at all costs should never be acceptable in an athletic program.

Deviance and Violence

Is deviance and violence out of control? A quick glance at the sport pages over the past few years would lead one to believe that deviance and violence in sport is out of control. The media coverage of on-the-field rule violations and violence and off-the-field behavior would like the reading public to assume that participants in sport (e.g., athletes, coaches, and spectators) are devious and violent people.

The commonly reported examples of deviance include cheating, gambling, shaving points, throwing games or matches, engaging in unsportsmanlike conduct, fighting (violence), taking performance-enhancing drugs, and generally finding ways to avoid rules. Over the years, these types of deviance have become a serious problem in most sports because of pressures to per-

form and win that have been heightened by increased commercialization and television coverage.

Violence among spectators is influenced by violence on the field of play as well as crowd dynamics, the situation at the event itself, and the overall historical and cultural context in which spectators live. Coaches, as well as reactions to violence by other athletes and teammates, have encouraged violence on the field of play by athletes and by the cultural context in the way an athlete lives. High school athletic associations continue to try to reduce violence on the field or court and in the stands.

Many of the high school athletic associations are trying hard to improve sportsmanship in interscholastic athletics. The sportsmanship programs are aimed toward athletes, coaches, and spectators. The sportsmanship programs are designed to eliminate cheating, gambling, fighting, violation of rules by athletes and coaches, and to encourage spectators to behave as ladies and gentlemen while attending contests. The Indiana High School Athletic Association (IHSAA) in collaboration with the Indiana Farm Bureau Insurance Company has developed a statewide scholarship program for schools that demonstrate good sportsmanship. In addition, they actively supported the sportsmanship theme through championship advertisements, sportsmanship seminars for athletes, coaches, and parents, and a sportsmanship presence on the IHSAA website.

Eligibility

Who plays and who does not? The answer to this question often causes heated debates and court challenges. The most common factors used in determining whether or not a person can participate include ability (disability), academic standing, age, citizenship, educational affiliation (private, public, or charter schools), gender, grade in school, height, place of residence, and weight. Eligibility rules are often challenged because of arbitrariness. High school students have contested eligibility (transfer) rules when their families have moved from one school district to another and they have been found they are ineligible to play varsity sports. High school athletic associations have established eligibility rules to ensure a fair competitive situation for all student-athletes.

Participation in interscholastic athletics is voluntary and a privilege in the reasoning of the courts, which may be extended at the discretion of the school board and the state high school athletic association. When eligibility standards are challenged in the courts, they must, in most circumstances, withstand only rational basis scrutiny. This means that if the requirements are rationally related to the purpose of activity and not arbitrary, capricious, or unjustly discriminatory, they will be upheld by the courts (Wong, 2003).

Academic Eligibility (No Pass, No Play)

Academic eligibility has gained a great deal of attention with the increase in NCAA academic requirements and the ability of students to meet the NCAA Clearinghouse standards for future collegiate participation. Realizing that the age group served by high school represents an interval in human development that can be turbulent and complex, high school athletic associations have been concerned with educating the whole person. Therefore, the primary focus of the secondary school should be to provide educational opportunities for its students in accordance with the requirements set forth by state education departments. This academic training should progress toward an adequate education and ultimately in earning a high school diploma. Participation in interschool programs is a privilege for which

reasonable standards should be established and enforced for the educational and personal welfare of the students who participate. If students cannot successfully carry and pass a normal minimum load of formal classroom work and simultaneously undertake the extra demands upon time and energy required by interschool participation, they should postpone their commitment to interschool programs and concentrate time and effort on achieving in the classroom. On the basis of these premises, minimum academic achievement requirements have been established by high school athletic associations. These minimum academic eligibility standards promoted the establishment of higher educational standards, upgraded student academic performance, countered public criticism of schools for low expectations and low student achievement, and enabled schools to use athletic participation as a motivator for better classroom performance and achievement.

High school athletic associations use a variety of means of demonstrating academic eligibility for athletic participation in high schools including grade point average (GPA), courses passed in previous and/or current semesters, courses passed in previous year, percent daily attendance, enrollment in the minimum number of periods, and maintaining a grade of 70 percent in each class during a six-week grading period to stay eligible for the next six-week grading period. Thus, a variety of standards are used by different states to demonstrate academic qualification for athletic participation in high schools.

For example, Indiana requires a student to complete five courses (e.g., English, mathematics, social studies, life science, chemistry, physics, or history) with a "D" or better grade to maintain athletic eligibility. This is a 60 percent average. It does not meet the minimum NCAA Clearinghouse standards.

Further, in 1985, the Texas legislature passed a statute requiring students to earn a grade of 70 percent in each class during a six-week grading period to stay eligible for the next six-week grading period. This statute has been known as the "no pass, no play rule". This law was contested in court and upheld. However, in 1995, the Texas legislature modified the law to make it more permissive, allowing failing students to rejoin the team if they were passing after three weeks. It further allowed failing students to practice or rehearse during a suspension period.

While "no pass, no play" rules have garnered a great deal of opposition for a variety of good and bad reasons, it is not fair to allow a student to participate in sports at the high school level not meeting the minimum NCAA Clearinghouse standards. High school athletic administrators should encourage high school athletic associations and school boards to increase academic standards for participation to at least the minimum NCAA Clearinghouse standard. This would allow those students who have chosen to moving on to higher education a chance at further sport participation.

Age Eligibility (Longevity)

High school athletic associations have developed rules of longevity to eliminate the problem of red shirting (see red shirting). Longevity rules determine the limits for participation in terms of semesters/years (i.e., eight semesters within four years or eight consecutive semesters) allowed to complete competition and a maximum age (i.e., 18 or 19) beyond which interscholastic competition may not continue.

The longevity rules are designed to equalize competition and have been defended on the grounds that it prevents older, more mature students from compromising the health and safety of the younger student-athlete, that 19- or 20- year-old students are not the average high school student, and that it eliminated the possibility of athletes red shirting in order to gain competitive advantage.

While longevity rules eliminate the problem with aging athletes, it causes another problem—discrimination toward a select group of students, the mentally disabled. The high school athletic association's longevity rule often prevents mentally disabled students from participating in extracurricular activities during their junior and senior years. These students often need extra time to finish high school. When contested by these students, courts have ruled that when participation in interscholastic sports is included as a component of the IEP (Individual Education Plan) as a related service, the privilege of competing in interscholastic sports is transformed into a federally protected right. In general, if participation in interscholastic athletics is not a component of the student's IEP, the court would rule the student has no constitutional right to participate in interscholastic sports.

The athletic administrator with athletes that are mentally handicapped should work cooperatively with the special education teachers and coordinators to ensure students have the opportunity to participate through their senior year. This means developing an appropriate IEP for each student who participates in athletics.

Red Shirting

Red shirting is the practice of delaying a student-athlete's competition in order to extend the athlete's career. Red shirting is an effective strategy to take advantage of an extra year's growth and maturity, and skill development. This practice is common in intercollegiate programs, but high school athletic associations' rules do not permit the practice because it is contrary to the educational mission. Further, the practice creates unfair competition advantages, dangerous mismatches, and unwarranted exclusion of peer student-athletes.

However, high school athletic associations recognize illness and/or injury and academic determinations of grade level as legitimate reasons as exceptions to the rules precluding red shirting and make appropriate allowances. In general, courts have agreed with the rational argument that red shirting regulations preserve the privilege of interscholastic athletic competition, consistent with their educational mission (Ness, 2003).

Transfer

The privilege of participation in interschool athletics should fundamentally be available to bona fide students in school districts where their parents or legally established guardians reside. Standards governing residence and transfer are a necessary prerequisite to participation in interschool athletics because: (a) they protect the opportunities of bona fide students to participate, (b) they provide a fundamentally fair and equitable framework in which interschool athletic competition, in an educational setting, can take place, (c) they provide uniform standards for all schools to follow in maintaining athletic competition, (d) they support the educational philosophy that athletics is a privilege that must not be permitted to assume a dominant position in a student's or school's program, (e) they keep the focus of educators and students on the fact that students attend school to receive an education first and participate in athletics second, (f) they maintain the fundamental principle that a high school student should live at home with his parents or legally appointed guardian and attend school in the school district in which the parents or guardians live, (g) they reinforce the view that the family is a strong and viable unit in our society, and as such, is the best place for students to live while attending high school, (h) they serve as a deterrent to students who would transfer schools for athletic reasons and to individuals who

would seek to recruit student athletes to attend a particular school for the purpose of building athletic strength, (i) they serve as a deterrent to students running away from or avoiding an athletic conflict or discipline that has been imposed, and (i) they protect school programs from losing students who have established an identity as an athlete and, as such, are contributors to the overall school program and image.

There are many legitimate reasons for transfers including family relocations caused by new employment, divorce, or relocating from a small rural school to a larger suburban school to gain additional academic opportunities (i.e., expanded elective academic courses in mathematics and sciences). These reasons and others constitute a basis for exceptions within the transfer rules.

Transfer rules are popular targets for legal challenges based on claims of violations of equal protection, freedom of religion, right to travel, and due process. In general, the courts have upheld transfer rules under rational judicial scrutiny. Considering that no fundamental right has been compromised, nor any suspect class established, the transfer rule need only be rationally related to the purpose stated above to be upheld by the court. However, if the student/athlete can establish fraud, collusion, or arbitrariness the possibility exists for a successful challenge.

Equity

Equity is an important issue facing public high schools. It is imperative that public high schools not discriminate against any student. The most common areas of discrimination over the years have focused on age, gender, disabled students, homeschoolers, race, and, religion. However, gender and home-schoolers have been hot issues recently and will be discussed below.

Gender

Gender equity has been an issue since the early seventies and before. The issue focuses on opportunities for equal access to participation by both genders. Title IX (1972) has opened many doors for young girls and women to participate in sport in the public school arena. Over the past 30-plus years, most of the inequities and barriers for young women have been eliminated in interscholastic athletics. Title IX reads as follows:

"No person in the United States shall, on the basis of sex, be excluded from participation in, be denied the benefits or, or be subjected to discrimination under any education program or activity receiving Federal financial assistance" (Title IX of the Educational Amendments, 1972).

In 1970 there were over two million men and boys participating in high school athletics and less than 800,000 women and girls. In 2005 there were over 2.8 million men and boys participating and over 2.3 million women and girls. It is projected that by 2010 the number women and girls will exceed the number of men and boys participating in high school athletics.

Recent trends include issues related to protecting members of discontinued men's teams (e.g., diving, gymnastics, and wrestling) and having the opportunity to participate without facing sexual harassment. It is clear that Title IX protects the participation rights of the historically underrepresented gender. In the athletic world, the underrepresented gender is female.

Title IX protects students, teachers, and coaches from sexual harassment, which is not only a Title IX violation but also criminal offense when it involves a young adult. Title IX has a prohibition against sexual harassment and it defines one method specially – quid pro quo. This is harassment based on a bargain or proposition where the coach offers the student-athlete something for performing a sexual favor. For example, Coach Jones offers Sally increased playing time, if she has sex with him. In sexual harassment cases, the sex of the perpetrator and the victim are not relevant, and civility is not required (*Onscale v. Sundowner Offshore Services*, 1998).

Gender equity requires that the selection of sports and levels of competition effectively accommodate the interests and abilities of members of both sexes. High school athletic associations and public high schools need to continue to focus on participation opportunities for all boys and girls. The challenges that high schools face include (a) facility equity (e.g., girls' softball field vs. boys' baseball field [see *Daniels v. Brevard County, 2001*] or girls' soccer field vs. boys' soccer complex), (b) equity in scheduling (i.e., scheduling girls' activities in nontraditional times of the year [see *Rideway v. Montana High School Association* [1988], *Lambert v. West Virginia State Board of Education* [1994]), (c) girls on boys teams (e.g., football, soccer, and wrestling), and (d) boys on girls teams (e.g., volleyball). The common examples of facility inequity are that the boys' facilities had announcer's booth, batting cages, concession stands, lights, press boxes, restrooms, scoreboards, covered and secured storage areas.

Home Schoolers

A current issue facing many public schools today is whether or not to permit home schoolers to participate in sports and other activities in their district's public schools. Many people believe that home-schooled students should be able to participate in school-sponsored extracurricular activities for many reasons. In Indiana, there are an estimated 23,455 Indiana students being taught at home in 2005-2006, from among 1.1 million school-age kids statewide, according to the Indiana Department of Education. That is up from 143 children the state recorded as being home-schooled in 1984-85. Nationally, the reported number of home schoolers increased by almost 30 percent between 1999 and 2003, to an estimated 1.1 million.

This is a complex policy area involving state legislatures, state associations, local school districts, and the legal system (see *McNatt v. Frazier School District* [1995], *Bradstreet v. Sobol* [1995], *Davis v. Massachusetts Interscholastic Athletic Association* [1995]). There is no national legislation to provide guidance in this area of policy development leaving states and others to decide.

If a home-schooled student wants to interact and participate in a school-sponsored sport, he must be ready to take on many conflicts. Local school boards nationally have had to make policy decisions that negatively affect these students. A home schooler from the Tamaqua School District (PA) wanted to play basketball for the Tamaqua Area School. The school board denied his request. On February 15, 2000, the Tamaqua Area School Board voted to formalize its policy. In spite of some opposition, the new policy bans home schoolers from taking part in district programs or extracurricular activities.

In the Tamaqua schools, as well as in all the public schools in Pennsylvania, the school districts are required to give home schoolers access to curriculum and books as requested. However, state law allows individual school districts to decide whether or not to make district activities available to home schoolers.

Questions continue to emerge and policy continues to evolve in this complex area as home-schooled students in different states seek the opportunity to participate (Killeen, 2002). The questions include:

- Is it fair to deny home schoolers the chance to play when their families pay taxes that fund public education? Some would say they made the choice freely not to attend public school and knew that they would not be eligible to play

sports for the local high school or any high school for that fact.

- Is it fair for home schoolers to take regularly enrolled students' positions on teams? An interesting question, since foreign exchange students who are in the country for one year or less do just that–they take positions of regularly enrolled students. So why not home schoolers?

- What educational message is sent when it is acceptable for home schoolers to play sports with, but not go to school with, other students?

- Should coaches be encouraged and allowed to recruit good home schooler athletes to strengthen their high school teams?

Funding (Soaring Costs)

The costs related to operating a high school athletic program have increased dramatically in the past 20 years. The number of sports offered in an athletic program has increased from as few as 10 to over 20, the number of coaches employed has doubled, and participants continue to increase annually. The changes in demographics have fueled the soaring costs of operations. Generally, school districts allocate dollars from the general fund to compensate coaches, construct and maintain facilities, and provide transportation, except for the driver compensation. The athletic departments are required to raise revenue to meet additional expenditures including awards, driver compensation for team travel, officials, uniforms, equipment, and game management personnel. Some athletic departments are required to raise funds for construction of new sport facilities.

High schools generate revenue generally through ticket sales, program sales, advertising, sponsorships, various fundraising activities (e.g., golf tournaments, awards dinners, etc.), and booster clubs. Often these efforts fall short and the department is faced with either cutting sports, requiring parents to donate funds to the booster club, assessing equipment fees, or assessing fees to play (except in California or South Dakota).

The issue facing all high schools large and small, poor and affluent is a soaring cost to operate interscholastic athletic programs. The future is not bright for financing interscholastic athletics. Gate receipts are not keeping up with the operational costs. Athletic administrators are looking for creative ways to add other revenue streams, including advertising, sales of licensed products, sponsorships, and pay-to-play; but is pay-to-play the best method to solve the growing problem? Will pay-to-play create more problems then it solves?

A recent poll in Wisconsin found that 269 out of 493 schools were charging participation fees. Carroll County, Maryland became the first school system near Baltimore to implement sports fees. In Strongsville, Ohio, students will have to pay $120 per sport with a cap of $240 for a multisport athlete. At Overlook Middle School near Worcester, Massachusetts, soccer now costs $342 and field hockey $389. Meanwhile, some schools that already charged fees are upping the ante this year. In Minnesota, five high schools in the Anoka-Hennepin area raised fees by $80 per sport, bringing the charge for football to $290 and basketball to $332 (Brown, 2002).

Some schools in California ask for donations because students cannot be required to pay fees there. A 1984 state Supreme Court ruling deemed student activities to be part of a district's education program. Fees are also banned in South Dakota, where the state attorney general in 1995 cited a state statute that says "Privileges of the public schools shall be free" (Brady & Giler, 2004).

Pay to Play

As sports teams begin practice across the country each year, many parents and student athletes are realizing that it may take more than just talent to make the cut. Increasingly, schools are charging participation fees to be on a team; a trend that educators and sports advocates say is a danger to the concept of public education and the overall effort to get more kids involved in athletic activities (Brown, 2002; Brady & Giler, 2004).

USA TODAY surveyed state high school sports associations and found 34 states in which associations say at least some school districts are charging students to play sports. Associations in 16 states plus the District of Columbia say they do not have, or are at least unaware of, schools that charge user fees. Pay to play, as it is commonly called, is not new. But the number of public schools that impose it is growing, an assertion that state associations base mainly on anecdotal evidence — what they hear informally from schools — because most states do not track how many schools charge fees (Brady & Giler, 2004).

One that does count is Kansas, where pay-to-play districts have grown from 29 to 50 to 55 in the last three years; about 18 percent of the state's 302 school districts. Michigan has 760 high schools; 558 returned a survey last year and 126 of those said they charged user fees, more than double the number from a decade ago. Missouri counted for the first time this spring and found 50 high schools with user fees (Brady & Giler, 2004).

Fees typically are $75 to $100 nationally and more often are charged for sports than for clubs and activities. Fees are often waived or reduced for students in federal free or reduced-lunch programs and sometimes are capped at several hundred dollars for families with children in several sports.

In Worcester, Massachusetts, for example, Oakmont Regional High School charges student athletes more than $1,000 to play football (Brown, 2002). Although some schools allow exceptions for athletes who cannot afford the fee, or provide an athletic participation fund, parents and administrators have raised concern about creating a two-tier system at a public school in which some kids have to pay and others do not. Moreover, it is awkward, at the very least, for a student to have to claim financial hardship to a coach or athletic department. Participation fees are unfair for families who cannot afford them. It could make a big difference for some kids when they decide if they want to (a) go out for a team, (b) get into trouble during the idle hours, or (c) quit school.

Moreover, the implementation of pay-to-play seems to lead to lower participation at a time when participation is rising in schools that do not charge to play sports. The implication is that playing a sport at a public high school is a privilege to be paid for, not something earned through effort. Further, there is some drop-off in participation when pay-to-play is implemented. Phil Curtin, former football coach at Oakmont Regional High School in Massachusetts, says he resigned before the 2003 season partly because of the pressures of pay to play. Oakmont was 8-3 in 2000 with 50 players. The team's record slipped to 4-7 and 3-8 in the next two seasons as the number of players dwindled to half. "I would probably still be there." if not for pay to play, Curtin says (Brady & Giler, 2004).

Further, some parents feel that because they are paying they have the right to control when their child plays in a game. There are some aggressive parents out there, and this can cause problems. Parents who pay for their children to play sometimes believe that should guarantee playing time. The Michigan High School Athletic Association puts out a primer on fees that says: "All of the conditions of being a team member apply as if the fee did not exist — and that includes playing time" (MHSAA, 2004, 37).

Pressure to Win

Most people play a sport for the thrill of having fun with others who share the same interest, right? But it's not always fun and games. Often student athletes who play competitive sports have had thoughts that go like this at one time or another: "Man, I can't believe I let the ball in the goal, and I know from the look in coach's eyes he wasn't happy."

Coakley (2003), Eitzen and Sage (2003), and Sawyer (2006) suggest there can be a great deal of pressure in high school sports applied to athletes by coaches, parents, and peers. Much of the time it comes from the feeling that a parent or coach expects you to always win. But sometimes it comes from inside, too. Some players are just really hard on themselves. And individual situations can add to the stress. Maybe there is a recruiter from the athlete's number-one college scouting on the sidelines. Whatever the cause, the pressure to win can sometimes stress the athlete to the point where the athlete just does not know how to have fun anymore (Martens, 2001; Sawyer, 2006; Seefeldt, 1998). Perhaps it could even be the reason why the athlete has not been playing as well lately.

The athletic administrator being aware of this situation should develop or seek assistance from outside consultants to develop a series of workshops focusing on how to overcome and prevent undue pressure to win. These workshops should be for athletes, coaches, and parents. The role of athletics should be to have fun and learn how to win and lose gracefully.

School Prayer

Organized prayers by coaches have been determined to be unconstitutional by the Supreme Court. The practice violates the concept of separation of church and state. The coach is an agent of the school, thus the organized prayer is determined to be school sponsored. School sponsorship of a religious message is not appropriate, because it tells members of the audience who are non-adherents that they are outsiders.

However, a student-led prayer in the locker room or on the field or court remains a legally gray area, unless a school official (i.e., the coach) has organized the prayer. It has been argued that students have a free speech right to initiate prayers. The Federal courts have ruled that student-led prayer can be just as coercive and involuntary as teacher-led prayer and therefore should be banned like teacher-led prayer in the public schools since 1962 (Sawyer, 1997). Yet, the right to private acts of devotion, even in school, is protected. Nothing in the Constitution prohibits any public school student from voluntarily praying at any time before, during, or after the school day.

In the southern states public expressions of religious faith are part of the daily routine. These Christian individuals and organizations have promoted prayer and other religious activities in the school. However, they are in direct conflict with individuals and groups (i.e., American Civil Liberties Union) who have claimed that the First Amendment to the Constitution specifically prohibits religious practices of any kind under the jurisdiction of the public schools. In 1996, a Federal Appeals court struck down a Mississippi law that allowed student-led prayer in public schools. The panel said the law suggests to the students that state wants them to pray (Sawyer, 1997).

Specialization

This is the age of specialization — and the decline of the three-sport athlete — in high school sports. It is the age of heightened intensity and competition — and increased spending by school districts and parents. Athletic directors and coaches share a consensus that today's high schoolers are more skilled than ever before. The changes have created a "professional" youth sports model designed to churn out elite athletes. That has placed added pressure on teenage athletes to train harder — and specialize earlier — if they hope to keep up.

The competition has spawned a cottage industry of instruction and training to help kids reach their goals. The athletic instruction/training industry is estimated nationally to be a $4 billion business — and growing steadily in Minnesota and many other states. It is common to see kids not only specializing in one sport; but, specializing in one position within that sport at a very young age. There are fewer and fewer three-sport athletes in high schools. Parents are much more involved. Consequently, kids are much better players. Elite club or AAU all-star teams exist in almost every sport, starting with children as young as early grade school. Opportunities for self-improvement are as limitless as the athlete's work ethic and parents' checkbook. Camps and clinics exist for goalies and quarterbacks, for soccer players and jump shooters, for wrestlers and volleyball players. Children can choose between day camps, overnight camps, instruction intensive camps, and specialized skill camps (e.g., pitching, batting, quarterback, and more).

Specialized training centers have become a staple of high school training, especially among suburban athletes whose parents have the disposable income for such extras. They offer supervised workouts by personal trainers who combine conditioning with strength, agility and speed training plus a recruiting service that attempts to link athletes with college coaches by making physical profiles available on the Internet.

Sportsmanship

The world of sports never has been perfect. Problems have ranged from spitballs to steroids, from fixed games to brawls between athletes and fans. The origins of many of these troubles are difficult to pinpoint and eliminate, but lack of sportsmanship is not among them. Who hasn't complained about a referee's call? Who hasn't heard someone holler, "Hey Coach! You're an idiot!" Who has not seen competing athletes go nose to nose, ready to start throwing punches, before being separated?

Sportsmanship might seem like an odd concept in these days of million-dollar contracts and 24-hour-a-day television replays. But on the high school and youth levels, the troubles are—or at least should be—more manageable. Young athletes are not playing for money, their coaches certainly are not doing it for the paycheck, and nothing is truly on the line except pride and tradition. Yet problems persist.

Recently, 116 boys' soccer players were ejected from Minnesota high school games. In addition, 136 players were ejected from boys' hockey games. The pressure to succeed, the pressure to win, the pressure to grab the golden ring of a college scholarship or a professional career has warped our sports world. Do theater owners allow people to scream, throw objects, and start fights at movies or concerts? Of course not. So why is it accepted at sporting events?

In quiet ways, away from the madding crowd, individuals and organizations are working toward more and better sportsmanship in almost all of the state high school associations. These associations are attempting to generally define sportsmanlike behavior as striving to succeed but committed to playing by the rules and observing ethical standards that take precedence over strategic gain when the two conflict. This view is universally admired, but fair play sometimes conflicts with the quest for victory. Here in lies the dilemma for coaches, administrators, parents, and student-athletes.

Substance Abuse

Substance abuse is not new to athletes. Evidence indicates that athletes have sought and used performance-enhancing drugs for centuries. Athletes in Greece and Rome used a variety of potions and substances, including hallucinogenic mushrooms, believed to improve physical performance. Strychnine and brandy was the potion of choice among European distance skaters in the 1700s and distance runners during the 1800s. Other drugs, including opium, alcohol, caffeine, strychnine, ethyl ether, and nitroglycerine, also were used during this period (Coakley, 2003).

High school students do abuse drugs (e.g., alcohol, caffeine, nicotine, and others) and use performance-enhancing drugs (i.e., steroids). The use pattern increases proportionately as the pressure to win accelerates. There are two basic answers to this problem. The first is to develop a sound comprehensive drug policy, and secondly reduce the amount of pressure placed upon student-athletes to win.

Drug Testing

A growing trend in high schools is to deter the use of performance-enhancing and/or recreational drugs. High schools nationwide have enacted a drug policy that includes drug testing. Drug tests today are much more sophisticated and yield much more information than whether or not the student-athlete is using drugs. This intrusion into the individual's privacy rights raises an issue for organizations wishing to tests student-athletes (Wong, 2003). A comprehensive drug policy should include drug education, prevention, rehabilitation, and testing.

The leading case in drug testing of interscholastic student-athletes is *Vernonia School District v. Action* (1995). The U.S. Supreme Court found in this case that the school's interest in deterring drug use by school children was an important state interest. The court concluded that a drug problem largely fueled by the role model effect of athletes' drug use, and of particular danger to athletes, is effectively addressed by the drug testing of athletes. Courts since this case have ruled in favor of drug-testing programs as long as they fulfill a compelling need and the reasonableness requirement, the objectives necessitating the implementation of a drug testing program will outweigh the potential invasion of privacy of the student-athletes. Finally, the *Vernonia* case clearly stated that athletes can be compelled to produce a urine sample.

Drug testing of high school students exploded after the Supreme Court ruled upon the *Vernonia* case. One of the main concerns about drug policies is the failure to provide sufficient due process to the student-athlete who tested positive. The key components of a sound drug policy include a clear drug-testing procedure, a clear definition of probable cause or reasonable suspicion, confidentiality, due process, and sanctions to be imposed.

Drug Prevention

Many state associations (e.g., Illinois, Indiana, Michigan, New York, Ohio, Pennsylvania, and others) and high schools nationwide have developed and implemented drug prevention programs for athletes. These programs have focused on alcohol, nicotine, recreational drugs, and performance-enhancing substances.

The NFHS encourages state associations to be proactive regarding drug prevention. The philosophy statement of the NFHS states: "... students should be encouraged and supported in their efforts to develop and maintain a lifestyle free from tobacco, alcohol, and other drugs." Further, NFHS members associations "... recognize the use of these substances as a significant health problem for students, resulting in negative effects on behavior, learning, and the total development of each individual" (http//:www.nfhs.org).

Athletic administrators should be the leaders in developing and implementing a drug prevention program for their athletes. The resolution of this problem certainly affects the health and safety of the athletes. It also provides the administrator and coaches an opportunity to make a difference in the lives of the athletes by enabling them to make wise behavioral choices relative to drugs.

Summary

Interscholastic sports have been intertwined in public education for over 100 years. Nearly every secondary school is engaged in some interschool sports competition. Many people feel that participation in sport has important educational benefits. The student-athlete benefits from adult supervision, by self-confidence enhancement, by learning to play by the rules, by working together with teammates toward a common goal, by being task and achievement oriented, by working hard to stay academically eligible, and by learning to win and lose.

There is a contrary view that is critical of sport as now constituted within the schools. The critics assert that sport detracts from educational goals. These same critics assert that although athletic participation may lead some individuals to be good sports, it may lead others to be bad sports. Although some play be the rules, others circumvent them. Most athletic programs have integrity, but there is hypocrisy in others.

There are a number of critical issues facing interscholastic sports. They include, but are not limited to: amateurism, budget shortfalls, cheating, deviance and violence, equity, pressure to win, sport specialization, and substance abuse. The future of interscholastic sports will depend upon how schools deal with excessive pressure to win.

References

Brady, E., & Giler, R. (2004). To play sports, many U.S. students must pay. http//:www.usatoday.com/sports/prep/2004-07-29-pay-to-play_Xhtm. (2006).

Brown, J. (2002). Will pay-to-play ruin school sports? http://www.csmonitor.com/2002/0920/p12s01-alsp.html. (2006).

Coakley, J.J. (2003). *Sport in society: Issues and controversies.* (8th ed). Boston: McGraw-Hill.

Eitzen, D.D., & Sage, G.H. (2003). *Sociology of North American sport.* (7th ed.). Boston: McGraw-Hill.

Foster, S.B. (2003). Religious issues. In D.J. Cotton, & J.T. Wolohan (Eds.). *Sport law for sport managers* (3rd ed.), (pp. 524-534). Dubuque, IA: Kendall-Hunt.

Keller, I.A., & Forsythe, C.E. (1984). *Administration of high school athletics.* (7th ed.). Englewood Cliffs, NJ: Prentice Hall.

Martens, R. (2001) *Successful coaching.* (3rd ed.). Champaign, IL: Human Kinetics.

Michigan High School Athletic Association (2004). *Association Bylaws.* http://www.mhsaa.org. (2006).

Ness, R.G. (2003). Eligibility issues. In D.J. Cotton, & J.T. Wolohan (Eds.), *Sport law for sport managers (3rd ed.),* (pp. 524-534). Dubuque, IA: Kendall-Hunt.

Sawyer, T.H. (1994). Religious issues. In D.J. Cotton, & T.J. Wilde (Eds.) *Sport law for sport managers* (pp. 349-361). Dubuque, IA: Kendall-Hunt.

Sawyer, T.H. (2006) *Indiana LANSE.* (3rd ed.). Terre Haute, IN: Press-Time Graphics.

Seefeldt, V. (Ed.). (1998). *Michigan PACE.* Indianapolis, IN: Benchmark Press.

Title IX, Education Amendments (1972), Civil Rights Act. (1964).

Wong, G.M. (2002). *Essentials of sports law.* (3rd ed.). Westport, CT: Praeger.

NOTES

CHAPTER 9

Recreational Sport

Sport within the United States reflects a multifaceted socioeconomic system. Further, it represents a tremendous diversity in participation throughout the lifecycle. Traditionally, recreational sport has been described in a variety of ways including extramural sport, intramural sport, recreational programming, physical recreation, physical activity, and fitness programming. Recreational sport is a broad programming foundation for social, cultural, sport, and special event opportunities in a recreational setting. There are a number of settings that support recreational sport opportunities in the United States (See Chart 9.1).

Social programming in recreational sport fosters congenial, non-competitive participation in a common interest. It emphasizes human reaction and often takes the form of banquets, parties, dances, dining, and other social activities as components of the sport experience, whereas cultural programming in recreational sport provides opportunities for individuality, creativity, and self-expression such as art, dance, drama, literary, and music activities.

Sport programming in recreational sport provides opportunities for participants and spectators to enjoy sport in one of four levels—professional, athletic, recreational, and educational. Professional sport in this environment includes marketing sport events with an emphasis on entertainment and a financial remuneration to highly skilled participants. Athletic sport provides high levels of competition for those participants who excel in a specific sport (i.e., travel teams in community youth programs that select only the top players to participate on the teams) while recreational sport includes programming sport activities for fitness and fun. Finally, educational sport includes teaching sport skills, strategies, and knowledge to prepare students through academic courses. The emphasis is on knowledge and performance as measured against a standard for credit through a formally prescribed course.

This chapter has been designed to describe the role of recreational sport in America. Further, the discussion will focus on the various structures of recreational sport organizations, their roles and functions, financing of programs, and major issues facing these organizations.

Recreational Sport Settings

1. City or municipal
2. Educational (e.g., public or private school intramural programs, campus recreational sport programs)
3. Military (e.g., Moral, Welfare, and Recreation (MWR) services in the military)
4. Not-for-profit Business and Quasi-Public Organizations (e.g., Boys and Girls Clubs, YMCAs, YWCAs, YMHAs, YWHAs, etc.)
5. Commercial Recreation Businesses (i.e., commercial recreation entrepreneurs have established sole proprietorships, partnerships, and corporations in specific sport areas including boating, bowling, dance, fishing, gymnastics, handball, martial arts, racquetball, tennis, etc.)
6. Correctional Recreation Services (i.e., state and federal correctional facilities)
7. Private Clubs (e.g., country club offering golf, swimming, and tennis or an Elks club offering bowling, golf, swimming, and tennis)
8. Corporations (i.e., most corporations with over 500 employees has an Employee Services Unit within the human resources department offering employee recreation opportunities and much more to promote employee health, morale, and productivity)
9. Public Parks and Forests (i.e., government lands and facilities providing facilities for boating, camping, hiking, skiing, swimming, and much more)
10. Commercial Vacations and Attractions (i.e., lodging facilities offering extensive sport-theme special events and regular sport scheduling, and attractions such as theme parks offering aquatics, sport leagues, clinics, tournaments, etc.)
11. Churches

Chart 9.1
Recreational Sport Settings in the United States

Learning Objectives

Upon completion of this chapter, the reader should be able to:
- Discuss the scope and value of recreational sport in America.
- Describe the various professional associations that support recreational sport in America.
- Discuss how recreational sport are funded in America.
- Outline the various challenges that recreational sport administrators face in America.

Governance

Recreational sport is governed differently by each enterprise (see Chart 9.1) that supports recreational sport. In the ensuing section, a general outline will be provided regarding the governance of the public and private enterprises involved in recreational sport.

Organizational Structure

The enterprises that coordinate the recreational sport in each setting have different structures. These structures will be discussed below:

The *city* or *municipal* and *county* governmental structures provide funds, facilities, and leadership for recreational sport programming. These structures are tax-based. However, the current economic climate has required these government structures to assess fees to supplement declining tax revenues. The recreational sport programs offered in this setting are available to all residents. Most often, there is a director of recreational sport reporting to a superintendent of parks and recreation for the city or county. However, the actual titles may differ by community or setting.

The *educational* setting includes public schools, private schools, and institutions of higher education. Each educational enterprise has goals that focus on student academic development. These governmental structures provide funds, facilities, and leadership for recreational sport programming. These structures are tax-based except for private schools and colleges and universities that recover the cost through tuition. Like the city, county, and municipal governments, the current economic climate has required these government structures to assess fees to supplement declining tax revenues as well. The recreational sport programs offered in this setting are available to all students. Often in public and private schools, the administration of recreational sport programs becomes the responsibility of the department of physical education and sometimes the athletic director. While in higher education, the responsibility for recreational sport has shifted from the department of physical education or athletics to the vice president for student services. In most cases, there is a director of recreational sport or intramurals.

Recreational sport in the United States military is the responsibility of *Morale, Welfare, and Recreation* (MWR) *Services.* Each of the four branches of the military and the coast guard are responsible for the MWR services. These services are funded by taxes and self-generated funds. MWR services provide facilities and leadership for recreational sport programming. The recreational sport programs offered in this setting are available to all members of the Armed Forces, their families, and retirees. There is a director of MWR services, usually a civilian, on each military installation and within each branch of the service, there

is a distinct overall organizational chart dividing the MWR into divisions for many reasons as well as competition and championship series offered in each sport.

Each state and federal government has a department focused on **corrections.** The organizational structure for each state and the federal correctional system are slightly different. These governmental structures provide funds, facilities, and leadership for recreational sport programming. These structures are tax-based. The recreational sport programs offered in this setting are available to all inmates. Most often there is a director of recreation reporting to an assistant warden or superintendent in charge of programming.

Private clubs provide a variety of recreational sport opportunities for their membership. Private clubs may limit their membership based on facility capacity, socio-economic status, ethnicity, or religious beliefs. Examples of private clubs include golf clubs (country clubs), racquet and tennis clubs, civic or social clubs (e.g., Elks Club), and aquatic or swimming clubs. The sport activities and facilities are the primary attraction and, through dues and supplementary fees, yield much of the income necessary for maintaining the operations and leadership. Most often, there is golf or tennis professionals or head swimming coaches in charge of the sport activity who report to a club executive director or president and a board of directors.

Nonprofit businesses and quasi-public organizations provide for community needs, not provided by a government entity, such as youth development and youth recreational sport programming. These organizations include, but are not limited to: Boys' and Girls' Club, YMCAs, YWCAs, YMHAs, YWHAs, Boys Scouts, Girls Scouts, and other similar organizations. These organizations are governed by a national organization. Local entities provide funds, facilities, and leadership for recreational sport programming. These structures are not taxed-based. The recreational sport programs offered in this setting are available to all members and non-members who pay higher fees. There generally is an executive director who reports to a board of directors. The executive director has a recreational sport director who oversees recreational sport programming.

Commercial recreation businesses have grown rapidly because of the market demand for sport-specific enterprises and the declining tax-based support for public recreational sport programs. Many commercial recreation entrepreneurs have established sole proprietorships, partnerships, and corporations in specific sport areas, including boating, bowling, dance, fishing, gymnastics, handball, martial arts, racquetball, tennis, etc.. These commercial structures are in business to make a profit. The membership fees and other financial tools (i.e., advertisement, concessions, retail sales, and sponsorships) provide the funding, facilities, and leadership for the recreational sport programming. These structures are not taxed based. The recreational sport programs offered in this setting are available to paying customers. There generally is an owner or executive director. The executive director normally reports to a board of directors or owner.

Corporations for over 70 years have provided employee recreational sport opportunities. It has transitioned from what was once known as industrial recreation to a broader umbrella term called employee services. Under the new umbrella, employee services include the employee store, community services, convenience services, dependent care, recreation programs, recognition programs, special events, travel services, voluntary benefits, and wellness (fitness). Employee recreational sport programs exist in a majority of corporations with 500 or more employees. Most programs emphasize fitness and extensive recreational sport programs

offered on-site and through cooperation with community agencies. The corporation provides funds, facilities, and leadership for recreational sport programming. These structures are not tax-based. However, the current economic climate has required some of these structures to assess fees to supplement the corporate allocations. The recreational sport programs offered in this setting are available to all employees, their families, and retirees. Most often, there is a director of employee services and an associate director with responsibilities for recreational sport programming. The director generally reports to the chief administrator in charge of human resources.

Public lands and forests owned by local, regional, state, and federal governments offer sport involvement opportunities in both informal and structured formats. The government provides extensive facilities to accommodate boating, camping, hiking, skiing, swimming, and other sport interests developed by the agency or through a commercial contractor. These governmental structures provide funds, facilities, and leadership for recreational sport programming. As tax-based structures, they are required to assess fees to supplement declining tax revenues. The recreational sport programs offered in this setting are available to all residents. Generally, there is a park or forest superintendent who oversees assistants in charge of recreational sport programming. The superintendent reports to a state agency or governor or county commissioners or mayor and/or park board or city manager.

Vacations and *attractions* focusing on recreational sport have become a great economic boom for the tourist and travel industry. A variety of accommodations including hotels, motels, resorts, and cruise ships offer extensive sport-theme special events and regular sport scheduling (e.g., Walt Disney World, Disney Cruise Line). Attractions such as theme parks (e.g., Disney World, Disney Land, MGM Studios,

Sea World, Busch Gardens, and others) offer many sport-oriented experiences, either on-site or nearby. The organizations in these settings provide funds, facilities, and leadership for recreational sport programming. These structures are not tax-based. The recreational sport programs offered in this setting are available to all customers. The director of recreational sport reports to the park executive director who reports to a chief executive officer.

Churches of all denominations are developing recreational sport programs and build new recreational sport complexes within new churches or adjacent old churches. This new movement is focusing on the younger generations rather than on the baby boomers. The church provides funds, facilities, and leadership for recreational sport programming. These structures are not tax-based. However, the current economic climate has required the churches to assess fees to supplement other revenues. The recreational sport programs offered in this setting are available to all members and their families. Most often, there is an assistant minister or lay director for recreational sport who report directly to the minister.

Function

The function of all of these entities within each setting (see Chart 9.1) is to provide the highest quality program within the setting. The programs and the quality of their application are a result of the commitment and philosophy of the setting. The service to be provided by each entity encompasses sport delivery through a combination of activities, facilities, and personnel (paid or volunteer) with participant interest and satisfaction foremost in mind.

There are two key reasons that these organizations provide recreational sport services. The first is to encourage participation and second is to design and deliver services for profit (Mull, Bayless, Ross, & Jamieson, 1997). Further, the two approaches are not mutually exclusive. Many settings are interested in providing quality service to sustain and expand participant involvement and maximizing enjoyment and profit.

Authority

The various organizations that provide recreational sport have authority established by legislation (e.g., state or federal), bylaws, the organization's constitution, or articles of incorporation. For example, city/municipal, state, or federal government entities report to city councils, county councils, or state or federal agencies. For-profit and not-for-profit organizations report to boards of directors, regents, or trustees. Table 9.1 outlines the various ways authority is established in the various organizations providing recreational sport programs.

Funding

Recreational sport program revenue sources vary according to political priorities, participant needs and interests, and organization philosophy. Recent changes in the economy have stimulated discovery on new non-traditional revenue sources to maintain and expand current levels of programming including sale of advertising, licensed merchandise, and sponsorships. The traditional forms of revenue include bonds, concessions, fund-raising, gifts and donations, grants (i.e., government or private), leases, taxes, United Way funding, and user fees. Table 9.2 describes the common revenue sources for the various organizations providing recreational sport programs.

National Governing Bodies

Recreational sport programs have a variety of national professional governing bodies. These bodies include the American Association for Physical Activity and Recreation (AAPAR), American Corrections Association (ACA), American Logistics

Table 9.1
Authority for Recreational Sport Entities in Various Settings

Recreational Sport Setting	Authority
City/Municipal	Legislation, City Council + Park and/or Recreation Board
Educational Entities	School Board, Board of Trustees
Military	Air Force, Army, Marines, Navy, Coast Guard, Department of Defense, Legislation
Correctional	State Departments of Corrections, Federal Bureau of Prisons
Private Clubs	Bylaws, Constitution, Board of Directors, Articles of Incorporation
Nonprofit Businesses	Bylaws, Constitution, Board of Directors, Articles of Incorporation
Commercial Businesses	Bylaws, Constitution, Board of Directors, Articles of Incorporation, Stock Holders
Corporations	Bylaws, Constitution, Board of Directors, Articles of Incorporation
Public Lands and Forests	Legislation (i.e., state or federal)
Vacations and Attractions	Bylaws, Constitution, Board of Directors, Articles of Incorporation, Stock Holders
Churches	Bylaws, Constitution, Board of Directors, Articles of Incorporation

Association (ALA), Employee Services Management Association (ESM), National Association for Sport and Physical Education (NASPE), National Correctional Recreation Association (NCRA), National Intramural-Recreational Sport Association (NIRSA), National Recreation and Park Association (NRPA), and the International Health, Racquet, and Sportsclub Association (IHRSA). Each of these associations provides its members with research, teaching, presenting, continuing education, and publishing opportunities as well as promoting quality recreational sport programs.

American Association for Physical Activity and Recreation (AAPAR).

AAPAR was founded in January 2006. It was a merger of the American Association for Active Lifestyles and Fitness (AAALF) and the American Association for Leisure and Recreation (AALR). AAPAR is one of five member-based associations within the American Alliance for Health, Physical Education, Recreation, and Dance (AAHPERD). It is composed of 12 national councils or professional interest areas.

There are 10 of the 12 councils that impact the area of recreational sport including the Council for Adventure and Outdoor Education/Recreation, Aquatics Council, Fitness and Wellness Council, Council for Lifelong Recreational sport, Adapted Physical Activity Council, Council on Aging and Adult Development, Children, Youth, and Families Council, Professional Recreation Council, Safety and Risk Management Council, and the Council on Facilities and Equipment.

AAPAR is a member-based association. Its mission is "dedicated to enhancing quality of life by promoting creative and ac-

Table 9.2
Funding for Recreational Sport Entities in Various Settings

Recreational Sport Setting	Funding Source(s)
City/Municipal	Taxes, User Fees, Retail Sales, Concessions, Sponsorships, Grants, Bonds, Leases
Educational Entities	Taxes, User Fees, Retail Sales, Concessions, Sponsorships, Grants, Bonds
Military	Taxes, User Fees, Retail Sales, Concessions, Sponsorships
Correctional	Taxes
Private Clubs	User Fees, Retail Sales, Concessions
Nonprofit Businesses	User Fees, Retail Sales, Concessions, Sponsorships, Gifts and Donations, United Way, Special Events, Leases
Commercial Businesses	User Fees, Retail Sales, Concessions
Corporations	User Fees, Retail Sales, Concessions
Public Lands and Forests	Taxes, User Fees, Retail Sales, Concessions, Sponsorships
Vacations and Attractions	User Fees, Retail Sales, Concessions
Churches	User Fees, Gifts and Donations, Grants

tive lifestyles through meaningful physical activity, recreation, and fitness experiences across the lifespan with particular focus on community-based programs" (http://www.aahperd.org/aapar).

The association's revenues include membership dues, services fees, certification fees, and sale of publications and licensed products. Like most service organizations, it receives donations, seeks grants to provide services, organizes fundraising events, and negotiates sponsorships. It is a not-for-profit, tax-exempted 501 (c)3 professional association headquartered in Reston, VA. AAPAR has over 8,000 members.

American Corrections Association (ACA)

For more than 125 years, the American Correctional Association has championed the cause of corrections and correctional effectiveness. Founded in 1870 as the National Prison Association, ACA is the oldest not-for-profit, tax-exempted association developed specifically for practitioners in the correctional profession. During the first organizational meeting in Cincinnati, Ohio, the assembly elected then-Ohio governor and future president Rutherford B. Hayes as the first president of the Association (http://www.aca.org).

The Declaration of Principles developed at the first meeting in 1870 became the guidelines for corrections in the United States and Europe. At the ACA centennial meeting in 1970, a revised act of Principles, reflecting advances in theory and practice, was adopted by the Association. At the 1954 Congress of Correction in Philadelphia, Pennsylvania, the name of the American Prison Association was changed to the American Correctional Association, reflecting the expanding philosophy of corrections and its increasingly important role within the community and society as a whole. Today, the ACA has more than 20,000 active members (http://www.aca.org).

American Logistics Association (ALA)

The *American Logistics Association* (ALA) is a voluntary, nonprofit organization of manufacturers, manufacturers' representatives, brokers, distributors, publishers, and other companies that sell or provide products and services to the military resale systems and MWR/Services. At ALA, the term "military resale systems" is used as a broad term that includes all military exchanges and commissaries, Department of State stores, Veterans Canteen Services, as well as all of the armed forces' Morale, Welfare, and Recreation (MWR) activities that involve a product or service. A global organization, ALA is represented by members in countries around the world. ALA members are diverse, with companies of all sizes in a wide variety of industries, but all members have one commonality: *Members are advocates for military total quality of life* (http://www.ala-national.org).

ALA is governed by a set of bylaws and a code of ethics, which can only be modified by a majority vote of the voting members of the association. The governing body of the association is the board of directors, which is comprised of 13 individuals, all members of ALA. Of the 13 board members, nine are elected by the membership; one is appointed by the board; one is the immediate past chairman; and two are elected by the chapter presidents. Elections are held annually in October. In addition to the Board, ALA has three councils, chapter presidents, and various committees. The Commissary Council, Exchange Council, and MWR/Services Council are each chaired by at least one board member. Any member of the Association may volunteer to participate on one of these councils, which meet four to six times annually to discuss issues and problems within the industry and propose solutions that will benefit all (http://www.ala-national.org).

Employee Services Management Association (ESM)

The Employee Services Management Association (ESM), initially formed as the National Industrial Recreation Association (NIRA), later changed its name to the National Employee's Services and Recreation Association (NESRA), has as its mission to "enhance the profession by expanding the knowledge of employee services through innovative programs and resources" (http://www.esmassn.org). It is a membership based nonprofit, tax exempted professional association headquartered in Oak Brook, Illinois with over 4,000 members.

The association has revenue streams that include membership dues for professionals and corporations, certification fees, service fees, conference fees, and sales of licensed products and publications. It also receives advertising revenues, donations, seeks grants for the provision of services and development of products, and negotiates sponsorships. ESM association is governed by a set of bylaws and a code of ethics, which can only be modified by a majority vote of the voting members of the association. The governing body of the association is the board of directors, which is comprised of 13 individuals, all members of ESM Association. The ESM is divided into five regions including Northeast, Midwest, Southeast, Southwest, and Western. There are active state chapters in Arizona, California, Connecticut, Florida, Illinois, Indiana, Michigan, Nevada, New York, North Carolina, Pennsylvania, Texas, and Washington (http://www.esmassn.org).

The ESM promotes ten components of a well-rounded employee services program. The ten components include employee stores, community services, convenience services, dependent care, recreation programs, recognition programs, special events, travel services, voluntary events, and wellness (http://www.esmassn.org).

International Health, Racquet, and Sportsclub Association (IHRSA)

The International Health, Racquet, and Sportsclub Association (IHRSA) is a trade association serving the health and fitness club industry. IHRSA's mission is to grow, protect, and promote the health and fitness industry, and to provide its members with benefits that will help them be more successful. IHRSA members are high-quality, for-profit businesses operating in the health, racquet and sportsclub industry. IHRSA members consist of:

- Club Members: 6,500 in over 67 countries
- Associate Members: 604 Industry Suppliers

IHRSA's initiative consists of a solution to the growing public health crisis of obesity and overweight people. IHRSA proudly represents and supports this goal through initiatives that help promote healthy, active lifestyles, such as Get Active America!, 120 Million by 2010, and its newest initiative: 'I Lost It at the Club' (http://www.ihrsa.org). IHRSA is a primary defender and promoter of the health club industry in Washington, D.C. and in state capitals across the country. IHRSA's Public Policy agenda is both defensive and offensive. It seeks to prevent the government from doing things that are harmful to your business, and to strengthen initiatives that will help grow your business.

National Association for Sport and Physical Education (NASPE)

NASPE is the preeminent national authority on physical education and a recognized leader in sport and physical activity. NASPE is a nonprofit, tax-exempted professional membership association that sets the standard for practice in physical education and sport. Its 17,000 members include K-12 physical education teachers, coaches, athletic directors, athletic trainers, sport management professionals, researchers, and college/university faculty who prepare physical activity professionals. It is the largest of the five national associations that make up the American Alliance for Health, Physical Education, Recreation and Dance (AAHPERD). NASPE envisions a society in which all individuals are physically educated and participate in lifelong physical activity. Further, the mission of NASPE is to enhance knowledge, improve professional practice, and increase support for high-quality physical education, sport, and physical activity programs through research, development of standards, and dissemination of information.

National Intramural-Recreational Sport Association (NIRSA)

NIRSA was founded in 1950 as the National Intramural Association. In 1975, the name was changed to the National Intramural-Recreational Sport Association. NIRSA is dedicated to providing its members with research, teaching, presenting, and publishing opportunities and promoting quality recreational sport programs on college and university campuses. It is a nonprofit, tax-exempted professional association located in Corvallis, Oregon. NIRSA has nearly 4,000 members.

The mission of NIRSA "is to provide for the education and development of professional and student members and to foster quality recreational programs, facilities, and services for diverse populations" (http//:www.nirsa.org, 2002).

NIRSA is a membership organization. Membership is a major source of funding. The association also receives donations and grants. Further, the association has a foundation mandated to support the mission of NIRSA. Finally, NIRSA has a third legal entity, a taxable, business-oriented component, which receives revenues from advertising, sponsorship, sales of licensed products, and sport club championships.

National Recreation and Park Association (NRPA)

The NRPA's mission is "to advance parks, recreation, and environmental conservation efforts that enhance the quality of life for all people" (http://www.nrpa.org). It provides leadership through its 70 member Board of Trustees comprising citizens and professionals who represent the diverse areas and disciplines within the parks and recreation industry. The NRPA is comprised of 10 individual branches (e.g., Armed Forces Recreation Society [AFRS] and American Park and Recreation Society [APRS]) and sections representing everything from aquatics to natural resources to recreational sport to recreation therapy. The association is divided into eight regions representing the 52 states affiliates. The NRPA has approximately 22,000 members. It is a non-profit, tax-exempted, 501(c)3 professional association located 36 miles west of Washington, D.C. between Dulles International Airport and Leesburg, Virginia.

The NRPA has a diverse revenue stream including membership dues, accreditation fees, certification fees, consulting and service fees, and sales of licensed products and publications. Further, the NRPA receives advertising revenue, donations, seeks grants for the development of services and products, and sponsorships.

Finally, the NRPA is an advocate for recreation and park programming nationwide, develops and monitors national accreditation and certification programs, organizes national forums and conferences for recreation and park professionals annually, facilitates and encourages the development of publications and supports research efforts in a wide array of endeavors, and works diligently to develop a variety of programs and partnerships.

Recreational Sport Issues

There are a number of issues that face recreational sport industry and managers that will be discussed below including accessibility, funding, competition for limited facilities in some settings and within communities, event management, facility development and financing, and injury and risk management.

Accessibility

Since 1990, the public sector has been diligently working to make recreational sport facilities and programs accessible to the persons with disabilities. The Americans with Disabilities Act (1990) has as its purpose "to provide a clear and comprehensive national mandate for the elimination of discrimination against individuals with disabilities." ADA focuses on eradicating barriers, by requiring public entities to consider whether reasonable accommodations can be made to remove any barrier created by a person's disability (Wong, 2002). The law does not clearly define "reasonable accommodation." There in lies the major problem generating numerous law suits against public entities. These accommodations apply to not only facilities but also programmatic barriers for the disabled. For example, recreational sport swimming programs offered in a local municipal aquatic facility that is not handicapped accessible. The city or municipality does not have the necessary funding to make the aquatic facility handicapped accessible for the small number of handicapped children wishing to participate in the swimming program. The city or municipality claims that it is not a "reasonable accommodation" to retrofit the aquatic facility for so few children.

Title III (ADA, 1990) provides that "no individual shall be discriminated against on the basis of disability in the full and equal enjoyment of the goods, services, facilities, privileges, programs, advantages, or accommodations of any place of public accommodation by any person who owns, leases, or operates a place of public accommodations" (ADA, 1990, U.S.C. Section 12182). According to the ADA, the following private entities are considered public accommodations: motion picture houses, theaters, concert halls, stadiums, other places of exhibition or entertainment, camps, gymnasiums, health spas, bowling alleys, golf courses, or other places of exercise or recreation. Based on the "public accommodation" clause, most private/commercial recreational sport programs are impacted by ADA. Therefore, the private/commercial recreational sport organizations must make their facilities and programs handicapped accessible. The only exception to this law is a truly private organization that is only open to a very select group of people. These groups have a Constitutional Right to Freedom of Association. However, each year that goes by, fewer and fewer of these private clubs are in existence.

The recreational sport manager must be aware of the Americans with Disabilities Act and its impact on recreation sports facilities and programming. The requirements are the same for both the public and private sector in regard to recreational sport. Therefore, when developing either facilities or programs, the recreational sport manager must ensure that accessibility is guaranteed to disabled persons.

Funding

Since the early 90s, tax revenues have either decreased or stayed status quo for many taxing jurisdictions within states, at the state level, and the federal level. Tragically when tax dollars become tight, one of the first services to be reduced are parks and recreation programs. This includes recreational sport programs. The taxes that generate the most funds are property, income, sales, and special assessments. The general public is generally not in favor of having

taxes increased or new special assessments added (e.g., Proposition 13 in California and the Palesky proposal in Maine).

This reduction in tax support for recreational sport programs has resulted in a shift of many programs to the private sector. The public sector has realized that depending on tax revenues is a bad fiscal policy. Public programs have begun assessing user fees, which at the same time has placed a major financial burden on low-income and single-parent families with multiple children. The user fee policy is slowly moving the recreational programs out of reach of these citizens.

Many public programs have instituted other financial strategies to keep from assessing user fees or keeping them as low as possible. These strategies include, but are not limited to: seeking gifts and donations to provide recreational sport scholarships for the financially disadvantaged, leasing facilities to private groups, generating commercial sponsorships to underwrite the cost of personnel, equipment, facilities, or programs, contracting with outside contractors to provide concessions for recreational sport programs, increasing other fund-raising activities, and seeking community block grants from the federal government.

College and university funding for campus recreation programs is a mixture of student fees and tuition revenue. As the cost of higher education continues to increase nationwide in both public and private education, the amount of dollars available for campus recreation programs from the general fund continues to decline. The trend is for these programs to become self-supporting as much as possible. This means that student fees continue to increase to cover the costs of facility construction and operations. Many programs have expanded offerings including providing concessions, in-house advertising, merchandise sales through proshops, opening facilities to faculty and students and their families for a fee; offering, for a fee, numerous non-credit instructional courses such as health and fitness and adventure courses, equipment rentals, and more. The future ensures that these programs on college and university campuses will eventually become profit centers as well as recreational sport centers for the campus. They have become very good recruiting tools, and many studies suggest that they also enhance retention efforts as well. Finally, on a number of private campuses, the recreational sport programs have become auxiliary enterprises similar to the operation of bookstores, dining facilities, and residence halls.

Funding will continue to be a major concern for public recreational sport programs offered by cities/municipalities, state agencies, federal agencies, and colleges and universities. The private programs will continue to grow and broaden their revenue streams as they grow. Therefore, recreational sport managers will need to be creative in developing alternate revenue streams beyond tax revenue in order to continue to provide recreational sport programs for all parties within these programs.

Competition for Limited Facilities

Competition for recreational sport facilities has been a common problem on college and university campuses that do not have separate facilities devoted to recreational sport programs. The trend for the past 20 years has been to develop separate recreational sport facilities. For example, for decades the recreational sport program has shared with academics and athletics the meager physical activity facilities at Indiana State University. During the 2005-06 academic year, the students approved a student fee of $125 per semester for a new recreational sport facility. The new facility will open during the 2007-08 academic year. This facility will be devoted to recreational sport as its number-one priority. Since it will be an auxiliary enterprise, academics

and athletics can request to rent space when available for its programs. Further, over the past few years, the Department of Recreational sport has been granted space for the following outdoor facilities to be devoted to recreational sport: flag football, soccer, and softball fields.

It is important for the recreational sport manager on a campus that does not have separate facilities to work closely with the academic and athletic programs in order to carve out time for shared use of the limited facilities on campus. Further, the manager needs to cooperate and collaborate with the academic and athletic administration to develop use policies and procedures such as procedures for priority status, for bumping programs, scheduling, outsider use, equipment use, and safety/risk management issues. Finally, the manager needs to work closely with the student body and central administration to develop plans for a standalone recreational sport center financed through students fees, faculty and staff fees, outsider fees, facility and equipment rental fees, sale of licensed merchandise, concession sales, fees for non-credit fitness and wellness classes, bond referendums, and sponsorships and advertisements.

Community recreational sport programs are always challenged, particularly during the winter months, with limited facilities. Many youth sport programs are organized and operated by not-for-profit organizations (e.g., Boys and Girls Clubs, YMCAs, YWCAs, elementary, middle, and high schools, and municipal government facilities) but the responsibility for community adult programs often falls on the shoulders of the department of parks and recreation or departments of recreation. Basketball, ice hockey, soccer, swimming, and flag football all cause great challenges for these entities. Most city/municipal recreation programs do not own indoor basketball facilities and rely heavily upon the local school buildings after hours. Outdoor facilities are also crunched by similar activities using the same facilities such as field hockey, lacrosse, and soccer. This is a challenge in many schools because of the need to provide space for after-school programming sponsored by the school. Therefore, the same cooperation and collaboration mentioned above with the college and university programs needs to be exhibited at this level as well for the scarce facilities.

Facility Development and Financing: The greatest growth in recreational sport program facilities is within the private or commercial sector. This has been stimulated by the marked increase in private/commercial recreational sport programs. Gifts and donations, merchandise sales, commercial sponsorships, and user fees support these programs and facilities.

The facilities within the public sector, except colleges and universities, have not kept pace with the recreational sport programs needs. The maintenance funding for the current facilities found in the public sector has been drastically reduced and in a number of cases eliminated entirely due to a reduction in tax revenues. This is true at both the state and federal levels.

Since the mid-eighties, there has been a steady growth in the development of stand-alone campus recreation facilities. The initial growth influenced private college campus administrators as a new means of recruiting and retaining students. This effort met with great success for the private colleges. This was followed by similar growth on the public campuses in the mid-nineties. This growth has not been only on four-year campuses. Most two-year campuses either have built or are building recreational sport facilities as well. Most of these facilities have been built with the aide of mandatory student fees. The students through a general referendum have approved these fees, in most cases. Further, the fees generally cover the cost of the bond issue or mortgage and operations of the facilities.

The major challenges for facility development are found in the public sector. Recreational sport facilities are not a high priority for cities/municipalities, state, or federal agencies. Taxpayers are not willing to pay for new or renewed recreational sport facilities presently. These facilities need to be maintained and expanded but this can only be done through alternate sources of funding. The public recreational sport manager will need to be very creative in finding the financial resources for facility development in the future. The financial plan for these upgrades and new facilities will need to be a combination of taxes (e.g., hotel/motel (bed tax), restaurant, sales tax, etc.), private donation, federal grant dollars, corporate donations (e.g., public parks and recreation facilities adjoining corporate facilities with an agreement for shared usage), shared usage with public schools both sharing the costs of the facilities, user fees, rental fees, concession sales, licensed merchandise sales, and planned giving.

Event Management

Event management, whether it is a sport tournament, road race, triathlon, or diving, gymnastics, or swimming meet, requires a great deal of planning and preparation. These events may be regularly scheduled events or special events that happen only occasionally. To satisfy the expectations of all consumers, recreational sport directors must ensure that policies and procedures regarding event management exist (e.g., alcohol control, crowd control, emergency medical procedures, risk management, security, scheduling, supervision, and many more). The policies and procedures that should be in place include decision making, financial requirements (e.g., fees, other revenue streams, expenditures, etc.), minimum staffing needs, paid and volunteer (e.g., emergency medical personnel, officials, supervisors, etc.), expectation of personnel, equipment requirements, facilities and space needs, risk management, emergency management, crowd control, media relations, use of logos, marketing and sponsorships, sale of licensed products, physical setup and tear down, and problem solving.

Injury and Risk Management

Recreational sport programs have thousands of participants involved in many different activities, all of which can cause personal injury to the participants. Sport injuries are very common. America, like no other country in the world, encourages its population when injured to sue the other party or parties to cover the cost of the injury. There are literally thousands of civil suits each year against recreational sport facilities and the personnel who operate these facilities. Most of the suits are settled out of court at great expense to recreational sport entities and the insurance industry. Therefore, recreational sport managers should attempt to minimize the possibility of being injured while participating in or watching a recreational sport event by requiring participants to wear protective equipment, reading and signing waiver or release to participate forms, ensuring that participants are taught proper techniques by trained and certified coaches or instructors, strictly enforcing rules, ensuring that all facilities are safe, providing safe equipment, and providing the necessary warnings so the participate can legally assume a risk.

The recreational sport director, with a risk-management committee, should develop a risk-management plan that is composed of segments related to emergency management, crowd control, alcohol management, security, and disaster management. Further, the director should ensure that accurate and detailed records are kept and maintained regarding all incidence and injuries. Medical information should be gathered and maintained on all participants as well as physician releases to participate. Finally, the director must ensure proper supervision of all areas and restrict access to unsupervised areas.

Summary

Sport within the United States reflects a multifaceted socioeconomic system. Further, it represents a tremendous diversity in participation throughout the lifecycle. Traditionally, recreational sport has been described in a variety of ways, including extramural sport, intramural sport, recreational programming, physical recreation, physical activity, and fitness programming. Recreational sport are a broad programming foundation for social, cultural, sport, and special event opportunities in a recreational setting. There are a number of settings that support recreational sport opportunities in the United States. Further, there are a number of issues that face recreational sport managers that will be discussed below, including accessibility, funding, competition for limited facilities on college and university campuses and within communities, event management, facility development and financing, and injury and risk management.

References

American Association for Physical Activity and Recreation. (2006). http://www.aahperd.org/aapar. (2006).

American Corrections Association. http://www.aca.org. (2006).

American with Disabilities Act. (1990). 42 U.S.C. Section 12101 et seq.

American Logistics Association. MWR Services. http://www.ala-national.org/mwr. (2006).

Employee Services Management Association. http://www.esmassn.org. (2006).

Mueller P., & Reznik, J.W. (1979). *Intramural-Recreational sport: Programming and administration.* (5th ed.). New York: John Wiley & Sons.

Mull, R.F., Bayless, K.G., Ross, C.M., & Jamieson, L.M. (1997). *Recreation sports programming.* (3rd ed.). Champaign, IL: Human Kinetics.

National Association for Sport and Physical Education. http:///www.aahperd.org/naspe. (2006).

National Intramural-Recreational Sport Association. http://nirsa.org. (2006).

National Recreation and Park Association. http://
nrpa.org. (2006).

Sawyer, T.H. (2001). *Employee services management:
A key component of human resource management.*
Champaign, IL: Sagamore Publishing.

Wong, G.M. (2002) *Essentials of sport law.* (2nd ed.).
Westport, CT: Praeger.

NOTES

CHAPTER 10

Intercollegiate Sport Governance

What is it exactly about intercollegiate sports that can draw six-digit crowds to certain football games? Why are grade school athletes dreaming about college sports scholarships even before high school enrollment? No matter that intrinsic mystery factor of collegiate athletics that keeps so many individuals invested worldwide, no one can deny the United States culture's devotion to collegiate athletics.

Collegiate athletics are everywhere. Fans view games from far and wide, not necessarily in the stadium. College sports are broadcast over network and cable television, radio and the internet worldwide making each game accessible to many. It is hard to walk ten feet without seeing a college hat, jacket, sweatshirt, or bumper sticker symbolizing a fan's favorite team. Collegiate organizations even sell teddy bears, flags, and mugs. College sports are a conversation at the water cooler or an ice-breaker on a first date. Playing on a sports team for a college may even be the way into a business firm. Collegiate sports affiliations are a step ahead in networking. Athletes who have not even been to col-

lege feel the impact; coaches motivate high school athletes with the pursuit of college scholarships and letters from colleges become status and bragging rights for high school seniors.

This popular link between higher education and sport is not unique to the United States, but collegiate athletics are most notoriously known as American. Even more remarkable is the fact that college basketball and football are followed with the same or more enthusiasm as their professional counterparts. Because of the enormity of collegiate athletics, the development of an elaborate organization and affiliate organizations to administer championships, organize conferences and regions, and ensure level playing fields became an urgent necessity. Intercollegiate sport governance serves as the backbone of collegiate athletics. So what exactly are intercollegiate sport organizations, and who do they govern? What are their functions and what issues do they face in the process? The following chapter is a comprehensive guide to the behind-the-scenes organizations that govern collegiate sport.

Learning Objectives

Upon completion of this chapter, the reader should be able to:

+ Identify the intercollegiate sport governing bodies, know the characteristics that make each unique, and the member population each serves.
+ Understand the organizational structure of each governing body and themes of organization that link the different intercollegiate associations.
+ Know how each organization functions for its members, the source of funding to implement these functions, and what authority each has.
+ Gain a thorough knowledge of issues every intercollegiate organization must face including academic eligibility, performance enhancing substances and violence on and off the field.
+ Trace the history of gender equity in sport.

Identification of Intercollegiate Governing Bodies

Collegiate athletics came first; before any development of intercollegiate sport governing bodies, colleges administered their own competitions void of formality. As collegiate sport grew, the need for an umbrella organization grew as well. The NCAA, or National Collegiate Athletics Association, developed and remains the largest and oldest organization. When the NCAA established itself and a pattern for serving a broad range of member institutions, the need for more specific organizations to cater to institutions feeling neglected in the NCAA system became apparent. Other intercollegiate sport organizations cultivated. The NAIA, the National Association of Intercollegiate Athletics supported smaller institutions before the NCAA

broke into divisions. The NJCAA, the National Junior College Athletics Association, served the community college population. The NCCAA directs intercollegiate competition with a Christian perspective for institutions religious in nature.

National Collegiate Athletics Association

The game of football inspired the beginning of the National Collegiate Athletics Association, popularly known as the NCAA. In the early 1900s football started becoming a very dangerous game. Mass formations and gang tackling (now outlawed) caused a multitude of serious injuries and deaths. Theodore Roosevelt urged the development of an association in charge of ensuring athletic safety in amateur sport (NCAA, *History*). He called for two White House conferences: the first in early December 1905, representatives from thirteen colleges made changes to football rules and the second in December 28, 1905, 62 members founded the Intercollegiate Athletic Association of the United States (IAAUS). In the following year, March 31, 1906, the IAAUS constitution became official.

In 1910, the IAAUS renamed and carried on as the NCAA. This association acted as a discussion group and rule-making body until 1921 when it held the first national championship. The first championship was contested in men's outdoor track and field and the title was won by the University of Illinois (NCAA, *History*). Until this time the Penn Relays, established in 1893, was considered the only competition that brought together collegiate contestants from every part of the country. The first NCAA Men's College Basketball Championship tournament was held with 5,500 fans in attendance at Northwestern University's Patton Gymnasium in Evanston, Illinois in 1939. That year, Oregon beat the

Ohio State Buckeyes 46 to 33 in the final game to win the national championship (NCAA, *History*). The National Invitational Tournament (NIT) was very popular in the eastern United States and rivaled the NCAA basketball tournament until 1950. Gradually the NCAA expanded to hold national collegiate championships for many other sports. The first college basketball games to be televised took place at Madison Square Garden in 1940. The University of Pittsburgh defeated Fordham, 57 to 37, and NYU beat Georgetown, 50 to 27 (NCAA, *History*).

Since the advent of television, the popularity of college basketball has exploded. As the NCAA grew, issues such as television rights and postseason play interference with academics dominated collegiate play. An important reform to control these issues occurred in 1951. Walter Byers was named executive director of a newly founded national headquarters to deal with NCAA expansion issues. The NCAA has reorganized several times: separating into three divisions in 1973, and separating Division I football into Division I-A and Division I-AA in 1978. In 2006, the NCAA renamed the sects of Division I football; Division I-A became Division I FBS (Football Bowl Subdivision) and Division I-AA became FCS (Football Championship Subdivision). The NCAA does not hold a championship tournament for Division I FBS football, a topic that has stirred controversy. Currently, the Bowl Championship Series—an association of the conferences who compete in Division I FBC football, bowl games and the sports media—collates a series of polls to determine the two teams that will play in the National Championship Game.

Prior to 1980 the Association for Intercollegiate Athletics for Women (A.I.A.W.) governed women's collegiate sports in the United States. The NCAA started to include women championships in 1980. By 1982 however, all divisions of the NCAA offered national championship events for women's athletics and most members of the AIAW joined the NCAA.

The NCAA currently resides as the largest and oldest association managing intercollegiate sports. The NCAA is an organization comprised of members (individual colleges and college conferences) and a national office (about 350 employees). The NCAA holds 88 championships in 23 sports; more than 40,600 student-athletes compete annually for national titles.

Canadian Interuniversity Sport

The NCAA is the largest collegiate athletic organization in the world, and because of the incredible popularity of college sports among fans in the United States, it is far more prominent than most national college sports bodies in other countries. Although the United States is best known for their collegiate sports system, other countries partake and have formed intercollegiate sport organizations. The CIS, Canadian Interuniversity Sport, is the Canadian version of the NCAA, the national governing body of university or large college sport.

Founded in 1906, the organization began as the CIAU, the Canadian Interuniversity Athletics Union, but only provided competition to two provinces, Ontario and Quebec (CIS, 2007). From 1906-1919, the CIAU grew into the CIAU Central, an organization that expanded across the nation. Officials renamed the organization in 2001, Canadian Interuniversity Sport, or the CIS. Current membership includes the majority of degree-granting universities in Canada. Over 10,000 athletes compete in 11 sports vying for Canadian National Championship titles (Hums, 2004).

Like the NCAA, the CIS makes a commitment to quality coaching, services, and facilities, intertwined with quality academics. Funding opportunities for athletes, however, marks the most notable difference between the CIS and NCAA. The CIS offers limited athletic scholarships: The most any university can offer an athlete is full tuition compared to NCAA scholarships which may include total college fees, travel, housing and books. And although the CIS caters to large universities, the organization itself maintains a smaller more modest budget than the NCAA (CIS, 2007).

National Association of Intercollegiate Athletics

The National Association of Intercollegiate Athletics, or the NAIA, began as an amateur basketball tournament for small colleges in Kansas City, Missouri. In 1937, a group of area business leaders, including Emil S. Liston, Dr. James Naismith, and Frank Cramer saw an opportunity to develop exciting amateur competition for local fans. What began as an eight-team tournament grew to a 32-team tournament by the next year. At the time, the NCAA had not split into three divisions. Small colleges and "big-time" football and basketball schools were lumped together competing for the same national championships. In an effort to provide a level playing field and a league catering to small colleges, tournament officials formally organized in 1940 as the NAIB, the National Association of Intercollegiate Basketball. In 1952, the NAIB became the NAIA when the league began to include other sports.

The NAIA made its mark in history by its groundbreaking decision to include minorities in collegiate athletics. In 1948, even before its inclusion of other sports, as the NAIB, the league was the first to offer black student-athletes participation in postseason games. In 1953, the NAIA was the first to include historically black institutions. In 1980, the NAIA was again the first to establish national championship competition for female athletes. This particular association paved the way for equity in sport. The NAIA launched its most recent project to impact society in 2000, the Champions of Character. This program seeks to generate a setting where all involved with athletic competition, coaches, fans, and athletes alike demonstrate five core values: "respect, integrity, responsibility, servant leadership, and sportsmanship" (NAIA, *Champions of Character*).

The NAIA grew in popularity and split into two football divisions to accommodate its member institutions in 1970. When the NCAA created Division II and Division III athletics, the pace changed and the NAIA began to lose members to the reinvented NCAA. Member institutions slowly withdrew over the years, but in 1995, colleges began to withdraw more rapidly. The association had enough members to keep the 1991 decision for a division split for men's and women's basketball, but in 1997, the NAIA eliminated separate divisions for football because of the lack of schools fielding football teams.

The NAIA currently serves 282 colleges in the United States and Canada in 14 regions. The NAIA sponsors 13 sports: men's football, soccer, women's volleyball, cross country, basketball, swimming, indoor and outdoor track and field, men's wrestling, men's baseball, women's softball, golf and tennis. Its headquarters reside in Olathe, Kansas.

National Junior College Athletic Association

The National Junior College Athletic Association (NJCAA) is an association of community or two-year college athletic departments throughout the United States. In 1937, in Fresno, California, West Coast junior college representatives saw a need for a separate athletics association to accommodate schools very different from the four-year institutions. Their goal was to establish an organization that would promote and supervise a national program consistent with the educational objectives of junior colleges.

May 14, 1938, the NJCAA constitution became official and representatives began collaborating to form the first NJCAA competition, a track and field meet. Hosted by Sacramento in 1939, the meet started as a West Coast competition and gradually expanded. In 1941, when Denver, Colorado served as host, the meet included competition from Mississippi.

Today the association encompasses 24 separate regions and ironically, many of the community colleges in California, the origin of the NJCAA, do not partake in the NJCAA. With 16 sports for men and 14 for women, the NJCAA has had to create up to three divisions for certain sports to accommodate the member colleges. Men's baseball, basketball, baseball, softball, men's golf and women's volleyball have all expanded to three divisions under the NJCAA. Cross country, outdoor track and field, soccer and tennis stretched to two divisions. Bowling, football, half marathon, ice hockey, lacrosse, swimming, diving, wrestling and women's golf remain competing in one division.

National Christian College Athletic Association

The National Christian College Athletic Association provides championships to universities, colleges, and Bible colleges who share Christian values and a unique perspective for sport competition. Collegiate sports are an opportunity for Christian fellowship and ministry with an emphasis on fair play and clean competition, not a win-at-all costs attitude. The root of its philosophy begins with three ideals:

"Athletics are a means to an end, not an end in themselves.
"The process is as important as the performance.
"The person (student-athlete) is more important than the program."
(NCCAA, *History and Philosophy*)

The plan for a Christian college association began in Canton, Ohio, 1966, in reaction against the perceived increasing corruption of collegiate athletics. The idea came to fruition in 1968 as a men's basketball tournament in Detroit, Michigan. In 1973, the league began to launch other sports, developing national competition in cross country, track and field and men's soccer. In 1975, the NCCAA developed a non-scholarship Division II basketball to provide a level playing field for small Bible colleges.

The NCCAA currently serves approximately 100 members non-exclusively. Many of the member institutions also belong to the NAIA. The association holds championships in men's baseball, basketball, cross country, men's golf, indoor and outdoor track and field, soccer, tennis, men's football, women's volleyball and softball. The NCCAA functions out of headquarters in Greenville, South Carolina.

Governance

The governance philosophy for intercollegiate athletics has evolved over its years of existence. What once was simply a one-vote per institution method has developed into national offices, presidential councils, and committees. In general, to cover all aspects of collegiate sport, each intercollegiate organization has developed a leadership committee in charge of legislation and voting, committees in charge of a general area of sport, and more specified committees within those committees. Although the governance philosophies are similar in comparison, they also differ in many ways as well. The NCAA, NAIA, NJCAA, and NCCAA maintain governance methods very specific to the needs of each individual organization. From organizational structure to funding, the following sections are an exploration of each of these governance philosophies.

Organizational Structure

Collegiate athletics began as informal competition in desperate need of organization. As collegiate sport organizations developed and grew to meet the needs of collegiate athletics, it became apparent that the organizations themselves also required structure and formality. The organizational structure of the intercollegiate governing bodies is symbolic; the types of representatives from member institutions included on the various levels of legislation reflect the ideals of that particular sport organization. Pay attention to how each organization may differ in structure, but also be aware of who the intercollegiate sport organizations incorporated and why.

NCAA

Since its beginnings, the NCAA has expanded rapidly, impacting organizational structure. Tracing its structural history reveals initial organization and later reorganization, not just into three divisions, but for voting policies as well. Each of the three divisions has its own organizational structure and authority. Representatives from the separate governing bodies form the NCAA Executive Committee, the governing umbrella over all three divisions. To understand the organizational structure, it is important to start first at the bottom-tier divisional structure. Although the divisions maintain separate structure, the organi-

zation of each is similar. August 1, 1997 marked the beginning of this new division-specific structure, a four-level approach for Division I and three-level approach for Divisions II and III to governance.

A group of institutional CEOs, college presidents, manages all legislation in each division. This reform raised the influence and involvement of college presidents in inter-collegiate athletics. The difference between divisions for this particular tier is only in name: Division I calls this group the Board of Directors, Division II and Division III named it the Presidents Council.

Each division's legislature covers a wide range of affairs; a committee developed to aid the decision-making process of the Board of Directors and Presidents Council. The Management Council of each division receives information from lower committee reports covering specific division activities. This group also provides information to the Board or Council as advisories. Each division calls this section the Management Council, but Division III athletics strayed from Division I and Division II with a decision to include college presidents and student-athletes on the council. Division I and II only allow athletics administrators and faculty athletics representatives.

Cabinets and committees complete the four-tier structure for Division I athletics. Cabinets are in charge of one specific area, such as eligibility or academic dealings. Committees report to the Cabinets. Committees may have jurisdiction over one particular sport or rules within each specific area. For Divisions II and III, there is no middle man; just committees exist to report to Management Councils and investigate specific areas.

Voting may be the biggest divider in divisional legislation. The Board of Directors and Presidents Councils are not the only individuals to officially vote on policy. Direct representation from the member institutions has a vote as well. Division I legislation allows one vote to each conference, not just each institution, while Divisions II and III still allow one representative from each institution to vote.

An all-encompassing governing body acts as an umbrella over the whole NCAA, all divisions. Representatives from the divisional structure are plucked to make the NCAA Executive Committee, the governing body of the NCAA as a whole. Members from the Division I Board of Directors and both Division II and Division III Presidents Council make up the voting population of the Executive Committee. The NCAA Executive Director and Chairs of Divisions I, II, and III Management Councils serve on the committee, but do not vote. The Committee also includes over a dozen association-wide committees that cover association-wide areas like Research, Women's Athletics, Sportsmanship and Ethical Conduct to name a few.

NAIA

The Council of Presidents, aside from the member institution population, is con-sidered the leadership of the NAIA. It contains both voting and non-voting/independent members. Like the NCAA, the NAIA involves CEOs, collegiate presidents, in the lead positions of governance and legislation voting. The 14 regions of the NAIA elect one to three CEOs to represent the region in the Council of Presidents. Each member, aside from the independent members, is allowed one vote. An Administrative Committee called the Corporate Advisory Board, a committee composed of a chair, the NAIA administrative head, and three additional members, manages this particular council. Three additional councils form the National Coordinating Committee, the bulk of NAIA governance, in charge of more specific management.

The three councils are the Council of Administrators, the Council of Faculty Athletics Representatives, and the Council of Affiliated Conferences and Independents. The individual three have a general theme to cover. The NAIA then divided these councils into more specialized committees. The more specific smaller commit-

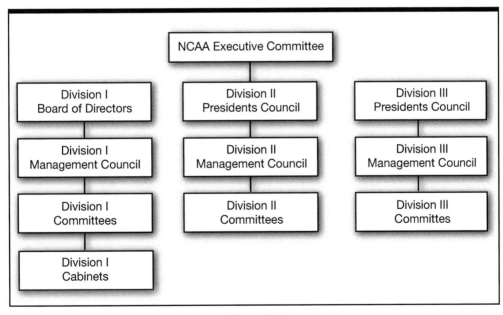

Figure 10.1
NCAA Organizational Structure

tees contribute to the overall theme of the larger committees.

The Council of Athletics Administrators deals with the business aspects of sport. Made up of the Chairs of each of the 14 regions and two elected members, this council controls the business side of sport with NAIA value in mind. The Athletics Directors Association, the Athletics Trainers Association, the Conduct and Ethics Committee and the NAIA Coaches Association mark four specific committees through which the Council of Athletics Administrators operates.

The NAIA remains a strong proponent of the student-athlete. The Council of Faculty Athletics Administrators, also known as the Faculty Athletics Representatives Association (FARA), ensures that academics and educational experience stay a priority. This council contains a group of officers in charge of the rest of the representatives: chair, first vice chair, second vice chair, sec-

retary, and parliamentarian. The roles of chair, first vice chair, and second vice chair rotate, the representatives attending the yearly national convention elect the secretary, and the parliamentarian remains as the explicit advisor once elected. This group of officers manages representatives from each region, three elected members, four independent members and a college registrar. Sub-committees include the Constitution and Bylaws Committee, Faculty Athletics Representatives, National Eligibility Committee, and the Registrars Association.

Organization is the key to running regional and national championship events successfully. The Council of Affiliated Conferences and Independents Sports Division, region and conference separation, as well as contributing to sports information and national athletics awards. The council is led by a chair, chair-elect, vice chair, and secretary. Conference representatives from each region and three representatives from

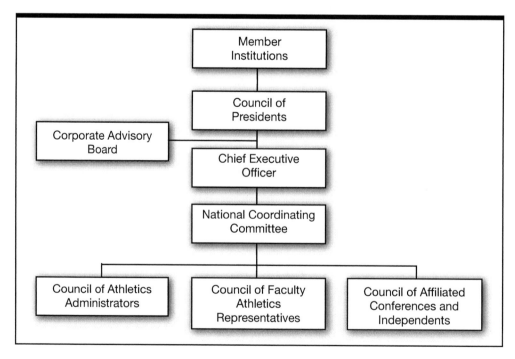

Figure 10.2
NAIA Organizational Structure

individual institutions form six committees: the Alignment Committee, Association of Affiliated Conferences, Association of Independents, Awards/Hall of Fame Committee, Divisions of Competition Committee and Sports Information Directors. This particular council extends its leadership into each region with regional management committees in governing each region.

NJCAA

A board of directors meets annually to vote on NJCAA policy and amendments to the constitution and bylaws. The regional directors, representatives from each region of both men's and women's junior college athletics, and four chief executive officers, elected from four geographical districts by CEOs of member colleges, compose the board. Each member of the board has one vote and a two-year term. The board meets annually, and the Executive Committee implements annual decisions year-round while the board is not convening.

The Executive Committee not only exercises the powers of the board between meetings, but this committee also appoints directors and representatives of the NJCAA for all national tournaments and meets. Members of the Executive Committee include NJCAA officers: a president, two vice presidents, and two secretary-treasurers. The president presides at annual meetings, executive meetings and any special meetings held, makes decisions on issues not covered in the Constitution and Bylaws, and delegates responsibility. The vice presidents cover any absences of the president and supervise committee work. The secretary-treasurers keep official records, including meetings and finances, and keep files of any official correspondence. Also in the Executive Committee are two regional directors from the men's and women's programs (four in total) for a two-year term and one CEO for a one-year term.

An Executive Director of the National Office, the only paid position of the NJCAA governing body, handles all business affairs. The tasks encompass a broad range of duties. An attorney-at-law, appointed independently, advises the board of directors,

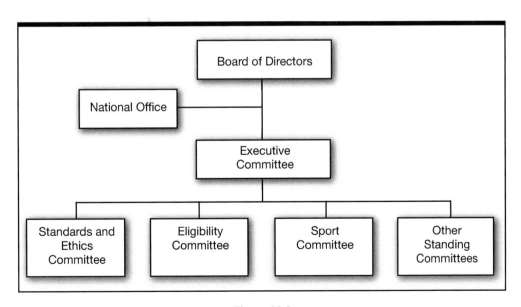

Figure 10.3
NJCAA Organizational Structure

the Executive Committee, and the National Office when needed.

The three committees mentioned oversee three general areas: business affairs, policy changes, implementing those changes and supervising. More specific committees called standing committees inform the board of directors in the decision-making process in more specific areas among other tasks. Twenty-nine standing committees for each sport and each important issue the NJCAA cover issues ranging from awards presentations to finance. A few examples include the following:

♦ The Standards and Ethics Committee investigates complaints of alleged violations and issues warnings, probations, and suspensions.

♦ The Eligibility Committee makes policy recommendations, receives requests for changes in policy and implements official decisions made by the board of directors.

♦ Individual sport committees are in charge of selecting All-America teams and recommending changes for conducting national championships.

NCCAA

The NCCAA elects a board of directors to direct legislation. This group meets twice a year, and although it is considered the leader of the association, it is important to remember that the NCCAA is like the NCAA and NAIA, bottom-up organizations where the member population or representatives from the member popula-

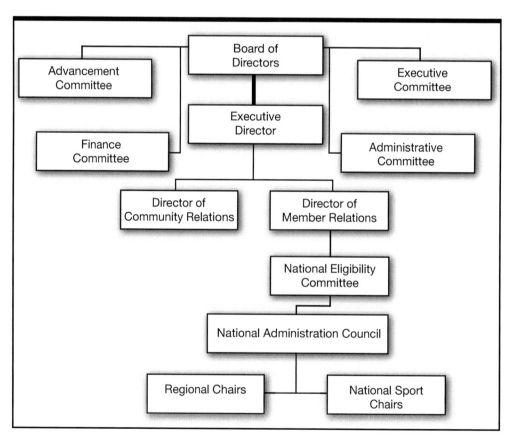

Figure 10.4
NCCAA Organizational Structure

tion are completely active in the legislation process and considered the true head of the organization.

Officers of the board of directors include a president, first-vice president, and second-vice president. The president is very active in a three-year term serving on all other secondary committees as a non-voting member, as chair of the Administration Committee and plays a crucial part in the national awards process. The first-vice president assumes presidential duties when the president is absent or cannot fill the term. The first-vice also assists the Administration Committee, chairs the National Eligibility Committee and serves a three-year term. The second-vice president acts as the secretary for meetings, is active on the Administration Committee and prepares national awards for presentation.

Other officers include the executive director, director of member relations and director of community relations. Each has their own specific task to aid NCCAA process. The executive director leads the administration of the National Office. The director of member relations addresses all matters including member institutions. This involves a multitude of responsibilities: schedules, arrangements for championship events, and even appeals processes. The director of community relations coordinates local and national fundraising, and maintains the organization website.

The Advancement Committee, Finance Committee, Administration Committee (different from the National Administration Committee) and Executive Committee are more issue-specific focus groups of representatives from colleges in the NCCAA. The Administration Committee and the National Eligibility Committees play an important role in the sanctions and appeals process.

The National Administration Council is composed of sport chairs and regional chairs. Sport chairs and regional chairs are the extension of the governing body into the membership institutions. Sport chairs deal with issues of their respective sport and regional chairs act as eligibility agents.

Function

Each organization functions differently according to its membership base. The NCAA has a completely different mission from the NCCAA. An association's list of functions or duties varies from budget size to core sport philosophy. The members of the diverse intercollegiate sport organizations do share at least one thing in common: they are all educational institutions. That theme is present in all organization duty: how to incorporate sports as an aid to higher education.

NCAA

NCAA function begins with values. From these philosophical ideals, the NCAA develops practical function. These ideals are reflected in a public mission statement:

"Our purpose is to govern competition in a fair, safe, equitable and sportsmanlike manner, and to integrate intercollegiate athletics into higher education so that the educational experience of the student-athlete is paramount" (NCAA, *Our Mission*).

Balance and excellence are at the forefront of NCAA value. The NCAA wishes for each individual athlete to pursue excellence not only in competition, but in education as well. The NCAA believes in the complete person, stressing balance in academics, sport and social life. Sportsmanship, respect for participant involvement, reigns as the NCAA code of conduct, while equity policy guides the inclusion for all races and genders as student-athletes, coaches, and administrators. Other values consist of leadership, strengthening a student's identity with an institution, and respecting the independence of each individual college.

The NCAA uses these values as the foundation for practical implication meaning, the organization hopes that each action reflects a commitment to its values. The functions of the organization involve a wide range of activities from enacting legislation to solve national sporting dilemmas to representing member institutions to the state and federal governments to supporting community service programs. The NCAA released 15 services shown in Table10.1.

NAIA

The NAIA views academics and athletics as a partnership: athletics are not revenue generation, but a way to enhance the educational experience. The organization involves mostly smaller colleges not profiting from "big-time" collegiate sports like the NCAA.

The purpose of the National Association of Intercollegiate Athletics is to promote the education and development of students through intercollegiate athletic participation. Member institutions, although varied and diverse, share a common commitment to high standards and to the principle that participation in athletics serves as an integral part of the total education process (NAIA, NAIA Official Handbook).

The NAIA is faced with the same tasks as all intercollegiate organizations: conducting sport-related business, organizing championships, protecting educational integrity in athletics programs, accepting members and sorting the members into divisions, regions and conferences. The NAIA associates with a ground-breaking reputation: The first to include black players in postseason play and the first to include women. Part of the newest groundbreaking agenda is the Champions of Character. The NAIA

developed this program to positively affect character, the first program of its kind in intercollegiate athletics. Champions of character operate with five core values: respect, integrity, responsibility, servant leadership, and sportsmanship.

NJCAA

The NJCAA acts as the governing body for sport on the junior college level. The NJCAA's general goal is to "promote and foster junior college athletics on intersectional ad national levels so that results will be consistent with the total education program of its member institutions" (NJCAA, NJCAA's Purpose Statement). The challenge for the NJCAA is to meet the needs of a diverse group of student-athletes from traditional and non-traditional backgrounds. Substance-free competition and equity, specifically gender equity, for active junior colleges are two issues at the forefront of the NJCAA mission.

The NJCAA seeks to provide a competition environment free from substance abuse. Therefore, the NJCAA requires member institutions to implement drug and alcohol awareness programs. The association forces colleges to form policies to deal with drug use from the abuse of alcohol and tobacco, to the abuse of performance-enhancing drugs like steroids. The colleges must have a treatment for violators, a system for the review of questionable behavior and the eventual suspension for those guilty of substance abuse.

The NJCAA supports equity on all levels of the association, from coaches to players to administrators to those employed at the headquarters. Specifically for women, the NJCAA firmly stands behind fair quantity and quality of female participation in junior college athletic programs. In an effort to impact young female students, the NJCAA stresses the inclusion of women in leadership roles of the women's division of sports. The association en-

Table 10.1
NCAA Function

- Enact legislation to deal with athletics problems when the problems spread across regional lines and when member institutions conclude that national action is needed.
- Interpret legislation adopted by the membership.
- Combine to represent intercollegiate athletics in legislative and regulatory matters on the state and Federal levels. This involvement includes such areas as Federal taxes affecting college athletics, antibribery and gambling laws, television, international competition, and Federal aid to education affecting sports and physical education.
- Provide financial assistance and other help to groups that are interested in promoting and advancing intercollegiate athletics.
- Promote their championship events and all intercollegiate athletics through planned activities of the NCAA national office. In addition to general public relations activities, the Association publishes The NCAA News and dozens of other publications on behalf of its members.
- Compile and distribute football, basketball, baseball, ice hockey, men's and women's lacrosse, and women's softball and volleyball statistics. Regular-season records are maintained in women's volleyball, football and basketball; championships records are maintained in all sports in which the members sponsor NCAA championship competition.
- Maintain committees to write and interpret playing rules in 13 sports.
- Conduct research as a way to find solutions to athletics problems. These efforts include surveys about academics, television, postseason events, athletics and recreational facilities, sports injuries and safety, recruiting, financial aid, playing seasons, the cost of intercollegiate athletics, and the effects of participation on the student-athlete.
- Annually produce, in conjunction with NCAA Productions, special programs for television along with television coverage of NCAA championships not carried by a national network. This operation includes a library of films and videotapes of more than 100 titles available for purchase and rental, plus the NCAA Television News Service, which supplies information to television and cable networks.
- Maintain a compliance services program that assists members in conducting institutional self-studies through a central resource clearinghouse and counseling agency to answer questions about intercollegiate athletics and athletics administration.
- Administer insurance programs, including a lifetime catastrophic injury insurance program, to ensure that member institutions can provide protection for student-athletes during competition, practice and travel. The Association also arranges disability insurance protection for elite student-athletes.
- Promote and participate in international sports planning and competition through membership in the U.S. Olympic Committee, USA Basketball, the United States Collegiate Sports Council, The Athletics Congress (track and field), the U.S. Volleyball Association, and the U.S. Baseball, Gymnastics and Wrestling Federations.
- Sanction postseason competition and certify certain noncollegiate contests to protect their institutional interests and those of their student-athletes.
- Support several community service programs, including NYSP (National Youth Sports Program), and offer Youth Education through Sports (YES) Clinics at numerous NCAA championship locations.
- Administer national and international marketing and licensing programs to enhance intercollegiate athletics and to expand youth development programs.

courages colleges to hire capable females to lead female sports whenever possible.

NCCAA

The NCCAA recognizes the profound impact of collegiate athletics and uses it to provide and support positive religious programs. The NCCAA functions as an organization to offer ministry and outreach opportunities and a positive Christian experience through sport participation.

"The NCCAA is an association of Christ-centered collegiate institutions whose mission is to use athletic competition as an integral component of education, evangelism, and encouragement" (NCCAA, *Faith-Based Competition*).

Part of the NCCAA's function is to supply athletes with a "game plan" through colleges and coaches to balance a caring relationship with family, school, church, and society. The NCCAA provides colleges with dedicated and caring leadership, national competition, discipleship programs, and conferences on current key issues in a young adult's life. One of the most important and well-known functions of the NCCAA is the national and international outreach and ministry programs. Besides what colleges do for service on an individual level, each year at NCCAA national championships, staff, coaches and student-athletes perform approximately 2,000 hours of Christian outreach. Over 4,000 NCCAA student-athletes and coaches have received NCCAA funding for sport ministry trips.

Authority

Intercollegiate sport organizations share the same type of authority over membership institutions. The NCAA, NAIA, NJCAA, and the NCCAA are all "bottom-up" organizations. Members elect volunteers to represent colleges and college conferences in policy voting and decision making. The job of the national office is not to "run" the NCAA, but to implement resolutions made by the collection of volunteer representatives. Any authority is given by the membership institutions.

National offices exist as a headquarters for a number of reasons. The first is to ensure fairness throughout the organization. Each association includes a compliance department and its role depends on its budget. The NCAA is able to employ many more positions than the NJCAA for example, and therefore has the capabilities to be more involved. Officers organize and run annual meetings, conduct voting and arrange championships.

Requirements for Membership

Each sport organization makes strides to maintain its foundation philosophy. One such stride to shape and mold the organization is to require certain qualities in members. The requirements each institution must fulfill before joining reflects the values of the sport organization. Having requirements and a theme for membership is also important to create a level playing field for competition.

NCAA

Members of the NCAA are institutions, not individual athletes, coaches, or administrators. An institution that belongs to the NCAA fits a number of membership requirements. The NCAA includes institutions with a purpose to provide higher education: the institution must be recognized by the regional academic agency. Institutions are willing to operate according to the rules and regulations of the NCAA bylaws, and also adhere to NCAA rule enforcement programs. Athletically, NCAA colleges must offer at least one sport for both men and women in each of the sport seasons (fall, winter, and spring).

Over one thousand members are categorized into five classifications: active institutions, provisional institutions, conferences, affiliated organizations and corresponding memberships. Each active member begins as a provisional member. Provisional status is awarded to those institutions that fit educational requirements for membership in the application process. This particular category of membership is limited to three years. Once deemed active, member institutions are then allowed to compete in NCAA championships, and vote on legislation and other member benefits as prescribed in the NCAA bylaws. Conferences are a group of members that share an active membership with the NCAA to compete in national championships, and a conference membership to compete in conference championships. Member conferences must have a minimum of six member institutions (to be recognized as a voting member conference of the NCAA). There are 32 conferences at Division I level and three independent schools. Reasons for institutions to join a conference include: revenue sharing, television contracts, corporate sponsorship, and scheduling advantages.

Conferences gain a vote in legislation when they meet competitive and legislative standards designated by the NCAA bylaws. Affiliated members are nonprofit organizations directly related to one of the NCAA sports such as Coaches' Associations and Sports Information Associations. One nonvoting delegate represents these types of organizations in the NCAA convention. Corresponding members include institutions or organizations that do not fit the requirements for any type of membership but still wish to receive official NCAA publications and mailings.

The development of three separate sects called divisions within the NCAA has defined the organization and allowed members to choose from the themes of participation. In an effort to serve the wide range of members and participants, the NCAA designated these three divisions with separate legislation.

In 1973, NCAA reorganization became official; the NCAA separated into three divisions: Division I, Division II, and Division III. The number of varsity sports, the playing schedule, football spectator attendance, and financial athlete support policy are the main themes sorting the divisions. Each division still operates under the legislation of the nationwide association.

Division I schools must provide at least seven sports for men and women, while Division II and III require a minimum of five for each gender. All divisions are required to have two team sports for both males and females. Division I programs must meet the minimum for financial support for athletes and not exceed the maximum. Division II programs provide limited financial support, but also provide student loans and employment opportunities. Division III athletes are awarded no financial support.

Each division has contest and participation minimums. Division I schools must play 100 percent of the minimum number of contests against Division I opponents; anything over the minimum number of games has to be 50 percent Division I. Men's and women's basketball teams have to play all but two games against Division I teams. Men's basketball teams must play one-third of all their contests in the home arena. Schools that have football are classified as Division I FBS or I FCS. FBS teams have to meet minimum attendance requirements, on average 15,000 people in actual or paid attendance for every home game. For Division II, football and men's and women's basketball teams must play at least 50 percent of their games against Division II, Division I FBS, or Division I FCS opponents. There are no attendance requirements for football, or home contest requirements for basketball, and for sports other than football and basketball, there are no scheduling

Table 10.2
NCAA Division I Conferences

Division I FBS (Football Bowl Subdivision)
Atlantic Coast Conference
Big East Conference
Big Ten Conference
Big 12 Conference
Conference USA
Mid-American Conference
Mountain West Conference
Pacific Ten Conference
Southeastern Conference
Sun Belt Conference
Western Athletic Conference

Division I FBC (Football Championship Subdivision)
Atlantic Ten Conference
    (This conference will disband its football section in 2007, when its
    football members begin play in the Colonial Athletic Association.)
Big Sky Conference
Big South Conference
Gateway Football Conference
Great West Football Conference
Ivy League
Metro Atlantic Athletic Conference
Mid-Eastern Athletic Conference
Northeast Conference
Ohio Valley Conference
Patriot League
Pioneer Football League
Southern Conference
Southland Conference
Southwestern Athletic Conference

Division I Non-football
America East Conference
Atlantic Sun Conference
Big West Conference
Colonial Athletic Association
    (This conference will begin sponsoring Division I-AA football in 2007).
Horizon League
Mid-Continent Conference
Missouri Valley Conference
United Basketball Conference
West Coast Conference

requirements. Division III policy places no emphasis on spectator attendance or meeting particular Division I-III scheduling competition. The focus is to maximize sport opportunities for student-athletes.

NAIA

Like the NCAA, members are not individual athletes, coaches or administrators, but are individual four-year or upper-level two-year institutions awarding undergraduate degrees in the United States and in Canada. Members are divided into two categories: active and associate. Both types must respect the NAIA constitution and by-laws, pay fees, and gain official acceptance from the Council of Presidents. The two categories diverge according to their regional credentials as an academic institution. The active members are accredited, while the associate members are not. The associate members also do not share the same rights in the organization. Associate members do not participate in postseason play, vote on policy, serve on committees, or participate in national awards.

NJCAA

The NJCAA requires community colleges to submit an application for membership along with membership dues. The application includes mandatory information like names of athletic directors, coaches, and trainers to ensure the organization of the athletics program. Like the NCAA, member institutions must be recognized and accredited by the regional education program. The NJCAA is exclusive to community colleges only.

NCCAA

Each collegiate athletics association has their own specific theme for membership: the NCAA attracts this population, the NAIA serves this population, the NJCAA forms competition for community colleges and the NCCAA attracts colleges with Christian priorities. In order to form a religious-based band of colleges, the NCCAA is exclusive to religious, regionally accredited institutions.

Sanctions and Appeals Process

Competition, in many ways, brings out the best in student-athletes and institutions. But when being competitive means breaking policy, a level playing field, the very foundation of sport organizations, is sacrificed. Intercollegiate sport organizations hope to curb violations with education and prevention, but if a college or athlete does commit an infraction, official sanctions and appeals processes exist. In general, the process involves notification to the college that a violation has occurred and a procedure for appeal if the college feels the grounds of the accusation are not justified.

NCAA

The Sanctions and Appeals process for the NCAA begins with categorizing infractions. A secondary violation includes isolated or inadvertent actions with minimal recruitment or competitive advantages for the institution in violation. Major violations include all other violations, especially those with major recruiting or competitive advantages. Once the violation has been categorized, the NCAA notifies the institution in question before any penalty consideration.

The institution's opportunities for response depend on the violation. If the action is a secondary violation, the institution may provide a written appeal to the Vice President for Enforcement Services or choose to appear before the designated appeals committee. Institutions with a pending major violation can only appeal with an appearance before the appeals committee.

The Infractions Appeals Committee is the official appeals committee for the NCAA. This committee hears and acts upon the appeals of major and secondary violations (if a letter has not been sent). The Management Council appoints five members: one from the general public void of any connection with an institution, and four membership representatives from different institutions and conferences. None may be from the board of directors. Each serves a term of three years. Aside from judging the institution appeal, the Infractions and Appeals Committee has privileges to amend legislation involved with appeals cases. The amendments are reviewed and approved by the Management Council.

NAIA

The NAIA does not differentiate violations like the NCAA, but instead deals with infractions according to their type. But even before the investigation, the Chief Executive Officer of the institution reported to be in violation is notified. Through one of two committees, depending on the type of violation, the NAIA conducts formal investigations.

The Council of Presidents has the authority to enforce policy among member institutions, but designates investigation authority and splits the responsibility for the sanctions and appeals process into two separate committees: the National Eligibility Committee and the National Conducts and Ethics Committees. The National Eligibility Committee deals with cases involving eligibility, and the National Conduct and Ethics Committee processes all other sanctions and appeals.

Before the committees decide for a punishment, the institution has the right to appeal. The National Eligibility Committee and the National Conducts and Ethics Committee will accept the appeal on one of three acceptable arguments. The institution must provide new or additional evidence, must prove the decision reached is arbitrary, or prove that bias or discrimination existed somewhere along the investigation.

NCCAA

A topic not yet addressed in the chapter involves similarities between intercollegiate sport organizations. Though each sport organization runs independently of the other does not mean that ideas or concepts were not adopted from one to another. Similarities in legislation in policy exist between sport organizations because a lot of the ideas have been reused. The NCCAA's sanction and appeal process authority designation mirrors that of the NAIA.

The board of directors for the NCCAA has full authority over member institution sanctions, but designates that authority to two separate committees: the National Eligibility Committee, dealing with eligibility cases, and the Administration Committee, dealing with all other ethics cases. The NCCAA, however, strays from the NAIA in the notification process.

The full institution staff is notified after the investigation and sanction decision. By the time the university receives notice, the appropriate committee has already set a punishment for the violation: a warning, reprimand, probation, withholding a student athlete, or other measures. The request for appeal must be made in writing to the National Eligibility Committee, the Administration Committee, and copied to the Executive Director and Director of Member Relations within 30 days of the notification. The appeal must contain lengthy reason for appeal and documentation.

The appeal will be returned with one of two decisions. The committee will either render the appeal void or will accept the appeal and re-open the case to investigate a possible different outcome.

NJCAA

Compared to the other organizations, the NJCAA's appeals process is longer. Member institutions have up to three chances to appeal sanctions to three different audiences. The National Office issues sanctions and punishments to a member institution in question. The NJCAA includes specifically, that no individual may appeal a decision made by the National Office; the member institution in question must present the appeal.

The process begins with a written challenge to the National Office. Challenges must include member identification, and a number of support documents including bylaw citations, a factual basis, and a jurisdictional basis. The challenge must also include the name and address of other membership institutions affected by the decision. The National Office, upon receiving the appeal, responds with a written judgment also including bylaw citation and support documents. This decision is effective immediately.

If the member institution is not satisfied with the decision of the National Office, the second step is an appeal to the Executive Committee. The member institution must produce reasons for appeal in a written document to the Executive Director and the corresponding regional director. The Executive Committee receives the appeal document, the initial challenge to the National Office, and any notes and documents from the National Office in accordance with the decision. The member institution then has a choice between an oral and written appeal. In an oral hearing, the president resides and committee members reach a decision by a roll call vote. The Executive Committee must submit a written copy of the verdict to all affected member institutions. If the college chooses the written appeal only, the Executive Committee must send a written decision within 14 days of the complete received information. The judgment is final and effective immediately.

If the member institution again is not satisfied with the decisions of the National Office or the Executive Committee, the member institution can appeal once more. Upon the third appeal, the NJCAA selects an independent arbitration service. The NJCAA representatives and the member institution engage in a court-like hearing complete with testimony, lawyers, and a court reporter; an expensive option. This hearing occurs in the NJCAA office in Colorado Springs, Colorado. The arbitration decision ends the appeal process. The member institution may not overturn this decision.

Funding

National championships are extravagant affairs and the main event for the intercollegiate sport organizations. Where does the money come from to run an event successfully? Each intercollegiate sport organization is non-profit, any surplus funds are cycled back into the membership institutions. Where to direct surplus finances is not as big a concern as to how to completely fund intercollegiate sport. The funding issues the intercollegiate sport organizations faces can be found in the funding section of sport issues.

NCAA

How does a nationwide non-profit organization provide the financial support for all of its million-dollar events and programs? The NCAA sponsors nationwide championship games, association-wide programs, pays management salary, supports the NCAA foundation, and provides for other special events. Although the NCAA is non-profit in nature, the organization manages to fund these expensive tasks by drawing money from a number of different areas. NCAA Division I football and basketball attract a lot of television attention, and therefore the television rights to these games are important. Selling the television rights is among the revenue operations to fund the NCAA. Others include championships, royalties, investments, sales and services, and philanthropic contributions.

Financially, the NCAA towers above the other intercollegiate sport organizations. For the 2006-2007 college sports calendar, the NCAA budgeted $564 million for revenues and also for expenses (since the NCAA is a non-profit organization). Television rights and marketing rights fees provided for $508.3 million of the revenue. The NCAA, therefore, was able to allocate $389.8 million to Division I programs,

24.7 to Division II and 17.9 million to Division III. Student-Athlete Welfare programs gained 22.6 million, membership programs and services added 72.6 million, administrative services received 22.8 million and finally, contingencies and reserves gained 13.6 million (NCAA, *Budgeted Revenue and Expenses*).

NAIA

The NAIA is a similar organization to the NCAA, a mirror to the Division II section of the NCAA. But the NAIA does not share the popularity or the high-profile television coverage. The NAIA, also a nonprofit organization, raises money through collection of fees: membership fees, championship revenues and merchandise. The NAIA also collects fees for running national championships, and shares net revenue with member institutions.

NJCAA

The NJCAA, like the NAIA, cannot rely on popularity for success in financing. This organization collects institution dues according to the number of students enrolled in the school, and a separate coach's association fee. The NJCAA sells official merchandise, and includes many opportunities for partnership advertising on their website. Businesses wishing to support the NJCAA through advertising can place an ad in the *NJCAA Handbook and Casebook*, the *JUCO Review*, on the organization website, on championship tickets, and even on official hotel room keys for championship events. The NJCAA provides many opportunities to advertise at championships, including public announcements and space in programs.

The organization recognizes the expensive nature of collegiate sport and includes fundraising opportunities for community colleges on the website. A college team may raise money in cooperation with a business. One example involves

ESPN magazine. If students sell a $20 subscription, $12 go to the team budget.

NCCAA

The NCCAA operates financials much like the NAIA. Its focus is not on individual fund raising for athletic teams. The NCCAA raises money through college dues, championship fees, and championship revenues. The NCCAA has such a unique purpose compared to the other colleges and relies heavily on sponsorships and donations. College for college, the NCCAA has the largest donation pool. The NCCAA also includes a "Preferred Vendors" link, including an advertisement partnership for businesses wanting involvement with the NCCAA.

Intercollegiate Sport Issues

Without question, collegiate athletics has had an intense influence on society and culture. Leaders designed collegiate sport organizations with the intent to positively affect and mold such a significant tradition. It is important, though, to recognize how athletics have shaped collegiate sport organizations as well. Athletics has grown so quickly that often it is difficult for sport organizations to stop issues before they start. In many cases, the sport organizations conform to alleviate new sport conflicts arising year after year.

Academic Eligibility

Participation in today's college sports requires hard training and long practice hours, which often harm the academic standing of certain student-athletes (Soltz, 1986). All four of the mentioned collegiate governing bodies have made strides to protect the academic integrity of their membership institutions. Part of the fight to ensure academics are a priority in athletic programs has been providing academic standards for eligibility, the right to participate. Each association has its own set of requirements and methods dealing with this particular issue, but all associations share a common theme: athletes must meets standards prior to entry into a college to participate and must also maintain standards to keep participating.

The academic success rate of NCAA Division I student-athletes had deteriorated to an alarmingly low level in the 1970s and 1980s (Kiger & Lorentzen, 1986). In past years, many NCAA Division I collegiate institutions have routinely violated their own academic policies by admitting high school athletes who are poorly prepared for college level work and who are unlikely ever to receive a college degree (Sperber, 1990). Some coaches had broken the rules and violated the ethical boundaries for admissions and eligibility by using fraudulent transcripts, altering admissions tests, granting grades for phantom courses, and counseling student-athletes to take courses that would help them retain their eligibility but not move them toward graduation (Sack, 1984).

More selective post-secondary institutions have implemented dual admissions policies to accommodate the personnel demands of college athletic programs (Sack, 1984). Often the term "student-athlete" has been the object of disdain, as media and fans bemoan a perceived contradiction in the title given to those who play intercollegiate sports while pursuing a college education (Sack, 1984).

In response to the public outcry over this situation, a committee of the American Council on Education formulated for the NCAA the legislation known as Bylaw 5-1-J (Proposition 48) and later changed to Bylaw 14.3. In January 1983, the NCAA Division I member institutions voted by a two-to-one margin to accept this more stringent academic standard for students participating in Division I intercollegiate sports (Bauman & Henschen, 1986).

According to Bylaw 14.3, as of August 1986 freshman student-athletes who want to participate in sports at any of the nation's 277 Division I meet certain criteria. This bylaw defines a qualifier as one who is a high school graduate and meets the following criteria:

> Presented a cumulative minimum grade point average of 2.00 (based on a maximum of a 4.00 scale) in a successfully completed core curriculum of at least 11 [specific] academic courses...as well as a 700 combined score on the SAT verbal and math sections or an 18 composite score on the new ACT (Judge, 1992).

Although Bylaw 14.3 was enacted to help reduce the criticism college athletics was receiving, it has not gone without criticism itself (Wood, 1989). Over the past 20 years, the NCAA has been under fire to modify the initial eligibility standards to correct some of the shortcomings of the original bylaw. The NCAA has worked hard to improve this bylaw and has modified the initial eligibility standards for incoming freshman. Currently, the NCAA requires a high school student to have taken 13 core courses and meet a minimum standardized test score and grade point average. In 2007-08 the number of core course required will be increased to 14 and that number will rise to 16 core courses in 2008-09. The standardized test score and grade point average are considered together on a sliding scale. For example, a student with a 2.3 GPA must score at lease a 900 on his SATs. A student with a GPA 2.5 or higher must score an 820 on his SATs. To evaluate and determine an athlete's eligibility, the NCAA formed an external body, the NCAA Initial Eligibility Clearinghouse. Students register with the clearinghouse by filling out forms and submitting high school transcripts and standardized test scores. Colleges contact the clearinghouse for status on a student's eligibility.

NCAA division I institutions have also built elaborate academic support centers and hired academic counselors and professional staff to help student-athletes succeed off the court and in the classroom. Academic and other support services for student-athletes that are often provided: tutoring expenses, study table and class advising, on-campus student development and career counseling, drug rehabilitation program expenses, and counseling expenses related to eating disorders. Institutions cannot provide typing, word processing, or editing services or costs for student-athletes.

The NAIA, on the other hand, requires high school students to meet two of three objectives. The first is a minimum 2.0 grade point average on a 4.0 scale, the second is graduation in the upper half of the class, and the third is a minimum of 18 on the enhanced ACT or 860 on the SAT.

The NCCAA also evaluates high school students based on three points: students must meet two of the three like in the NAIA. To become eligible a student must score a minimum of 18 on the Enhanced ACT or 860 on the SAT, must graduate with a 2.0 or higher grade point average, or graduate in the upper half of the high school graduating class. The high school of graduation must be accredited. If not, the student may be accepted into the college in good standing and participate the following semester.

Academic eligibility out of high school for community college athletic participation must encompass a broad range of students, both traditional and non-traditional. High school graduates must simply graduate from an accredited institution. Since NJCAA member institutions include non-high school graduates, the NJCAA must establish academic requirements for non-high school graduates as well. Non-high

school graduates must have received a high school equivalency diploma or must pass a national test like the GED. Students who have completed the requirements for high school early or are still completing high school and are enrolled in at least 12 credits maintaining a 1.75 GPA or higher have potential eligibility. Those students who have not yet completed their high school requirements must have the high school principal and college president sign the NJCAA High School Waiver form. If a student has not met any requirements, but has been able to enroll in the junior college, the student can establish eligibility by passing one full term of college (12 credits) with a 1.75 GPA or higher. This type of student cannot participate until the student's high school class has graduated.

Gender Equity

After more than six decades of collegiate sport organization and national competition for males, females still had no opportunity for formal collegiate sport in the United States. In Canada, however, female sport organization originated in 1923 as the Women's Intercollegiate Athletics Union. Male and female sport in Canada eventually merged into the CIS. Women in United States collegiate sport formally began when a group of female physical educators organized as the Commission on Intercollegiate Athletics for Women in 1967. In 1971, this organization evolved into the Association of Intercollegiate Athletics for Women (AIAW), an organization that provided national collegiate championships. The NAIA was the first male-dominated organization to include female athletics, but it wasn't until the NCAA made strides to include women that issues began to arise.

Female athletics had been making a splash on the collegiate scene. Sport organizations realized that female sport could be profitable. The NCAA lured members of the AIAW away from their original membership by cutting costs to national team championships and offering television coverage. The AIAW could not compete. The result was a hostile takeover. With no way to provide television coverage and a failed lawsuit against the NCAA, the AIAW, an institution ran by women for women, folded in 1982.

Women's sports received significantly less funding and fewer participation opportunities. The inequity became very apparent, and on June 23, 1972, the United States Government enacted Title IX legislation:

"No person in the United States shall on the basis of sex, be excluded from participation in, be denied the benefits of, or be subjected to discrimination under any education program or activity receiving Federal financial assistance" (Title IX, 2006).

Title IX legislation was developed to ensure both males and females equal participation and opportunities in educational institutions supported by the government. Enforcing Title IX became the next issue and still remains an issue today. A system was needed to evaluate an institution's compliance. After 1979, the "three-prong test" stood as the general interpretation of Title IX. Under this rule, an institution must provide athletic opportunities that reflect the student enrollment numbers. An institution must also demonstrate expansion for athletic opportunities for women, and provide "full and effective accommodation of the interest and ability" of females. Today, the NCAA Task Force exists to ensure all institutions are meeting the athletic demands of successful female programs.

The implementation of the Title IX policy has created strong advancement for female sport, but gender inequities still exist on the individual college level. Certain colleges still have more sports available for women than for men, but the total number of participation opportunities is significantly geared toward men. Sports like ice hockey and football are traditionally offered to men only. Budgets and coaching salaries are still higher for male sports. Most athletic department positions, from athletic directors to coaches, are held by men. Women also are not making much progress into senior administrative roles. In 1999, women held almost 39 percent of the 19,124 athletics administration jobs at NCAA institutions, up from 35 percent in 1995, when the study was first conducted (Suggs, 2000). But only 17 percent of the 995 athletics directors in the study were women. The number of women coaching women's sports is 42.4 percent the lowest ever (Suggs, 2000). That number has steadily declined from a little over 90 percent in 1972. Women also held only three percent of the head-coaching jobs—and seven percent of the assistant positions—for men's teams (Suggs, 2000). But the number of female assistant coaches is at an all-time high 5,811 (Suggs, 2000).

Some disagree that exact equality is the answer. If it is true that more males than females desire to play at the collegiate sport level, why should the funding, support, and opportunities be equal? Instead of a "full and effective accommodation", is Title IX a policy forcing participation and overcompensating? Schools looking for a quick answer to equality are forced to spend less on non-revenue male sports than they would have before. Sports like wrestling and men's track and field are being discontinued by many universities. Should an equality policy exist that detracts from sport programs? The debate is still out on Title IX.

Funding

Because collegiate athletics involve many different types of expenditures, such as uniforms and travel, and home contest expenses, spending can add up if not carefully monitored. Budgets are the responsibility of each individual member institution, but in an effort to keep collegiate organizations from overspending intercollegiate organizations employ committees to regulate spending. For example, the NCAA employs a Finance Committee in charge of solving monetary issues.

The Finance Committee has implemented several policies for two main reasons. College teams have a maximum roster size depending on the sport, a maximum number of games on the schedule, strict start and finish dates for practice, and efficient scheduling to minimize travel expenditures. The first reason for these policies is to aid colleges in budgeting. The second is to level the playing field among colleges with different athletic funding opportunities. Some big Division I universities might be able to afford bigger rosters, more trainers on trips and more coaches. Maintaining maximum standards also keeps colleges with bigger athletic budgets from obtaining competitive advantages.

Finance Committees cannot solve every funding issue in collegiate athletics. The truth of the matter is, sports on all levels deal with financial setbacks. One myth in collegiate funding is that revenue sports like football fund non-revenue sports like track and field. This myth is false; the cost for Division I FBS football is astronomical. In the Mid America conference, to keep Division I FBS football status, colleges like Ball State University, Bowling Green State University, Ohio University, and Western Michigan University have dropped men's track and field programs. Coaches were out of jobs and student-athletes had to quit or transfer to find a new place to study, train, and compete.

Gambling

All four sport organizations stand against gambling with zero-tolerance policies. The policy extends past gambling on collegiate sports to gambling period. No student involved with collegiate athletics may knowingly place a bet, receive a bet, offer information to aid a bet, or partake in gambling on any level. If gambling penetrates the NCAA, students and student-athletes, suddenly the theme for intrinsic sport takes a backseat to the money to be made on any important game. These organizations not only wish to preserve collegiate sport reputation, but also want to protect college students from the dangers involved with gambling. Gambling attracts organized crime and young impressionable college students are vulnerable. Also, gambling is a danger to the integrity of sport. Organizations want to completely prevent athletes from throwing a championship to receive money or to win their own bets.

The NCAA has taken an active approach not only to punish perpetrators, but to prevent their existence with education, publicizing the issue, and holding athletes accountable. The NCAA holds private educational meetings with Final Four participants and encourages individual colleges to inform their athletes of the policies and dangers associated with gambling. The NCAA has also enacted a media campaign and web postings. The NCAA holds anyone with impact on the game accountable. Championship officials are subjected to thorough background checks, and athletes sign affidavit forms prior to championships.

Performance Enhancement

All aspects of collegiate sport have grown since its beginning in the early 1900s and the use of performance-enhancing supplements/drugs is no exception. The NCAA defines two types of supplements: nutritional supplements and performance-enhancing supplements. Nutritional supplements are designed to supplement a diet with vitamins and minerals. Performance-enhancing supplements are designed to enhance athletic performance. Collegiate sports organizations use policies of education and enforcement to curb the recent explosion in performance enhancement use and abuse. While the majority of athletes limit their supplement use to protein shakes and multivitamins, some branch out into other areas of performance-enhancing supplements and even drugs.

These organizations follow the banned substance list of Olympic and National/International Sport Federations, along with the Federation Internationale du Sport Universitaire (FISU) which governs the World University Games held every two years. The NCAA bans stimulants, anabolic agents, diuretics, street drugs, and urine manipulators. The list includes a number of stimulants like ephedra, and several derivatives of steroids. Collegiate administrations not only oppose the use of these substances by athletes but also hold coaches, trainers, and any employee of the college affiliated with athletes accountable by prohibiting any encouragement practices.

Programs for education and enforcement are enacted as soon as an athlete steps on campus prior to an athlete's clearance to play. Athletes attend mandatory educational meetings informing them of the banned substance list and the consequences of illegal substance use. Student-athletes also sign consent forms demonstrating their knowledge of the banned substance list, drug-testing policies, and the penalties associated with a failed drug test.

In a January 2006 report released by the NCAA, amphetamine drug use among student athletes has continually increased since 1997, with the majority of users claiming a desire to improve their athletic performance as their primary motivation. Amphetamines make up one of the classes of supplements on the NCAA's banned substances list, which includes more than 100 different drugs. While the use of these drugs is monitored closely, there are many substances, such as creatine or protein powder, that athletes can use without any legal implications. It has been reported that as many as 13 percent of all collegiate athletics have used creatine (Armsey, 1997). Creatine is a nutritional supplement that is purported to be a safe ergogenic aid in adults.

Illegal substances present an obvious issue, but the collegiate associations also wish to control the use of legal supplementation. In 2000, NCAA banned university athletic programs from giving creatine to student-athletes. Substances like creatine, HMB, and numerous caffeine drinks like Red Bull are supplements that may aid strength and endurance development but are not on the banned list.

Some of the rules are a bit confusing. Caffeine is legal for use outside of competition, but caffeine appears on the banned substance list for competition. Note that caffeine at high concentration levels is banned by the NCAA and other national and international sport-governing bodies. It is unlikely for an athlete to reach prohibited levels through caffeine-containing sports drinks, but other beverages, dietary supplements, and medications contain caffeine and additional stimulants. The mixture of these products and caffeinated sports drinks could cause problematic caffeine levels. A positive test is a possibility if it is used in very high quantities prior to competition. These aids are readily at a student-athlete's fingertips; most are sold at the nearest mall. However, although most of these supplements are not illegal in athletic competition, their safety over time is not an exact measure. For this reason, intercollegiate sports issues do not prohibited these substances, but prohibit the distribution by a college or encouragement to use this particular type of substance to student-athletes.

Drug Testing

Drug testing can be conducted by member institutions throughout the year and is often conducted by the governing bodies like the NCAA. Drug-testing policies and programs differ with each member institution. Bigger universities with copious athletic budgets may choose to conduct randomized testing throughout the year. But no matter the institution, all athletes participating in national championship play are subject to testing. Usually, drug testing at a championship will include a random team or athlete and those teams or athletes placing first and second. The test involves a urine sample following the conclusion of competition. A failed drug test at a championship means suspension carrying into the following season and revoking a championship finish.

The NCAA Division I Drug-Testing Program was created, implemented, and approved in 1986 to protect the health and safety of student-athletes and to ensure that no one participant might have an artificially induced advantage or be pressured to use chemical substances. The NCAA competition testing program was first applied at the Men's and Women's Cross Country championships (November) 1986. Since 1999, NCAA drug-testing programs have been administered by an independent organization, The National Center for Drug Free Sport. The Center selects NCAA postseason events for testing and submits the confidential testing schedule to the NCAA president for approval on behalf of the NCAA Executive Committee. Each NCAA championship is tested at least once every five years. The Center provides collectors, supplies, on-site support and administrative services for the program. Athletes who test positive for any banned substance are ruled ineligible by their schools for at least 365 days. They also lose one year of eligibility.

Drug testing was designed to provide a deterrent to the use of banned substances, but prevention is hard to quantify. Since the NCAA began its year-round drug-testing out of competition program in 1990, national drug-use studies have shown a decrease in steroid use in football. The national average has dropped from 8.4 percent in 1985 to three percent in 2001. Support for continued drug testing is high. According to the 2001 NCAA year-round drug-use study, 17 percent of the athletes surveyed said that the threat of NCAA drug testing discouraged them from using banned

substances, and 56.5 percent of athletes stated that they agreed that all college athletes should be tested by the NCAA. The NCAA released drug-testing results after the August 2002 to June 2003 year. Of 9,256 year-round samples, 1513 championship samples and 22 exit tests collected, only 103 came back positive. Football and track athletes were subject to random year-round testing, while all other sports were only randomly subjected to testing at championships and bowls. Results from the recent expansion to year-round drug testing for all sports, have not yet been released (NCAA, *NCAA Health and Safety*).

Since some of the drugs on the NCAA banned substances list can be purchased at health food stores, like the General Nutrition Center, and found in over-the-counter nutritional supplements, student-athletes are easily susceptible to failing a test. The Food and Drug Administration does not strictly regulate nutritional supplements so they are not guaranteed to be safe and pure. Sometimes the nutritional supplements contain banned substances and are not listed on the label, making it tricky and confusing to tell what is legal and what is not. Some herbal products in supplements may contain banned substances such as ephedrine or androstendione. Collegiate institutions have focused on providing information to student-athletes to ensure that they are familiar with the banned list and that they are cognizant of the punishments.

Performance-enhancing drugs are not the only substance-abuse issue intercollegiate sport organizations attempt to control. Street drugs like cocaine, heroine, and marijuana are increasingly popular among groups of students on college campuses. College athletes are not exempt from the peer pressure and addictive nature of the drug scene. Although these substances do not enhance performance unfairly (cocaine is the exception because it is a nervous system stimulant), intercollegiate institutions include these substances in drug tests throughout the year. Intercollegiate institutions stand in regulation with the United States government. These street drugs are illegal, and by including them on the drug test, intercollegiate sport organizations share the same zero-tolerance policy. Also, intercollegiate organizations associate with character-building methods; to not be just an activity in a student's life, but to be a positive action. Drug use violates the codes of behavior held by intercollegiate sport organizations. These organizations want to be a support for academics. Taking these types of drugs interferes with academic success as well.

The intercollegiate sport organizations have made policy against alcohol as well. Even though alcohol is legal for about half of student-athletes, those over 21, alcohol is included in championship and university drug tests. If an athlete wins a championship, the trophy is stripped if the student is caught with alcohol in the system. If an athlete tests positive for alcohol on the university level, the individual institution decides the punishment, usually not in the same severity of a failed drug test due to doping or street drug use. The use of alcohol on any school or intercollegiate sport organization-sponsored event is strictly prohibited. Athletes caught with alcohol or caught sneaking to bars on trips have had scholarships revoked and seasons cut short.

Rule Enforcement

Member institutions vote on policy and elect officials from their own member-base to implement policy and legislation.

The road from an idea to legislation may be complicated and differ with the themes of each intercollegiate organization, but the NCAA, NAIA, NJCAA, and NCCAA all have one issue in common: rule enforcement. What happens to the rule once implemented? How do the organizations ensure each individual institution adheres to the long list of regulations?

The first solution to this particular issue is prevention. Like with specific issues such as doping, drug abuse, or gambling, intercollegiate sport organizations hope that education will prevent issues. Education may start at the student-athlete level, but it does not stop there. Administrators and coaches attend informational seminars for concerns ranging from recruiting to designated practice hours. Prevention does not solve every problem.

To serve as intercollegiate athletics police, each organization maintains a compliance department. The compliance department of each organization refers to the employees devoted to ensuring that all institutions abide by the rules. The organizations with significantly less financial resources like the NAIA, NCCAA, and NJCAA rely on self-reporting and individual collegiate integrity for fairness; their compliance departments do not contain any full-time employees. The NCAA, however, has a Vice President for Enforcement Services assisted by six directors and over 20 enforcement representatives, all full-time employees geared towards ensuring rule enforcement.

The main problem with compliance departments is financial. An investigation involves a first-hand look at the problem, many official documents, and the development of a case much like those in the judicial court system. Any particular incident involves many college employees. Member institutions complain that although the NCAA has over 20 hired employees, conducting proper investigations may need many more than that. And for associations who rely on self-report and volunteer compliance departments, the worry can be even greater. Many NCAA division I universities hire full-time compliance directors, often with a law degree or legal background, to help deal with issues like: personnel, recruiting, eligibility, financial aid, awards and benefits, and practice and playing seasons.

Amateurism

Amateurism was once an Olympic Sport Governance issue; the United States Olympic Committee suspended athletes from the Olympic Games for accepting money for performance. After the USOC changed the policy on amateurism and allowed professional athletes to compete in the Olympics, the NCAA and the other intercollegiate sport organizations remained as the prominent amateur sports organizations. In recent years, professionalism has extended into the collegiate ranks. Athletes are trying to play professionally out of high school, collegiate athletes are more and more suspending their own eligibility to join professional teams, and competitive college coaches are recruiting foreign athletes who may have been professional at one time.

In the fall of 2006, the NCAA implemented a plan to protect the amateurism of college sport. The plan involved a change in the NCAA Initial-Eligibility Clearinghouse. NCAA President Myles Brand authorized the addition of the Amateurism Certification to the Clearinghouse for Division I and II recruits official as of August 1, 2007. Division III amateurism will be the responsibility of each individual institution.

When high school, transfer, or foreign athletes register with the Initial-Eligibility Clearinghouse before official recruitment for academic clearance, they will also find a new questionnaire, the first step to the amateurism certification process. This questionnaire will include general questions navigating an athlete's sport history. The final certification notice occurs two to three months prior to enrollment.

The NCAA has also selected certain rules for athletes to follow in order to receive amateur status and collegiate eligibility in the certification process. Three main points exist for Division I and Division II athletes:

- An athlete may not receive benefits from an agent of any kind,
- An athlete must not agree to be represented by an agent,
- An athlete must have complied to the "organized-competition" rule.

The three main points of eligibility serve the two divisions. Division I rules for amateurism extend even farther. Division I recruits must never have:

- had a contract with a professional team,
- received salary for participation,
- accepted prize money about actual and necessary expenses,
- played with professionals
- participated in professional tryouts,
- practiced or competed with professional teams.

Sport Agents

A majority of student-athletes graduate and begin careers in fields other than sports. Athletes who have excelled in collegiate competition have lucrative opportunities to compete as professionals. Athletes in a variety of sports may sign multimillion-dollar deals to play professionally. Sport agents are the middle men and women negotiating deals for the athletic contract and taking a cut of the money. It's an occupation that has become increasingly competitive with the increase in sport star salaries and increases in sport agent pay. Because of the multitude of athletic talent at Division I schools, the NCAA has been forced to take a stance on the interaction of sport agents with college student-athletes.

In order to protect the amateurism of collegiate athletics, the NCAA has limited student-athletes' interactions with sport agents while athletes are still eligible for participation. As stated by NCAA Bylaw 12.3,

"A student may not agree verbally or in writing to be represented by an athlete agent in the present or in the future for the purpose of marketing the student-athlete's ability or reputation" (NCAA, 2006-2007 NCAA Division I Handbook).

The athlete may talk or socialize with the agent, but may not accept benefits of any kind: transportation, free meals or otherwise. To add, the athlete may not accept benefits from agents, financial advisors, runners, or non-agents who befriend the athlete for an agent and distribute different types of benefits.

The NCAA has jurisdiction over athletes and eligibility, but who controls the agents? Because of the increasing number and competitive tactics, states had passed different laws to protect athletes and institutions. In 1997, the lack of uniformity of each individual state's law caused the formation of the Uniform Athlete Agents Act. The act became official in 2000, providing a uniform system for regulating athlete agents. The agents must register within the state, reveal identity and history as an agent (including criminal history) and may not provide inaccurate information. A student-athlete who has signed a contract has 72 hours to notify the institution and 14 days to cancel the contract and continue their collegiate eligibility.

Violence on and off the Field

The NCAA not only denotes education a priority, but also demands students follow a code of behavior. The NCAA and other intercollegiate organizations are committed to the idea that each athlete is a role model and each individual represents the institution. Intercollegiate organizations feel that eliminating violence on the field is important, and aiding in the fight against violence off the field is just as necessary.

Section 2.4 of the NCAA Division I Manual named "Principle of Sportsmanship and Ethical Conduct" addresses the code of

behavior demanded of athletes to follow. Certain key behaviors include: "respect, fairness, civility, honesty and responsibility" (NCAA, 2006-2007 NCAA Division I Handbook). Violence obviously violates this code. What happens when student-athletes make the mistake of acting violently on the field?

Section 2.4 also includes a policy deeming individual institutions responsible. "It is the responsibility of each institution to a) establish policies for sportsmanship and ethical conduct in intercollegiate athletics" and b) educate (NCAA, 2006-2007 NCAA Division I Handbook). This policy forces each institution to sanction any athletes responsible, but any decision made must be made in accordance with the member conference and as a reflection of the NCAA.

The 2006 NCAA Division I football season faced two institutions with a shockingly violent situation to deal with. In the University of Miami and Florida International University football game, rivals, a brawl broke out between teams. This was not just any fight: players used helmets and crutches to harm players from the opposing team. Immediately, referees ejected 13 players: eight from FIU and five from Miami. The aftermath provided institution presidents, athletic directors and coaches with the tough decision to punish players.

Florida International in accordance with the Sun Belt Conference kicked two players off the team and suspended 16 others "indefinitely". FIU president lifted the suspension about a month later, and the 16 finished the season. Miami suspended 13 players in accordance with the Atlantic Coast Conference for only one game and suspended the individual swinging his helmet for four games. Players issued public apologies and both teams mandated community service. The institution leaders of Miami involved players with services like developing sportsmanship programs with local high schools. FIU players all would have to complete ten hours of anger-management classes and 50 hours of community service (ESPNnews, 2006).

Intercollegiate organizations also encourage a code of behavior for those in charge of student-athletes: coaches, administrators, and anyone affiliated with the athletics programs. In both situations, neither coach acted violently and both addressed the situation with full apology. Were the coaches responsible for the violent actions of their players? FIU football coach Don Strock resigned mid-season, but continued to coach the team until the end of the season. It is not clear whether the brawl had anything to do with the resignation. The University of Miami fired coach Larry Coker at the end of the same year. He had worked 12 years at the institution and won a national championship in his first year. Again, it is unclear whether the brawl had anything to do with this particular firing, but many pointed fingers and linked both situations (ESPNews, 2006).

Intercollegiate sport organizations make contributions to aid the fight against violence off the field, and not just as community service for athletes in violation. The NCAA's Youth Leadership Program in Iowa is an example of the effect intercollegiate sport organizations can have on a community. The University of Iowa Athletics department worked with community service agencies and school districts in Iowa City and Cedar Rapids to coordinate summer leadership schools and after-school programs to curb growing violence in the surrounding community. The program sent kids with free time to a structured safe environment.

Summary

Collegiate athletics have had a profound impact on United States culture. Each season can be associated with a collegiate athletics schedule: in the fall it's football time, and winter commences the NCAA basketball tournament brackets. And in turn, spectators and fans impact collegiate sport. Each purchased hat and ticket means a bigger athletics department budget. The grand-scale facilities even smaller private institutions afford and the expansion of rosters and sports on the NCAA schedule are a donation from a fan or partnership with business leadership taking interest in collegiate athletics.

This investment in and continual expansion of collegiate athletics also demands leadership to govern and legislate. For collegiate athletics, this type of guidance is found in intercollegiate sport organizations like the NCAA, the NAIA, the NJCAA, and the NCCAA. As complex as the operations of these organizations can be, they are simply structured groups of member institutions banned together by national championships and themes for participation.

Member institutions elect representatives from their own member-base, form new policy, and confront new sport issues each year. Issues like academic eligibility, gender equity, performance enhancement, and many others continue to reappear as governing bodies try to maintain a firm grip. Intercollegiate sport organizations will become even more important to securing safety and level playing fields in the future as collegiate sport continues to grow and evolve.

References

Armsey, T.D. (1997). Nutritional supplements: Science vs hype. *The Physician and Sports Medicine, 25* (6), 76-92.

CIS. (2007). *Programs and services.* Retrieved March 28, 2007, from http://www.universitysport.ca/e/about/index.cfm#top

Bauman, S., & Henschen, K. (1986). A cross validation study of selected performance measures in predicting academic success among collegiate athletes. *Sociology of Sport Journal, 3,* 366-371.

ESPNews. (2006). *Brawl to blow images of Miami, Florida International*. Retrieved December 1, 2006, from http://www.sports.espn.go.com/epn/wire?section=ncf&id=2629905

ESPNews. (2006). *Community service ordered for Miami players in brawl*. Retrieved December 1, 2006, from http://www.sports.espn.go.com/ncf/news/story?id=2639253

Hums, M.A., & MacLean, J.C. (2004). *Governance and policy in sport organizations*. Scottsdale, AZ: Holcomb Hathaway Publishers.

Judge, L.W. (1992). The academic success rate of Proposition 48 student-athletes: A study of a Midwestern university, *Academic Athletic Journal, Fall*, 30-46.

NAIA. (2005). *About the NAIA*. Retrieved December 15, 2006, from http://www.naia.cstv.com/member-services/about/

NAIA. (2005). *Champions of sharacter*. Retrieved December 1, 2006, from http://naia.cstv.com/champions-character/

NAIA. (2005). *Championship sports*. Retrieved November 30, 2006, from http://www.naia.cstv.com/member-services/championships/

NAIA. (2005). *Focus on students*. Retrieved November 30, 2006, from http://www.naia.cstv.com/member-services/students/

NAIA. (2005). *Member institutions*. Retrieved December 1, 2006, from http://www.naia.cstv.com/member-services/institutions/

NAIA. (2005). *NAIA history*. Retrieved December 15, 2006, from http://http://www.naia.cstv.com/member-services/about/history.htm

NAIA. (2006). *NAIA Official handbook*. Retrieved December 14, 2006, from http://www.graphics.fansonly.com/schools/naia/member-services/pubs/handbook/2006-2007_Official_Handbook.pdf

NCAA. (2003). *Historical outline of multidivision classification*. Retrieved December 18, 2006, from http://www1.ncaa.org/eprise/mainadministrator/Historical_Outline.pdf

NCAA. (2005). *Youth leadership program in Iowa*. Retrieved December 1, 2006, from http://www1.ncaa.org/eprise/main/membership/ed_outreach/champs-life_skills/Newsletters/Newsletters/aug05_newsletter.pdf

NCAA. (2005). *NCAA health and safety*. Retrieved March 28, 2007, from http://www1.ncaa.org/membership/ed_outreach/health-safety/index.html

NCAA. (2006). *2006-2007 Budgeted revenue and expenses*. Retrieved December 20, 2006, from http://www1.ncaa.org/org/finanace/pie_charts

NCAA. (2006). *2006-2007 NCAA Division I manual*. Retrieved December 1, 2006, from http://www.ncaa.org/library/membership/division_i_manual/2006-07/2006-07_d1_manual.pdf

NCAA. (2006). *2006-2007 NCAA Division II manual*. Retrieved December 1, 2006, from, http://www.ncaa.org/library/membership/division_i_manual/2006-07/2006-07_d2_manual.pdf.

NCAA. (2006). *2006-2007 NCAA Division III Manual*. Retrieved December 1, 2006, from http://www.ncaa.org/library/membership/division_i_manual/2006-07/2006-07_d3_manual.pdf

NCAA. (2006). *Frequently asked questions*. Retrieved December 20, 2006, from http://www1.ncaa.org/membership/ach/index

NCAA. (2006). *History*. Retrieved December 1, 2006, from http://ncaa.org/about/history.html

NCAA. (2006). *Member conference*. Retrieved December 1, 2006, from http://www.ncaa.org/membership/membership_svcs/membership_breakdown.html

NCAA. (2006). *Membership*. Retrieved December 1, 2006, from http://www2.ncaa.org/portal/about-ncaa/membership

NCAA. (2006). *NCAA Active member definition*. Retrieved December 1, 2006, from http://www.ncaa.org/about/active.html

NCAA. (2006). *NCAA Amateurism certification*. Retrieved December 20, 2006, from http://www1.ncaa.org/membership/ach/index

NCAA. (2006). *NCAA Championships*. Retrieved December 6, 2006, from http://www.ncaa.org/about/champs.html

NCAA. (2006). *Our mission*. Retrieved December 1, 2006, from http://www2.ncaa.org/portal/about_ncaa/overview/mission.html

NCAA. (2006). *NCAA Corresponding member definition*. Retrieved December 1, 2006, from http://www.ncaa.org/about/corresponding.html

NCAA. (2006). *NCAA Provisional member definition*. Retrieved December 1, 2006, from http://www.ncaa.org/about/provisional.html

NCAA. (2006). *Overview*. Retrieved December 1, 2006 from http://www2.ncaa.org/portal/about_ncaa/overview/

NCAA. (2006). *NCAA Affiliated member definition*. Retrieved December 1, 2006, from http://www.ncaa.org/about/affiliated.html

NCAA. (2006). *Services provided*. Retrieved December 5, 2006, from http://www.nacc/org/about/services.html

NCAA. (2006). *What's the difference between division I, II and III?*. Retrieved December 5, 2006, from, http://www.ncaa.org/about/div_criteria.html.

NCCAA. (2006). *Faith-based competition*. Retrieved November 30, 2006, from http://www.thencaa.org/competition.html

NCCAA. (2006). *NCCAA Administrators and coaches code of ethics.* Retrieved November 30, 2006, from http://www.thencaa.org/codeofethics.html

NCCAA. (2006). *History and philosophy.* Retrieved November 30, 2006, from http://www.thencaa.org/history.html

NCCAA. (2006). *About the NCCAA.* Retrieved December 1, 2006, from http://www.thencaa.org/about.html

NCCAA. (2006). *Division I NCCAA Handbook.* Retrieved December 15, 2006, from http://www.thencaa.org/div1hand.html

NCCAA. (2006). *Division I NCCAA Handbook table of contents.* Retrieved December 1, 2006, from http://www.thencaa.org/div1hand.html

NCCAA. (2006). *Division I NCCAA Handbook table of contents.* Retrieved December 1, 2006, from http://www.thencaa.org/div2hand.html

NCCAA. (2006). *NCCAA Application for membership.* Retrieved December 1, 2006, from http://www.thencaa.org/Downloads/Member%20Application.doc

NJCAA. (2006). *NJCAA's Purpose statement.* Retrieved December 1, 2006, from http://www.njcaa.org/purpose.cfm

NJCAA. (2006). *National office.* Retrieved December 1, 2006, from http://www.njcaa.org/about.cfm

NJCAA. (2006). *Committee Members- Officers.* Retrieved December 1, 2006 from http://www.njcaa.org/officers.cfm

NJCAA. (2006). *Officers-elections.* Retrieved December 1, 2006, from http://www.njcaa.org/election-info.cfm

NJCAA. (2006). *History.* Retrieved December 1, 2006, from http://www.njcaa.org/history.cfm

NJCAA. (2006). *Membership-benefits/eligibility.* Retrieved December 1, 2006, from http://www.njcaa.org/members.cfm

NJCAA. (2006). *NJCAA Fund-raising opportunities.* Retrieved December 1, 2006, from http://www.njcaa.org/fundraising.cfm

NJCAA. (2006). *Advertising opportunities with the NJCAA.* Retrieved December 1, 2006, from http://www.njcaa.org/advertising.cfm

NJCAA. (2006). *Sponsorship opportunities with the NJCAA.* Retrieved December 1, 2006, from http://www.njcaa.org/sponsorship.cfm

Title IX. (2006). *Title IX.* Retrieved December 1, 2006, from http://en.wikipedia.org/wiki/Title_IX

Sack, A. (1984). Proposition 48: A masterpiece in public relations. *Journal of Sport and Social and Social Issues, 8*(4), 1-3.

Soltz, D.F. (1986) *Athletics and academic achievement: What is the relationship? MASSP Bulletin, 70*(492), 20, 22-24.

Sperber, M. (1990). *College sports inc.: The athletic department vs. the university.* New York: Holt, Rinehart & Winston.

Suggs, W. (2000). *Top posts in sports programs still tend to go to white men.* Retrieved March 28, 2006, from http://chronicle.com/weekly/v46/i39/39a05301.htm

Thompson, R. (1986). Improving the academic performance of athletes. *NASP Bulletin, 70*(492), 15-16, 18-19.

Wood, T. J. (1989). Successful academics and athletics: Can it be done? *Athletic Administration, 3*, 12-13.

NOTES

CHAPTER 11

Governance of Professional Sport

It has been reported by sociologists (Coakley, 2004; Eitzen & Sage, 2004) and psychologists (Loy & Kenyon, 1969; Cox, 1998) that sports have taken on a central role in the daily lives of millions of Americans, sometimes even exceeding politics, community service, religion, or family in importance. For example, more Americans watched the January 1999 Super Bowl (133 million) than had elected President Bill Clinton in 1998 (48 million; (Sawyer, Hypes, & Hypes, 2004). The national obsession with pro sports is partly documented in financial terms.

The professional sports industry has grown into one of the most significant mass entertainment industries in American society. In 2005, the *Sport Business Journal* estimates the 164 franchises in professional baseball, basketball (men and women), football, hockey, lacrosse, and soccer (men and women) were estimated to be worth over $18 billion (Sawyer, et al., 2004). The gross national sports product, GNSP, today is around $145 billion and is predicted to be in the $170 billion range by the year 2010 (Sawyer, et al., 2004). This would make it the sixth largest industry in North America. A December 2005 study in the *Sports Busi-ness Journal* estimated the size of the American sports industry to be $243 billion.

The emergence of sports as such a major social force is a relatively recent phenomenon. Swanson & Spears (1995) suggest that modern sports fans would scarcely recognize the American sports scene during the years immediately following World War II. Professional sports had a modest, even provincial quality about them. Only professional baseball and boxing event attracted substantial national attention. Major League Baseball teams were confined to the Northeast and upper Midwest since they traveled only by train. The National Football League (NFL) had been formed in 1922 but paled in comparison to baseball and college football in popularity. The National Basketball Association (NBA) was formed from the merger of two competing leagues in 1950; but, like football, it took a distinct backseat to the college game. The National Hockey League (NHL) had been founded in Canada in 1917 but was slow to capture American audiences.

The incredible success of pro sports in the second half of the twentieth century was due primarily to two changes in U.S. society. First, the economic boom that followed World War II created a larger, more affluent middle class. Swanson and Spears (1995) indicate that the economic growth produced not only substantially higher levels of discretionary income but also more leisure time. Pro sports were just one of many aspects of popular culture—along with entertainment staples such as movies and music—to flourish in America's new consumer culture (Sage, 1998). Television was the second factor that propelled professional sports to national significance. By 1960, television sets were in almost 90 percent of American households (Swanson & Spears, 1995). Sporting events, which had traditionally been local affairs that fans paid to attend, now became national events that millions of viewers could enjoy for free. This had several effects on pro sports. First, individual sports teams gained much wider fan bases since a far larger number of people were able to watch the games. Second, some sports—notably boxing and minor league baseball—were devastated by drop offs in attendance as fans stayed home to watch televised events instead. Third, the games themselves were changed in various ways to better fit a television format. For example, "TV timeouts" were introduced in basketball (Wiggins, 1995).

But by far the greatest effect that television had on the four major sports leagues, Major League Baseball, the NFL, the NBA, and the NHL was to make them much more profitable than ever before (Stoldt, Dittmore, & Branvold, 2006). As regular-season games and national championship events, such as the World Series and the Super Bowl, drew (and continue to draw) increasingly larger TV audiences, television networks were able to demand increasingly higher rates from advertisers. Thirty seconds of advertising time during the 2001 Super Bowl, for example, cost an estimated $2 million (Stoldt, et al., 2006). The TV networks, in turn, have to pay the major pro sports leagues enormous sums for broadcasting rights. In 1980, for example, Major League Baseball earned $80 million from local and network television. In 1990, this figure increased to $612 million, and in 1996 it was $706 million. In 1998, CBS, Fox, ABC, and ESPN paid the NFL a combined $17.6 billion for eight years of broadcasting rights (Howard & Crompton,2004).

Many critics have charged that the very success of pro sports threatens to alienate some fans as the cost of supporting their favorite team escalates. Broadcasting fees typically account for less than half an individual team's revenue in these leagues; ticket sales, concession stand sales, stadium advertising, and licensed merchandise provide the rest. From 1991 to 2000, ticket prices for the four major pro sports increased 80 percent, four times faster than the Consumer Price Index, which gauges the average rate of inflation (Gorman & Calhoun, 1994). While some critics argue that the leagues are exploiting fans in order to increase owners' profits and players' salaries, economists point out that the leagues are charging what the free market will bear. In other words, attending pro sports games may cost what it does simply because fans are willing to pay so much (Sage, 1998).

Learning Objectives

Upon completion this chapter, the reader should be able to:

- Identify the various professional sports and their governing bodies.
- Discuss what constitute a professional sport.
- Define, explain, and discuss the development of professional sport.
- Identify and describe the various pieces of legislation impacting professional sports.

- Document the significance of the relationship between television and professional sport.
- Describe the major revenue sources for a professional sport.

Professional Sports as a Mirror of Society

While pro sports may be a form of escapism for individual fans, pro sports can, like other seemingly trivial aspects of popular culture, provide meaningful insights about society as a whole. The close observer of contemporary American sports can learn much about the national condition. Sports have become a microcosm of national life (Gorman & Calhoun, 1994).

For example, pro sports have served as an important arena for civil rights. Jackie Robinson's breaking Major League Baseball's color barrier in 1947 is now recognized as one of the seminal events in the early civil rights movement. Thirty years later, tennis champion Billie Jean King's defeat of self-proclaimed male chauvinist Bobby Riggs became one of the most celebrated events of the feminist movement. These and countless other triumphs demonstrate how pro sports reflect one of America's most cherished values: equality of opportunity. Yet a close examination of pro sports also shows how pervasive discrimination still is (Wong, 2002).

In addition to reflecting American society, pro sports often represent American culture to the rest of the world. Sports may be America's most successful export to the world. Michael Jordan is arguably the most famous man on the planet. America's most visible symbol has, over the 20th century, evolved from the Stars and Stripes to Coke to the Nike Swoosh. Whatever the world thinks of America, it loves our games (Sage, 1998; Coakley, 2004; Eitzen & Sage, 2004).

Like the rest of popular culture, the sports world is characterized by change. To maintain their enormous popularity, the major sports leagues and the individual teams that compose them are constantly adapting to new technologies and changing public tastes. The formation of new professional leagues such as the Women's National Basketball Association and the Women's United Soccer League may signal a new era for women's sports and the emergence of extreme sports in the early 1990s may signal a new emphasis on individuality in U.S. culture.

The Development of Professional Sport

Professional sports leagues in North America are "closed corporations" limited to a fixed number of teams known as "franchises." Only a vote of the existing constituent franchises can admit more teams; when this occurs, a new franchise place is put up to bid among would-be owners. With a few exceptions, these franchises enjoy a geographical monopoly in a particular location. This system started with the formation of the National League in 1876, a reaction to the instability of its predecessor organizations (Swanson & Spears, 1995).

Although league members generally operate as independent entities, separate from the league itself, they are largely creations of the league. Only the few oldest teams in the National Hockey League, for example, existed before becoming part of the NHL or its former rival, the World Hockey Association (http://www.NHL.com/history). The rest of the teams were created *ex novo* as expansion teams or as charter members of the WHA, which merged into the NHL in 1979.

Exceptions to the ownership structure described above do exist. Major League Soccer is technically not an association of franchises, but a single business entity. The team owners are actually shareholders in the league. The league, not the individual teams, contracts with the players. The short-lived XFL football league did not have independently owned teams. All teams were owned by the league. During the labor struggles in the National Hockey League in 2004, the entire league, including all franchises, could have been purchased for $3.8 billion.

Because North American pro teams are so closely tied to their leagues, they almost never play games outside of the league. The best teams in a given season reach a playoff tournament, and the winner of the playoffs is crowned champion of the league (and in the case of the four major professional sports leagues, "world champion"). The league develops its own rule book and sets the conditions under which players join and change teams.

Baseball uses the National Association of Professional Baseball Leagues (NAPBL), which is composed of minor league and independent league teams, to develop young baseball talent. Currently, Minor League Baseball accounts for approximately 73 percent of professional baseball. The remaining 27 percent are the teams of "independent" baseball, leagues, and teams not affiliated with Major League Baseball (http://www.minorleaguenews.com/history/baseball/2005/04/04/01.html).

Although most minor league teams are independently owned, each minor league team is affiliated with a major league team that hires and pays the players and coaches and assigns them to a given level in its minor league hierarchy (e.g., A, AA, or AAA; (http://www.mlb.com). The independent league teams are not affiliated with a major league team. These teams are responsible for player and coaching staff payrolls. Professional ice hockey has a system somewhat similar to baseball's, while the National Basketball Association (European and Asia Leagues) and National Football League each operate developmental leagues as well.

The system of league organization described above developed in Major League Baseball in the 19th century and was later adopted by other North American sports leagues. Outside of North America, the American system of organizing sports leagues is sometimes referred to as "franchising". North Americans themselves refer to major league teams as franchises, but have no need for a name for their system of league ownership, since all major leagues operate on the same principles.

History of Women in Professional Sports

While women have been actively participating in sport, the number of women who organize sports events has been gradually on the increase.

In women's professional sports, individual sports, such as golf, bowling, and billiards have a much longer history than team sports. For example, one of the oldest histories of women's professional sports in the United States is in golf. In 1950, the Ladies Professional Golf Association (LPGA) was established, and it became an international organization in 1970s. This kind of organization set up a standard whether or not the professional sport prospers. The LPGA continues to grow, and the total prize money for the year 1997 reached $3,020,000 (http://www.lpga.com). In the case of bowling, the Professional Women's Bowling Association (PWBA) was established in 1959 and the Ladies Professional Bowlers Tour (LPBT) started in 1981 (http://www.pwba.com). As for Billiards, The Women's Professional Billiard Association was established in 1976 (http://www.wpba.com).

On the other hand, women's professional team sports have had a difficult time surviving and stabilizing compared to individual sports. Some people argue that the masculine image of team sports has inhibited women from participating in them for a long time. The rest of this section briefly overviews the history of women's major professional team sports in the United States.

Women's Baseball

Since many men were on the battlefield during the Second World War, the All-American Girl's Professional Baseball League (AAGBL), in place of Major League Baseball, was created in 1943 to provide entertainment to people exhausted by the war. It reached almost one million in 1948. Yet, when the war ended and Major League Baseball players came back home, female baseball players were obliged to return to the roles of housewives at home. AAGBL lost its audience, struggled with finances, and ceased to exist in 1954.

Forty years later, in 1994, a businessman in Atlanta struck a $3 million sponsorship deal with Coors and formed a women's professional baseball team called the Colorado Silver Bullets. About 20 members were selected from 1,300 baseball players nationwide for this team. The Bullets played games with men's semiprofessional teams and regional teams. In 1997, the Ladies League Baseball was born and it included four teams, the Bullets fought with them (http://www.coloradosilverbullets.org).

The Ladies League Baseball changed its name into the Ladies Pro Baseball and added two teams into the league in 1998. However, after the first month, the league was suspended and faced financial difficulties with its sponsors. The Bullets have not operated also since 1998 as Coors terminated its contract (http://www.coloradosilverbullets.org).

Women's volleyball

The Women's Professional Volleyball Association was established in 1986. The association organized professional six-player indoor volleyball leagues and beach volleyball leagues, such as Budlight Pro Beach Volleyball League in 1997, in which four teams participated. It was unfortunate that the Women's Professional Volleyball Association dissolved in April 1998.

Women's basketball

The first women's professional basketball league in the United States was created in 1976. The league consisted of eight teams. It was very popular, as the average attendance of 1,200 per game suggests, and the games were televised, too. The league did not survive the following year, however, since some teams were faced with financial problems and the league lost its audience. In 1980 and 1984, the league made a fresh start but did not last long.

The Women's National Basketball Association (WNBA), which emerged in January 1997, has been doing well. WNBA consists of 12 teams, with six Eastern Conference teams and six Western Conference teams. During the first year, attendance reached one million and 65 million people watched the games on TV. It should be noted that Mikiko Hagiwara, a former player of Japan Energy, became a member of Phoenix Mercury (http://www.wnba.com).

There are many countries where women's professional basketball leagues exist besides the United States, such as Italy, Germany, Spain, and Brazil. Many Americans players went overseas, and some WNBA players play basketball in foreign countries during WNBA's off-season.

Women's softball and soccer

The first women's professional softball league was established in 1976, but it only lasted for four years because of its financial reasons and failure in marketing. In 1994, the Women's Professional Fastpitch emerged to prepare a rebirth of the professional league which came into existence with six teams in 1997. The teams were divided into two groups, had 66 games a year, and the winners of both groups participated in a play-off. Several games were on the air. Another team joined the league in 1999, and the league will consist of 18 teams in five years (*Sports Business Journal*, 2001).

There was a proposal to create a professional league in women's soccer for several years but it has been put off due to the lack of financing. A professional league was formed after the 1999 Women's World Cup; however, it failed after the initial year of operation.

Prospect for the future

As we have seen, individual professional sports, such as golf and tennis, have been a success and taken root in the United States. However, as for team sports, most women's leagues and organizations have struggled to survive, but the WNBA has started to gain the public's attention recently. WNBA's success can be attributed to the fact that women's sports have been gradually accepted in U.S. society. Once the organizations and systems are formed to pave the way for further acceptance, the next step will be to take a substantial action. Learning from past failures, the management of organizations must be able to attract more spectators to women's professional sports in order for women's professionals to have a success in a variety of sports and for women's sports to permeate the whole society.

Identification of Professional Sports and Their Governing Bodies

As of 2005, there is no universally accepted definition or list but the following four North American professional leagues are always defined as the major leagues: (see Table 11.1 for a detailed listing of all professional sports in America).

The Big Four

- The National Football League (32 clubs as of 2006, founded in 1920). The NFL partially absorbed the All-America Football Conference in 1949 and merged with the American Football League in 1970. (http://www.nfl.com)
  - The NFL Europe League (six teams founded in 1991) is an American football league which operates in Europe backed by the NFL. (http://www.nfl.com/europeleague)
- Major League Baseball (30 clubs as of 2006, formally founded in 1920 though constituent leagues began cooperation in 1903). MLB is divided into the American League (founded in 1901) and the National League (founded in 1876). The two are effectively merged on an organizational level. (http://www.mlb.com)
  - Minor League Baseball (19 leagues with 198 teams) is backed by MLB. The 19 leagues are divided into triple A (three), double A (three), single A (seven), Rookie (five), and winter (one).
  - Independent League Baseball (six leagues with 54 teams) is not backed by MLB (http://www.independentleague.com).
- The National Basketball Association (30 clubs as of 2006, founded in 1946). The NBA partially absorbed the rival American Basketball Association in 1976 (http://www.nba.com).
  - The NBA Developmental League (12 teams founded in 2001). The D-League is the NBA's officially sponsored and operated developmental basketball organization. Known until summer 2005 as the National Basketball Development League (NBDL), the D-League

started with eight teams in the fall of 2001. In March 2005, NBA commissioner David Stern announced a plan to expand the D-League to 15 teams and develop it into a true minor league farm system, with two NBA teams sharing each D-League team. For 2006-07, the league will have 12 teams, with each D-League team being affiliated with between one and three NBA teams (http://www. nba.com/NBA_Developmental_ League).

- The National Hockey League (30 clubs as of 2006, founded in 1917). The NHL partially absorbed the rival World Hockey Association in 1979 (http://www.nhl.com).

Others

- Major League Soccer (12 teams as of 2006, founded in 1993 with the inaugural season 1996). The MLS is the top soccer league in the U.S. in the American Soccer Pyramid. It is a sanctioned by the professional division of the United States Soccer Federation, which is a member of FIFA. As of 2007, it will include Canada with the addition of a team from Toronto, Ontario (http://www.mls.com).
- Major Indoor Soccer League (six teams, founded in 2001, two inactive teams, and two expansion teams for 2007). In the summer of 2001, the National Professional Soccer League disbanded. The six surviving teams organized into Major Indoor Soccer League as a single-entity structure similar to Major League Soccer. In 2002, the MISL absorbed two teams from the World Indoor Soccer League followed by a third team in 2003 (http://www.misl.com).
- Major League Lacrosse (10 teams founded in 1991, inaugural season 2001). The league was divided into the American Division — Boston, Bridgeport (moved to Philadelphia in 2004) and Long Island — and the National Division — Baltimore, New Jersey and Rochester — from 2001 until 2005. The league played a 14-game regular season its first two years; in 2003, the schedule was cut to 12 games. The MLL plans to add two more western expansion teams in 2008. Cities under consideration are Columbus, Dallas, Portland, Salt Lake City, San Diego, Seattle, and St. Louis (http://www. majorleaguelacrosse.com).

- Professional Golf in the U.S. is divided into two major associations – Professional Golfers' Association of America (1916), and Ladies Professional Golf Association (1950).
  - Professional Golfers' Associations are found in many countries worldwide such as the Professional Golfers' Association of America (1916) or Professional Golfers' Asssociation of South Africa. The two largest golf organizations in the world, the PGA Tour and the PGA European Tour are now independent of the PGAs which established them (http://www.pga.com).
  - Ladies Professional Golfers Association is now the oldest ongoing women's professional sports organization in the U.S. The organization is known best for operating the LPGA Tour, a series of weekly golf tournaments for elite female golfers from around the world (http://www.lpga.com).
- United States Tennis Association (USTA) is the national governing body for the sport of tennis. It was established in 1881 and initally called the United States National Lawn Tennis Association. The USTA Pro Circuit is the world's largest professional tour for tennis develoment (http://www.usta.com).

- National Pro Fastpitch (seven teams founded in 2003). The National Pro Fastpitch was formerly known as the Women's Pro Softball League (WPSL), which replaced the Women's Pro Fastpitch (WPF) Tour. The WPF started in 1995, chnaged its name to WPSL in 1998 and suspended operations in 2001. It re-emerged as the National Pro Fastpitch in 2003 (http://www.npf.com).
- Arena Football League (19 teams founded in 1987) Arena football is a sport invented by Jim Foster, a former executive of the United States Football League and the National Football League. The AFL launched in 1987 (http://www.arenafootball.com).
  - af2 (short for arenafootball2) is the name of the Arena Football League's minor league, which started play in 2000. Like most other minor sports leagues, the Af2 exists to develop football players, and also to help players adapt to the style and pace of arena football. In addition, the af2 is similar to other minor leagues because af2 teams play in smaller cities and smaller venues. While the AFL is played in larger cities like Los Angeles, Philadelphia, New York and Chicago, the af2 fields teams in cities such as Wilkes-Barre, Bakersfield, Spokane and Anchorage (http://www.arenafootball.com/af2).

These four leagues are often referred to as the Big Four, although there is a significant enough disparity in the popularity and revenues of the NHL compared to the other three leagues that the NFL, MLB, and the NBA could be separately categorized as the Big Three (Howard & Crompton, 2003). Compared to the other three leagues, the NHL has struggled to find support in the Southern United States which has led some sports fans in this region to dispute

Table 11.1
Professional Sports in America

Baseball	Open Wheel Racing
Basketball (MW)	Indy Racing League
Beach Volleyball (MW)	Drag Racing
	Formula One racing
Billiards (MW)	Tractor Pulling
Body Building (MW)	Truck Racing
Bowling (MW)	LeMans Series
Boxing	Motorcycle racing (MW)
Curling (MW)	Motocross
Cycling (MW)	Grand Prix Motorcycle series
Darts	Superbike Racing
Disc Golf	Marathon Racing (MW)
Equestrian (MW)	Racquetball (MW)
Figure Skating (MW)	Rodeo (MW)
Football	Roller Hockey (MW)
Golf (MW)	Skiing (MW)
Hockey	Snowboarding (MW)
Horse Racing (MW)	Soccer
Lacrosse	Surfing (MW)
Motorsports (MW)	Tennis (MW)
NASCAR Nextel Cup Series	Triathlon (MW)
NASCAR Busch Series	Volleyball (M)

the NHL's status as a major league. Yet the NHL continues to expand into the southern region of the United States. However, since the NHL is the only other team sports league in the North America to generate multibillion-dollar revenues, the league is closer financially with the three more popular leagues than any other North American team sports league. Furthermore, in spite of a season-long lockout in 2004, the NHL returned in 2005 with even stronger revenues than before the lockout.

In terms of overall league revenue, the NFL, MLB, and the NBA rank as the three most lucrative sports leagues in the world (in that order). Based on June 2006 exchange rates, the NHL ranks as the world's fifth most lucrative league, slightly behind the FA Premier League in English soccer (Howard & Crompton, 2003). It is worth noting, however, that the Premier League has only 20 clubs, depending on exchange rates and what is defined as revenue the Premier League's average per-team revenues are very close to, and could be ranked ahead of the NBA's.

Soccer is very popular in North America, although none of the past attempts to establish a premiere professional league have been extremely successful. The current premiere league, Major League Soccer, has not yet (in spite of its name) achieved major league status in the eyes of North American fans. Some of the top American and Canadian professionals opt to play in Europe rather than for MLS, such as seasoned USA striker Brian McBride. The U.S. men's team has performed respectably in recent international competitions and has been in the last five World Cup finals.

Governance

Organizational Structure

Each professional sport has its own structure and system of governance. How-

ever, in general, the structure includes a league commissioner, board of governors, or committee structure composed of the team owners, and a central administrative unit.

The central league operations may involve a wide variety of functions, including, but not limited to: (a) scheduling games, (b) hiring and training league referees, umpires, or other officials, (c) producing, managing, and marketing league events (as opposed to team events), (d) disciplining players or team employees, (e) marketing the league's marks and logos, (f) maintaining and marketing the broadcast programming, (g) marketing league and player products, (h) negotiating and servicing league-wide broadcasting arrangements, labor contracts, and sponsorship agreements, (i) developing press relations for and marketing of the overall league, (j) recording and compiling league statistics, (k) dealing with college and university officials and/or minor or developmental league personnel, (l) conducting centralized lobbying with federal and state governments, (m) coordinating legal, accounting, and business services, and (n) conducting negotiations and dealings with other outside organizations (e.g., IOC or USOC; (Cozzillio & Levinstein, 1997).

The team administrative unit, in general, includes such positions as general manager, assistant general managers, directors/managers of concessions, grounds, marketing, office operations, player development, public relations, security and safety, sponsor relations, stadium operations, team operations (e.g., clubhouse, staff, travel, umpires, videographers, and others), and ticket sales (i.e., box office and group sales). Each of the middle management areas has a number of staff, some full-time and others are seasonal.

The individual teams' responsibilities center around operations in their own geographic areas and activities that primarily impact their own operations. For example, each team is likely responsible for: (a) negotiations for arena, stadium, or facility leases, (b) securing training, off-season, practice, and/or preseason facilities, (c) marketing and selling season tickets and individual game tickets to their regular and preseason home games, (d) marketing luxury suites, party suites, club seats, and ticket packages, (e) conducting press relations for, and marketing of, its individual team, (f) producing the home games (including broadcasting, half-time activities, game-day promotions, team cheerleaders, bands, or other music for the game), (g) negotiating local television and radio contracts, and (h) hiring team employees and players.

The leagues are divided into divisions, generally based on geographical regions of the country (e.g., east, central, and west). For example, in baseball, there are two leagues (American and National) with six divisions (east, central, and west in each league) and 30 teams. Each league has a president who reports to the commissioner, who works at the behest of the owners. The commissioner represents the interests of all parties associated with professional baseball. The parties include owners, players, fans, television networks, corporate sponsors, host cities and venues, and the minor leagues.

Minor League Systems

All the major leagues are distinguished from the minor league systems they utilize to develop and train personnel.

- Although MLB clubs have recruited many players from the Japanese leagues, the vast majority of MLB players are developed through the minor league baseball system. Prospective players traditionally were drafted or (before the first MLB draft in 1965) signed to a contract with a MLB team directly after high school and then assigned to the appropriate minor league level for development. With the growth of college baseball in the past few decades,

more and more players opt to play at the collegiate level and delay entry into the MLB draft. Individual teams' large scouting staffs have given way to smaller staffs and subscriptions to commercial player scouting services. Entering the majors directly from high school or college is almost unknown; most of the few who have were quickly reassigned to the minors after disastrous MLB debuts.

- College and high school basketball produce most of the NBA's talent, though minimum age rules have ended the NBA's practice of drafting players directly from high school beginning in 2006. The NBA D-League supplies the NBA to an extent, though NBA teams more frequently recruit talent from European and Latin American professional leagues.

- Semi-pro football and minor leagues, such as the Continental Football League, once flourished up to the 1950s but today the source for almost all NFL players is college football. The NFL does maintain its own six-team minor league, NFL Europe, which also serves the dual purpose of introducing the game of American football in European markets. NFL teams also recruit a number of players from indoor leagues and occasionally sign players from the Canadian Football League.

- Each NHL team has an affiliate in North America's top-tier minor hockey league, the American Hockey League, and in lower leagues such as the Central Hockey League or ECHL. For decades, the traditional route to the NHL went through the Canadian Hockey League (CHL) generally regarded as the world's premier competition for 15- through 20-year-olds. In recent decades, NHL teams have drafted and/or signed prospects from top European amateur and professional organizations and a growing number of NHL hopefuls are forgoing the professional CHL in favor of NCAA Division I college hockey. Regardless of which route hockey players take to sign an NHL contract, almost all are initially assigned to an affiliate in their NHL team's minor league system for development (http://www.nhl.com).

Authority and Operations

The working relationships between teams in a league are conducted according to provisions of league constitutions and bylaws. Each team incurs its own expenses for player salaries, arena, stadium, or facility leasing, uniforms, travel, insurance, equipment, and other operations costs. The league office usually absorbs the expense of employing and training officials and pays those expenses out of league revenues or passes them through to the individual teams to share the costs. Each team, by nature, is entitled to keep its own revenues from such sources as ticket sales, sales of sponsorship rights, sales or rental of luxury or party suites, facility agreements, parking fees, concessions, sales of licensed goods, sale of naming rights, and sales of local broadcasting rights. However, most leagues have some sort of revenue sharing that commonly involves such items as sales of team or league products, sales of national television broadcast rights, and revenues or profits from post-season playoffs and/or championship games.

Major Revenue Sources for a Professional Sports Team

The primary revenue sources for professional sport teams include media contracts, gate receipts, concessions and restaurant rights, licensing and merchandising revenues, naming rights, parking fees, public financing for stadiums, and sponsorship packages. Each of these revenue sources will be discussed briefly below:

1. Media revenues are generated through sales of package rights to local networks. The broadcast revenues generated through network and cable sales are collected by the league and shared with the teams.

2. Gate receipts account for the majority of revenue for teams. Each team sells season ticket packages, pre-season ticket packages, partial season ticket packages, individual tickets, group ticket packages, luxury suites, party suites, club seats, box seats, and field seats.

3. Concessions and restaurant rights include stationary concession stands, portable concession stands, luxury restaurants, luxury and party suite catering, club seat catering, concession sales in the stands, and beer and soda rights.

4. Licensing and merchandising revenues are generated through the sale of licensed products (e.g., bats, balls, hats, T-shirts, sweat shirts, and souvenirs).

5. Naming rights are generally a multiyear contract for a corporation to secure the rights to name the arena or stadium. The agreements range in length from five to 30-year for $2 to $5 million a year (e.g., RCA Dome in Indianapolis, $2 Million a year for 10 years; Conseco Fieldhouse in Indianapolis, $2.5 million a year for 10 years; Financial, Inc. Stadium in Tampa, $3.8 million for 10 years; Pac Bell Ball Park in San Francisco, $50 million over 24 years).

6. Parking fees generate a large sum of income from the spectators. Often, VIP parking is included in the luxury suite and club seat packages.

7. Public financing of arenas and stadia through government revenue bonds, tax revenues, advantageous lease agreements, waiver of property taxes, free

land, investments in infrastructure, and in-kind services, such as police support.

8. Sponsorship sales are payment by corporations to pro sport teams and leagues in exchange for advertising rights such as signage and promotions related to the team or league.

Major Legislation Impacting Professional Sports

There are a variety of federal statutes that impact professional sport leagues and teams. The legislation will be identified below and described briefly:

1. Antitrust legislation, since 1970, has played an important role in influencing the business of the major professional sport leagues in America. This type of legislation, beginning in the late 1880s, was developed to promote competition and prevent monopolies that might lead to the suppression of competition. The first legislation passed under this category was the Sherman Antitrust Act (1890), which focuses on unfair monopolization and to protect the American consumer by promoting free and open market competition. The second major piece of legislation was the Clayton Act (1914) which provides a statutory exemption from the Sherman Act and declares that labor unions are not combinations or conspiracies in restraint of trade and, therefore, insulates them from retribution for certain labor practices, such as striking or picketing. The player issues related to this legislation include reserve clause, free agency, draft, compensation system, and right of first refusal (Wong, 2002).

2. Labor relations law is derived from statutory law, judicial decisions and interpretations, constitutional rights, and administrative decisions by agencies of the U.S. government. Key legislation in these area includes: (a) Clayton Act (1914) which exempted unions from the Sherman Act, (b) Norris-LaGuardia Act (1932) limited the power of the federal government to issue injunctions and to limit union activity, (c) Wagner Act (1935), later called the National Labor Relations Act (amended 1947), gives employees the right to join or assist unions without fear of employer retribution, and (d) Taft-Hartley Act (1947), officially referred to as the Labor Management Relations Act, which prohibits unions from pressuring employees to join or assist a union or unionization drive. This legislation governs all collective bargaining in professional sports (Wong, 2002).

3. Agency law outlines the fiduciary relationship between the agent who agrees to act for and under the direction or control of the principal (player). The functions of the player agent include negotiating contracts and endorsements, counseling, managing financial matters, marketing, resolving disputes, and planning. As of 2002, there were Uniform Athlete Agent Acts passed by 18 states with 12 pending (Wong, 2002).

4. Intellectual property law assists owners of teams and leagues to protect their property interests in all of the merchandise for sale to the general public. The key pieces of legislation include the Lanham Act or the Federal Trademark Act (1946), which protects registered names, logos, and symbols associated with sports organizations and the Copyright Act (1976) which protects the expression of ideas such as music played at sporting events, the media guides or programs sold at sporting events, and even the sporting event itself recorded or broadcast for

television or radio (Wong, 2002).

5. Sports broadcasting Act (1961) immunizes from antitrust liability the pooled sale of telecasting rights by the four major professional sports leagues. It allows the leagues to negotiate television packages but it also restricts the ability of the leagues to define the geographical areas into which the pooled telecasts may be broadcast (Wong, 2002).

6. Professional and Amateur Sports Protection Act (1992) makes it unlawful for: (a) a government entity to sponsor, operate, advertise, promote, license, or authorize by law or compact or (b) a person to sponsor, operate, advertise, promote, pursuant to the law or compact of a government entity, a lottery, sweepstakes, or other betting, gambling, or wagering scheme based, directly or indirectly (through the use of geographical references or otherwise), on one or more competitive games in which amateur or professional athletes participate, or are intended to participate, or on one or more performances of such athletes in such games (26 USC 3701, 188).

Professional Sport Issues

Professional sports are facing a number of major issues that can impact a league's or team profitability. These issues include broadcasting issues such as Internet rights, siphoning, home taping, domestic and international piracy of satellite transmissions, blackouts, handheld pagers, and satellite distribution, collective bargaining, employment diversity, facility financing, franchise stability, franchise locations, gambling, higher player salaries, ownership restrictions, substance abuse, television exposure, violence, and weathering challenges from rival leagues. Each of these issues will be discussed briefly below.

Broadcasting Issues

Owners and general managers of professional teams should be aware of each of the following issues, which include Internet rights for sport broadcasts, siphoning of sport events from network television to pay television, home taping of copyrighted events, domestic and international piracy of satellite transmissions, blackouts of scheduled programs, handheld pagers, and satellite distribution of sports games. These issues will briefly be discussed below:

Internet rights – The topic of who owns Internet rights for sports broadcasts is an area of litigation that so far has not been fully explored. The Internet is rapidly changing the way television and sports are marketed and utilized (Wong, 2002).

Siphoning – Siphoning is shifting of programs from standard broadcast television to pay cable or subscription television. With expansion of pay television options offered on cable systems in the United States, this has become a more heated topic. The Home Box Office case (*Home Box Office v. FCC*, 567 F.2d 9 [D.C. Cir.], *cert. Denied*, 434 U.S. 829 [1977]) allows professional sports teams to put together pay cable packages for their games that would not have been possible under the FCC rules (Wong, 2002).

Home taping – As sport events are being broadcast, viewers are able to tape them from their television sets. The Supreme Court (*Sony Corporation of America v. University City Studios*, 104 U.S. 774 [1984] held that home taping does not constitute copyright infringement. For sports teams, this means that they will probably not be able to gain any royalty fees for the taping of their games from television (Wong, 2002).

Domestic and international pricey of satellite transmissions – Domestic pricey is an increasingly important area of concern, especially with the expansion of the availability of satellite technology, anyone with an "earth station" is able to intercept, or "pirate", sports broadcasts. Some of the most common offenders are bars trying to attack a clientele who otherwise might not be able to view the game.

The laws governing international satellite piracy are much more lenient than the laws in the United States. Some foreign governments (e.g., China and North Korea) have been known to sanction satellite piracy (Wong, 2002).

Blackouts – Since a 1973 FCC ruling, blackouts have been effectively eliminated and allow more fans to watch professional sports (Wong, 2002). It also had a positive impact on television advertising during the games based on the number of fans watching a game.

Handheld pagers – The court in *NBA v. Motorola, Inc.* (105 F.3d 841, 2d. Cir. 1997) held that real-time updates of the NBA scores were not an infringement upon the copyrights owned by the NBA. This decision has had an enormous effect upon the broadcasting of sports on the Internet. With this case as precedent, Internet sports sites are able to provide real-time sports scores for their visitors without fear of infringing upon copyrights (Wong, 2002).

Satellite distribution – In 1992, the Cable Television Consumer Protection and Competition Act (1992) was passed by Congress. It states

> It shall be unlawful for a cable operator, a satellite cable programming vendor ... to engage in unfair methods of competition or unfair or deceptive acts or practices, the purpose ... of which is to hinder significantly or to prevent any multi-channel video programming distributor from providing satellite cable programming ... to subscribers or consumers.

This act protects consumers right to view sports programming especially when one cable system attempts to block another entity from broadcasting its programming (Wong, 2002).

Collective Bargaining

Swanson and Spears (1995) indicate the professional athletes began seeking union representation over a hundred years ago. However, there was not an official players union until the mid-1950s. Professional sports since that time has been subject to continued labor conflict, most recently the NHL lockout in 2005. Over the years each players association of the major four leagues has been involved in at least one work stoppage and hundreds of games have been cancelled due to strikes (players or officials) and lockouts (management).

Contracts in professional sports are different from most other forms of unionized employment in that employees can negotiate their own contracts. In most professional sports leagues, the collective bargaining agreement sets a minimum salary and perhaps a maximum salary (a cap); but, players and their agents are free to negotiate within such parameters. One notable exception is the WNBA, which has a salary scale based on seniority and draft position (Wong, 2002).

The major labor issues for professional sports include free agency, salary caps (hard and soft), calculation of salary cap, and arbitration. Table 11.2 outlines the major work stoppages in the major four. The key issue causing the strike or lockout dealt with compensation issues.

Employment Diversity

Women and minorities are losing ground in professional sports employment reversing a trend toward greater diversity. Every professional sport had lower averages for employing women compared to 2001 and minority hiring slipped as well (Lapchick, 2003). In the 12th issue of the "Racial and Gender Report Card" (2006) found minorities (Blacks, Asians, Latinos, Pacific Islanders, and American Indians) lost ground in most of the top management positions in professional sports, including general managers and team vice presidents. The two most noteworthy highlights from the report were that: (a) Black Entertainment Television founder and CEO Robert Johnson was awarded the right to purchase the NBA's new Charlotte, North Carolina, franchise, which made him the first black majority team owner in pro sports and (b) there was an all-time high of 24 head coaches/managers who were minorities in the four biggest professional leagues. Finally, the professional sport leagues need to continuously be aware the need for diversity in employee ranks.

Facility Financing

Economic development strategies which focus on sports are controversial, and for good reasons. Programs based on plans to construct a new sports venue or lure a professional team to an area are often justified by touting the potential economic benefits of such a move. However, research in this area indicates such benefits are often greatly exaggerated or even false. Scholars of the issue who do believe sports strategies have positive effects tend to emphasize the non-economic benefits of them although economic the advocates of specific stadium proposals highlight benefits. A difficulty with how economic impacts of sports facilities or teams are measured only aggravates the controversy over the potential of sports as an economic development strategy.

Advantages of public financing: Proponents of public financing of sports claim that sports facilities and teams generate tax revenue for the area, causes direct spending by teams and owners in an area, create new jobs, and contribute to community development. In addition, they claim that stadiums are more attractive to tourists and shoppers than heavy industry (another potential eco-

nomic development tool) and new stadiums lead to improved infrastructure in an area. Advocates of sports-based development strategies also point out that many economic studies of sports facilities show negligible or negative impacts on examined facilities that were built in suburban areas. They emphasize that most of the stadiums built in the last decade differ fundamentally from those studied in past studies; the new stadiums and arenas tend to be built in urban areas and are often part of an urban development strategy. Furthermore, they include new stadium technology, such as expanded luxury seating, restaurants and bars, catering, and theme activities.

Disadvantages of public financing: Professor Andrew Zimbalist of Smith College criticized the idea that sports facilities' economic impact is significant in his article "The Economic Impact of Sports Teams on Cities". In the essay, he also finds that the main recipients of the public largesse are the owners and players; they reap millions while "the city cannot even cover its incremental debt service with rent and other stadium revenues" (Zimbalist, 1996, 10).

Another key argument is that owners and players may not live in an area and spend money, as was feared in the case of the Houston Oilers football team moving to Nashville. John J. Siegfried, a professor of economics at Vanderbilt University, claims that only about 100 people in high paying jobs, including management and players, are employed by an NFL franchise, and most of those will not live in Tennessee (Siegfried 1996, 31). As a result, potential economic benefits from their direct spending will not be realized in the area targeted for economic development.

In "Sports Stadiums and Area Development: A Critical Review", Robert Baade and Richard Dye discounted proponents of stadium construction argument that jobs would be created by noting that the type of jobs created would be generally low-wage and seasonal, including ticket sellers, restaurant and bar workers, and taxi drivers. They argue that a city engaged in such a strategy would gain a comparative advantage in that sector of labor, as compared to a neighboring area that encouraged a sector utilizing high-skilled workers and high-technology, which Baade described as "growth-producing jobs" (Baade and Dye, 1988, 272).

Stability of Professional Team Franchises

All four major leagues exhibit the stability of most of their franchises. No team from any of the four leagues has collapsed outright in decades. However, the Montreal Expos came very close, the team's relocation was the first in Major League Baseball since 1972, when the Washington Senators moved to Texas, becoming the Texas Rangers. The franchise was owned by Major League Baseball from 2002 until mid-2006. However, in 2006 a new ownership group was selected headed by Theodore N. Lerner (http://www.mlb.com).

Although all four major leagues have had at least one franchise relocate to another city in the last decade, relocation of teams is generally uncommon compared to other leagues. It should be noted that all four major leagues have had frequent franchise collapses and relocations in their early histories; but, these events ceased occurring with regularity by the time the leagues reached "major" status.

The last of the "big four" to fold outright were the original Baltimore Bullets in 1955 while the last team to cease operations was the Cleveland Barons (formerly the California Golden Seals) which was merged into the Minnesota North Stars organization in 1978, two years after moving to Ohio from California. However, this merger was officially dissolved in 1991 and the franchise was resurrected as the San Jose Sharks. The last NHL team to fold outright was the New York Americans in 1942. The NBA

and NHL did, however, merge with rival leagues in the 1970s. During these mergers, only a few American Basketball Association and World Hockey Association franchises survived; the remaining ABA and WHA franchises went out of business (Swanson& Spears, 1995).

The last NFL team to fold was the Dallas Texans in 1952 (http://www.nfl.com), and no MLB team has folded since 1899, when four National League teams ceased to exist. The four leagues all expanded within the last decade and currently have either 30 or, in the case of the NFL, 32 teams. The newest major league team is the Charlotte Bobcats who joined the NBA in 2004. The newest NFL team is the Houston Texans who became the NFL's 32nd team in 2002 after the NFL was unable to find a viable ownership group and stadium plan in Los Angeles. The newest NHL teams are the Columbus Blue Jackets and Minnesota Wild, who began play in 2000, while the newest MLB teams are the Arizona Diamondbacks and Tampa Bay Devil Rays, who joined the NL and AL respectively in 1998 (http://www.nfl.com).

The major sports leagues in the United States and Canada are unique compared to most leagues outside North America in that there is no promotion and relegation system. The same teams compete in the leagues each year. The worst teams are not relegated each year to a second-tier league, to be replaced by the best teams from the second-tier league. One could even argue the worst teams are *rewarded* for their futility, as the worst teams receive a higher position in the following year's draft for new players, which in football and basketball usually consists of players who have played the sport in college. A notable result of the "closed shop" aspect of the major leagues is that the franchises have average book values that are considerably more.

Recent expansion franchises have commanded huge entry fees that are generally held to represent the price the new team must pay to gain its share of the existing teams' often guaranteed revenue streams. The Houston Texans paid an unprecedented $700 million to join the NFL. By comparison, the Charlotte Bobcats paid $300 million to join the NBA. The Diamondbacks and Devil Rays paid $130 million each to join MLB while the Blue Jackets and Wild paid $80 million each to join the NHL (http://www.nfl.com).

Many sports analysts and owners believe that 30 is the optimal number of teams for a major league, which is only two below the maximum number any league has ever had. Thus, future expansion is by no means certain, especially by the NFL which is already over the 30-team limit. The NFL is still anxious to return to Los Angeles (see below); but many believe that NFL officials would privately prefer to re-locate an existing team in order to avoid altering its current eight four-team division alignment. Even if expansion franchises could continue to command huge fees as more teams join the leagues, the owners' share of the fees is constantly reduced. Even if large markets remain without a team, a point could still be reached where one-time expansion revenues are offset by chronic stresses such as a drain on the talent pool (which could have a noticeable impact on the quality of play and, thus start turning off fans) and saturation of the national television market (if the leagues are unable to negotiate higher fees from the television networks, then additional teams will simply cause the existing television revenue to be split into smaller shares).

Locating Professional Franchises

Major leagues tend to have franchises only in the largest cities and most heavily populated market areas with nearly all franchises in metropolitan areas of at least one million and with most in metro areas having populations over two million. This typically means at least one franchise (and often two) in each of the New York City, Chicago, and Los Angeles areas. There are two major exceptions: The NFL has not had a franchise in L.A. since 1995 and the Green Bay Packers survive in professional sports' smallest metropolitan area (less than 300,000) thanks to a unique community ownership and their proximity to the larger Milwaukee area, not to mention the loyalty of their fanbase. The Packers are also the last remaining link to the NFL's small-town Midwest roots. Many such teams existed in the NFL before 1934; since then, only the Packers remain (http://www.nfl.com).

The Utah Jazz is located in the smallest television market of any U.S. team (the Green Bay Packers' television market includes the much larger city of Milwaukee 120 miles / 200 km to its south). The Jazz relocated during a turbulent period in NBA history and have enjoyed strong support from a very large geographical area devoid of other major sport teams (http://www.nba.com). Utah is also the least populous state with an NBA team.

Professional sport leagues, as we know them today, evolved during the decades between the Civil War and World War II when the railroad was the main means of intercity transportation. As a result, virtually all major league teams were concentrated in the northeastern quarter of the United States within, roughly, the radius of a day-long train ride. No MLB teams existed south or west of St. Louis; the NFL was confined to the Great Lakes and the Northeast and the NBA (which didn't exist before 1946) spanned from the Quad Cities to Boston (Swanson & Spears, 1995).

The NHL remained confined to six cities in the Northeast, Great Lakes, and eastern Canada, although several West Coast-based teams did compete for the Stanley Cup in the era before the Cup competition was limited to NHL teams. During the 1910s and into the 1920s, the pro teams in Western Canada and the USA Pacific Northwest were on a par with those in Quebec and Ontario. From 1914 to 1927, the Stanley Cup was an eastern vs. western championship. (Before 1914, the Stanley Cup was a challenge cup, and some western teams did mount challenges, including one from the remote Yukon Territory); http://www.nhl.com).

As travel and settlement patterns changed, so did the geography of professional sports. With the arguable exception of the western hockey teams that competed for the Stanley Cup in the early 20th century, there were no major league teams in the far west until after World War II. The first west coast major-league franchise was the NFL's Los Angeles Rams who moved from Cleveland in 1946. The same year, the All-America Football Conference began play with teams in Los Angeles and San Francisco. Baseball would not extend west until 1958 in the controversial move of both New York-based National League franchises. The NBA would follow in 1960 with the move of the Minneapolis Lakers to Los Angeles while the NHL would not have a west coast presence until it doubled in size in 1967 (Swanson & Spears, 1995).

Since then, as newer, fast-growing Sunbelt areas such as Phoenix and Dallas became prominent, the major sports leagues expanded or franchises relocated (usually quite controversially) to service these communities. Most major areas are well-represented with all but seven continental U.S. metropolitan agglomerations over one million people hosting at least one major sports franchise. As of 2006, the largest metropolitan area without a major professional sports franchise is California's Inland Empire. However, since this area is adjacent to the San Diego and Los Angeles metro areas and serves as a local market for those teams, no major league franchise is likely to move there without purporting to represent the L.A. and/or San Diego markets as well.

The most populous independent metropolitan area outside of a major franchise's local market is the Hampton Roads region of Virginia, nearly 200 miles from the nearest major sports teams in Washington, D.C. It previously hosted a successful franchise in the American Basketball Association. Virginia is also the most populous state without a team within its borders (http://www.nba.com).

Another large metropolitan area without any major league franchises is Las Vegas, which is expected to surpass the Hampton Roads area in metropolitan population before the 2010 Census to become the largest metropolis without a franchise. Despite the area's explosive growth, all four leagues are wary of placing a team there due to the city's legal gambling industry, which includes sports betting. In the U.S. especially, as contrasted with Europe, for a professional sports organization to have any association, real or perceived, with gambling has been taboo ever since the 1919 World Series scandal, and all four leagues forbid its personnel to have any type of contact or association with anything related to gambling of any kind (http://www.nba.com).

Gambling

The success of the professional sports industry hinges on maintaining a high level of integrity so that the public has no doubt about the outcome of the event. Wong (2002) suggests that if people were to believe there was a connection between the teams and the players and organized gambling, the integrity of the game could be damaged. In 1989, MLB banned Pete Rose from baseball for the remaining years of his life for gambling on the Cincinnati Reds to win when he was the team manager as an example to others. Further, MLB sought and received assurances from Walt Disney Company that it would not allow gambling on its cruise ships before approving the sale of the Anaheim Angels to Disney (Wong, 2002).

Table 11.2
Major Four Leagues Work Stoppages

Year	League	Stoppage	Dates	Issue
1968	NFL Lockout	Walkout	Fall	Increased pension fund
1970	NFL	Strike	July	Increased pension contributions
1972	MLB	Strike	April 2-14	Salary arbitration established; Increased pension fund
1974	NFL	Strike	Fall	Owners keep Rozelle Rule
1975	NFL	Strike	August	Owners break strike
1976	MLB	Lockout	March 1-17	Owners accept free agency
1980	MLB	Strike	March 26-April 3	Salary arbitration preserved; Increased pension fund
1981	MLB	Strike	June 12-July 31	Compensation rules for free agency severely limited
1982	NFL	Strike	September-November	Increased minimum salaries; No percentage of revenue for players
1985	MLB	Lockout	March	Minimum salary raised; Salary arbitration experience raised from 2 to 3 years
1987	NFL	Strike	Fall	Players abort strike; sue owners on antitrust grounds
1990	MLB	Lockout	March	Number of players eligible for salary arbitration expanded
1992	NHL	Strike	April	Player compensation systems
1994/5	NHL	Lockout	August-January	Rookie salary cap; revised salary arbitration rules; free agency changes
1994/5	MLB	Strike	August-April	Agreed to begin season without a CBA; 1994 World Series cancelled
1995	NBA	Lockout	September	Salary cap/free agency
1996	NBA	Lockout	July	Salary cap
1998/9	NBA	Lockout	July-January	Cap on rookie salaries, limit on "Larry Bird" raises, increase in minimum salary
2004/5	NHL	Lockout	August-May	Salary cap

While the MLB does not allow owners to own any interest in gambling operations, the NBA, NFL, and NHL all allow their owners to own legal gambling operations, as long as they are not involved in any activity that includes taking bets on legal games (Wong, 2002). However, all leagues ban coaches, players, and other personnel from making promotional appearances involving casinos and gambling cruises.

Finally, leagues may have no clear policy concerning the gambling interest for their owners; they have worked hard to keep people from gambling on their games through state lotteries and offshore sports books. The leagues lobbied for the passage of the Professional and Amateur Sports Protection Act (PASPA; (1992) and for the Internet gambling Prohibition Act (1999). It is clear any connection to gambling raises serious concerns for the leagues.

High Player Salaries

The average annual salary for players in the four major leagues is about $2.9 million in 2004; although player salaries can range from $300,000 for backup players to $20 million for superstars.

- NBA players have the highest average player salaries of the four leagues at $4.9 million; however, their teams also have the smallest rosters (http://www.nba.com).
- The NFL has the highest average team payroll and a salary cap that will exceed $100 million for the first time under the new collective bargaining agreement with the NFL's players union. However, NFL payrolls distributed among rosters that are far larger than the other three leagues making their players among the lowest paid on the average at $1.3 million (although this average is likely to increase under the new CBA; (http://www.nfl.com).
- Following the settlement of the 2004-

05 NHL lockout, NHL players were also due to be paid about $1.3 million on average, although, this, too, is set to increase because the lockout did not have the adverse effect on league revenues that was expected (http://www.nhl.com).
- MLB is in the middle at about $2.5 million per player (http://ww.mlb.com).

Ownership restrictions

All four major leagues have strict rules regarding who may own a team and also place some restrictions on what other sort of activities the owners may engage in. To prevent the perception of being in a conflict of interest, the major leagues generally do not allow anyone to own a stake in more than one franchise, a rule adopted after several high-profile controversies involving ownership of multiple baseball teams in the 1890s. There was one recent exception to this rule: after being blocked in their bid to eliminate or "contract" two franchises in 2001, Major League Baseball purchased the Montreal Expos from its owners. Although MLB eventually relocated the team to Washington, D.C., the franchise (now known as the Nationals) remained owned by the other 29 MLB clubs. In May 2006, the team was sold to a local group lead by Theodore N. Lerner (http://www.mlb.com).

All four leagues grant some sort of territorial exclusivity to their owners, precluding the addition of another team in the same area unless the current team's owners consent, which is generally obtained in exchange for compensation and/or residual rights regarding the new franchise. For example, to obtain the consent of Baltimore Orioles owner Peter Angelos to place an MLB team in Washington (which is about 35 miles from Oriole Park at Camden Yards), a deal was struck under the terms of which television and radio broadcast rights to Nationals games are handled by the Orioles franchise, who formed a new network (the Mid-Atlantic Sports Network) to produce and distribute the games for both franchises on local affiliates and cable/satellite systems (http://www.mlb.com).

Some leagues, such as the NFL, have even stronger ownership restrictions. The NFL currently forbids large ownership groups or publicly traded corporations from purchasing NFL teams. This policy allows the league office to deal with individual owners instead of boards of directors although the Packers' ownership group was grandfathered into the current policy. The NFL also forbids its majority owners from owning *any* sports teams (except for soccer teams) in other NFL cities; and prohibits owners from investing in casinos or being otherwise involved in gambling operations. (NFL owners may freely own soccer teams without league restrictions because Lamar Hunt won a court challenge stemming from his investment in the old North American Soccer League. Hunt currently owns three teams in Major League Soccer, one based in Kansas City—where he owns the Chiefs—and also teams in Dallas and Columbus; (http://www.nfl.com).

Regarding territorial rights, the main concern for many team owners has become television revenue, although the possibility of reduced ticket sales remains a concern for some teams. Because the National Football League shares all of its television revenue equally, and most of its teams sell out their stadiums with little difficulty, some NFL owners are seen as being less reluctant to share their territories. For example, the return of the NFL to Baltimore in 1996 attracted no serious opposition from the Washington Redskins organization.

Substance Abuse

Soaring paychecks for top athletes and pharmacological advances have conspired to increase the prevalence of performance enhancing drugs in professional and Olympic sports in recent years. At the same time, an influx of money into college athletics has helped deepen pervasive corruption in this area. Individual athletes face tough ethical choices about how to get ahead amid systematic cheating and gross pay inequities among athletes, with cheaters often obtaining the biggest rewards.

"WINNING ISN'T EVERYTHING, it's the only thing." This often repeated comment of a famous National Football League coach, the late Vince Lombardi, captures an attitude held by many fans and athletes: sports is always about winning. This urge to win at all costs encourages the intrusion of drugs into sports. For if winning is everything, then many athletes will do anything to win. Sometimes, doing anything means doing drugs.

One of the most exciting sports stories in recent years was the attempt to break Roger Maris's single-season home run record in baseball. On September 8, 1998, Mark McGwire of the St. Louis Cardinals made history by hitting his 62nd home run. The popular McGwire, who finished the season with 70 home runs, was widely celebrated for his feat. However, many people believe that McGwire's achievement was tarnished by a revelation some weeks earlier that he had been using androstenedione, a compound that temporarily boosts levels of the male sex hormone testosterone. "Andro" is believed by some to promote muscle buildup and recovery; McGwire had taken it as part of his power lifting exercise regimen. It is legal to buy androstenedione as a "dietary supplement" in the United States; although, many medical experts believe it is essentially similar to artificial forms of testosterone (steroids) that are illegal in the United States without a doctor's prescription. Androstenedione is banned by many sports organizations outside of baseball including the National Football League (NFL) and the International Olympic Committee (IOC). Despite the fact that

McGwire's actions were legal and within the rules of Major League Baseball, many sports observers were dismayed. "In raising his testosterone to reach Maris' record," wrote syndicated columnist Derrick Z. Jackson, "McGwire has lowered the values of his sport. No longer is it the best man who wins. It is the best-enhanced man." (In August 1999, McGwire announced that he had stopped using the substance. He hit 65 home runs in the 1999 season.)

The McGwire controversy led MLB to revise its drug policies in cooperation with the players association. The Barry Bonds controversy continued the substance abuse drama in MLB. The professional leagues will be faced with substance abuse concerns for years to come.

Television Exposure

All four of the major sports have had television contracts with at least one of the original "big three" U.S. broadcast television networks (CBS, NBC, and ABC) since those networks' early years, indicative of the sports' widespread appeal since their inception. Regular-season games, as well as important contests such as championship and all-star games, are often televised in prime time. In the last generation, fast-growing cable and satellite networks have taken a larger chunk of the major sports' pie. The four major sports now have entire sports networks dedicated just to each of them (such as the NFL Network).

Comparing the sizes of television contracts, the NFL is by far the largest (reportedly $2.2 billion U.S. for the 2001 season) with the NBA and MLB second and third ($500 million and $479 million respectively). The NHL is in a distant fourth place ($120 million), a disparity those who wish to exclude the NHL from the major leagues often point to. However, the NHL began airing games on NBC starting in January 2006 and the NHL Network is now available to a large percentage of U.S. cable and satellite subscribers. In addition, many regular season NHL games are broadcast on regional sports networks (such as FSN) which can vary on contract worth by region or team (*Sports Business Journal*, 2006).

Violence

Violence in sports involves intentional aggressive violence. Competitive sports, such as baseball, basketball, football, ice hockey, lacrosse, and soccer may involve aggressive tactics but actual violence in sports falls outside the boundaries of good sportsmanship. Violence in sports may include threats, verbal abuse, or physical harm and may be carried out by athletes, coaches, fans, and spectators. Violence outside of sports may include assault, assault and battery, battery, murder, rape, and sexual abuse.

There are a number of incidents, either during an athletic event or outside of sports, that raise the public's interest and concern about athletes who are charged with criminal offenses. Violence within the context of sports is a familiar subject. Many people consider the punishment of fines and suspensions of violent action to be minor when compared to the nature of conduct within sport. Violence in the professional ranks that rises to a concern includes player against player, player versus fan violence, player versus official, and off-the-field conduct.

Weathering Challenges from Rival Leagues

All of the majors have bested at least one rival league formed with the intention of being just as "big" as the established league, often by signing away star players and by locating franchises in cities that were already part of the existing league. In many cases, the major leagues have absorbed the most successful franchises from its failing rival, or merged outright with it.

- Major League Baseball withstood the challenge of the Federal League in 1914 and prevented the Continental League from getting off the ground in the early 1960s by awarding franchises to some of the proposed CL cities. Before World War II, black players were not allowed to play Major League Baseball, and various rival Negro Leagues sprung up to showcase black players' talents; although no official cross-league play took place, white and black players often faced off in postseason barnstorming tours where the Negro League players showed themselves to be MLB players' competitive equals. After Jackie Robinson broke the major league color barrier in 1947, the influx of black stars into the major leagues drained the Negro Leagues of talent and eventually caused their collapse (http://www.mlb.com).

- The NBA withstood the challenge of the American Basketball Association in the 1960s and '70s, absorbed four of its most successful franchises (Denver Nuggets, Indiana Pacers, New York Nets, and San Antonio Spurs), and adopted several of the ABA's rule variations, most notably the three point shot (http://www.nba.com).

- The NFL has fought off the most rivals throughout the years. The most notable rival was the American Football League, which existed from 1960-1970 before merging with the NFL. In the AFL's last years, it achieved parity with the NFL: AFL teams won two of the four pre-merger Super Bowl games and TV ratings and in-person attendance for the two leagues were about the same. The America Football League name was previously used by several shortlived leagues back in the 1920s and 1930s. Another strong rival to the NFL was the All-America Football Conference of 1946-1949, which also merged with the NFL. Other rival football leagues were the World Football League of 1974-1975, the United States Football League of 1982-1985, the Canadian Football League's American franchises of 1993-1995, and the XFL of 2001. All told, 13 of the NFL's current 32 franchises were absorbed from a rival league — all 10 AFL franchises of the 1960s, the Cleveland Browns and San Francisco 49ers from the AAFC, and the St. Louis Rams (originally based in Cleveland and later relocated to Los Angeles) of the 1936 AFL. Another three NFL franchises have been added or moved to USFL cities since the USFL's demise in 1986, these being Phoenix, Jacksonville and Baltimore (http://www.nfl.com).

- Prior to the challenge of the World Hockey Association, the NHL prevented the old Western Hockey League from achieving parity with the NHL by doubling in size in 1967. The WHA was in existence from 1972-1979, and upon its demise, the four strongest teams joined into the NHL: the Edmonton Oilers, the Quebec Nordiques (now the Colorado Avalanche), the New England Whalers (later renamed the Hartford Whalers and now the Carolina Hurricanes), and the Winnipeg Jets (now the Phoenix Coyotes). A few WHA players became NHL stars after the merger, including Mark Messier, Wayne Gretzky, Mark Howe, and Mike Liut. The WHA initially attracted star players such as Bobby Hull and Derek Sanderson to its teams by offering substantially higher salaries than did the NHL at the time; to compete for free agents, NHL teams were forced to match this salary escalation, bringing hockey players' salaries to parity with those of other North American professional athletes (http://www. nhl.com).

Summary

The professional sports industry has grown into one of the most significant mass entertainment industries in American society. In 2005, the *Sport Business Journal* estimates the 164 franchises in professional baseball, basketball (men and women), football, hockey, lacrosse, and soccer (men and women) were estimated to be worth over $18 billion (Sawyer, et al., 2004). The gross national sports product, GNSP, today is around $145 billion and is predicted to be in the $170 billion range by the year 2010 (Sawyer, et al., 2004). This would make it the sixth largest industry in North America. A December 2005 study in the *Sports Business Journal* estimated the size of the American sports industry to be $243 billion.

The emergence of sports as such a major social force is a relatively recent phenomenon. Swanson & Spears (1995) suggest that modern sports fans would scarcely recognize the American sports scene during the years immediately following World War II. Professional sports had a modest, even provincial quality about them. Only professional baseball and boxing events attracted substantial national attention. Major League Baseball teams were confined to the Northeast and upper Midwest since they traveled only by train. The National Football League (NFL) had been formed in 1922 but paled in comparison to baseball and college football in popularity. The National Basketball Association (NBA) was formed from the merger of two competing leagues in 1950; but, like football, it took a distinct backseat to the college game. The National Hockey League (NHL) had been founded in Canada in 1917 but was slow to capture American audiences.

Professional sports are facing a number of major issues that can impact a league's or team's profitability. These issues include broadcasting issues such as Internet rights, siphoning, home taping, domestic and international piracy of satellite transmissions, blackouts, handheld pagers, and satellite distribution, collective bargaining, employment diversity, facility financing, franchise stability, franchise locations, gambling, higher player salaries, ownership restrictions, substance abuse, television exposure, violence, and weathering challenges from rival leagues.

References

Baade, R. A., & Dye, R.F. (1988). Sports stadiums and area development: A critical review. *Economic Development Quarterly, 2*(3), 265-275.

Coakley, J.J. (2004). *Sport in society.* (8th ed). New York: McGraw-Hill.

Cox, R.H. (1998). *Sport psychology: Concepts and applications.* (4th ed.). New York: McGraw-Hill.

Eitzen, D.S., & Sage, G.H. (2003). *Sociology of North American sport.* (7th ed.). New York: McGraw-Hill.

Howard, D.R., & Crompton, J.L. (2003). *Financing sport.* (2nd ed). Morgantown, WV: Fitness Information Technology.

http://www.arena football.com. (2006).

http://www.arenafootball.com/af2. (2006).

http://www.minorleaguenews.com/history/baseball/2005/04/04/01.html. (2006).

http://www.independentleague.com. (2006).

http://www.lpga.com. (2006).

http://www.majorleaguelacrosse.com. (2006).

http://www.mlb.com. (2006).

http://www.misl.com. (2006).

http://www.mls.com. (2006).

http://www.nba.com. (2006).

http://www.nba.com/NBA_Developmental_league. (2006).

http://www.nfl.com. (2006).

http://www.nfl.com/europelegaue. (2006).

http://www.npf.com. (2006).

http://www.nhl.com. (2006).

http://www.pga.com. (2006).

http://www.usta.com. (2006).

Gorman, J., & Calhoun K. (1994). *The name of the game: The business of sports.* New York: John Wiley & Sons.

Loy, J.W., Jr., & Kenyon, G.S. (1969). *Sport, culture, and society.* New York: MacMillen.

Parks, J.B., & Quarterman, J. (Eds.) (2003). *Contemporary sport management.* (2nd ed.). Champaign, IL: Human Kinetics.

Sage, G.H. (1998). *Power and ideology in American sport.* (2nd ed.). Champaign, IL: Human Kinetics.

Sawyer, T.H., Hypes, M.A., & Hypes, J.A. (2004). *Financing the sport enterprise.* Champaign, IL: Sagamore Publishing.

Siegfried, J.J. (1996). Does Nashville need a publicly funded football stadium? *Tennessee's Business, 7* (1-2), 31-36.

Stoldt, G.C., Dittmore, S.W., & Branvold, S.E. (2006). *Sport public relations.* Champaign, IL: Human Kinetics.

Swanson, R.A., & Spears B. (1995). *History of sport and physical education in the United States.* (4th ed.). New York: McGraw-Hill.

Wiggins, D.K. (1995). *Sport in America from wicked amusement to national obsession.* Champaign, IL: Human Kinetics.

Wong, G.M. (2002). *Essentials of sports law.* Westport, CT: Praeger.

Zimbalist, A. (1996). The economic impact of sports teams on cities. *Tennessee Business, 7* (1-2), 9-16.

NOTES

CHAPTER 12

Motorsports Governance

Motorsports are sporting activities that combine a body of steel, aluminum, or fiberglass, or a combination of all three with an engine of various sizes. These mechanisms race over land, snow, water and/or ice and in the air at amazing speeds. Motorsports include auto racing, air plane racing, powerboat racing, motocross (motor cycle) racing, snowmobile racing, and truck racing. In America the most popular by far is auto racing, in particular NASCAR series racing and Indy Car racing.

Auto racing, also known as automobile racing, autosport, or motorsport, is a sport involving racing automobiles. It began in France in the late nineteenth century and is now one of the world's most popular and, perhaps, the most thoroughly commercialized spectator sport. Auto racing began almost immediately after the construction of the first successful petrol-fuelled autos. In 1894, the first contest was organized by Paris magazine *Le Petit Journal*, a reliability test to determine best performance. That first race now is called *Paris to Rouen 1894*. Competitors included factory vehicles from Karl Benz's Benz & Cie. and

Gottlieb Daimler and Wilhelm Maybach's DMG. A year later, the first real race was staged in France, from Paris to Bordeaux. First over the line was Émile Levassor but he was disqualified because his car was not a required four-seater (Swanson & Spear, 1995).

The first auto race in the United States, over a 54.36 mile (87.48 km) course, took place in Chicago, Illinois on November 2, 1895 with Frank Duryea winning in 10 hours and 23 minutes beating three petrol-fuelled cars and two electric. The first trophy awarded was the Vanderbilt Cup (Swanson & Spear, 1995).

Learning Objectives

Upon completion this chapter, the reader should be able to:

- Identify the various categories of motorsports in the United States.
- Discuss how motorsports is governed.
- Understand how motorsports is fi-

nanced.
*   Identify and discuss the issues facing motorsports.

Identification of Motor Sports Governing Bodies

There are two leading marketers and promoters of motorsports entertainment in the United States. They are Speedway Motorsports, Inc. (SMI) and International Speedway Corporation (ISC). The information below describes these two motorsport marketers and promoters:

Speedway Motorsports, Inc. (SMI)

SMI is a leading marketer and promoter of motorsports entertainment in the United States. SMI owns six premier speedway facilities in growing markets across the country and has one of the largest total permanent seating capacities, with the highest average number of seats per speedway, in the motorsports industry. Speedway Motorsports also provides souvenir merchandising through SMI Properties, manufactures and distributes smaller-scale, modified racing cars through 600 Racing, as well as broadcasts syndicated racing programs through Performance Racing Network. SMI is located in Concord, NC and is listed on the NYSE under the symbol TRK. As of December 31, 2005, total permanent seating capacity was approximately 775,000 located at the facilities seen in Table 12.1 (http://www.speedqaymotorsports.com).

Table 12.1
SMI Facilities

Atlanta Motor Speedway in Georgia
Bristol Motor Speedway in Tennessee
Infineon Raceway in California
Las Vegas Motor Speedway in Nevada
Lowe's Motor Speedway in North Carolina
Texas Motor Speedway in Texas

SMI derives revenue principally from the following activities:

*   sales of tickets to motorsports races and other events held at our speedways,
*   licensing of network television, cable television, and radio rights to broadcast such events,
*   sales of sponsorships, facility naming rights, and promotions to companies that desire to advertise or sell their products or services surrounding our events, and
*   commissions earned on sales of food, beverages, and hospitality catering and sales of souvenirs and other motorsports related merchandise, and rental of luxury suites during events and other track facilities (http://www.speedqaymotorsports.com).

In 2004, SMI derived approximately 80 percent of its total revenues from NASCAR-sanctioned events. SMI has experienced substantial growth in revenues and profitability as a result of the following factors:

*   continued improvement, expansion, and investments in SMI facilities,
*   SMI participation in the consolidated NASCAR television and ancillary rights agreements,
*   growth in sponsorships through consistent marketing and promotional efforts, and
*   the overall increase in popularity of NEXTEL Cup, Busch, Craftsman Truck, IRL, NHRA, CCWS, and other motorsports events in the United States.
*   Debuting on Wall Street in February 1995, Speedway Motorsports, Inc. (NYSE:TRK) became the first motorsports company to be publicly traded on the New York Stock Exchange. The

Company has continuously pursued a successful five-pronged business strategy. This business strategy includes enhancing and improving speedway facilities, maximizing broadcast and sponsorship exposure, increasing the daily usage of the facilities, growing 600 Racing, Performance Racing Network, zMax, and looking for new opportunities for additional motorsports facilities through construction or acquisition (http://www.speedqaymotorsports.com).

The SMI Board of Directors follows certain guidelines and has established committees to ensure that Speedway Motorsports, Inc. conducts itself in a manner pleasing to its shareholders. In order to ensure the integrity of the board of directors, all members serving on committees are independent of the company and management.

International Speedway Corporation (IMC)

Bill France Racing, Inc., established in 1953, signed the initial contract to secure land for construction of Daytona International Speedway on Nov. 8, 1957. Thus, Daytona International Speedway Corporation (now International Speedway Corporation) was born.

Today, International Speedway Corporation, a publicly held company (Nasdaq: ISCA – news, OTC Bulletin Board: ISCB - news), is a leading promoter of motorsports activities in the United States currently promoting more than 100 events nationwide.

ISC currently owns and/or operates 11 of the nation's major motorsports facilities (see Table 12.2; (http://www.iscmotorsports.com).

ISC also owns and operates MRN Radio, the nation's largest independent sports radio network, DAYTONA USA, the "Ultimate Motorsports Attraction" in Daytona Beach, Florida, the official attraction of NASCAR, and subsidiaries which provide catering services, food and beverage concessions, and produce and market motorsports-related merchandise under the trade name "Americrown".

Included among the events conducted by ISC at its facilities are:

Table 12.2
International Speedway Corporation Facilities

Daytona International Speedway in Florida (home of the Daytona 500)
Talladega Superspeedway in Alabama
Michigan International Speedway located outside Detroit
Richmond International Raceway in Virginia
California Speedway near Los Angeles
Kansas Speedway in Kansas City, Kansas
Phoenix International Raceway in Arizona
Homestead-Miami Speedway in Florida
Martinsville Speedway in Virginia
Darlington Raceway in South Carolina
Watkins Glen International in New York
Nazareth Speedway in Pennsylvania
Indirect 37.5 percent interest in Raceway Associates, LLC, which owns and operates
    Chicagoland Speedway and Route 66 Raceway near Chicago, Illinois.

- Stock car and/or truck races sanctioned by NASCAR, Automobile Racing Club of America (ARCA) and International Race of Champions (IROC),
- Open-wheel events by the Indy Racing League (IRL),
- Sports car races by the Grand American Road Racing Association (Grand American), International Motorsports Association (IMSA), and Sports Car Club of America (SCCA),
- Motorcycle events by the American Motorcyclist Association (AMA), and
- Go-kart races by the World Karting Association (WKA) (http://www.iscmotorsports.com).

Categories of Autoracing

There are five major categories of autoracing (motorsports) in the United States. They include drag racing, open wheel racing, rallying, road racing, sport car racing, and stock car racing. Table 12.3 lists other categories of motorsports that are smaller in magnitude. Each of the major categories will be briefly discussed below:

Drag Racing

Drag racing was organized as a sport by Wally Parks in the early 1950s through the National Hot Rod Association (NHRA). The world's largest and loudest auto racing organization is located in Glendale, California. Parks initially started NHRA as a means of getting hot rodders off the streets and on to legal dragstrips. Since those early days, NHRA has evolved into the largest promoter of professional drag-racing in the world. Today, with more than 300 dedicated employees, NHRA offers drag racing opportunities for hot rod enthusiasts of all levels, from kids ages 8-17 in the NHRA O'Reilly Auto Parts Jr. Drag Racing League all the way up to the top of the professional ranks with the organization's $50 million NHRA POWERade Drag Racing Series (http://www.nhra.com).

More than 140 member tracks across North America host NHRA competitions in NHRA's seven geographic regions. In addition to the marquee POWERade Series, which crisscrosses the United States, making 23 stops in 21 cities over the course of nine months, NHRA offers popular weekly grassroots programs at many of its member tracks. One of the most popular is the NHRA Street Legal Drags presented by American Automobile Association (AAA) program, which offers the opportunity to compete in grudge-match-style drag racing. Serious weekend warriors can compete at their local track in the Summit Racing Series, which crowns national champions each season. Two developmental series are available for those who are interested in a career as a touring pro: the NHRA Lucas Oil Drag Racing Series and the NHRA Xplōd Sport Compact Racing Series (http://www.nhra.com).

Table 12.3
Other Categories of Motorsports

Autocrossing	Autograss	Board track racing
Demolition Derby	Dirt Speedway Racing	Dirt track racing
Drifting	Folkrace	Grand Prix Truck Racing
Ice Racing	Int'l Sporting Code	Rallycross
Road racing	Short track Mtr Racing	Slalom
Snowmobiling	Solo	Sprint car racing
Street racing	Motocross	

NHRA's key business partners include the Coca-Cola Co., whose POWERade brand sponsors the top touring series and Lucas Oil Co. and Summit Racing Equipment, which both sponsor key developmental touring series. All of NHRA's major series receive television coverage from NHRA's exclusive multimedia partner, ESPN Inc. A sample of the active official sponsors involved in the sport include Budweiser, Sears Craftsman, Fram, Pontiac, Checker Schuck's Kragen, MBNA America, and GMC. In an independent survey conducted by *Sports Business Journal* in 2003, NHRA was ranked high in a variety of categories reflecting sponsor satisfaction, including Best Value for the Money where NHRA was ranked first among 16 major sports, including the NFL, NBA, MLB, and NASCAR (http://www.nhra.com).

Open Wheel Racing

Open wheel is a term for cars, usually purpose-built racecars, with the wheels located outside the car's main body, as distinct from cars which have their wheels below the body or fenders in the manner of most street cars, stock cars, or touring cars. Open-wheel racing includes many types and levels of motor racing including Formula One, American Championship Car Racing (Champ Car World Series, Indy Racing League), sprint car, midget car, and others.

Since 1916, there has been a United States national automobile racing championship for drivers of single seater (commonly referred to as open wheel) cars. This championship has been run by several different sanctioning bodies since 1909. The Indianapolis 500 has been a round of the National Championship since its inception in 1911.

Sanctioning Bodies

- From 1909 to 1955, the championship was sanctioned by the Contest Board of American Automobile Association (the AAA). AAA introduced the first championship for racing cars as early as in 1905, but it was cancelled after a couple of serious incidents. Barney Oldfield was leading the championship at the point it was cancelled.

- From 1956 to 1978, the championship was sanctioned by the United States Automobile Club (the USAC), a body formed by the then-owner of the Indianapolis Motor Speedway, Tony Hulman.

- In 1979, there were two championships run by two sanctioning bodies, USAC and CART (Championship Auto Racing Teams), which was a body formed by most of the existing team-owners. As all the top teams were allied to CART, the CART championship became the de-facto championship.

- In 1980, USAC and CART jointly formed the Championship Racing League (CRL) to run the National Championship; but the management of the Indianapolis speedway disliked the idea. The CRL was abandoned before any races were run and CART exclusively sanctioned the championship. In 1981 and 1982, the Indianapolis 500 was not included as a points-paying round of the National Championship; although all the top drivers and teams competed anyway. One further race was run by USAC at Pocono Raceway in 1981. This race was not supported by many CART teams and even included some dirt-track cars. After this, USAC withdrew from sanctioning, except for the Indianapolis 500 which they continued to run. USAC ceremonially named the '500' as part of their 'Gold Crown' championship, an essentially meaningless title as the race was the only round, and allowed the race to be included in the CART championship.

- From 1983 to 1995, stability returned and the championship was run by CART, with USAC organizing at Indianapolis.
- In 1996, Tony Hulman's grandson, Tony George, the owner of the Indianapolis track and the '500', created the Indy Racing League (IRL), a separate championship that includes the Indianapolis 500 as a round. The IRL's results are either listed alongside the existing National championship or treated as an entirely separate entity and not included.
- CART continued running the existing championship until the organization folded at the end of 2003.
- The rights to CART's assets were purchased by a consortium called Open Wheel Racing Series (OWRS) in 2004 and the former-CART series was renamed the Champ Car World Series.
- Formula One, abbreviated to F1, and also known as Grand Prix racing, is recognized as the highest class of auto racing in the world. The "formula" in the name is a set of rules that all participants and cars must meet. The F1 season consists of a series of races, known as Grand Prix, held usually on purpose-built circuits and, in a few cases, on closed city streets. The results of each race are combined to determine

two annual World Championships, one for drivers and one for constructors (http://www.formula1.com).

Grand Prix motor racing has its roots in organized automobile racing that began in France as far back as 1894. It quickly evolved from a simple road race from one town to the next to endurance tests for car and driver. Innovation and the drive of competition soon saw speeds exceeding 100 mph; but, because the races were held on open roads, there were frequent accidents with the resulting fatalities of both drivers and spectators (http://www.grand-prix.com; (see Table 12.4 for Grand Prix races).

Champ Car, a shortened form of "Championship Car", has been the name for a class of cars used in American Championship Car Racing for many decades. It is also the common name for the Champ Car World Series, an Open Wheel World Championship mainly based in North America that was formerly known as CART or Championship Auto Racing Teams. The series was formerly known as the CART PPG IndyCar World Series and the CART FedEx Championship Series.

The Indy Racing League, better known as IRL, is the sanctioning body of a predominantly American based open-wheel racing series. Its centerpiece is the Indianapolis 500. The IRL is owned by Hulman

Table 12.4
Grand Prix Races

Avus Grand Prix	Bari Grand Prix	Belgian Grand Prix
Belgrade Grand Prix	Coppa Acerbo	Coppa Ciano
CzechGrand Prix	Donington Grand Prix	Dutch Grand Prix
French Grand Prix	German Grand Prix	Hungarian Grand Prix
Italian Grand Prix	Milan Grand Prix	Mille Miglia
PrixMonaco Grand Prix	Moroccan Grand Prix	Penya Rhin Grand
San Sebastian Grand Prix	Spanish Grand Prix	Swiss Grand Prix
Targa Florio	Tripoli Grand Prix	Tunis Grand Prix
United States Grand Prix	Vanderbilt Cup	Zandvoort Grand Prix

and Co., which also owns the Indianapolis Motor Speedway complex. The IRL was brought about in 1994 by Tony George and was created with a breakaway group of drivers from CART, which had coordinated Indy car racing since 1979 when CART broke away from the United States Auto Club (USAC). George designed IRL as a lower-cost open-wheel alternative to CART, which had come to be technology-driven and dominated by a few wealthy multicar teams much like in Formula One. The IRL developed a consistent engine package and chassis rules that have produced some of the closest finishes in any racing series. Ironically, the series is now dominated by many of the same wealthy multicar teams that once dominated CART (http://www.irl.com).

Rally Racing

Rallying, or rally racing, involves highly modified production cars on (closed) public roads or off-road areas run on a point-to-point format where participants and their co-drivers "rally" to a set of points, leaving in regular intervals from start points. A rally is typically conducted over a number of stages of any terrain that entrants are often allowed to scout beforehand. The co-driver uses the "pacenotes" to help the driver complete each stage as fast as possible, reading the detailed shorthand aloud over an in-car intercom system. Competition is based on lowest total elapsed time over the course of an event (http://www.nasarallysport.com).

The top series is the World Rally Championship (WRC); but, there are also regional championships and many countries have their own national championships. Some famous rallies include the Monte Carlo Rally and Rally Argentina. Another famous event (actually best described as a "rally raid") is the Paris-Dakar Rally. There are also many smaller, club level, categories of rallies that are popular with amateurs, making up the "grass roots" of motorsports.

Road Racing

In sports car racing, production versions of sports cars and purpose-built prototype cars compete with each other on closed circuits. The races are usually conducted over long distances, at least 1000 km, and cars are driven by teams of two or three drivers (and sometimes more in the U.S.), switching every now and then. Due to the performance difference between production-based sports cars and sports racing prototypes, one race usually involves many racing classes. In the U.S., the American Le Mans Series was organized in 1999 featuring GT, GTS, and two prototype classes, LMP1 (Le Mans Prototype 1) and LMP2.

Another series based on Le Mans began in 2004, the Le Mans Endurance Series, which included four 1000 km races at tracks in Europe. A competing body, Grand-Am, which began in 2000, sanctions its own set of endurance series, the Rolex Sports Car Series and the Grand-Am Cup. Grand-Am events typically feature many more cars and much closer competition than American Le Mans. Famous sports car races include the 24 Hours of Le Mans, the 24 Hours of Daytona, and the 12 Hours of Sebring (http://www.grandamerican.com).

The Grand American Road Racing Association was established in 1999 to return stability to major league sports car road racing in North America. As the organization begins its seventh season of competition in 2006, Grand American is universally regarded as one of the world's fastest-growing motorsports organizations. Grand American is located in Daytona Beach, Florida on the same corporate campus that is also home to NASCAR, International Speedway Corporation (ISC), and Daytona International Speedway but it operates as its own stand-alone corporation with a group of independent investors and its own board of advisors. Among the company's investors are several of the key people behind NASCAR's success but Grand American offers an entirely different product that features extremely competitive sports car racing on historic road and street circuits and in major market speedways throughout North America.

Stock Car Racing

Stock car racing is the American variant of touring car racing. Usually conducted on ovals, the cars look like production cars, but are in fact purpose-built racing machines that are all very similar in specifications. Early stock cars were much closer to production vehicles; the car to be raced was often driven from track to track.

The main stock car racing series is NASCAR (see Table 12.5 for an outline of NASCAR Series), and among the most famous races in the series are the Daytona 500 and the Pepsi 400. NASCAR also runs the Busch Series (a junior stock car league) and the Craftsman Truck Series (pickup trucks). NASCAR also runs the Featherlite series of "modified" cars, which are heavily modified from stock form. With powerful engines, large tires, and light bodies, NASCAR's oldest series is considered by many to be its most exciting. There are also other stock car series like IROC in the United States and CASCAR in Canada (http://www.nascar.com).

Other Forms of Motorsports

There are other forms of motorsports besides the very popular auto racing that should be recognized. These other forms include motocross, truck racing, motorboat racing, air racing, and snowmobile (snow cross) racing. Each of these forms will be discuss briefly below:

Motocross

Motocross (often shortened to (MX) or MotoX) is a form of motorcycle racing or all-terrain vehicle racing held on enclosed off-road circuits and is widely considered the world's most popular form of motorcycle racing. Motocross is derived from the French and was originally called Scrambling when the sport was invented in the UK. The first known race took place at Camberley, Surrey in 1924. The name "motocross" is a combination derived from the words "Motorcycle" and "Cross Country". Motocross is often abbreviated as MX (http:www.amamotorcross.com).

AMA Pro Racing, which was formed in 1994 to respond to the growth of motorcycle racing in United States holds many events, among which the AMA Superbike, AMA Supercross, AMA Motorcross, and AMA Flat Track http:www.amamotorcross.com).

Finally, Supermoto is a recent invention involving racing Motocross bikes on a part concrete, part off-road track, with "road" tires instead of off-road tires. Some tracks for these race events have jumps, berms, and whoop-dee-doos just like true motocross tracks. For special events, the Supermoto track may incorporate metal ramps for jumps that can be disassembled and taken to other locations. Supermoto races may take place at modified go-kart tracks, road racing tracks, or even street racing tracks. There are also classes for kids such as the 85cc class (http://www.supermotorcross.net).

Table 12.5
NASCAR SERIES

- Nextel Cup
- Busch Series
- Craftsman Truck Series
- Dodge Weekly Series
- Regional Racing
  - Grand National Division
  - Touring Division
  - AutoZone Elite Division
  - Special Event Division
- NASCAR Canadian Tire Series
- NASCAR Mexico Corona Series

Truck Racing

Grand Prix Truck Racing is a form of motor racing that runs race modified versions of heavy trucks on racing circuits. This type of racing is popular in Europe (http://www.truck-grand-prix.de/).The sport started over 20 years ago and enjoyed great success, but declined in the 1990s. However, in the last few years, the profile of truck racing in Europe and the UK has increased and currently over 30 teams regularly compete. The sporting regulations came under the control of the FIA later to ensure that the vehicles conform to the layout and original style of the truck whilst defining the safety standards required to race (http://www.truckracing.de/).

Maximum race speed is restricted to 100 mph for safety reasons and a minimum weight limit is 5500kgs. Races start from a rolling start and commonly, races last from eight to 12 laps. Although a non-contact sport, due to the closeness of trucks to one another during races, minor collisions can occur. However, injuries to drivers are very rare.

Unlike other forms of motorsport, race trucks look like and conform to regulations to ensure that major components used are the same as their road going counterparts. All drivers must hold a race licence issued by the Motor Sports Association or the national motorsport body from the driver's country. The makes of truck currently represented in truck racing cover most of the common marques over the last 20 years. The regulations allow for trucks to compete in two classes so trucks with less sophisticated engine management systems, suspension, and braking systems can compete effectively (http://nascar.com/craftsman).

The NASCAR Craftsman Truck Series is a popular NASCAR racing series that features modified pickup trucks. The idea for the Truck Series dates back to 1993 when a group of off-road racers made a prototype for a NASCAR-style pickup truck. These were first shown off during the 1994 Daytona 500, and a number of demonstration races were held during the season. These trucks proved to be extremely popular, and it led to NASCAR creating the series, originally known as the "Super-Truck Series", in 1995 (http://www.nascar.com/craftsman).

While a new series, it managed to garner quite a significant amount of support from prominent Winston Cup people immediately. The series became known as the Craftsman Truck Series in 1996. By 1998, most of the short tracks were phased out in favor of speedways of one to two miles in length and more of the races were held at tracks that hosted Cup and Busch events concurrently; but some races were held with Champ Car and Indy Racing League events. Most of the first drivers in the series were veteran short trackers who had not made it into the other NASCAR series. It is worth noting that most of the early champions have used their titles to become Nextel Cup regulars at one point in their careers. As the years went on, a number of younger drivers debuted in the series, using the series as a springboard for their racing careers. Kyle Busch was 16 when thrown out of a 2001 Craftsman Truck Series race in Fontana, CA by CART (which sanctioned the Marlboro 500 that weekend) because tobacco sponsorship regulations prohibited competitors under 18 in any race during the meet and resulted in a 2002 NASCAR minimum age requirement of 18. Most races nowadays will last around 250 miles at larger tracks, 150 to 200 miles at most others, and 200-250 laps around the shortest tracks (http://www.nascar.com/craftsman).

Motorboat Racing

There are five common forms of motorboat racing including (a) drag boat racing, (b) hydroplane racing, (c) jet spring boat racing, (d) offshore powerboat racing, and

(e) F1 Powerboat racing. Each of the theses forms will be discussed briefly below.

Drag Boat Racing. This form of boat racing is similar to auto drag racing, which takes place on water rather than land. Instead of two cars, two boats race each other over a straight quarter-mile course (http://f1boat.com). One difference between auto and boat drag racing, the boats begin from a short rolling start rather than a standing start. The International Hot Boat Association (IHBA) indicates the premier category of drag boat racing is the Top Fuel Hydroplane class, which is a water-based equivalent to Top Fuel Dragsters capable of covering a quarter mile of water in less than five seconds with a terminal speed of approximetly 250 mph. There are other categories of drag boats based on various engine configurations. The biggest event on the drag calendar is the IHBA World Finals, which takes place in Phoenix (http:///www.ihbaracing.com).

Hydroplane Racing.   Hydroplane racing, commonly known as hydro racing, is a sport involving racing hydroplanes on lakes and rivers. It is a popular spectator sport worldwide and one of the more commercialized sports. There are three racing circuits for hydrplanes, including limited racing (for boats classified as either F-125, F-250, F-350, or F-500), unlimited racing (normally F-750 engines), and stock outboard racing (utilizing both hydroplane and runabout or monoplane hulls with racing engines that use a service outboard powerhead and a racing lower unit with a direct drive). The U.S. governing body is UIM powerboat racing (http://www.apbaracing.com).

Jet Sprint Boat Racing. This is a form of racing where trailerable speed boats, powered by water jet propulsion rather than by conventional propellers, race in shallow water. The courses are generally artifical watercourses characterized by many tight turns. The racing format is a sequence of time trails. This type of motorboat racing is very popular in Austrialia. The jetboat was invented in New Zealand. It has not yet caught on in the United States.

Offshore Powerboat Racing. This type of motorboat racing is characterized by large, ocean-going powerboats. The race is typically point-to-point racing. This is an elite sport because of the size of the boats and the amount of fuel required to participate make it an expensive sport.

In Europe, Middle East, and Asia offshore powerboat racing is led by the UIM regulated Class 1 while in the U.S., the leadership is split among the SBI/APBA/UIM and the OSS races. Although there are team sponsors, the sport is still an amateur sport financed mainly by a mixture of private funding and commercial sponsors. The sport is moving more to a circuit racing style, which makes for a better TV and spectator experience.

F1 Powerboat Racing. Inaugurated in 1981, the F1 Powerboat World Championship is similar to Formula 1 car racing, and similar rules apply. Each F1 Powerboat race lasts approximately 45 minutes following a circuit marked out in a selected stretch of water, usually a lake, river, or sheltered bay. Qualifying periods decide the formation of the grid and timing equipment records the performance of competitors to decide the final classification and all-important allocation of championship points (http://www.f1boat.com).

The characteristics of F1 powerboat racing include (a) a grand prix-style event, similar to Fomula One automobile racing, in which teams compete in 13 venues around the world each season, (b) most races take place along a track of approximately ¼ mile with multiple turns, over which the boats can reach 140 miles per hour, (c) the races are longer than most power boat races at approximately 45 minutes but still shorter than most automobile races, (d) the F1 powerboats use a tunnel hull catamarans that are capable of both high speed and exceptional maneuverability weighing 860 pounds, including 260 pounds of engine, and (e) the F1 boats are powered by a Mercury V6 two stroke that propels the boat to 62 mph in less than four seconds and to a maximum speed of over 136 mph (http://www.f1boat.com).

Air Racing

This is a motorsport that involves small airplanes and is practiced worldwide. Unlike auto racing, corporate sponsorship and broadcast media coverage is much less. The sport began in 1909 in Reims, France. The race lasted one week flying from France to England. Later, an air race from England to Australia was instituted. In 1921 the U.S. instituted the National Air Meets (later called Races) which operated until 1939. From 1939 until 1949, the Cleveland Air Races continued the spirit. In 1947, an all-women Transcontinetal Race dubbed the "Powder Puff Derby" was established and ran successfully until 1977. In 1964, the first Reno Air Races (so-called National Championship Air Races) were organized and are still successful today. The Reno affair includes races for six different classes of aircraft, civil airshow acts, military flight demonstrations, and a large static aircraft display. Other promoters have run various pylon racing events across the nation including races in Mojave, California, Hamilton, California, Phoenix, Arizona, and Tunica, Mississippi (http://www.airracinghistory.freeola.com/redbull.htm).

The newest entrant into the air race arena is the Red Bull Air Race Series. The competitors participating fly singly through a series of gates, between which they must perform a prescribed series of aerobatics maneuvers. These events are usually held over water near large cities (http://www.airracinghistory.freeola.com/redbull.htm).

Formula One air racing class is without question the most successful class in the 86-year history of airplane racing. It has seen more races, more pilots, and more airplanes than all other racing classes combined in a half-century lifetime and has experienced not one important change in its rules in all that time. Moreover, it is the only formal air racing class to be exported from the U.S. to Europe and the only class to be recognized by the International Aeronautics Federation (FAI), the world governing body for competitive aviation (http://www.airracinghistory.freeola.com/Formula%20One%20Air%20Racing.htm).

Snowmobile (Snocross) Racing

The most popular form of snowmobile racing is snocross. Snocross racing with its high-flying aerial displays and short-track is both spectator and television friendly. A snocross track features tight turns, banked corners, and a variety of bumps allowing racers to catch "big air" in full view of the spectators. The World PowerSports Association (WPSA) assists racers, manufacturers, and sponsors in benefiting from the rapidly expanding sport of professional snowmobile racing. Its mission is to bring the sport of snowmobile racing to its highest levels (http://www.wsaracing.com).

Governance

The governance of motorsports rests with the racing teams, marketers and promoters, and sanctioning bodies. The key to entities of motorsports are racing teams. Without the racing teams, there would be no motorsports as we know it today.

The anatomy of a racing team consists of four major parts: the main office, the garage, the driver, and track side on race day.

- The main office personnel include the owner (sometimes serves as CEO), the chief executive officer, the chief financial officer, directors of public relations, marketing, human resources, and purchasing and logistics.

- In the garage, there is a fabricator (builds new parts for race cars or bikes), shop manager (builds and maintains backup car or cycle), chief mechanic (oversees race car or cycle preparations), and transportation personnel.
- The personnel on track side on race day include pit stop coach, human performance specialist (oversees diet and physical conditioning of the driver), mechanics (work as pit crew during race, responsible for daily aspects of mechanical preparation), engineers (chief, support, data acquisition, and electronics who conduct engineering operations and assist in mechanical maintenance), and race day spotter (keeps driver informed during races).
- The driver is the person who drives the car in the race (drives as fast as humanly possible).

Sanctioning Motorsport Bodies

Automobile and Truck Racing

There are three major sanctioning bodies in motorsports. These three include the National Association for Stock Car Auto Racing (NASCAR), the National Hot Rod Association (NHRA), and the United States Automobile Club (USAC). Each of these will be briefly discussed below.

The National Association for Stock Car Auto Racing (NASCAR) is the largest sanctioning body of motorsports in the United States. The three largest racing series sanctioned by NASCAR are the NEXTEL Cup, the Busch Series, and the Craftsman Truck Series. NASCAR also oversees seven regional series and one local grassroots series. NASCAR sanctions over 1,500 races at over 100 tracks in 38 states, Canada, and Mexico. In 1996, 1997, and 1998, NASCAR also held exhibition races in Japan (http://www.nascar.com). Table 12.6 lists the NASCAR sanctioned race tracks in the United States.

Beginning as regional entertainment in the Southeastern U.S., NASCAR has grown to become the second most popular professional sport in terms of television ratings inside the U.S., ranking behind only the National Football League. Internationally, NASCAR races are broadcast in over 150 countries. It holds 17 of the top 20 attended sporting events in the U.S. and has 75 million fans who purchase over $2 billion in annual licensed product sales. These

Table 12.6
NASCAR Race Tracks

Martinsville Speedway	Talladega Superspeedway
Bristol Motor Speedway	Dover International Speedway
Kansas Speedway	Michigan International Speedway
Lowe's Motor Speedway	Atlanta Motor Speedway
Texas Motor Speedway	California Speedway
Michigan Speedway	Richmond International Raceway
Darlington Raceway	Pocono Raceway
Indianapolis Motor Speedway	New Hampshire Internat'l Speedway
Phoenix International Raceway	Infineon Raceway
Watkins Glen International	

fans are considered the most brand-loyal in all of sports and, as a result, Fortune 500 companies sponsor NASCAR more than any other sport (http://www.nascar.com).

NASCAR's headquarters are located in Daytona Beach, Florida; although, it also maintains offices in four North Carolina cities: Charlotte, Mooresville, Concord, and Conover as well as New York City, Los Angeles, Arkansas, and international offices in Mexico City, Mexico, and Toronto, Canada. NASCAR and UTI cooperated and opened a technical school in North Carolina called NASCAR Technical Institute where aspiring students train to be NASCAR mechanics.

The National Hot Rod Association (NHRA) is the largest sanctioning motor sports body in the world. The NHRA was formed to prevent people from street racing. Illegal street racing is not drag racing. Since it was founded by Wally Parks in 1951, NHRA has been dedicated to safety while providing millions of racing fans with The Extreme Motorsport™. This is the fastest and most spectacular form of entertainment on wheels. Finally, with 80,000 members and more than 35,000 licensed competitors, NHRA is a thriving leader in the world of motorsports (http://nhra.com).

The United States Automobile Club (USAC) is an open-wheel auto racing sanctioning body. From 1956 to 1979, the USAC sanctioned the United States National Championship and from 1956 to 1997, it sanctioned the Indianapolis 500.

The USAC was formed when the American Automobile Association (AAA) withdrew from auto racing following the 1955 Le Mans disaster. USAC became the arbiter of rules, car design, and other matters for what it termed *Championship* automobile racing. This term, which sounds rather generic, in fact became a term of art describing a car built to be used in the highest level of USAC racing. For a while, there were separate series of specifications for

Championship cars designed to be run on dirt rather than paved tracks (http://www.usac.com).

USAC also became the sanctioning body for many lower levels of motor racing, including sports cars, sprint cars, midget cars, and others. Some of these series were used somewhat as a developmental league for Championship racing.

USAC was not particularly popular with a large segment of drivers, team owners, and crew members who often found its rules, procedures, and judgments to be rather capricious and arbitrary. This feeling of ill will came to a head in the late 1970s and led to a break between USAC and most of the Championship team owners and drivers who formed their own organization, Championship Auto Racing Teams (CART), which began operation in 1979. Unsurprisingly, litigation ensued, in large part over which group had the right to use the term "Championship". This was eventually resolved, in favor of CART. After an attempt to form a new championship, called the Championship Racing League (CRL), vetoed by Indianapolis Speedway management, the USAC and CART eventually settled into a relatively peaceful co-existence with the USAC continuing to sanction the Indianapolis 500 and CART including the race in its schedule. In 1996, when CART and the newly formed Indy Racing League split open-wheel racing into two different series, USAC became the sanctioning body of the Indy Racing League (http://www.usac.com).

Motocross

The American Motorcyclist Association is a U.S. organization of over 274,000 motorcyclists which organizes numerous motorcycling activities and campaigns for motorcyclists' legal rights. The organization was founded in 1924 and now has over 1,200 chartered clubs. It is the largest motorsports organization in the world overseeing 80 professional and more than 3,700 amateur events each year. The AMA also maintains the Motorcycle Hall of Fame (http://www.amamotorcross.com).

PowerBoat Racing

The sport is governed by the Monaco-based Union Internationale Motonautique or U.I.M. (International Power Boating Association). Nicolo di San Germano has been responsible for promoting the F1 World Championship since 1993 and has expanded the sport's geographical reach and its global stature.

Air Racing

FAI is the world air sports federation, founded in 1905. It is a non-governmental and not-for-profit international organization with the basic aim of furthering aeronautical and astronautical activities worldwide. FAI activities include the establishment of rules for the control and certification of world aeronautical and astronautical records. FAI establishes regulations for air sporting events that are organized by member countries throughout the world. FAI also promotes skill, proficiency, and safety in aeronautics. FAI confers medals, diplomas, and other awards to those who have contributed to the achievement of these aims as well as for work done in the restoration of old aircraft (http://www.fai.org).

Snowmobile Racing

The sport is governed by the World PowerSports Association (WPSA), which organizes, promotes, and regulates a variety of snowmobile competitions. The WPSA assists racers, manufacturers, and sponsors who benefit from the rapidly expanding sport of professional snowmobile racing. Its mission is to bring the sport of snowmobile racing to its highest levels (http://www.wsaracing.com).

Motorsport Funding

Motorsport funding is as complicated as funding for a major professional sport team. The revenue streams are similar for motorsports. The revenue streams include:

- Racing Teams
  - Corporate sponsorships
  - Sale of licensed products
- Marketers, Promoters, and Race Tracks
  - Corporate sponsorships
  - Naming rights
  - Sale of licensed products
  - Broadcast rights
  - Ticket sales
    - Luxury suites
    - Party suites
    - Club seats
    - Upscale seating (e.g., Club One at the Atlanta Motor Speedway, Champions Club at the Homestead-Miami Speedway and Michigan International Speedway, Speedway Club at Lowe's Motor Speedway and Texas Motor Speedway, and Octane at the Phoenix International Raceway)
- Concessions
- Premier restaurants
- Beverage rights (beer and soda)
- Travel packages (air fare, hotel, track transportation, and tickets)

MotorSports Issues

There are two key issues facing motorsports. These issues are tobacco sponsorships and the dramatic growth of NASCAR. Each of these issues will be discussed below.

Tobacco Sponsorships (Auto and Truck Racing in U.S.)

In order to effectively limit children's exposure to cigarette advertising, many countries are attempting to limit tobacco advertising and sponsorship at sporting events. These efforts are fueled by the theory that limiting the exposure of children to "anti-health" advertising will cause a decline in the number of children who take up smoking. Countries have targeted advertising at sporting events to lower the risk of exposure to youths who presumably associate sports, and therefore smoking, with that which is "cool".

These new restrictions are creating controversy in the sporting industry including motorsports (i.e., Winston Cup Series in NASCAR now the Nextel Series), a venue to which the tobacco companies turned as an alternative to television advertising. Those who oppose advertising tobacco products at sporting events argue that sports exemplify "life and vitality," while tobacco kills more and more people every year. Proponents of tobacco sponsorship of sporting events argue that tobacco sponsorship should be legal since tobacco itself is legal (http//:www.naag.org/issues-tobacco.php).

Tobacco advertising on television has been prohibited in the United States since 1971, pursuant to the Cigarette Labeling and Advertising Act (CLAA). Congress has twice failed at banning tobacco sponsorship of sporting events: the Tobacco Control and Health Protection Act (TCHPA) and the Protect Our Children from Cigarettes Act (POCCA). Both Acts were strongly opposed by supporters who believed the laws violated the First Amendment.

In the mid 1990s, the state Attorneys General sued the tobacco industry to recover state Medicaid funds paid out for illness and disease caused by smoking. The suit revealed that, as part of industry plans to gain and retain customers, the industry misled the public about both the health risks and the addictive nature of tobacco use. The court's ruling of tobacco industry responsibility resulted in the 1998 Master — or Multistate — Settlement Agreement (MSA) ordering the industry to pay almost $200 billion to the states by 2025 (http//:www.naag.org/issues-tobaco.php).

After the Master Settlement Agreement, sponsorship became increasingly important to tobacco companies. Establishing themselves as companies that were committed to doing business differently, showing that they cared about the public and were altruistic was important to them. Following the MSA, tobacco companies launched major public relations campaigns utilizing television and print media touting their commitment to the community. These public relations campaigns also provided an opportunity for tobacco companies to get their names on television for the first time in 30 years (http//:www.naag.org/issues-tobaco.php).

The MSA restricts commercial tobacco sponsorship in the following ways:

- Limits tobacco companies to one brand-name sponsorship per year.
- Prohibits brand name sponsorship of events with a significant youth audience or team sports (football, basketball, baseball, hockey, or soccer).
- Prohibits sponsorship of events where the paid participants or contestants are under age 18.
- Bans tobacco brand names from stadiums and arenas (http//:www.naag.org/issues-tobaco.php).

Commercial sponsorship promotes the sponsoring company's brand name, such as in the previous NASCAR Winston Cup or the Marlboro Team Penske. Commercial sponsorship of athletic, musical, artistic, or other cultural event includes the use of the brand name either as part of the event or to advertise or promote sales. The goal of this type of sponsorship is to sell the product, increase exposure to a brand name, associate a brand with an event or lifestyle, normalize tobacco use, and promote the tobacco company as a supporting member of the community.

The Impact

Both commercial and corporate giving sponsorship sustain the image of tobacco use as socially acceptable and of tobacco companies as legitimate members of the community. In addition, commercial sponsorship has the same effect as other forms of tobacco advertising; it directly promotes a product that can addict and kill its user.

Studies have demonstrated the relationship between tobacco industry sponsorship and youth smoking behavior.

- Tobacco company sponsorship has the same effects on children as traditional tobacco product advertisement and promotion.
- Teenagers who can readily name a cigarette brand and who own a tobacco-company promotional item are more than twice as likely to become established smokers than other adolescents.
- Approximately one-third of adolescent experimentation with smoking results directly from tobacco advertising and promotion.
- Tobacco sports sponsorship, in particular, influences youth attitudes and behaviors related to smoking, increases brand awareness, links brands and sports, and associates cigarette brands with the excitement of the sporting event, evoking positive attitudes about smoking and smoking behavior.

What are racing teams and race tracks doing to confront changes in tobacco sponsorships? They will slowly seek replacement sponsors, such as technology sponsorships. American society, as a whole, is beginning to recognize the dangers of tobacco use. For many years motorsports have welcomed sponsorships from tobacco companies. This is changing not just in North America but around the globe.

NASCAR Growth

Can the dramatic growth continue? Will sponsors continue to support NASCAR? Will the TV rights continue to grow? Will there be new tracks in cities list New York and Seattle? Will current tracks continue to expand? Will the fan base continue to grow?

Fans are responsible for NASCAR's exponential growth since 1995 (See Table 12.7) and they are the ones officials are hoping will fuel future growth. In 1995, an estimated 5.3 million people attended Winston Cup races. Nine years later, 6.8 million attended races in NASCAR's newly renamed top series—the Nextel Cup (http://www.nascar.com).

Television ratings also have grown. More than 37 million fans watched the Daytona 500 in February, which drew a rating of 11.4 on NBC, the highest ever rating for a NASCAR event. In 1995, the rating for the season's most popular race was 7.8 (http://delawareonline.com).

New tracks are being planned for New York City and Seattle. Tracks recently opened near Los Angeles, Chicago, Kansas City, and Las Vegas. It is no longer a Southern sport. In 1995, nine of 31 races were held outside the South. In 2004, 18 of 36 races were held across the United States. "To sustain its growth, NASCAR must continue to reach out to mainstream America just like the NFL has," said Humpy Wheeler, president of Lowe's Motor Speedway in Charlotte, N.C.

This means exciting personalities; great, close racing; improved facilities; more entertainment around

Table 12.6
NASCAR Growth
1995-2004

Fan base: +19%	From 63 million to 75 million
Retail sales: +250%	From $600 million to $2.1 billion
Nextel Cup events: +16%	From 31 to 36
Weekend attendance: +28%	From 5.3 million to 6.8 million
Events on network TV: +420%	From 5 to 26
Avg. TV viewership: +83%	From 3 million to 5.5 million

races (don't let them watch grass grow while they wait!); interactive TV where you can race in the race itself; better advances in TV technology like Fox has introduced; and continued growth in media intensity in the top five markets, particularly New York City. (http://www.nascar.com)

An example of the dramatic growth in NASCAR can be illustrated by the Dover International Speedway experience: When Dover International Speedway opened in 1969, it was one of the few tracks located outside of NASCAR's Southeast base. Back then the facility held 10,000 people. Now it holds about 140,000 and is expected to expand again over the next five years. "There has been a lot of growth in a new audience of younger fans who might not be as familiar to NASCAR as our traditional fans," McGlynn said. "The older demographic will always be there, but the new group of fans is responsible for the explosion. Their expectations are different. They have higher standards for their sporting experiences and we are finding a way to accommodate them." At Dover, officials recently announced a five-year plan, known as the "Monster Makeover," to improve the facility by installing skyboxes, having better food and beverage stations, and building an outdoor concert area (http://www.doverspeedway.com).

Changes in NASCAR are being made to attract new fans. None of these changes is being made with "diehard" NASCAR fans in mind. It's all about the new fans. And NASCAR is getting them like never before. If it's not in track improvements, then it's by introducing the "Car of Tomorrow", which will debut next year in 15 of 36 races, and full time by 2009. In reality, the "Car of Tomorrow" is designed to bring back images of the car of yesterday, when there was side-by-side racing instead of a bunch of cars drafting the leaders and not being able to pass because of a car's aerodynamics (http://www.nascar.com).

"The Car of Tomorrow is going to help NASCAR more than anything," says NASCAR. "These cars we have now are aero beasts ... hard to drive with all sorts of unfixable problems. The new car will get us back to more real side-by-side racing." Or, it's in the three-year-old playoff system called "The Chase for the Nextel Cup," where the top 10 drivers from the first 26 races will compete for the overall championship over the final 10 races of the season (http://www.nascar.com).

NASCAR also has extended its reach to Hollywood, whether it's in commercials from its sponsors or in upcoming movies such as the auto racing farce starring comedian Will Ferrell, *Talladega Nights: The Ballad of Ricky Bobby*. All of this, of course, is directed at younger fans. The question is, will it draw the younger fans?

Will NASCAR be successful in new markets and sustain the dramatic growth, such as the biggest population centers in the United States, such as Staten Island in New York City and just outside Seattle? After years of negotiations, neither track has gotten off the ground. California Speedway added a second race in 2004 after selling out its one race a year since its opening in 1997. The speedway has not filled its capacity of 92,000 since. Estimates had the attendance at 70,000 for its race in March. This speedway is centrally located for a population of approximately 17 million who are within a two-hour drive. However, NASCAR is not worried about catching on in those areas. It will just take time, much as it did for Dover to catch on, which did not really happen until the mid-1980s.

Summary

Motorsport racing refers to anything machine that is propelled by an engine over land, water, or snow and in the air. In the U.S., the biggest commercial and spectator motorsport is auto followed by truck racing namely the NASCAR series and Indy Racing. But there are a number of other professional motorsports that are thriving, including motocross, motorboat racing, air racing, and snowmobile racing. Each of these professional motorsport venues are governed by national or international bodies. The most common funding mechanisms are private funding, spectator involvement, television contracts, and corporate sponsorships.

There are two key issues facing motorsports. These issues are tobacco sponsorships and the dramatic growth of NASCAR.

References

http://www.airracinghistory.freeola.com/Formula%20One%20Air%20Racing.htm. (2006).

http://www.airracinghistory.freeola.com/redbull.htm. (2006).

http://www.apba-racing.com. (2006).

http://www.amamotocross.com. (2006).

http://www.autosport.com. (2006).

http://www.champboat.com. (2006).

http://www.delawareonline.com. (2006).

http://www.doverspeedway.com. (2006).

http://www.fai.org. (2006).

http://www.F1boat.com. (2006).

http://www.grandamerican.com. (2006).

http://www.inbaracing.com. (2006).

http://www.iscmotorsports.com. (2006).

http://www.motocross.com. (2006).

http://www.naag.org/issues_tobacco.php. (2006).

http://www.nasarallysport.com. (2006).

http://www.nascar.com. (2006).

http://www.nhra.com. (2006).

http://www.speedwaymotorsports.com. (2006).

http://www.supermotocross.net. (2006).

http://www.truckracing.de/. (2006).

http://www.truck-grand-prix.de/. (2006).

http://www.usac.com (2006).

http://www.ussmokeless.com. (2006).

http://www.wsaracing.com. (2006).

Swanson, R.A., & Spears B. (1995). *History of sport and physical education in the United States.* (4th ed.). New York: McGraw-Hill.

NOTES

CHAPTER 13

Olympic Sport Governance

Spectators flock to the Olympic Games. The triumph of victory and the agony of defeat resound through the unsullied stadium as competitors from around the world scrape for the chance at a medal. Those lucky audience members able to grab a seat go to see the best athletes in the world. Pretend for a minute you are there to see the Olympic Games. The athletes, the coaches, the stadium, the Olympic rings, and the feeling you get when you see the Olympic flame; how did it all get there? For every concession, T-shirt, uniform, television broadcast, or security line are numerous individuals belonging to several different organizations all working together planning from years in advance up to the very last event. And where do these committees find all the money to pull off this type of worldwide event successfully? What issues might stand in the way? This chapter shines some light behind the scenes on governing organizations and entities and the politics that often accompany putting on an event of the magnitude of the Olympic Games.

Learning Objectives

Upon completion this chapter, the reader should be able to:

- Identify the Olympic Sport Governing Bodies, what makes each unique, and what specific instances caused each governing body to reorganize.
- Understand the financial issues the governing bodies face with raising money and sponsorships.
- Know the steps to elect each host city for the Olympic Games.
- Understand why the image of the Olympic Games is so important and what politics stand in the way.
- Describe the need and follow-through plan for the Games' security.
- Identify historical doping cases and the organizations formed to control athlete illegal substance use.

Governance

The Olympic Games represent an extraordinary sporting, social, cultural, and environmental legacy for the host city, the region, and the country. The Olympic Games is a unique event centering global interest on its host city. The financing of the Games has changed dramatically since Munich (1972), and economic interests and effects are increasingly paramount. To understand the placement of every security officer, the qualification of every athlete in the Games, and the many millions of small details needed to put on the Olympic Games, it is important to start with the basics. A worldwide competition means organization on the international level, the national level and coordination between the two. The International Olympic Committee, known as the IOC, resides over international sport affairs with an adopted document, the Olympic Charter. Countries participating in the Olympics establish National Olympic Committees, known as NOCs. The United States government developed the Ted Stevens Olympic and Amateur Sports Act (1973) that set the guidelines for the U.S. National Olympic Committee known as the "United States Olympic Committee". The national sport organization adopted the USOC Bylaws as guidelines for operation. Through the coordination of the national organizations, and the international organizations the Olympic issues like the host-city selection process can be handled appropriately.

The International Olympic Committee

The International Olympic Committee developed out of a growing interest in the Ancient Olympic Games. Pierre de Coubertin and Demetrius Vikelas led this developing interest into action. On June 23, 1894, in a meeting in Paris, the idea of a "modern" Olympic Games became a series of steps to its actual implementation. At this meeting, the International Olympic Committee was developed in order to organize such an event. It was agreed at the same meeting that the Olympic Games would be held every four years with the first in Athens, Greece to commemorate the history of the event. To commemorate this date, June 23 is known as Olympic Day, a sort of "birthday" of the Olympic Movement. In many of the world's countries these days, the celebration often takes the form of fun runs.

IOC headquarters currently reside in Lausanne, Switzerland. It was Coubertin who chose this city in the midst of the First World War. In recognition of the long history that unites the IOC and Lausanne, the city received the title of Olympic Capital in 1993. Although the Olympic Games had a rough start in popularity second to world fairs, the IOC now heads the biggest and most popular international sporting competition. Acting as the supreme authority of the Olympic movement, the IOC ensures the Olympic Games but also doubles as an organization promoting ethics, education, charity, and the Olympic spirit in sports and in life.

The role of the IOC is to promote Olympism in accordance with the Olympic Charter. Olympism is a philosophy of life founded on the education of the body and mind through sport. The IOC is dedicated and committed to ensuring that its legacy is the best possible one. The International Olympic Committee governs the organization and operation of the Olympic Movement. The IOC has the final authority on all questions concerning the Olympic Games and the Olympic Movement. The IOC owns exclusive rights to the Olympic Games, the Olympic symbol, the Olympic flag, the Olympic anthem, the Olympic motto, the Olympic flame, and the Olympic torch. The IOC charges corporations a use of rights fee for use of any of the Olympic symbols mentioned above. The IOC is an international non-governmental organization that receives no public money. Its revenues come mainly from the sale of television rights for the Olympic Games and marketing programs. Up to 1980, the IOC had only a few employees. Its development over the last 20 years has led to a growth in its administration and expansion of it organizational facility. The Olympic House was built next to the Château (1986) and the west wing was extended some years later (1998).

International Federations

The International Federations govern their sport at a global level. They ensure the promotion and development of sport and the development of the athletes who practice it, at all levels. During the Olympic Games, the International Federations are responsible for the practical organization of the sports events on the program. All the technical aspects of a sport are their responsibility: the rules, equipment, venues, judging, etc. International Federations also conduct in and out of competition drug testing.

National Olympic Committees

The National Olympic Committees carry out many different functions in their respective countries from the development of sport at all levels, to the creation of educational programs, to the continued training of sports administrators. They are also responsible for developing and protecting the Olympic Movement and send a delegation of athletes to the Olympic Games. The National Olympic Committees ensure that all the programs carried out at a national level conform to the principles of the Olympic Charter. Although the Olympic Charter proclaims that the Olympics are contests among persons and not among nations, the IOC assigns to a variety of NOCs the mission of choosing national Olympic teams. In most cases, the NOCs do this by hold-

ing Olympic trials or by choosing athletes on the basis of their previous performances. From the start of the modern Olympic Games, male and female amateur athletes of every race, religion, and nationality have been eligible to take part.

NOCs also have the authority to designate cities that may bid to host Olympic Games in their respective countries. The United States Olympic Committee (USOC), through its board of directors, voted New York City as the United States candidate for the 2012 Olympic Games that were eventually awarded to London.

There are approximately 199 National Olympic Committees whose role is to spread Olympic values at a national level. There are NOCs throughout the world:

> 53 NOCs in Africa
> 42 NOCs in North, South and Central America
> 42 NOCs in Asia
> 48 NOCs in Europe
> 14 NOCs in Oceania

National Governing Bodies

Each International Federation recognizes a distinct National Governing Body in each country participating in the sport. National Governing bodies (NGBs) or national sports federations (NFs) are the organizations governing a specific sport within each country. For example, in the United States, USA Track and Field is the NGB for athletics (track and field) recognized by the International Association of Athletics Federation (IAAF), the international federation for track and field. Each NGB is responsible for approving and sanctioning competitions open to all eligible athletes in its country. USA Track and Field (USATF) is responsible for the management and direction of the United States Track and Field Championships. NGBs set the qualifying standards, national policies and eligibility requirements

Table 13.1
International Sport Federations

Summer Sports

Sport	Federation	Location	Website
Aquatics	Fédération Internationale de Natation	Lausanne, Switzerland	http://www.fina.org
Archery	International Archery Federation	Lausanne, Switzerland	http://www.archery.org
Athletics	International Association of Athletics Federations	Monte-Carlo Cédex, Monaco	http://www.iaaf.org
Badminton	International Badminton	Kuala Lumpur, Malaysia	http://www.internationalbadminton.org
Baseball	International Baseball Federation	Lausanne, Switzerland	http://www.baseball.ch
Basketball	International Basketball Association	Cointrin, Switzerland	http://www.fiba.com
Boxing	International Boxing Association	Lausanne, Switzerland	http://www.aiba.net
Canoe/Kayak	International Canoe Federation	Lausanne, Switzerland	http://www.canoeicf.com
Cycling	International Cycling Union	Aigle, Switzerland	http://www.uci.ch
Equestrian	Fédération Équestre Internationale	Lausanne, Switzerland	http://www.horsesport.org
Fencing	Fédération Internationale d'Escrime	Lausanne, Switzerland	http://www.fie.ch
Football (Soccer)	Fédération Internationale de Football Association	Zurich, Switzerland	http://www.fifa.com
Gymnastics	International Gymnastics Federation	Moutier, Switzerland	http://www.fig-gymnastics.com
Handball	International Handball Association	Basel, Switzerland	http://www.ihf.info
Hockey	International Hockey Federation	Lausanne, Switzerland	http://www.worldhockey.org
Judo	International Judo Federation	Seoul, Rep. of Korea	http://www.ijf.org
Modern Pentathlon	Union Internacionale de Pentathlon Moderne	Monaco, Monaco	http://www.pentathlon.org
Rowing	International Rowing Federation	Lausanne, Switzerland	http://www.worldrowing.com
Sailing	International Sailing Federation	Southampton, Great Britain	http://www.sailing.org
Shooting	International Shooting Sport Federation	Munich, Germany	http://www.issf-sports.org
Softball	International Softball Federation	Plant City, Florida	http://www.internationalsoftball.com
Table Tennis	The International Table Tennis Federation	Lausanne, Switzerland	http://www.ittf.com
Taekwondo	World Taekwondo Federation	Seoul, Rep. of Korea	http://www.wtf.org
Tennis	International Tennis Federation	London, Great Britain	http://www.itftennis.com
Triathlon	International Triathlon Federation	North Vancouver, Canada	http://www.triathlon.org

Table 13.1
International Sport Federations (continued)

Sport	Federation	Location	Website
Volleyball	International Volleyball Federation	Lausanne, Switzerland	http://www.fivb.ch
Weightlifting	International Weightlifting Federation	Budapest, Hungary	http://www.iwf.net
Wrestling	International Federation of Associated Wrestling Styles	Corsier-sur-Vevey, Switzerland	http://www.fila-wrestling.com

Winter Sports

Sport	Federation	Location	Website
Biathlon	International Biathlon Union	Salzburg, Austria	http://www.biathlonworld.com
Bobsleigh (Bobsled)	International Bobsleigh and Tobogganing Federation	Milan, Italy	http://www.bobsleigh.com
Curling	World Curling Federation	Perth, Great Britain	http://www.worldcurling.org
Ice Hockey	International Ice Hockey Federation	Zurich, Switzerland	http://www.iihf.com
Luge	International Luge Federation	Berchtesgaden, Germany	http://www.fil-luge.org
Skating	International Skating Union	Lausanne, Switzerland	http://www.isu.org
Skiing	International Ski Federation	Oberhofen/Thunersee,	http://www.fis-ski.com

Recognized Sports (not currently in the Olympic program)

Sport	Federation	Location	Website
Air Sports	Fédération Aéronautique Internationale	Lausanne, Switzerland	http://www.fai.org
Bandy	Federation of International Bandy	Katrineholm, Switzerland	http://www.internationalbandy.com
Billiard Sports	World Confederation of Billiard Sports	Sint-Martens-Latem, Belgium	http://www.billiard-webs.org
Boules	Confédération Mondiale des Sports de Boules	Gap, France	http://www.CMSBoules.com
Bowling	International Bowling Federation	Manila, Philippines	http://www.fig.org
Bridge	World Bridge Federation	Paris, France	http://www.worldbridge.org
Chess	World Chess Federation	Athens, Greece	http://www.fide.com
Dance Sport	International Dance Sport Federation	Barcelone, Spain	http://www.idsf.net
Golf	International Golf Federation	Far Hills, New Jersey	http://www.internationalgolffederation.org
Karate	World Karate Federation	Madrid, Spain	http://www.wkf.net
Korfball	International Korfball Federation	Zeist, Netherlands	http://www.ikf.org
Life Saving	International Life Saving Federation	Leuven, Belgium	http://www.ilsf.org
Motorcycle Racing	Fédération Internationale de Motocyclisme	Mies, Switzerland	http://www.fim.ch
Mountaineering and Climbing	The International Mountaineering and Climbing Federation	Berne, Switzerland	http://www.uiaa.ch
Netball	International Federation of Netball Associations	Manchester, Great Britain	http://www.netball.org

Table 13.1
International Sport Federations (continued)

Sport	Federation	Location	Website
Orienteering	International Orienteering Federation	Slu, Finland	http://www.orienteering.org
Pelota Vasca	Federación Internacional de Pelota Vasca	Pamplona, Spain	http://www.fipv.net
Polo	Federation of International Polo	Vineuil, France	http://www.fippolo.com
Powerboating	International Union of Powerboating	Monaco, Monaco	http://www.uimpowerboating.com
Racquetball	International Racquetball Federation	Colorado Springs, Colorado	http://www.international racquetball.com
Roller Sports	International Roller Sports Federation	Rome, Italy	http://www.rollersports.org
Rugby	International Rugby Board	Dublin, Ireland	http://www.irb.com
Squash	World Squash Federation	East Sussex, Great Britain	http://www.worldsquash.org
Sumo	International Sumo Federation	Tokyo, Japan	http://www.AmateurSumo.com
Surfing	International Surfing Association	La Jolla, California	http://www.isasurf.org
Tug of War	Tug of War International Federation	Hoensbrook, Netherlands	http://www.twif.org
Underwater Sports	World Underwater Federation	Rome, Italy	http://www.cmas.org
Water Ski	International Water Ski Federation	Unteraegeri, Switzerland	http://www.iwsf.com
Wushu	International Wushu Federation	Beijing, China	http://www.iwuf.org

for participation in their respective sports. NGBs are responsible for the preparation, development, and selection of the Olympic teams in their respective sports. The United States Olympic Trials are going to be staged in Eugene Oregon in 2008 for the selection of the United States Track and Field Olympic team. USATF will begin working with the local organizing committee in Eugene, approximately two years prior to the event to set all of the details in place to administrate the Olympic Trials for track and field.

Amateur Sports Act 1973 (USOC)

After the International Olympic Committee took shape as the international governing body of sport, the two represen-tatives in the IOC from the United States, James P. Sullivan and William Milligan Sloan, shaped an organization with its sole intent to organize athletes to partake in the Olympic Games. As years passed, the organization took different names and began to assume more responsibility. The United States government intervened to commence the formation of an official National Olympic Committee with a monopoly status corporate jurisdiction over amateur sport, a corporation and governing body for sport wrapped into one organization. What followed was the development of a policy for a governing body of United States amateur sport known as the Amateur Sports Act 1973, a set of codes for the United States Olympic Committee.

Table 13.2
USOC Sport Governing Bodies

Summer Team Sites

Sport	Federation	Location	Website
Archery	USA Archery	Colorado Springs, CO	http://www.usarchery.org
Badminton	USA Badminton	Colorado Springs, CO	http://www.usabadminton.org
Baseball	USA Baseball	Durham, NC	http://www.usabaseball.org
Basketball	USA Basketball	Colorado Springs, CO	http://www.usabasketball.org
Bowling	US Bowling Congress	Greendale, WI	http://www.bowl.com
Boxing	USA Boxing	Colorado Springs, CO	http://www.usaboxing.org
Canoe/Kayak	USA Canoe/Kayak	Charlotte, NC	http://www.usacanoekayak.org
Cycling	USA Cycling	Colorado Springs, CO	http://www.usacycling.org
Diving	USA Diving	Indianapolis, IN	http://www.usadiving.org
Equestrian	US Equestrian Federation	Lexington, KY	http://www.usef.org
Fencing	USA Fencing	Colorado Springs, CO	http://www.usfencing.org
Field Hockey	USA Field Hockey	Colorado Springs, CO	http://www.usfieldhockey.com
Gymnastics	USA Gymnastics	Indianapolis, IN	http://www.usa-gymnastics.org
Judo	USA Judo	Colorado Springs, CO	http://www.usjudo.org
Karate	USA National Karate-Do Federation	Saint Albans, WV	http://www.usankf.org
Pentathlon	USA Pentathlon	Colorado Springs, CO	http://www.usolympicteam.com/152.htm
Racquetball	USA Racquetball	Memphis, TN	http://www.usra.org
Roller Sports	USA Roller Sports	Lincoln, NB	http://www.usarollersports.org
Rowing	US Rowing	Princeton, NJ	http://usrowing.org
Sailing	US Sailing	Portsmouth, RI	http://ussailing.org
Shooting	USA Shooting	Colorado Springs, CO	http://usashooting.com/usashooting.cfm
Soccer	US Soccer	Chicago, IL	http://www.ussoccer.com
Softball	USA Softball	Oklahoma, OK	http://www.usasoftball.com
Squash	US Squash Racquets Association	Bala Cynwyd, PA	http://www.usa-squash.org
Swimming	USA Swimming	Colorado Springs, CO	http://www.usa-swimming.org
Synchronized Swimming	US Synchronized Swimming	Indianapolis, IN	http://usasynchro.org
Table Tennis	USA Table Tennis	Colorado Springs, CO	http://www.usatt.org
Taekwondo	USA Taekwondo	Colorado Springs, CO	http://www.usa-taekwondo.us
Team Handball	USA Team Handball	Colorado Springs, CO	http://www.usolympicteam.com/237.htm
Tennis	US Tennis Association	White Plains, NY	http://www.usta.com
Track and Field	USA Track and Field	Indianapolis, IN	http://www.usatf.org
Triathlon	USA Triathlon	Colorado Springs, CO	http://www.usatriathlon.org
Volleyball	USA Volleyball	Colorado Springs, CO	http://www.usavolleyball.org
Water Polo	USA Water Polo	Colorado Springs, CO	http://www.usawaterpolo.org
Water Skiing	USA Water Ski	Polk City, FL	http://www.usawaterski.org

Table 13.2
USOC Sport Governing Bodies (continued)

Weightlifting	USA Weightlifting	Colorado Springs, CO	http://www.usaweightlifting.org
Wrestling	USA Wrestling	Colorado Springs, CO	http://www.themat.com

Winter Team Sites

Sport	Governing Body	Location	Site
Biathlon	USA Biathlon	New Gloucester, ME	http://www.usbiathlon.org
Bobsled	USA Bobsled and Skeleton Federation	Lake Placid, NY	http://www.usbsf.com
Curling	USA Curling	Stevens Point, WI	http://www.usacurl.org
Figure Skating	US Figure Skating	Colorado Springs, CO	http://www.usfsa.org
Ice Hockey	USA Hockey	Colorado Springs, CO	http://www.usahockey.com
Luge	USA Luge	Lake Placid, NY	http://www.usaluge.org
Short Track	US Speed Skating	Salt Lake City, UT	http://www.usspeedskating.org
Skeleton	USA Bobsled and Skeleton Federation	Lake Placid, NY	http://www.usbsf.com
Skiing	US Ski and Snowboard Association		Park City, UThttp://www.ussa.org
Snowboarding	US Ski and Snowboard Association		Park City, UThttp://www. ussa.org
Speedskating	US Speed Skating	Salt Lake City, UT	http://www.usspeedskating.org

The culture of sports changed. The same codes enacted in 1973 were called into question. The policy of amateurism had grown into one of the biggest issues in sport. Athletes had been expelled for accepting money, while others sought loop holes through secret bank accounts. The sporting community began to rebel against the exclusion of professionals, some of the United State's best athletes. The participation in Paralympic sports began to grow, elite disabled athletes needed financial support, and the Amateur Sports Act of 1973 had not evolved to bear the growth in Paralympic sports. The Olympic Games are a coveted event sought after by many athletes, however, the Amateur Sports Act did not call for any lawsuit protection for the USOC. This particular organization is in charge of allowing qualified athletes the right to participate and athletes who became unhappy with decisions burned the USOC with lawsuits. In 1998, Senator Ted Stevens of Alaska sponsored an amendment to the act to solve such issues and others. The new Amateur Sports Act coined the Ted Stevens Olympic and Amateur Sports Act calls for the professional athlete acceptance into the Olympic Games, increased management and jurisdiction over Paralympic sports, increased support for disabled elite athletes, lawsuit protection for the USOC, and also increased athlete representation in the USOC. Once the United States Government set the parameters for the USOC with the Ted Stevens Olympic and Amateur Sports Act, the USOC set its own guidelines for operation, a document known as the USOC Bylaws. The development of the second document made the United States Olympic Committee official in 1961.

Organization of Olympic Sport Governing Bodies

Understanding how the Olympic sport governing bodies work is like appreciating how a car moves. Anyone can see what a car does, but to truly realize how a car runs, it is necessary to identify the parts and their functions. Further, anyone can turn on their television and see the Olympic Games: watch the sprinters race, the announcers comment and spectators cheer. But truly understanding how these International and National Olympic Committees run an event of this magnitude begins with understanding the "parts" or governing body organization.

International Olympic Committee

The International Olympic Committee includes the Session, the Executive board, and the Office of the President. At least once a year, the members meet at the general assembly called the Session. It is on the occasion of the Sessions that important IOC decisions are made. The Session includes the bulk of IOC members. Meeting annually, the Session elects new members and makes amendments to the Olympic Charter, the main document of the governing body. The Olympic Charter forms an umbrella over the Olympic Movement, including everything from a description of the Olympic ideals, rules and regulations for the Olympics, guidelines for IOC process, and the host city election procedure.

The Session elects the Executive Board, the organization containing the president, four vice presidents, and ten other members. Individuals included in the Executive Board serve a four-year term. While the Session meets just annually, the Executive Board oversees IOC function the rest of the year. The Executive Board is kept busy with tasks like appointing the director general (in charge of daily operation), maintaining finances, forming the topics discussed for the next Session meeting, and making sure that all Session decisions are properly implemented. All the rules that the Olympic Family members must follow are brought together in a document called the Olympic Charter. The IOC currently has over 100 active members. They can come from Olympic Family organizations, be administrators in the sports world, Olympic athletes, or independent personalities. The members elect the president of the IOC. He has a mandate of eight years, renewable once only for a further four years.

An elected president resides at the helm of the International Olympic Committee. Currently, a Belgian, Jaques Rogge, the president heads all IOC action, leads Executive Board meetings and acts as the official spokesperson. The president is elected by secret ballot vote conducted by members of the Session for an eight-year term. If re-elected at the end of this term, the president may serve for four more years with no option for re-election upon completion. The limit on the presidency term was adopted in 2002 along with the new rules for the Session. Since Dimitrius Vikelas of Greece was elected first president in 1894, the IOC has had eight presidents in its history. The United States has had one president, Avery Brundage, from 1952-1972.

United States Olympic Committee

The United States Olympic Committee is a larger organization encompassing more than 500 members both professional and volunteer. Based in Colorado Springs Colorado, the USOC breakdown involves a Board of Directors, Officers, a CEO, Committees, a General Assembly, and Members.

The Board of Directors contains four individual members, two members from the National Governing Bodies Council, two members from the Athlete's Advisory Council, and also includes the United States members of the IOC. The members of the IOC on the board are also directors by nature of the position. Each type of member is elected by the Nominating and Governing Committees. Board members serve a four-year term and may be re-elected for another two-year term. All board members are able

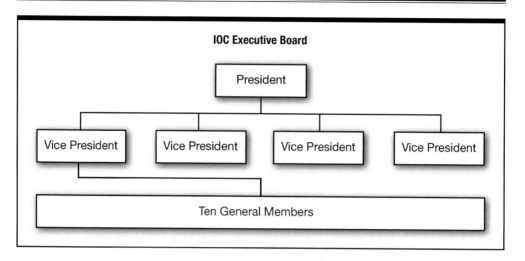

Figure 13.1
Organizational Chart for IOC

to vote on raised issues, electing officers, and policy amendments.

The Officers involve the chair of the board, vice president, and secretary positions. The Chair is a non-IOC member of the board selected by the Nominating and Governance Committee for a term of one to 18 months. After the initial term is served, the board then may re-elect the chair for a term agreed upon by the board. Another important fact about the chair is that it is a volunteer position. The vice president is voted in by existing board members mainly handling Bid City issues. The secretary and the secretary's term is designated by the CEO.

The chief executive officer of the USOC is employed by the board for as long as the board deems appropriate. The CEO manages all professional staff functions and business affairs. The CEO may sit in on board meetings but may not vote.

The USOC also designated four committees to aid USOC function: the Audit, Compensation, Ethics, and Nominating and Governance Committees. The Audit Committee contains at least three but not more than five members appointed by the board watching over the USOC's accounting affairs and press releases pertaining to these issues. The Compensation Committee contains at least three but not more than five members as well, also appointed by the board. This particular committee is in charge of developing and recommending CEOs and reviews the overall management action. The Ethics Committee contains five members, one from the board and four independent members elected by the Nominating and Governance Council. The Ethics Committee maintains the organization's compliance with the Code of Ethics. The Nominating and Governance Committee contains five members selected from five different groups. Each of these groups elects one member: the National Governing Body Council, the Athlete's Advisory Council, the corporation's Public Sector Board of Directors, the independent Commission on Reform, and the Corporation's Governance and Task Force. These five are responsible for electing a majority of the board.

The General Olympic Assembly meets once a year. The board determines the site and provides informational updates to members from membership organizations.

Function

The Olympic Games and national competitions are inarguably the most recognized functions of the International and United States Olympic Committees. Competitions of such magnitude involve a lot of organization and time, but in actuality, these contests only formulate a portion of committee function. Both governing bodies have expanded their mission past running successful sport competitions. The IOC and USOC expect to preserve many sport aspects off the field.

IOC

The IOC's mission includes many objectives included in the Olympic Charter. The IOC seeks to be an all-encompassing positive force, not just in athletics. The organization commits itself to ethics in sport on all levels, development of competitions, to the "celebration of the Olympic Games", to cooperation with related organizations, the promotion of women in sport, the importance of health, the elimination of doping, securing a future for sport, Olympic education and leaving a "positive legacy from the Olympic Games to the host cities and host countries". The IOC is involved in all issues in sport and tries to reach issues out of sport within countires participating in the Olympics (Olympic Charter, 2004).

USOC

The mission of the USOC as written in the bylaws is as follows: "To support United States Olympic and Paralympic athletes in achieving sustained competitive excellence and preserve the Olympic ideals, and thereby inspire all Americans" (USOC Bylaws. 2006).

Generally, the USOC represents the United States as its "national Olympic committee in relations with the International Olympic Committee and the Pan-Ameri-

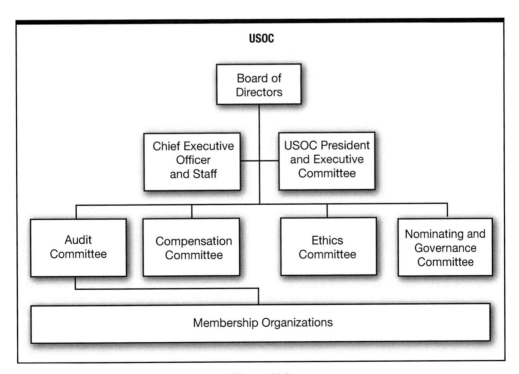

Figure 13.2
Organization Chart for USOC

can Sports Organization and as its national Paralympic committee in relations with the International Paralympic Committee" (Ted Stevens Olympic and Amateur Sports Act, 1998). The Act also elects financial obligation to amateur sport. The mission statement in the USOC Bylaws is a more specific response to the Ted Stevens Olympic and Amateur Sports Act designated function for the United States Olympic Committee and other national governing bodies. The section includes nine specific functions or duties. The USOC must (a)"develop interest and participation", (b) minimize schedule conflict between organizations, (c) keep athletes informed of policy changes, (d) distribute not only USOC rules but also of international sport organizations, (e) allow eligible athletes to compete in international competition, (f) provide separate programs for men and women encouraging female participation, (g) support disabled athlete participation, (h) "provide and coordinate technical information on physical training, equipment design, coaching, and performance analysis," and (i) maintain safety and the development of safety precautions (Ted Stevens Olympic and Amateur Sports Act, 1998).

Authority

The IOC and USOC are ambitious organizations with goals to function as all-encompassing sport governing bodies. Authority is an important issue in each committee's effectiveness; without the proper command of international and national sport, neither organization could place plan into action. The ideas behind the function of both committees are realized because both committees have the power to do so. It is important to understand that when a great deal of money is involved, as is with both the IOC and USOC, authority must be run like a business.

IOC

The International Olympic Committee is a parent organization intended to localize management and authority for the Games as well as to provide a single legal entity that owns copyrights, trademarks, and other intangible properties related to the Olympic Games. Nations that aspire to host the Summer Olympic Games or the Winter Olympic Games must bid for the organization with the IOC, which has the ultimate authority of deciding where the Games will be staged. The IOC members, representing most of the member countries, vote to decide where the Games will occur. The IOC is run by delegates from each country. Those delegates are appointed by the IOC themselves. Athletes and individual sport federations became involved in this process after several unaccountable, self-serving IOC actions leading to implacable criticism (notably by British journalist Andrew Jennings) as an unrepresentative, undemocratic, nepotistic, and unaccountable faction, largely run for the benefit of the delegates and having little to do with the ideals articulated in its charter. Efforts were made to clamp down on the obvious misbehavior of IOC delegates (who used their authority as voters for the host city to extract favors from bidders for the games). An advisory board of recently retired former athletes has been created but critics of the organization believe more fundamental reform is required.

USOC

The Ted Stevens Olympic and Amateur Sports Act (1998) designates the USOC authority. The USOC may serve as a "coordinating body for amateur athletic activity in the United States", will "represent the United States in the appropriate international sport federation", and "establish national goals and encourage the attainment of those goals" (Ted Stevens Olympic and Amateur Sports Act, 1998). USOC authority also involves the management of affairs pertaining to issues with international sport competitions on and off U.S. soil. Those affairs include recommending athletes for Olympic teams, coordinating sponsorship of athletes in international competition, and actually designating teams for non-major international competition. On U.S. soil, the USOC is in charge of amateur athletic competition including national championships and eligibility standards for those competitions.

The USOC, chartered by the United States government, has corporate authority as well. This gives the USOC the ability to "make contracts", accept donations to advance "corporate purposes", have rights to property, "to sue and be sued", and other basic corporate legalities (Ted Stevens Olympic and Amateur Sports Act, 1998). The USOC also has strict ownership of all Olympic symbols.

Requirements for Membership

With the authority to function as all-encompassing governing bodies, the IOC and USOC are faced with the task to choose members that reflect organization ethics and goals each election year. Guidelines for membership have evolved throughout the history of the organization in response to the ever-changing needs of sport and in some cases, blemishes on the reputations of the organizations. The IOC and USOC membership requirements diverge; membership for the IOC is defined by persons while the membership for the USOC is defined by organizations.

IOC

To begin the membership process, Coubertin, the first president, chose the first 15 members of the IOC. An independent committee selecting its own members, the first IOC members were all from Eu-

rope or the Americas, with the exception of one from New Zealand. IOC members are officially considered to be representatives from the IOC to their own nations, not delegates from their own countries to the IOC. Most members are elected to the IOC after serving on the National Olympic Committees (NOCs) of their own countries. The committee elected its first Asian member in 1908 and its first African member in 1910. Currently, members from European and North American countries still account for much of the IOC membership. IOC members must retire at the end of the year in which they reach the age of 80, unless they were elected before 1966, in which case they can serve for life.

After the 2002 corruption allegations for the Winter Games Salt Lake City bid, the International Olympic Committee reordered the membership election process. Up until 2002, the IOC members simply elected themselves with no official organization cap. As a result, membership access seemed limited to a business elite group of friends. This election process did not reflect the image of the Olympic Games and the corruption allegations sent the redesign into motion. Positions are still elected by the IOC General Assembly but the rules have changed: the organization has a 115 member cap, 70 positions are available for individual members, 15 are for Olympic athletes elected by fellow Olympic athletes at the Olympic Games, 15 are for members of National Olympic Committees, and 15 are for members of International Sport Federations on the Olympic Program.

USOC

Membership into the upper-tier offices of the USOC involves election. However, the USOC recognizes many member organizations able to send representatives to the General Assembly each year. The member organizations range from Boy Scouts to the U.S. Marine Corps in seven categories:

Olympic sport, Pan American sport, community-based multisport, affiliated sport, education-based multisport, and the armed forces. The board elects new organizations by choosing to recognize the groups. Organizations must be involved in the administration of at least one sport or competition on the program of the Olympic, Pan-American, or Paralympic Games. The organizations must promote participation, prepare for participation, or hold amateur athletic competition in the designated sports. Organizations with political or commercial involvement are ineligible;   but programs that have an amateur purpose may still be involved even if they also have a link to a political, commercial organization.

Sanctions and Appeals Process

A sanction is the penalty given to an athlete or other participant who is found to have committed an illegal act or offense against USOC or IOC guidelines. A sanction in national or international sport may involve a warning, a period of suspension from competition or involvement in that sport, or even a life ban for serious offenses. The sporting horizon of today is filled with stories about positive drug tests, B samples, designer drugs, blood doping, growth hormone, and illegal substance abuse. These types of infractions put sport-governing bodies in a compromising position to continually enact new legislation with penalties to deal with the current issues plaguing sport.

Until the late 20th centtury, the Olympics nominally only accepted amateur athletes. In the early years of the Olympic movement, amateurism was the target of scrutiny. Amateurism in sport has been delineated and redefined over the years, arousing substantial social and political sentiment. Olympic rules about amateurism caused many controversies over the years leading to issued sanctions. Governing bodies disqualified "professional" athletes and stripped them of their medals. Jim Thorpe was stripped of track and field medals for having taken expense money for playing baseball in 1912. Questions were raised about whether an amateur could be reimbursed for travel expenses, be compensated for time lost at work, be paid for product endorsements, or be employed to teach sports. Tennis was dropped from the Olympic program after 1924 amid turmoil over such issues as where to draw the line between amateurism and professionalism. These issues were not always completely resolved by the IOC, leading to confusion about the definition of professionalism in different sports. Successful Olympians from Western countries often had endorsement contracts from sponsors. Complex rules involving the payment of the athletes' earnings into trust funds rather than directly to the athletes themselves, were developed in an attempt to work around this issue but the intellectual evasion involved was considered embarrassing to the Olympic movement. The term "intellectual evasion" refers to the process by which athletes and coaches alike would use technicalities in the complex amateur legislation to appear innocent.

After the 1972 retirement of IOC President Avery Brundage, the Olympic amateurism rules were steadily relaxed, and in many areas, amount only to technicalities and lip service. In the United States, the *Amateur Sports Act* of 1978 prohibits national governing bodies from having more stringent standards of amateur status than required by international governing bodies of respective sports. Olympic amateurism regulations were eventually abandoned in the 1990s. Times have changed dramatically for Olympic athletes since then. Today's Olympic competition includes some of the highest-profile professional athletes in the world. Tennis returned as a medal sport in 1988. In 1996, the dream team in basketball captivated audiences in the Atlanta Games with a group of charismatic professional all stars. Just as the pattern of sanctions has changed for individual sports like tennis, the main sanctions issued in sport, as a whole, have switched focus.

The USOC and IOC now focus the majority of sanctions issued yearly to try to control the doping issue. *Doping* is defined as the use of drugs to enhance performance and direct the outcome of athletic performance. The stakes for winning on the world stages have raised over the years promulgating a win at all cost attitude. Unfortunately, there is an "arms race" between the developers of new performance-enhancing techniques and substances and the testing agencies. National and international governing bodies have legislated strict consequences for doping violations. In most cases, if an athlete is caught doping, he or she is initially banned from the sport for two years. The second offense is a lifetime ban. Certain NGB's, like USA Weightlifting for example, now issue a lifetime ban for the first doping offense. Weight lifting also reorganized the weight categories in 1998, eliminating "tainted records", in an effort to promote clean sport. Some organizations also impose financial penalties for failed drug tests. The U.S. Olympic Committee is also considering sanctions against coaches and others tied to athletes who test positive for illegal performance-enhancing substances. The USOC has no direct control over coaches, agents, trainers, and others who work with U.S. athletes in Olympic sports. Some work under the umbrella of national governing bodies that the USOC controls only through funding. Others are hired directly by the athletes. Measures to punish those affiliated with guilty athletes could include denying accreditation for the Olympic Games. The USOC also is considering denying coaches and others tied to doping cases access to its training centers.

Sanctions/penalties for a positive drug test can have a profound impact on the career of those involved. But the sport governing body that issues the sanction may not have the final say. The accused have an option: those found guilty may take their case to the Court of Arbitration for Sport for an appeal.

The Court of Arbitration for Sport (CAS), based in Lausanne, Switzerland, is an organization autonomous of any sports organization that provides for services in order to facilitate the settlement of sports-related disputes through arbitration or mediation by way of procedural rules adapted to the specific needs of the sports world. The CAS was created in 1984 and is placed under the organizational and financial authority of the International Council of Arbitration for Sport (ICAS). The CAS has almost 300 arbitrators from 87 countries, chosen for their specialist knowledge of arbitration and sports law. Around 200 cases are registered by the CAS every year. Any disputes directly or indirectly associated to sport may be tendered to the CAS. These may be disputes of a commercial nature (e.g, a sponsorship contract) or of a disciplinary nature following a decision by a sports organization (e.g, a doping case).

The intellectual evasion as mentioned previously when dealing with athletes and coaches accused of violating amateurism rules remains a constant theme in the doping issue as well. Drug tests are a very complicated and intricate procedure involving two samples, several seals to the samples, a spotter (someone watching the urine test completion at all times), and a laboratory to test the specimen. Athletes accused of doping, even if results show a failed test, use process technicalities and tampering to maintain innocence. For example, Tyler Hamilton, a United States cyclist, won the gold medal in the Athens Olympics and also failed a drug test. Because the "B" urine sample (back-up test sample) had been destroyed, he could not be pronounced guilty of doping. A month after the Olympic competition, he failed yet another test. USADA (the United States Anti-doping Agency discussed later in the chapter) imposed a two-year ban from the sport but Tyler Hamilton has taken his case to the Court of Arbitration once again for an appeal to prove his innocence. The trial is still impending. Is Tyler a victim of a poor drug test or is he instead victimizing the testing process and the Court of Arbitration?

Olympic Sport Issues

Behind every Olympic Games are a countless number of details; behind each and every detail is a process. Sport organizations like the IOC, NOCs, and International Federations strive for each step in the formation of the Olympic Games to run smoothly. The magnitude of this huge event renders this goal impossible. For every step and every process there are issues that complicate progress. From issues like the host city selection process to image and politics to the schedule and to substance abuse and doping, sport federations must not only be equipped to plan a monstrous event, but must also be prepared to handle all controversies.

Financing

The Olympic Games not only mean the spirit of sport and the pursuit of greatness; the festival means new grandiose sport facilities, Olympic team accommodations for every country, and salaries for those who organize it. The dollar amounts add up exponentially for a "spare-no-expense" event. Where does the money come from, how much is it and who does what when it accumulates? The amount of money needed to fund the Olympic Games and to also fund the organizations that work to hold the event not only adds up but causes issues.

The IOC oversees the financial pursuit to ensure the Olympic Games, NOCs, International Federations and the IOC itself have enough money to support a countless number of endeavors not just in Olympic years but in the off years as well. The IOC used to rely heavily on money generated through host city fund raising; but, in 1984, in the Summer Olympic Games in Los Angeles, of the $225 million raised, not one cent landed in the hands of the IOC treasury. After this disaster the IOC created the Marketing Commission to provide alternative monetary resources. IOC members, NOC members and International Federation members form the Marketing Commission. This particular committee stays busy reviewing and studying all possible avenues to market the Olympic Games and monitors the implementation of any marketing programs making that each move reflects the Olympic spirit. The Executive Board has final say on which programs will be set into action. The new plan succeeded in raising $3.6 billion after its implementation from 1997 through the 2000 Olympic Games. For the next preparation phase of the Olympic Games, the Marketing Commission refined their activity and was able to raise even more money. From the years 2001 to 2004, the Marketing Commission reported four main revenue sources: broadcast rights, licensing and other revenues, ticketing and sponsorship.

The Marketing Commission generated 53 percent of total income from selling the broadcast rights of the Olympic Games. Encompassing over half of the revenue, television is a major factor for financial support, $2,229 million worth. The IOC sells exclusive rights to more than 4,000 hours worth of coverage for free-to-air broadcasting only. The IOC has received higher offers for pay-per-view television rights, but turned them down. Television is not only the main financial support but also is the biggest worldwide promoter for the Games.

The IOC manages licensing and other revenues through the host-city Organizing Committees. This income includes the sale profit from products that display the official emblems and mascots of the Olympic Games. The IOC raises its money through the rights to the Olympic Games' symbols such as the flame and torch, the anthem, and of course, the Olympic rings. Only encompassing two percent of the revenue, these products still produced about $86.5 million from 2001-2004. The Organizing Committee also supervises the collection of ticketing profit. The sale of Olympic event and ceremony tickets generated $441 million in the same period of time and 11 percent of the IOC revenue.

The IOC has control of the second largest revenue gain, sponsorships. The IOC received $1,459 million (34 percent) in donation from various businesses supporting the Olympic Games and profiting from affiliation. The Marketing Commission developed programs, like the TOP program to "loan" use of special Olympic symbols while businesses are donating to the Olympic Games. Sponsorships will be discussed in the next section.

Altogether, from the years 2001-2004, the IOC raised $4,215.5 million. Ninety-two percent of the income is funneled to the Organizing Committees, NOCs and International Sport Federations. The money helps support these groups, but also covers necessary costs for the Olympic Games and Olympic teams from every participating country. Specifically, from 2001-2004, finances went to the Salt Lake Organizing Committee, the Athens Organizing Committee, and 199 NOCs.

The final eight percent funds IOC programs. The Finance Commission of the IOC guarantees that IOC finance abides by International Accounting Standards and mandates yearly external audits. This particular sect of the IOC also designs an efficient budgeting plan and strategy and informs the Executive Board of wise investments.

The USOC shares the same type of rights, but for the distribution of Olympic symbols in the United States. The USOC also raises money through the sale of Olympic products and through partnerships with corporations. After the funding disaster of the Los Angeles Olympic Games mentioned earlier, the USOC set up a trust fund called the United States Olympic Foundation. The initial endowment totaled $111 million and remains intact year to year. Each year it generates an annual grant varies around $5.5 million for the promotion of Olympic-related sports in the United States. Both organizations, the IOC and the USOC, rely heavily on sponsorships, a topic discussed in depth later in the chapter.

Host City Selection Process

From start to finish, the host city selection process involves a multitude of steps that all together took about two years to complete. The procedure is also ever-changing; the latest "two-phase" election proceeding was developed in December 1999 and implemented for the 2008 Games election.

The first phase starts in the National Olympic Committees, associations in charge of Olympic activity at the national level. From Albania to Zimbabwe, 199 NOCs encompass the globe. As the bidding process begins, the NOC of each country selects a city, and each selected city then becomes an applicant for the IOC to consider. Each applicant city attends a seminar, completes a questionnaire, and submits to an observer program by a team of experts. The IOC chooses 10 cities, named official candidate cities, for the second phase.

This final phase includes a Candidature file, a written document produced by each Candidate city, and visit from the IOC Evaluation Commission. As the final meeting draws near, reports are concluded. The IOC meets and votes. If majority rule is not reached in the first round of voting, the city with the lowest votes is dropped and the committee votes again until at last majority rule selects the Olympic Games host site.

Image and Politics of the Olympic Games

The Olympic Games are a worldwide symbol of excellence: in athletics and in character. The importance of maintaining the Olympic ideal, however, extends past competition. Part of the Olympic image is ensuring independence from any government or nation, building an organization free from fraud, and also to aiding in the fight for improving the state of the world. No matter what kind of extensive effort put forth to eliminate politics from an organization or an organization's image, political competition is inevitable. The Olympic Games are no exception. Politics exist within the IOC and countries in the past have used the Olympic Games to make political messages.

What does the IOC accomplish between Olympic Games? Besides the organization of the coveted world athletic competition, the IOC maintains a worldwide social responsibility. Part of this responsibility is an independence from all national government power and politics. The IOC seeks to operate without gain from any country in particular. For example, if the IOC comprised of only delegates from Europe, how might the Games and Game operation change in favor of European nations? Cultures across the world have different ways of life and governments. By staying independent, the IOC will not favor any culture or country in particular. This policy is important to maintaining fairness, but almost as important, being perceived as fair.

The IOC reaches out in many different ways. Calls to action are written within the Olympic Charter for not only speaking out on certain social issues but to act upon them as well. Among the issues at the forefront are world peace, tolerance of all cultures and races, and attention to poorer nations. An example of the IOC's interventions is the IOC's meeting with the Olympic Committee of the Democratic People's Republic of Korea and the Korean Olympic Committee to form one unified Olympic team for the Beijing Olympics in 2008. The IOC attempted to begin to unite the countries with a very traumatic history through sport September 5, 2006. IOC President Jacques Rogge stated, "Enormous progress was made towards the creation of a unified team for the Beijing 2008 Olympic Games" (IOC News, 2006). The image the IOC tries to project with these policies is to eliminate the idea of an organization geared toward sport alone. The organization wishes to be known as one that identifies a great responsibility to social issues and is beneficial to the world in many different ways other than uniting countries in competition. IOC Olympic Solidarity programs focus on instructional training for coaches in developing nations. Apart from providing funding through Olympic Solidarity, mainly on coaching clinics and sport training programs, the IOC also distributes funds to International federations like the IAAF for providing additional competitions to developing countries. For example, in 2001, the IAAF received a $6 million (IOC) grant, in the eyes on many observers for being a role model for other federations to follow by fighting the drug menace in sport.

The IOC has devoted a great deal of effort to maintaining its image of excellence. How well has the IOC preserved its reputation as a politics-free, socially conscience organization? The Olympic committee has had its fair share of negative press, which leads critics to question the IOC's image goals. Critics have attacked the Bid Selection Committee, policy to fill vacancies within the organization, and the lack of the inclusion of women. Within the committee, critics have identified alliances to assert political and majority power. Other image problems that the IOC encounters but may have less control over are how countries use the Olympic Games to achieve political goals. Countries may hold competitions to spark political involvement like when China held a dual match with the United States table tennis team. What followed was a series of foreign policy discussions between the two nations. Country leaders may use the Games to inspire national and cultural loyalty at the expense of other cultures or nations. For example, in the past, some Olympic competitions became Communism vs. Democracy instead of competitor vs. competitor. Other countries use the Olympic Games to send a political message worldwide by boycotting the Games.

Many Olympic Games in the past have been boycotted by many different countries for many different political reasons. In 1984, the Soviet Union and other Eastern Bloc Nations boycotted the Los Angeles Games in the Cold War period. Africa boycotted the 1976 Melbourne Games when the New Zealand rugby team toured apartheid South Africa. The United States is no exception from those countries using the Olympic Games to make a political statement. The Soviets invaded Afghanistan in 1979. Moscow had already been elected to hold the 1980 Olympic Games. President Carter tried to absolve political motive by professing the competition would be "dangerous to athletes" and stating "It should be remembered that in the United States and other free countries, the National Olympic Committees were independent of government control." But the "independent" decision was backed by the strong arm of the law, warning the revoking of passports of the athletes who went (CNN Specials, 1998).

All attacks have resulted in IOC movement. These situations have led to the expulsion of members and a conscience addition of women to IOC committees. The IOC has recently opened all of its meetings and documentation to the press. The IOC's worldwide image is not only very important to its reputation but also to its effectiveness as well. The Olympic Games thrive on the ideal of fair competition between nations. Because of this, the IOC has made extensive addition to the Charter and has taken significant measures to police its internal structure. No matter the effort, however, it is impossible to completely control politics within the IOC and the use of the Olympic Games for political visions. Therefore, political manipulation will always be a part of the image of the Olympic Games.

Reorganization

A lot of the International Olympic Committee's and United States Olympic Committee's structure and process is a response to mistakes, scandals, or failures that forced leaders to "reorganize." The term reorganization used in this context refers to the evaluation and change of a committee's internal structure. One historic scandal, the 2002 Winter Olympic bid disgrace, led to many changes.

Salt Lake City had been one particular United States city aggressively bidding for the host of the Olympic Winter Games. Since 1932 and up until 1998, Salt Lake City Organizing Committees, or the SLOC, had campaigned but failed to win the bid. Tom Welch and Dave Johnson, directors of the SLOC for the 2002 Olympic bid, decided to take an even more aggressive approach. Millions of dollars went to the bribery of International Olympic Committee members. The money was spent in several ways including Super Bowl Trips, $400,000 worth in scholarships to 13 beneficiaries, free medical care including plastic surgery, and more than $15,000 worth in expensive guns and skis. (CNN News, 1998) When the IOC announced the winner of the host-city Olympic bid for the 2002 Games, Tom Welch and Dave Johnson found their plan had worked; Salt Lake City would host the 2002 Winter Olympic Games.

Swiss IOC member Marc Hodler broke the scandal in December 1998. Investigations of the IOC, USOC, and SLOC ensued. Shortly after the investigation began, members of these organizations, including Tom Welch and Dave Johnson, resigned their posts. The reaction to this uproarious scandal involved a heavy "reorganization".

"There's an opportunity here to probably make some changes and do some things that probably should have been done long before; but, the evidence wasn't there and available to do it," USOC director David Schultz said. "So, I think there's a possibility here to perhaps make the Olympic movement stronger than it's ever been before" (CNN News, 1999).

The IOC followed through with major internal structure changes. The host city election process was amended including the elimination of IOC member visits to candidate cities. Membership to the IOC would include a cap of 115 members, 15 active Olympians, 15 International Federation members, 15 National Olympic Committee members, 70 individual members, and an age limit of 70 years. IOC member terms would last eight years renewable through election and the presidential term would be limited to eight years with re-election to a four-year term only. Various committees were created as well: the Nominations Committee for IOC membership, the IOC Ethics Commission, and the World Anti-Doping Agency. The IOC also opened meetings and financial reports to the media and for publication.

Security

The synchronized terrorist attacks on September 11, 2001, made it clear that security was an issue not to be taken lightly. The Olympics are the largest and most recognized worldwide event with the most worldwide attention and participation. The huge event not only involves coaches, athletes, and other delegates from many different countries but must house them as well. The IOC faces security challenges on many levels, and history reminds the Olympic organizing committees that security will always be an important concern. In Munich, 1972, Israelis and Palestinians residing in the Olympic village were killed in a hostage situation. Recently, in the United States at the Atlanta Summer Games, a bomb was detonated in the Olympic park. To prevent harm to all who participate or watch the Olympic Games, the IOC as well as the National Olympic Committee and Organizing Committees of the host city take many precautions.

The IOC oversees the process and ensures basic levels of security are given proper attention. The National and Organizing Olympic Committees set forth the emergency action plan. As spectators seek access to Olympic Games, they encounter handheld metal detectors and many security officers. Venues involved with the Olympic village such as practice sights, dining halls, and other designated areas have high security. The perimeter to the Olympic Village grounds are all closed with access through security like any airport. Only individuals with the proper accreditation can enter and leave the premises. The access pass is a photo ID and a list of sights permitted to that particular person worn around the neck. Those wishing to enter the premises must also surrender their belongings to X-ray screening or hand search.

Selection of New Olympic Sports

The Executive Board of the IOC has been voting new sports into the Olympic program since 1936. Only recently, the IOC made history in their policy by developing a systematic approach to evaluating and adding to the list of sports. In the Mexico session of 2002, the IOC formed limits: 28 sports, 301 events, and 10,500 athletes at most in each Olympic Games. The IOC also made a declaration to review the sports chosen and make changes to the list if necessary after each edition of the Olympic Games.

In response to the Mexico meeting, the Olympic Program Commission, a division of the IOC dedicated to reviewing the structure of the Olympic program, developed a list of 33 criteria to evaluate each sport. After careful consideration, the Executive Board of the International Olympic Committee validated the list on August 11, 2004. In the form of a questionnaire, the criteria are used as a survey to International Federations. And in turn, the feedback aids executives in the decision to add new sports to the Olympic Program.

The document titled "Evaluation Criteria for Sports and Disciplines" includes various themes. The first section, "History and Tradition", evaluates a sport background seeking answers to questions like past participation in the Olympics and its first international organization and contest. The second section, "Universality", tests the worldwide applicability of the sport. How many national federations are affiliated with the sport? How many countries include national competitions in the sport? The third section, "Popularity of the Sport", calculates a sports' spectator and media attention. The fourth and fifth sections, "Image-Environment" and "Athlete's Health", require the new sport to embrace policies like gender equity, fairness in outcome, positive impact on the environment, and anti-doping guidelines. The last two specific sections, "Development of the IF" and "Costs", assess the status of development programs in each federation available for the sport and also a budget to include the sport in the Olympic Games. The very last section titled "General" is an open forum for any other important considerations specific to the particular sport in question.

Under these guidelines, the Olympic Program Commission evaluates new sports

in question in a two-year process, and the Executive Board of the IOC makes the final decision with a vote. The IOC meeting in Singapore 2005 finalized the Olympic Program for 2012.

The exclusion of baseball and softball from the Olympic Games left two openings in the 28-sport cap of the program. Five "non-Olympic sports", sports that had not yet been in an Olympic Games, were appraised by the Olympic Program Commission. Roller sports, squash, golf, karate, and rugby made the list. The Executive Board then voted for two nominees. Majority ruled karate and squash. Rule 46 of the Olympic Charter, however, mandates that each sport included in the Olympic Games be an "Olympic sport". This called for another vote with a two-thirds majority necessary for karate's and squash's inclusion to the "Olympic sport" list. Both sports failed to gain the required amount of votes and did not make the program for 2012. If softball and baseball were to be nominated in the future, because they have already been in the Olympic program are considered "Olympic sports" and would not need the two-thirds vote.

Like every hot issue in sports, the selection of new sports to the Olympic program has a unique history. Many of the new sports added to the Olympic Program were included to promote opportunities for women in sport. Although Coubertin opposed the participation of women in the Olympics and no women competed in 1896, a few female golfers and tennis players were allowed to participate in the 1900 Games. Female swimming and diving were added to the 1912 Games, and female gymnastics and track-and-field events were first held at the 1928 Games. Women's Olympic sports have grown significantly since then, and currently women account for approximately half of the members of teams, except in teams from Islamic nations, where the level of female participation is generally lower. The inclusion of women in some Olympic sports is still evolving. Just recently in the 2000 Olympics in Sydney, Australia, women's hammer and pole vault made their debut as Olympic events in track and field.

Decertification of Olympic Sports

Since the beginning of the Olympics, the schedule of events has been continually changing. Just as sports are added, sports are subtracted. From 1900 to 1920, tug-of-war made the program list as an event of track and field. The 56 lb. weight throw in track and field was contested in 1904 at the Olympic Games in St. Louis and the 1920 games in Antwerp and discontinued there after. Polo, golf, rugby, and lacrosse thereafter are among the sports decertified over the history of the Olympics. Sport decertification made news in 2005 at the same Singapore session in which the evaluation criteria mentioned earlier was developed. Before the Executive Board considered squash and karate as additions to the Olympic program for 2012, two sports; baseball and softball, were previously decertified by Executive Board majority vote, leaving openings in the schedule.

On the last day of the Singapore session, President of the IOC Jaques Rogge announced his support for the decision. He highlighted the new criteria system for excluding baseball for its doping failures and softball for its lack of universal appeal. Both sports, though, remain Olympic sports because they had previously been a part of the Olympic Program, and if the issues of doping and universality are addressed in the future, softball and baseball may be readmitted in 2016.

At another IOC meeting in Turin on February 2006, the Olympic committee voted again on the reinstatement of baseball and softball for 2012. The proposal to keep the sports in the program was once again turned down.

Sponsorships

The International Olympic Committee relies heavily on corporations for the funding necessary to bring the event to life. Nearly 40 percent of marketing funds collected come from the relationship between the Olympic Games and sponsors. In turn, for their support, corporations receive exclusive marketing access. This relationship between a business and the Olympics comes in two forms: The Olympic Partner Program (TOP) and Suppliers.

Since 1985, TOP has held the exclusive marketing rights for both the summer and Winter Games. Corporations wishing to sponsor the Games enter a four-year deal with TOP, not only providing funding for the Games itself but also aiding support for years in between. The corporation then benefits from use of exclusive Olympic imagery, concessions, and showcase at the event, and other marketing tools worldwide. The IOC even designated a program solely to the promotion and recognition of these sponsors. Coca-Cola, McDonald's, and Visa are among the companies in the TOP contract with the Olympics for the 2006 Torino Games.

Suppliers of the Olympic Games provide other critical services but with limited marketing access. For example, since 1991, DaimlerChrysler has provided IOC member transportation to meetings across the globe and has also provided transportation for developing nations operating National Olympic Committees. Another supplier, Mizuno, outfits the IOC and Olympic Game staff.

Substance Abuse and Doping

The competitive drive can bring out the best and worst in athletes and coaches. Since the beginning of sport, participants have looked to foreign substances for an edge in competition. It had become more than necessary to enforce regulation of these types of substances; athletes had begun to use cocaine, alcohol, and other harmful materials. The 1930s marked history when synthetic hormones commonly and collectively known as steroids were invented. When cyclists began to die in competition because of the misuse of certain substances, the urgency for a drug test rose drastically and drug tests were implemented in the 1968 Olympic Games in Grenoble and Mexico.

Since the drug test had been introduced, the history of doping until the present is certain athletes trying to hide performance enhancement one way or another. Athletes used undetectable (at the time) doping substances like anabolic steroids. Even state-run government doping plans abused banned drugs and managed to escape drug tests. One hundred meter champion Ben Johnson tested positive for anabolic steroids at the Olympic Games in 1988 and reminded the athletic world that doping was still a big problem.

Substance abuse hit a climax in the sport of cycling in 1998 when police raided the Tour de France and found prohibited substances in bulk. As a result, the International Olympic Committee saw a great need for an independent international system or program to put a stop to the mishandling. From February 2 through February 4, the IOC held its first convention to regulate anti-doping. The conference led to the Lausanne Declaration, a demand in writing for an anti-doping organization. The World Anti-Doping Agency, also known as WADA, came to fruition on November 1999, with a goal to be fully functional by the Sydney Olympic Games in 2000. With the support, funding, and representatives not only from the IOC, but from government agencies all over the world, WADA has been a more effective means to a drug-free Olympic Games.

The organization focuses its attention to seven different priorities to ensure their vision of a doping-free world of sports.

WADA mandates universality. Each country or sport federation must adopt WADA policy and the association oversees implementation. At the helm, WADA has effort placed on coordinating anti-doping policy through an international website. For those countries that have limited anti-doping resources, WADA provides regional anti-doping organizations helping those countries work together. Another WADA mission is to prevent doping with educational programs and also with direct contact with elite athletes at major competitions. To keep athletes in check, WADA has implemented an out-of-competition testing program with no notice. Lastly, WADA continues to develop and improve the prohibited substance list and also the accuracy of the drug test itself.

Along with WADA, the United States has been continually fighting doping scandals. No story quite compares to the scandal USOC Doping Chief Wade Exum reported in year 2000. He alleged that 19 American medalists were permitted to compete at various Olympic Games from 1988 to 2000 despite having earlier failed drug tests. For years, insiders had speculated that U.S. athletes were not impervious to delving into doping to get an edge on the competition. American athletes often spoke publicly against illegal drug use in sport, cursing the sports regimes of East Germany and China for systemic doping practices. "There is no commitment to stopping the drug problem," said track and field star Carl Lewis in 2000. "People know the sport is dirty, the sport is so driven by records." This five-time Olympic medalist was among the athletes named in more than 30,000 pages of documents released by former U.S. Olympic Committee anti-doping chief to Sports Illustrated and several newspapers in 2003. More than 100 athletes from a number of different sports tested positive for banned substances between 1988 and 2000 but were exonerated by internal appeals processes. Exum made the initial allegations about the cover-ups in 2000, which led several sporting organizations, the IOC, IAAF, and the World Anti-Doping Agency, to pressure the USOC to re-examine how they conducted drug testing. Along with the worldwide movement's reconstruction, the United States Olympic Committee developed its own organization to fight doping, the United States Anti-Doping Agency, also known as USADA. Soon, the USOC turned over drug-testing responsibilities to the newly founded U.S. Anti-Doping Agency. Before the program's official implementation on October 1, 2000, the USOC made careful plan to organize its governing structure. Five members elected from outside the OSOC and four members elected from two different organizations within the USOC (the Athlete Advisory Council and the National Governing Body) made up USADA's Board of Directors. In 2003, the Board of Directors formed a new policy of election; the AAC and NGB would be able to nominate new members to the board; but, the actual election responsibility would be that of the board.

USADA's mission is not unlike that of WADA. Two million dollars a year is allocated for research to expand the prohibited substances list and to maintain the integrity of the drug test. Of all national anti-doping policies, USADA budgets the most. USADA also maintains an education program reaching athletes from the youth to the elite level. USADA is also in charge of both in- and out-of-competition drug testing meaning athletes do not have to be in a competition or a competitive season to be drug tested by USADA.

In 2006, Justin Gatlin, the current world record holder in the 100-meter dash and 2004 Olympic Gold Medalist failed a drug test after competing in the Kansas Relays. Gatlin announced on July 29, 2006 that he tested positive for testosterone or related substances. He agreed to cooperate with authorities and, in turn, escaped a lifetime ban from the sport. Gatlin's story sent shockwaves throughout the track and field community. USADA, in an attempt to clean up sport, has successfully caught several "dirty" champions; but, the reoccurrence of failed drug tests year after year has led the sporting community to question whether USADA has been effective at preventing illegal drug use.

Summary

For athletes in the Winter and Summer Games, the coveted worldwide competition comes once every four years. Is it possible that any other competition has as much worldwide clout and hype as the Olympics? The Olympic Games have become what they are today through the International Olympic Committee designing, defending, and amending the Olympic Charter. The USOC is the governing body actively promoting and protecting sport on United States soil. Overseeing all aspects of Olympic sport on the national and world level is a conundrum that involves thorough enthusiastic preparation. Although issues in sport, from financial concerns to illegal substance abuse, test and challenge the governing bodies and the sporting community, these issues also strongly shape IOC and USOC policy. These two very important and powerful governing bodies may never escape politics or negative attention but in response to these sporting issues, the IOC and USOC have evolved in constructive ways to fit the ever-changing sports horizon.

References

CBC. (2006). *Drugs and sport*. Retrieved on September 22, 2006, from http://www.cbc.ca/sports/indepth/drugs/stories/top10.html

CNN News. (1998). *'Thorough' Olympic bribery probe promised*. Retrieved on September 17, 2006, from http://www.cnn.com/US/98122/29/olympic.bribery.01/index.html

CNN News. (1999). *Salt Lake Olympics rocked by resignations, evidence of payments*. Retrieved on September 17, 2006, from http://www.cnn.com/US/9901/08/olympic.bribes.03/

CNN Specials. (1998). *Olympic boycotts*. Retrieved on September 14, 2006, from http://www.cnn.com/SPECIALS/cold.war/episodes/20/spotlight

Court of Arbitration for Sport. (2006). Retrieved September 30, 2006 from http://www.tas-cas.org/default.htm

Hums, M.A., & MacLean, J.C. (2004). *Governance and policy in sport organizations*. Scottsdale, AZ: Holcomb Hathaway Publishers.

IOC. (2006). *The finance commission*. Retrieved November 8, 2006 from http://www.olympic.org/uk/organisation/commission/finance/index.uk.asp

IOC. (2006). *The marketing commission*. Retrieved November 8, 2006 from http://www.olympic.org/uk/organisation/commissions/marketing/index_uk.asp

IOC. (2006). *National Olympic committees*. Retrieved August 11, 2006 from http://www.olympic.org/uk/organisations/noc/index_uk.asp

IOC. (2006). *Olympic programme*. Retrieved August 13, 2006, from http://www.olympic.org/uk/organisation/commissions/programme/full_story_uk.asp?id=1657

IOC. (2006). *The Olympic programme commission*. Retrieved August 11, 2006, from http://www.olympic.org/uk/organisation/commissions/programme/index_uk.asp

IOC. (2006). *Olympic sponsorship*. Retrieved August 7, 2006, from http://www.olympic.org/uk/organisation/facts/programme/

IOC. (2006). *Organization*. Retrieved August 13, 2006, from http://www.olympic.org/uk/organisation/ioc/index_uk.asp

IOC. (2006). *Organization: Evolution of its structure*. Retrieved on September 17, 2006, from http://www.olympic.org/uk/organisation/ioc/organisation/index_uk.asp

IOC. (2006). *Partner, product category, and Contact information*. Retrieved August 13, 2006, from http://www.olympic.org/uk/organisation/facts/programme/sponsors_uk.asp

IOC. (2006). *Suppliers*. Retrieved August 13, 2006, from http://www.http://www.olympic.org/uk/organisation/facts/programme/suppliers_uk.asp

IOC News. (2004). *IOC discusses revision of Olympic Games sports programme*. Retrieved August 11, 2006 from http://www.olympic.org/uk/organisation/commission/programme/full_story_uk.asp?id=845

IOC News. (2005). *News about Singapore 117th IOC session*. Retrieved August 7, 2006, from http://www.olympic.org/uk/news/events/117_session/full_story_uk.asp?id-1426

IOC News. (2005). *Procedure for the vote on the Olympic programme for the 2012 Olympic games*. Retrieved August 7, 2006, from http://www.olympic.org/uk/organisation/commissions/programme/full_story_uk.asp?id=1309

IOC News. (2005). *Singapore 2005: 2012 Olympic sport vote*. Retrieved August 11, 2006 from http://www.olympic.org/uk/news/events/117_session/full_story_uk.asp?id=1437

IOC News. (2006). *Two Koreas make progress in creation of unified team*. Retrieved September 14, 2006, from http://www.olympic.org/uk/news/olympic_news/full_story_uk.asp?-1893

IOC Olympic Games. (2006). *Beijing 2008 election*. Retrieved August 11, 2006 from http://www.olympic.org/uk/games/beijing/election_uk.asp

Masteralexis, L.P., Barr, C.A., & Hums, M.A. (1998). *Principles and practice of sport management*. Gaithersburg, MD: Aspen Publishing.

Olympic Charter. (2004). *Olympic charter*. Retrieved September 14, 2006, from http://multimedia.olympic .org/pdf/en_report_122.pdf

Olympic Games. (2006). Retrieved September 30, 2006 from http://www/encarta.msn.com/encyclopedia_761562380/Olympic_Games_(modern).html

Olympic Program Commission Report to the IOC Session. (2006). *Evaluation criteria for sports and disciplines*. Retrieved August 11, 2006, from http://multimedia.olympic.org/pdf/en_report_813.pdf

Ted Stevens Olympic and Amateur Sports Act. (1998). Chapter 2205- United States Olympic Committee. Retrieved September 14, 2006, from http://www/usolympicteam.com/ASA2000.pdf

The Hindu, (2001). *IAAF to get 6 million dollar subsidy*. Retrieved September 30, 2006 from http://www.hiduonnet.com/2001/08/05/stories/0705096j.htm

USA Today. (2006) USOC wants to sanction coaches. Retrieved September 30, 2006 from http://www.usatoday.com/sports/olympics/2006-07-13-usoc-doping–x.htm

USADA. (2006). *USADA mission*. Retrieved August 19, 2006, from http://www.usantidoping.org/who/mission.html.

USOC Bylaws. (2006). *Bylaws of the United States Olympic committee*. Retrieved September 14, 2006 from http://www.olympicteam.com/USOC_Bylaws_as_of_6232006.pdf

WADA. (2006). *WADA history*. Retrieved August 19, 2006, from http://www.wada-ama.org/en/dynamic.ch2?pageCategory.id=311

WADA. (2006). *A brief history of anti-doping*. Retrieved August 19, 2006, from http://www.wada-ama.org/en/dynamic.ch2?pageCategory.id=312

WADA. (2006). *Mission*. Retrieved August 19, 2006, from http://www.wada-ama.org/en/dynamic.ch2?pageCategory.id-255

NOTES

CHAPTER 14

Paralympics Sport Governance

Paralympics are an international competition among each nation's elite athletes with physical and sensory disabilities and is second in size only to the Olympic Games. The Paralympic Games and Paralympic Winter Games follow the Olympic Games and Olympic Winter Games at the same venues and facilities. The Paralympic Games have been contested since 1960 and now feature competition in 19 sports. The Paralympic Winter Games showcase four sports and were first held in 1976 (http://www.paralympic.org).

The Paralympics offers competition to athletes who are blind or visually impaired, have amputated limbs or similar impairments, have spinal cord injuries, and have motor impairments due to cerebral palsy, traumatic brain injury, or stroke. In certain sports, athletes with other physical disabilities may also compete (e.g., muscular dystrophy). Finally, there are opportunities for persons with intellectual disabilities as well.

An intellectual disability is a particular state of functioning that begins in childhood before age 18 and is characterized by significant limitations in both intelligence and adaptive skills as expressed in conceptual, social, and practical adaptive skills.

A person with an intellectual disability will usually have an IQ below 75 and significant limitations in adaptive behavior that impact the person's daily life and ability to respond to a particular situation or environment. Of the total population with intellectual disabilities, approximately 87 percent are mildly affected. Ten percent have moderate intellectual disabilities, and only three percent have severe disabilities.

Learning Objectives

Upon completion this chapter, the reader should be able to:

- Describe the differences between Paralympics and Special Olympics.
- Discuss the history of Paralympics.
- Outline the Paralympics governance system.
- Describe the govern structure for Deaflympics.
- Identify the various sports in the summer and winter games for both Paralympics and Deaflympics.

History of Paralympics

Sir Ludwig Guttmann organized a sports competition in 1948 that became known as the Stoke Mandeville Games involving World War II veterans with spinal cord injuries; in 1952, competitors from the Netherlands took part in the competition, giving an international notion to the movement. The first Olympic-style games for athletes with disabilities were held in Rome in 1960; officially called the Ninth Annual International Stoke Mandeville Games these were considered to be the first Paralympic Games. The first Winter Paralympics were held in Örnsköldsvik, Sweden in 1976 (http://www.paralympic.org).

The word "Paralympic" derives from the Greek preposition "para" ("beside" or "alongside") and the word "Olympics" (the Paralympics being the parallel Games to the Olympics). The word Paralympic was originally a pun combining 'paraplegic' and 'Olympic'; however, with the inclusion of other disability groups and the close associations with the Olympic Movement, it now represents 'parallel' and 'Olympic' to illustrate how the two movements exist side by side (http://www.paralympic.org).

Since 1988, the Summer Paralympics have been held in the conjunction with the Olympic Games in the same host city. This practice was adopted in 1992 for the Winter Paralympics and became an official policy of the International Olympic Committee (IOC) and the International Paralympic Committee (IPC) following a June 19, 2001 agreement. The Paralympic Games take place three weeks after the closing of the Olympics, in the same host city and using the same facilities. Cities bidding to host the Olympic Games must include the Paralympic Games in their bid and, typically, both Games are now run by a single organizing committee (http://www.paralympic.org).

In the 1996 Atlanta Games, athletes with intellectual disabilities were allowed to participate for the first time. However, following cheating in the 2000 Sydney Games, in which non-disabled athletes were entered in the Spanish Basketball ID team, such athletes were banned by the IPC. Following an anti-corruption drive, the International Sports Federation for Persons with an Intellectual Disability (INAS-FID) lobbied to have these athletes reinstated. Beginning in 2004, athletes with intellectual disabilities (a focus of Special Olympics as well, see Chapter 15) began to be re-integrated into Paralympic sport competitions; although, they remain excluded from the Paralympic Games. The IPC stated that it will re-evaluate their participation following the Beijing 2008 Paralympic Games (http://www.paralympic.org).

The International Paralympic Committee

The International Paralympic Committee (IPC) is the international governing body of sports for athletes with disabilities and acts as the International Federation for 12 sports. It supervises and co-ordinates the Paralympic Summer and Winter Games and other multidisability competitions, e.g., world championships. The IPC also supports the recruitment and development of athletes at local, national, and international levels across all performance levels.

The IPC was founded on September 22, 1989, as an international non-profit organization formed and run by around 160 National Paralympic Committees (NPCs) from five regions and four disability-specific international sports federations (IOSDs). The organization has a democratic constitution and structure composed of elected representatives. The four IOSDs are:

1. CP-ISRA: Cerebral Palsy International Sport and Recreation Association mission is to promote and develop the

means by which people throughout the world can have access to opportunities for participation in sport and recreational activities.

The CP-ISRA seeks to: (a) increase the number of National Members, (b) promote with and through them the value of sport and recreation for those with cerebral palsy or a related neurological condition (c) encourage and facilitate the organization and running of more World, National, and Regional Games, (d) work within the International Paralympic movement to ensure that those served are not disadvantaged on the world's sporting stage, and (e) challenge attitudes and assumptions and will work cooperatively with other organizations to achieve the organization's vision (http://www.cpisra.org).

2. IBSA: International Blind Sports Federation's goal is the full integration of the blind and visually impaired through sport at all levels (http://www.ibsa.en).

3. INAS-FID: International Sports Federation for Persons with Intellectual Disability was founded in 1986 with the aim to create a platform for athletes with intellectual disabilities who wish to perform their sports:
    +   in a competitive way,
    +   in open competition as at the Olympics, and
    +   according to the rules of the International Federations (for athletics the rules of the IAAF, for basketball those of FIBA, etc.) (http://www.inas-fid.org).

4. IWAS: International Wheelchair and Amputee Sports Federation is the funding and marketing division of the International Stoke Mandeville Wheelchair Sports Federation, which provides services to over 70 member nations. The headquarters are located at Stoke Mandeville where sport for people with spinal injuries began in 1945 after the Second World War (http://www.wsw.org.uk).

Whereas other international sports organizations for athletes with a disability are either limited to one disability group or to one specific sport, the IPC, as an umbrella organization, represents several sports and disabilities. The national sports organizations, which created the IPC, are convinced that the future of sport for persons with a disability lies in bringing together athletes with different abilities to hold joint competitions.

As time went by, multidisability competitions developed that later became included in the Paralympic Games. The Paralympics were growing fast and became important international sport events. The need to govern these games more efficiently and to speak with one voice to the IOC resulted in the foundation of the ICC, the "International Co-ordination Committee of World Sports Organizations for the Disabled", in 1982. Only five years later, the ICC was replaced by the International Paralympic Committee (IPC). It was the strong wish of the member nations to form this organization with a democratic constitution and elected representatives. The IPC was finally founded in Düsseldorf, Germany, in 1989 (http://www.paralympic.org).

The Winter Paralympics in Lillehammer in 1994 were the first Paralympic Games under the management of IPC. Today we look back on a history of the organization, which is rapidly developing and presently numbers around 160 member nations. The movement's growth is best exemplified through the phenomenal rise of the Paralympic Games. More countries competed at the ATHENS 2004 Paralympics (3806 athletes, 136 countries) than in the Munich 1972 Olympic Games. In Athens, the degree of media coverage was unprecedented. With interest in and acceptance for sport for persons with a disability growing, the expansion of the Paralympics is most likely to continue in the future (http://www.paralympic.org).

The IPC is currently composed of a General Assembly (its highest decision-making body, made up of the National Paralympic Committees (NPCs), International Federations (IFs), Regional Organizations (four International Organization of Sport for the Disabled [IOSDs] and Sports), a Governing Board, a Management Team in Bonn, and various Standing Committees and Councils. From 1989 (when the IPC was founded) to 2001, Dr. Robert D. Steadward held the office of IPC President. In December 2001, after the maximum of three terms in office, he was succeeded by the former Paralympian and President of the International Wheelchair Basketball Federation, Sir Philip Craven, MBE (http://www.paralympic.org).

Disability Categories

The International Paralympic Committee (IPC) has established the following disability categories that are used to determine eligibility for participation:

- Amputee: An athlete with a partial or total loss of at least one limb.
- Cerebral Palsy: People who have non-progressive brain damage, for example, cerebral palsy, traumatic brain injury, stroke, or a similar problem affecting muscle control, balance, or coordination.
- Intellectual Disability: An athlete who has a significant impairment in intellectual functioning with associated limitations in adaptive behavior. This category is currently suspended.
- Wheelchair: For all athletes with spinal cord injuries and other disabilities that

require them to compete in a wheelchair. Athletes must have at least 10 percent loss of function to their lower limbs.

- Vision-Impaired: Athletes who have a vision impairment ranging from partial vision (sufficient to be judged legally blind) to total blindness.
- *Les Autres:* French for *the others* and includes competitors with a mobility impairment or other loss of physical function that does not fall strictly under one of the other five categories. Dwarfism, multiple sclerosis, or birth deformities of the limbs, such as that caused by thalidomide, are examples of this.

Governance

In 2005, the Executive Committee was replaced by a Governing Board whose members were directly elected by the IPC General Assembly. There are four advisory Councils in addition to several Standing Committees. They are governed under a new IPC Constitution and a new electoral system. This will lead the 12 IPC sports toward more self-sustainability and eventually independence from the IPC. In addition to the NPCs and IOSDs, the sports and regional bodies will also become full members of the IPC. (see Chart 14.1 for organizational structure)

The IPC General Assembly (GA) is the highest authority of the International Paralympic Committee (IPC). It is the biannual assembly of all members of the IPC which are:

- International Sports Federations (IOSD Sports and IPC Sports)

An International Federation (IF) is an independent sport federation recognized by the IPC as the sole world wide representative of a sport for athletes with disabilitirs

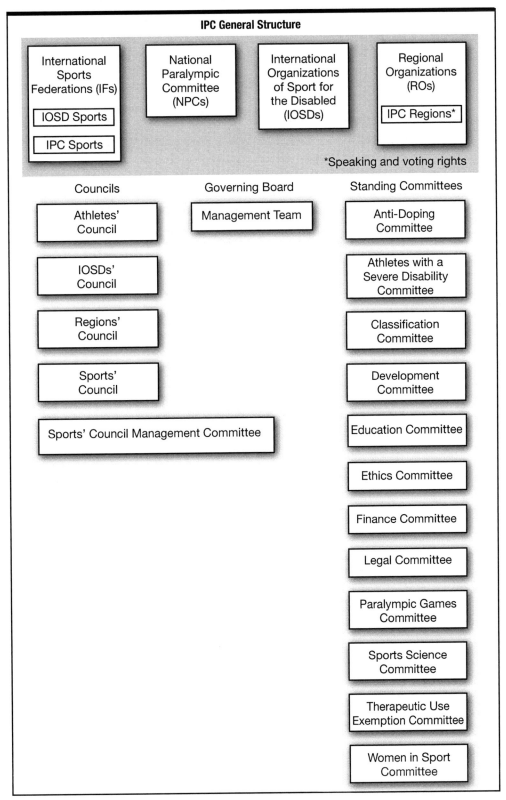

Chart 14.1
Organizational Structure of the IPC

that has been granted the status as a Paralympic Sport by the IPC.

Membership: The IPC currently recognizes six (6) IFs; the International Equestrian Federation (FEI), the International Wheelchair Basketball Federation (IWBF), the International Tennis Federation (ITF), the International Federation for Disabled Sailing (IFDS), the World Organization Volleyball for the Disabled (WOVD), and the World Curling Federation (WCF).

Function: To exercise technical jurisdiction and guidance over the competition and training venues of its respective sport, or sports, during the Paralympic Games.

- The National Paralympic Committees (NPCs)

A National Paralympic Committee (NPC) is a national organization recognized by the IPC as the sole representative of athletes with a disability in that country or territory to the IPC.

Membership: The IPC currently has 161 National Paralympic Committees.

Function: NPCs undertake the coordination and support of IPC activities and Paralympic Sport within their respective territory. They are also responsible for the entrance, management, and team preparation for the Paralympic Games and other IPC-sanctioned competitions.

- International Organization of Sport for the Disabled (IOSD)

An International Organization of Sport for the Disabled (IOSD) is an independent organization recognized by the IPC as the sole representative of a specific disability group to the IPC.

Membership: The IPC currently recognizes four (4) IOSDs: the Cerebral Palsy International Sports and Recreation Association (CP-ISRA), the International Blind Sports Federation (IBSA), the Interna-

tional Sports Federation for Persons with an Intellectual Disability (INAS-FID), and the International Wheelchair and Amputee Sports Federation (IWAS).

Function: IOSDs cooperate with the IPC in providing the disability specific expertise required to develop sport for athletes with disabilities from the grassroots level to elite level. They are the governing body for some of the disability specific sports participating at the Paralympic Games. The ISODs also coordinate their development activities with the IPC.

- Regional Organizations (IPC Regions)

A regional organization is an independent regional organization recognized as the sole regional representative of the IPC members within a specific region as recognized by the IPC.

Membership: The IPC currently recognizes three Regional Organizations: the African Sports Confederation of Disabled (Africa), the European Paralympic Committee (Europe), and the Oceania Paralympic Committee (Oceania). Until such time as an independent regional organization is created, the IPC has established a Regional Committee the Paralympic Committee of the Americas (for the Americas region) and the Asia Paralympic Council (for the Asia region) to act as the sole representative body in that region.

Function: Regional Organizations act as liaison with the IPC on behalf of its members in the respective region, organize Regional sports events, coordinate their development activities with the IPC, and provide support to the IPC membership in the respective region.

Governing Board

The Governing Board (GB) is the representative of the IPC Membership, elected at the General Assembly in accordance with nomination and election procedures adopted by the IPC Membership at the 2004 Extraordinary General Assembly. The GB is responsible for overseeing the affairs of the IPC in between meetings of the General Assembly (GA). Membership: The GB comprises 15 members including one president, one vice-president, ten members-at-large, one co-opted member (member without vote), one athletes' representative (ex-officio member with vote, elected by the Athletes' Council), and the CEO (ex-officio member without vote). The GB is chaired by the president and holds meetings at least three times a year. Function: The Governing Board is primarily responsible for the implementation of policies and directions set by the GA. Additionally, the Governing Board provides recommendations on membership (conditions for membership and fees) to the General Assembly, including motions received from members. It is also responsible for approving budgets and audited accounts, IPC Rules and Regulations, and membership of IPC Committees and the Paralympic Games.

Management Team

The IPC Management Team consists of the professional staff working under the direction of the CEO. With the authority delegated by the Governing Board, the CEO represents the board and the organization in all day-to-day business affairs and in all proceedings and negotiations of all types against courts and authorities. The CEO is responsible for the management of the organization, including the authority to directly employ, supervise, control, review the performance and terminate staff. The IPC Management Team is based at IPC Headquarters in Bonn, Germany. The team is comprised of departments: Executive Office, Paralympic Games, Sports and Relations with IPSFs, Marketing and Fundraising, Media and Communication, Medical and Scientific, Membership Relations and Services, Development, Finances, Administration and Human Resources.

IPC Standing Committees

The IPC's 12 Standing Committees are: Anti-Doping, Classification, Athletes for Severe Disability, Development, Education, Ethics, Finance, Legal, Paralympic Games, Sports Science, Therapeutic Use Exemption, and Women in Sport.

IPC Councils

The IPC's five Councils are: Athletes', OSDs' Regions', Sports', and Sports' Council Management Committee,

Paralympics Funding

The Paralympics is a nonprofit tax-exempt corporation. It receives its funding through the following sources:

- Individual donations (e.g., direct-mail solicitation, telephone solicitation, planned giving, online donations)
- Corporate donations (e.g., direct gift, matching gifts for employees)
- Corporate sponsorships (e.g., Coca-Cola, Home Depot, IBM, Kodak, McDonalds, Swatch, VISA, and many more)
- Grants from state and federal governments, corporations, and foundations
- Sale of licensed merchandise

The United States Paralympics (USP)

The Amateur Sports Act (Public Law 95-606) was adopted in 1978. This law was amended in 1998 to become the Olympic and Amateur Sports Act (OASA). Because of the efforts of Senator Ted Stevens of Alaska to shepherd this law through Congress, the 1998 amendments are often called the "Ted Stevens Amendments". The 1998 Stevens Amendments placed greater responsibility on the USOC and its constituent organizations to serve elite athletes with a disability, in particular Paralympic athletes.

U.S. Paralympics coordinates the preparation and selection of athletes to U.S. Paralympic Teams, both summer and winter, in conjunction with pertinent National Governing Bodies (NGBs) and other partner organizations. U.S. Paralympics also works with national and locally focused sport organizations that offer Paralympic programs to children and other developing athletes. Through these efforts, U.S. Paralympics promotes Olympic ideals throughout the American population, especially among those Americans who have physical disabilities.

The Paralympic Games have always been held in the same year as the Olympic Games. Since the Seoul 1988 Paralympic Games and the Albertville 1992 Winter Paralympic Games, they have also taken place at the same venues as the Olympics. On June 19, 2001, an agreement was signed between IOC and IPC securing this practice for the future. From the 2012 bid process onwards, the host city chosen to host the Olympic Games will be obliged to also host the Paralympics. The Chinese city of Beijing will host the next 2008 Paralympic Games whereas the Winter Paralympics 2010 will be in Vancouver, Canada. London will host the Paralympics in 2012 (http://www.usparalympics.org).

U.S. Paralympics and the United States Olympic Committee are working with Blaze Sports Clubs of America, the Department of Veterans Affairs, Brooke Army Medical Center (BAMC) in San Antonio, Texas, Walter Reed Army Medical Center (WRAMC) in Washington, D.C., Balboa Naval Medical Center in San Diego, and other partner organizations across the nation to establish ongoing Paralympic sport

opportunities for severely injured service members to enhance their rehabilitation, readiness, and lifestyle.

Paralympics Military Program

The program serves as a way of bringing Paralympic sport back to its roots. Its origins can be traced back to the time after World War II when it was used as a way of rehabilitating wounded soldiers.

At a Paralympic Military Summit, active duty service members and veterans who have sustained severe injuries, either in or out of combat, participate in various Paralympic sports. U.S. Paralympics national team coaches and athletes in each sport conduct clinics and organize competition for the participants.

The inaugural summit took place September 20-25, 2004, in Colorado Springs, Colorado, home of the U.S. Air Force Academy, Fort Carson, the United States Olympic Committee and U.S. Paralympics. Thirty-four veterans learned about, and competed in, six different Paralympic sports: cycling, fencing, shooting, sled hockey, table tennis, and sitting volleyball. The second Paralympic Military Summit took place in San Diego, California, November 8-13, 2005. Veterans attending the summit participated and competed in archery, sailing, swimming, track and field, strength and conditioning, and sitting volleyball (http://www.usparalympics.org).

Deaflympics

Formal international athletic competitions among the deaf began in 1924. These games have had three official names:

- International Games for the Deaf, 1924-1965 (alternately, International Silent Games)

- World Games for the Deaf, 1966-1999 (alternately, but rarely, World Silent Games)
- Deaflympics, 2000- to present. (De-Pauw & Gavron, 2005)

Officially, the games were originally called the "International Games for the Deaf" from 1924 to 1965 but were sometimes referred to as the "International Silent Games". From 1966 to 1999, they were called the "World Games for the Deaf" and occasionally referred to as the "World Silent Games". From 2000, the games have been known by their Current Name, "Deaflympics" (often mistakenly called the "Deaf Olympics"; (http://www.usdeafsports.org).

Though they are commonly called the "Deaf Olympics," that has never been an official name for these games since the International Olympic Committee has always refused to allow the use of the "Olympics" name for the deaf competitions. The main or "summer" games have been held on a quadrennial basis, except for three years between 1928 and 1931 (when the scheduling of the games was adjusted to avoid conflict with the International Olympic Games) and for the 10 years between 1939 and 1949 (caused by the disruptions of World War II). Paralleling the Winter Olympics, world winter games for the deaf were introduced beginning 1949, also on a quadrennial schedule except for the two years between the third (1957) and fourth (1959) Winter Games. This was done to put the Winter Games on a new schedule that did not conflict with the main deaf Games. Thus, the deaf Games now occur every two years, alternating between the main "summer" Games and the Winter Games and in the years between the regular Olympics and Winter Olympics (http://www.usdeafsports.org).

To qualify for the games, athletes must have a hearing loss of at least 55 decibels in their "better ear". Hearing aids, cochlear implants and the like are not allowed to be used in competition, to place all athletes on the same level. Other examples of ways the games vary from hearing competitions are the manner in which they are officiated. The football referees wave a flag instead of blowing a whistle. On the track, races are started by using a light flash instead of a starter pistol.

The Akron Club of the Deaf in Ohio sponsored the first national basketball tournament in 1945 at which time it established the American Athletic Union of the Deaf. The organization was later renamed the American Athletic Association of the Deaf and, in 1997, the USA Deaf Sports Federation (USADSF). Its purpose is to foster and regulate uniform rules of competition and provide social outlets for deaf members and their friends serve as a parent organization of national sports organizations, conduct annual athletic competitions, and assist in the participation of U.S. Teams in international competition.

The Federation had published a quarterly newspaper, *AAAD Bulletin*, since 1948 and established the Hall of Fame in 1952. Beginning in 1955, Athletes of the Year have been selected on an annual basis. The *Deaf Sports Review* magazine is also published by the organization.

Recognized as the only national athletic association to coordinate the participation of American deaf and hard of hearing individuals in international competitions, the Federation is affiliated with the International Committee of Sports for the Deaf (ICSD, formerly known as Comité International des Sports des Sourds – CISS) and has hosted the Summer Deaflympics in 1965 (Washington, D.C.) and 1985 (Los Angeles) and the Winter Deaflympics in 1975 (Lake Placid, NY) and 2007 (Salt Lake City).

All deaf and hard of hearing individuals with a hearing loss of 55 decibels or greater in the better ear are eligible. The use of hearing aids is prohibited in competitions. U.S. Team participants must be American citizens and members of the Federation in good standing. Figure 14.1 identifies the various sport organization involved with the Deaf Games.

Disabled Sports USA

A national nonprofit, 501(c)3, organization established in 1967 by disabled Vietnam veterans to serve the war injured DS/USA now offers nationwide sports rehabilitation programs to anyone with a permanent disability. Activities include winter skiing, water sports, summer and winter competitions, fitness and special sports events. Participants include those with visual impairments, amputations, spinal cord injury, dwarfism, multiple sclerosis, head injury, cerebral palsy, and other neuromuscular and orthopedic conditions (http://www.dsusa.org).

Disabled Sports USA was founded in 1967 by disabled Vietnam veterans. It was then called the National Amputee Skiers Association. In 1972 the National Amputee Skiers Association (NASA) was broadening its mission. No longer solely serving skiers, NASA needed a new name. They chose to call themselves the National Inconvenienced Sportsmen's Association. In 1976, NISA became the National Handicapped Sports and Recreation Association. The NHSRA name stuck until 1992 when the organization was renamed to National Handicapped Sports. In October 1994, after polling the organization's 80+ chapters and affiliates, the National Board of Directors approved the most recent name change to Disabled Sports USA (DePauw & Gavron, 2005).

According to Executive Director Kirk Bauer, "Disabled Sports USA" was selected for the following reasons:

- The word "disabled" brought the orga-

nization in line with current language used by the federal government. "Disabled" has become more universally accepted than "handicapped."

- Disabled Sports USA has become an organization of global importance. Disabled Sports USA fields teams to compete in the World Championships for track and field, cycling, volleyball, and swimming. It is now necessary to use "USA" rather than "National" to reflect this change in scope.

- Almost all of the U.S. Olympic Committee-member National Governing Bodies for able-body sports have "U.S." or "USA" within their name (such as USA Basketball, U.S. Skiing, and USA Volleyball). Disabled Sports USA is a Disabled Sports Organization member of the U.S. Olympic Committee (http://www.dsusa.org).

It is the position of DS/USA that the Disabled Sports Organizations (DSOs) be appropriately funded by the U.S. Olympic Committee (USOC) to conduct development programs necessary to produce athletes for the National Governing Bodies (NGBs).

It is the goal of DS/USA that the USOC ultimately become the National Policy Organization (NPO). The U.S. Disabled Sports Team (USDST) will serve in that role until the USOC can meet the requirements of the International Paralympic Committee (IPC) through legislation or other means.

National Disability Sports Alliance

The National Disability Sports Alliance (NDSA) is the National Coordinating Body for competitive sports for individuals with cerebral palsy, traumatic brain injuries and survivors of stroke. NDSA was origi-

Figure 14.1
Affiliated Sports

Selection of athletes and coaches to U.S. Teams for the Deaflympics, PANAMDES Games, and World Championships is based on parameters and requirements outlined in each sport's Athlete and Coach Selection Criteria which are available in the Participation Criteria section under the Athletes menu.

BADMINTON Ad Hoc Committee on Badminton
(vacant)
E-mail:
badminton@usdeafsports.org

BASEBALL Ad Hoc Committee on Baseball
Herman Fuechtmann, Chair
408 Bircher Avenue
South St. Paul, MN 55075-1007
E-mail:
Fuechtmann@usdeafsports.org

BASKETBALL (Apply as a NSO now!)

BOWLING Ad Hoc Committee on Bowling
Edward Abakumoff, Chair
c/o USADSF Home Office
102 North Krohn Place
Sioux Falls, SD 57103-1800
Phone: (605) 367-5761 TT
Fax: (605) 977-6625
E-mail:
bowling@usdeafsports.org

CYCLING United States Deaf Cycling
Association
Beverly Buchanan, President
Campus Life, Gallaudet
University
800 Florida Ave NE
Washington, DC 20002
Phone: (202) 448-6902 TTY
Fax: (202) 651-5757
E-mail:
Beverly.Buchanan@gallaudet.edu
Website:
www.usdeafcycling.org

GOLF US Deaf Golf Association
Claude Stout, President
18812 Lake Placid Lane
Germantown, MD 20874-6236
Phone: (301) 515-9492
E-mail:
president@usdeafgolf.org
Website: www.usdeafgolf.org

ICE HOCKEY American Hearing Impaired Hockey
Association
Cheryl Hager
4214 West 77th Place
Chicago, IL 60652-1205
Phone: (773) 767-1205
Fax: (312) 829-2098
E-mail: Cheryl@ahiha.org
Website: www.ahiha.org

MARTIAL ARTS American Martial Arts Association
of the Deaf
Dr. Frank Lala, President
AMAAD c/o Daniel Briones, Jr.,
Executive VP
PO Box 861
Upland, CA 91785
Exec VP Daniel Briones, Jr.:
EvPresident@amaad.com
Sec'y Cathy Lee:
Secretary@amaad.com
Website: www.amaad.com

ORIENTEERING Ad Hoc Committee on Orienteering
Billy Allaband
612 West 20th Street
Wilmington, DE 19802
E-mail:
WMAllaband@usdeafsports.org
Committee Members: Art
Bond, Tim Gilpatrick and
Joseph Ward

SHOOTING USA Deaf Shooting
Richard Soboleski, President
P.O. Box 383
Plantsville, CT 06479-0383
Phone: (860) 621-6972
Fax: (860) 276-3859
E-mail: lsoboleski@snet.net

SKI & SNOWBOARD United States Deaf Ski and
Snowboard Association
Edward Ingham, President
709 8th Street NE
Washington, DC 20002-3603
VideoPhone (VP): 202.546.7949
E-mail: President@usdssa.org
Website: www.usdssa.org

Figure 14.1
Affiliated Sports (continued)

SOCCER

USA Deaf Soccer Association
Ken Noll, President
3711 Sout State Route 157
Glen Carbon, IL 62034
E-mail:
knoll@usdeafsoccer.com
Website:
www.usdeafsoccer.com

SWIMMING

Ad Hoc Committee on Swimming
(vacant)
E-mail:
swimming@usdeafsports.org

TABLE TENNIS

Ad Hoc Committee on Table Tennis
(vacant)
E-mail:
tabletennis@usdeafsports.org

TEAM HANDBALL

USA Deaf Team Handball

Richard Jacobs, President
Contact person: Kellie
McComas, Logistic Coordinator
14519 - 112th Ave NE
Kirkland, WA 98034-4404
Phone: (425) 487-4816 - can
use VP
Fax: (425) 776-7483
E-mail:
KellieMcC@comcast.net
Website: http://members.tripod.
com/usadth/home.html

TENNIS

Ad Hoc Committee on Tennis
Howard L. Gorrell, Chair
261 North Franklin Street #514
Hanover PA 17331-2461
E-mail:
Gorrell@usdeafsports.org
Forum: http://sports.groups.
yahoo.com/group/USADeaf_
Tennis/

TRACK & FIELD

USA Deaf Track & Field

Thomas Withrow, President
9706 DuBarry Avenue
Glenn Dale, MD 20769-9285
Phone/Fax: (301) 464-1284
E-mail: TEWithrow@aol.com
Website: www.usadtf.org

VOLLEYBALL

Ad Hoc Committee on Volleyball
John Knetzger, Chair
2625 East Shorewood Blvd.
Milwaukee, WI 53211-2457
Fax: (414) 962-0671
E-mail:
Knetzger@usdeafsports.org

WATER POLO

Ad Hoc Committee on Water Polo
Jordan Eickman, Chair
E-mail:
Eickman@usdeafsports.org
Committee Members: Zeb
Jenkins and Duane Styles

WRESTLING

Ad Hoc Committee on Wrestling
Robert McConnell, Chair
102 North Krohn Place
Sioux Falls, SD 57103
Phone (V/TTY): (605) 367-5760
E-mail:
McConnell@usdeafwrestling.org
Website:
www.usdeafwrestling.org
Committee Members: Jay Innes
and Dusan Jaksic

YOUTH

Deaf Youth Sports Festival
Timothy Owens
PO Box 17565
Louisville, KY 40217-0565
E-Mail: Timo01@aol.com
Website: www.teammdo.org

nally formed as the United States Cerebral Palsy Athletic Association (USCPAA) in 1987. NDSA also provides programming for other physically disabling conditions such as muscular dystrophy and multiple sclerosis (http://www.ndsaonline.org).

As the National Coordinating Body for Cerebral Palsy sports, NDSA is responsible for conduct and administration of approved sports in the United States. NDSA formulates the rules, implements policies and procedures, conducts national championships in ten sports, disseminates safety and sports medicine information and selects the athletes to represent the United States in international competition.

Special Olympics

(See Chapter 15 for greater details)

The Special Olympics is an international organization that helps people with intellectual disabilities develop self-confidence and social skills through sports training and competition. The athletes can develop social relationships with their teammates and coaches during continuous training. The individuals will also have the opportunity to stay fit and healthy while improving their coordination and skill. Special Olympics was founded by Eunice Kennedy Shriver in the 1960s. The late Rosemary Kennedy, who suffered from mental retardation, is often credited as the inspiration for the Special Olympics (Shriver and Kennedy were sisters; (http://www.specialolympics.org).

Paralympics Issues

There are a number of issues to be considered, including, is the Paralympics and IOC partnership a boon or bust, can the challenges in marketing Paralympics be overcome, should there be an open class of competition, should the threshold for eligibility be minimum disability, should Paralympic sport athletes with severe disabilities be included, should a sport be capable of ownership by a body, are there adequate participation opportunities for women in the Paralympics, should the Paralympic games be down-sized, and are performance-enhancing activities a problem in the Paralympics? Each of these issues will be discussed briefly below:

The Paralympics and IOC Partnership Will Allow the Paralympics to Grow?

In terms of infrastructure, the Paralympics might seem to be in a win-win situation. However, when the Paralympics were a completely separate entity, no one demanded a highway expansion, a new transit system to the airport, or even a new permanent stadium. You would be hard-pressed to find any remaining indication of the event at the last autonomous Paralympics venue in New York (located near Nassau County Coliseum on Long Island). The 1984 Paralympics (originally called the International Games for the Disabled, since spinal cord athletes did not compete) used existing structures and temporary facilities, not out of political correctness, but out of sheer budgetary restraint and long before anyone thought of a "sustainable" Olympics (http://thetyee.ca/views/2006/07/paralympics/).

Before forming a relationship with the IOC, the Paralympics had not ventured into any other types of business relationships. The same cannot be said for the Olympic movement which finds it again mirroring a government in controversies about environmental and fiscal messes in the making.

The Paralympics joined with the Olympics partly to gain greater exposure to world TV audiences. In this, the Paralympics have failed miserably. Whether TV audiences find the sight of a wheelchair track event, in comparison to a major league baseball or hockey game, purely unappealing as sporting spectacle or because of a general, societal lack of acceptance of disability is hard to determine. However, the revenues generated from TV contracts (a major source of funds for the Olympics) have yet to become a reality for the Paralympics (http://thetyee.ca/views/2006/07/paralympics/).

Can the Challenges in Marketing Paralympics Be Overcome?

Approximately 20 percent (58 million) of the American population (300 million) have disabilities (U.S. Census Bureau statistic, 2006). The disabled community is conscious and loyal to brands. The significantly large segment of the population represented by the disabled attracts a large number of corporations (e.g., Coca-Cola, Home Depot, IBM, Swatch, Kodak, VISA, McDonalds, to name a few) who are willing to invest in the Paralympics nationally and internationally. Yet there are challenges faced by the Paralympics in this arena including equating a "person with a disability" with the term "athlete", being treated as a charity, and a large variety of sport forms makes it difficult to market Paralympics sports.

The key to solving many of these challenges is educating the general public and the corporate world about the Paralympics and the disabled athletes it services. Often, the general public confuses the Paralympics (i.e., physically and/or sensory disabled individuals) with Special Olympics (i.e., intellectually handicapped individuals who may also be physically challenged). Further adding to the confusion is persons with disabilities are often defined by their "disabilities" rather than their "abilities".

Those in the general public and in the corporate world who do not understand that the physically disabled person can also participate in sports recreationally as well as at the elite level, often ask: "How could someone in a wheelchair play basketball, bowl, ski, or swim, much less be an elite athlete?"

The challenge for the Paralympics sport managers is to educate the general public and the corporate world that a physically disabled person has many other abilities and can compete at the elite level using specially designed equipment and modified rules for the sport. Further, the sport managers need to demonstrate that these physically disabled athletes can provide exciting and inspirational entertainment (Grevemberg, Wolff, & Hums, 2001; Hums, 2001; LeClair & Wolff, 2001). Finally, the education needs to extend to demonstrating that the Paralympics provides opportunities for many different classifications of disabled including amputees, cerebral palsy, dwarfs, and visually handicapped, to name a few. Each of these individuals can and do participate in elite sports. But they are different and the general public and the corporate world need to clearly understand these facts.

Often individuals and corporations treat the Paralympics Games as a charity. It is not a charity nor should it be a charity. The sport manager should make it clear that showing support for these competitors gives athletes with disabilities a sense of respect and acceptance for what they are and what they can do. They are athletes just like those who participate in the Olympics. They are not charity cases and do not want to be treated that way.

Should There Be an "Open Class" or "Different Classes" of Competition?

Sidebar: Open Class is a class of athletes that has no specific classifications or qualifications. Different classes is a class by specific classifications or qualifications such as age, skill, experience, or type of disability.

According to the IPC Classification Code, classification is "simply a structure for competition that provides the framework for fair competition and aims to ensure that competitive success is determined by strategies, skills, and talent of athletes and teams and not solely due to the function determined by the athletes' physical, sensorial, or intellectual ability" (IPC Classification Code, 2006).

Classification is not the only means to ensure that competition is fair, with outcomes determined by ability rather than disability. Other gates also determine fairness including eligibility criteria and rules of play that govern participation in each individual sport. Eligibility criteria determines who is and is not eligible to participate in any govern activity and it is the classification system(s) that determine how those who are eligible are grouped together in ways to "neutralise" or "balance out" the effects of their disability. These systems differentiate groups by using such factors as age, gender, height, and disability.

It is clear there can be either an "open class" or "different classes." There is no single answer. What is appropriate for one situation may not be suitable for another and, again, it is the relationship between classification and eligibility that needs to be addressed initially. The organizers must weigh the variables and make decisions to ensure the primary objective (i.e., mass participation, talent identification, or elite competition) has the best possible chance of delivery.

Should the Threshold for Eligibility Be Minimum Disability?

The notion of minimum disability is related to both eligibility and classification. Many times, the final decision regarding eligibility is of an arbitrary nature. For example, what difference does a through-the-wrist amputation make to a middle-distance runner? How does a minimal visual impairment impact upon a B3's ability to throw a discuss? Is an athlete with cerebral palsy classified as C8 (high functioning, ambulatory) or a soccer player with ID really that different from many of the millions of other amateur players, all over the world, who play football for the love of it with only their dreams connecting them with interna-

tional competition and with no exception whatsoever of ever experiencing it firsthand (http://www.uksport.gov.uk/images/uploaded/vistas.pdf)?

If Paralympic sport is to be, and to be seen to be, a necessary alternative to Olympic sport, the significance of the difference must be apparent for all to see, and this suggests a broad band of segregation rather than a narrow and arbitrary line.

Should Paralympic Sport Athletes with Severe Disabilities Be Included?

For several years, the inclusion in Paralympic sport of athletes with severe disabilities has been a priority of the IPC. How is it, then, that very few of these athletes with severe intellectual disabilities (ID) are ever seen competing? How does IPC or INAS-FID explain the fact that most people with intellectual disabilities have no access to the truly elite competitions that are the bedrock of both the Olympics and Paralympic Games? If the answer is to be found in these athletes' inability to comprehend the nature and the requirements of elite performance, isn't the IPC at risk of an argument of circularity, with those ID athletes who are able to do so subject to accusations of insufficient intellectual deficit to meet the "minimum disability" requirements (http://www.uksport.gov.uk/images/uploaded/vistas.pdf)?

Should a Sport Be Capable of Ownership By a Body?

Boccia is a game being played that has all the characteristics of a mature sport (like basketball and football) capable of attracting and sustaining in equal measure the interest of recreational players and elite performers alike. However, it is most often associated with athletes with cerebral palsy. Why is this? Why has boccia not yet established itself alongside soccer, tennis, and swimming as a fully independent sport equally accessible to all people with or without disabilities and drawn to it from all walks of life? Could it be because boccia is deemed to be "owned by" (e.g., the organization that developed the sport appears to be the owner of the sport) the custodians of cerebral palsy sport? (http://www.uksport.gov.uk/images/uploaded/vistas.pdf)

Should there be "IPC sports"? Will "IPC sports" allow for the smooth and successful transition into independence? However, the very notion of an "IPC sport" suggests that a sport can be owned by a body. Sport should not be capable of ownership by any body other than that one body that is recognized as having a responsibilies for making it accessible to anyone with or without a disability who might wish to play it. The proper responsibility of the IPC is for classification and eligibility. A sport's ownership rights should be the exclusive preserve of those who practice it, boccia and the cerebral palsy athletes. Or should the sport be owned by these who would like to particpate in the sport?

Are There Adequate Participation Opportunities for Women in Paralympics?

Since 1972 and the passage of the Title IX legislation, every sport manager asks this question. The Paralympics, like all other organizations (e.g., intercollegiate athletics, interscholastic athletics, Olympics, Special Olympics, and youth sports), is attempting to create more participation opportunities for female athletes. There are a number of challenges facing women that do not necessarily impact men, such as cultural and religious mandates (e.g., other countries outside the United States, such as countries in the Middle East) that bar a women's involvement, lack of adequate financial resources, and familial pressures. Many of these challenges cannot be solved by the Paralympics. However, in an attempt to increase female participation, the

IPC, in 2000, introduced a number of initiatives including:

- Equity in allocation of country wild cards (extra athlete participation slots),
- Addition of viable events and disciplines for women,
- Equitable allocation of slots by sports and nation, and
- Emphasis on increasing awareness of sport and NPC leadership of issues related to women and sports (http://www.paralympic.org).

Hums & MacLean (2004) suggest, "Women with disabilities face a two-tiered challenge in sport; they are female athletes and they are athletes with disabilities" (p. 311). Therefore, it is important for sport managers to continue to improve opportunities for competition.

Should the Paralympics Games be Down-sized?

This is an annual question asked for the past few decades. There continues to be pressure (within the Paralympics movement and outside from the IOC) to contain or reduce the size and complexity of Paralympic Games. These pressures are also linked to the issues of classification and eligibility. If the number of disability groups is limited, it will directly impact the size of the games.

The dilemmas faced by the IPC include (a) there is no evidence of any intention to reduce the number of disability groups, (b) there is a continuous demand to admit new sports, and (c) there is financial and logistical pressure to resist any further expansion. Changes need to be made in the future in order to strengthen the Paralympic Games; but, such changes should not be based on financial, logistical, or political pressures. The changes should be made in the knowledge and belief that to do so is in the best interest of the sport and the athletes.

Are Performance-Enhancing Activities a Problem in the Paralympic Games?

Performance-enhancing activities are found in all amateur and professional sports, and the Paralympics is not an exception. The use of performance-enhancing substances is an area of great concern for the Paralympic movement. The IPC in 2001 established a special awareness campaign called "Doping Disables". The IPC says doping has no place in the Paralympic movement and the movement will never accept doping and must not be associated with it. With this said, everyone must recognize that some athletes, due to their disabilities or illnesses, are required to take medications every day of their lives. A common medicine taken is a banned substance – steroids. Therefore, the IPC has indicated that decisions must be made about what is appropriate use (medical reasons supported by a physician's authorization), as opposed to excessive use, of certain substances.

In 2001, the IPC signed a memorandum of understanding with the World Anti-Doping Agency (WADA) in order to take proactive approach to combat doping in sport for athletes with disabilities. The IPC is now a member of the WADA Board. Further, the WADA has independent observers present at the Paralympic Games to evaluate the doping control process (http://www.paralympic.org).

Summary

The Paralympic Games are an elite multisport event for athletes with disabilities. This includes mobility disabilities, amputees, visual disabilities, and those with cerebral palsy. The Paralympic Games are held every four years, following the Olympic Games, and are governed by the International Paralympic Committee (IPC). (The Paralympic Games are sometimes confused with the Special Olympics, which are only for people with intellectual disabilities.)

There are a number of issues to be considered including, is the Paralympics and IOC partnership a boon or bust, can the challenges in marketing Paralympics be overcome, should there be an open class of competition, should the threshold for eligibility be minimum disability, should Paralympic sport athletes with severe disabilities be included, should a sport be capable of ownership by a body, are there adequate participation opportunities for women in the Paralympics, should the Paralympic games be down-sized and, are performance-enhancing activities a problem in the Paralympics?

References

DePauw, K., & Gavron, S. (2005). *Disability sport.* Champaign, IL: Human Kinetics.
Grevemberg, D., Wolff, E.A., & Hums, M.A. (2001, May). *Integration of Paralympic sport in international sport federations: Comparative international models.* Presented at the annual conference of the North American Society for Sport Management, Virginia Beach, VA.
http://www.dsusa.org. (2006).
http://edweb6.educ.msu.edu/kin866/lawoasa.htm. (2006).
http://www.ibsa.es. (2006).
http://www.inas-fid.org. (2006).
http://www.ndsaonline.org. (2006).
http://www.paralympic.org. (2006).
http://www.specialolympics.org. (2006).
http://www.thetyee.ca/views/2006/07/paralympics/. (2006).
http://www.usdeafsports.org. (2006).
http://www.uksport.gov.uk/images/uploaded/vistas.pdf. (2006).
http://www.usparalympics.org. (2006).
http://www.wsw.org.uk. (2006).
Hums, M.A. (2001, April 2-6). There's gold for sponsors in Paralympic Games, too. *Street and Smith's SportsBusiness Journal, 3,* 44.
Hums, M.A., & MacLean, J.C. (2004). *Governance and policy in sport organizations.* Scottsdale, AZ: Halcomb Hathaway, Publishers.
LeClair, J., & Wolff, E.A. (2001, October). *The Unspoken Reality in the Contested Arena of Cultural and Policy Barriers to the Development of Sport for Athletes with Disabilities.* Presented at the annual conference of the North American Society for Sport Sociology, San Antonio, TX.

NOTES

CHAPTER 15

Special Olympics Governance

Special Olympics is an international nonprofit organization dedicated to empowering individuals with intellectual disabilities to become physically fit, productive, and respected members of society through sports training and competition. Special Olympics offer children and adults with intellectual disabilities year-round training and competition in 26 Olympic-type winter and summer sports. There is no charge to participate in Special Olympics. The Special Olympics is recognized as a tax-exempt organization under U.S. Internal Revenue Code Section 501(c)3.

Special Olympics indicates it currently serves more than 2.25 million persons with intellectual disabilities in over 200 programs in more than 150 countries. These numbers are the result of an overwhelming successful campaign that began in 2000. That year, Special Olympics made a bold commitment to reach two million athletes by the end of 2005 while simultaneously changing attitudes about people with intellectual disabilities around the world. Over the course of those five years, in addition to providing more than one million more athletes the opportunity to experience the joy of sport, Special Olympics transformed itself (http: www.specialolympics.org).

Today, Special Olympics stand as a leader in the field of sport for those with intellectual disability. (Note: The term "intellectual disabilities" is now used by Special Olympics; prior to 2004, the term "mental retardation" was used because of its specific meaning in clinical and academic settings. Note that other terminology — including cognitive delay intellectual handicaps, learning disability, mental disabilities, and mental handicaps — is used around the world.) It is a truly global movement with more than 500,000 athletes in China, more than 210,000 in India, almost 550,000 in the United States, more than 600 in Afghanistan, and 4,400 athletes in Rwanda. Special Olympics World Games were held in Ireland in 2003 and Japan in 2005 and, in 2007, China will host the World Summer Games. Most importantly, Special Olympics sharpened the focus on its mission as not just "nice", but critical, not just as a sports organization for people with intellectual disabilities, but also as an effective catalyst for social change (http://www.specialolympics.org).

Children and adults with individual disabilities who participate in Special Olympics develop improved physical fitness and motor skills, greater self-confidence, and a more positive self-image. They grow mentally, socially, and spiritually through their activities. Further, they exhibit boundless courage and enthusiasm, enjoy the rewards of friendship, and ultimately discover not only new abilities and talents but "their voices" as well.

Learning Objectives

Upon completion this chapter, the reader should be able to:

- Describe the history of the Special Olympics.
- Outline the governance of the Special Olympics.
- Discuss the philosophy and principles of the Special Olympics.
- Identify the various Special Olympic sports.
- Describe the funding for the Special Olympics.
- Identify and discuss the Special Olympics special programs.
- Identify the Special Olympic partners,

- Discuss the Special Olympics Sport and Empowerment Act of 2004.
- Discuss the Special Olympic issues.

History

The global Special Olympics movement got its start on July 20, 1968, when the First International Special Olympics Games were held at Soldier Field, Chicago, Illinois. But the concept of Special Olympics was born much earlier when Eunice Kennedy Shriver started a day camp for people with intellectual disabilities at her home in 1962.

Shriver believed that people with intellectual disabilities were far more capable than commonly believed and deserving of the same opportunities and experiences as others. So, in June 1962, she invited 35 boys and girls with intellectual disabilities to Camp Shriver, a day camp at Timberlawn, her home in Rockville, Maryland, to explore their capabilities in a variety of sports and physical activities.

Even before Camp Shriver, Eunice Kennedy Shriver already had a long-standing commitment to people with intellectual disabilities. She was instrumental in focusing the Joseph P. Kennedy Foundation on improving the way society deals with its citizens with intellectual disabilities and helping identify and disseminate ways to prevent the causes of intellectual disabilities. Shriver is executive vice president of the foundation, which was established in 1946 by her father and mother, Ambassador and Mrs. Joseph P. Kennedy, to honor their eldest son who was killed in World War II.

Using Camp Shriver as an example, Shriver promoted the concept of involvement in physical activity and competition opportunities for people with intellectual disabilities. Camp Shriver became an annual event and the Kennedy Foundation gave grants to universities, recreation departments, and community centers to provided

Camp scholarships to individuals with intellectual disabilities. In 1963, the foundation supported 11 similar camps around the United States. By 1969, the foundation supported 32 camps across the country that served 10,000 children with intellectual disabilities.

The movement grew beyond the Kennedy Foundation and, between 1963 and 1968, more than 300 camps similar to Camp Shriver were started. In the early 1960s, Dr. William Freeberg, then chairman of the Recreation and Outdoor Education Department at Southern Illinois University at Carbondale, Illinois, worked with the Kennedy Foundation to develop one-week workshops for recreation directors across the country. The workshops focused on the principles that everyone, including people with disabilities, benefits from recreation and everyone has talents and gifts to share with others. In 1965, 10 recreation teachers from the Chicago Park District attended one of Freeberg's workshops on a grant from the foundation. One of those teachers was Anne Burke.

By 1967, the Chicago Park District wanted to do more for people with intellectual disabilities, and Burke joined a team to assess the needs and how to address them. She proposed holding a citywide track meet modeled after the Olympics to raise awareness of the program. Freeberg, who had joined the team as a consultant, suggested they develop a proposal to submit to Shriver at the Kennedy Foundation.

Shriver immediately saw the potential of the idea and asked Burke to expand its scope to include more sports and athletes from across the United States. Shriver sent Kennedy Foundation staff to Chicago to work with Burke and the Chicago Park District to start planning and announced that the Kennedy Foundation would provide a grant to underwrite the event. On July 20, 1968, Shriver opened the Chicago Special Olympics (the First International Special Olympics Games), which were held in Chicago's Soldier Field, with 1,000 athletes with intellectual disabilities from 26 U.S. states and Canada competing in many sports. Special Olympics today is a global movement with more than 2.25 million athletes in 150 countries around the world (http://www.specialolympics.org).

"The Chicago Special Olympics prove a very fundamental fact," Shriver said in her Opening Ceremonies address. "The fact that exceptional children — children with mental retardation — can be exceptional athletes; the fact that through sports, they can realize their potential for growth." Shriver also announced a new national program — Special Olympics — to offer people with intellectual disabilities everywhere, "The chance to play, the chance to compete, and the chance to grow" (http://www.specialolympics.org).

Chicago Mayor Richard Daley, who attended the First International Special Olympics Games that day, said to Shriver, "You know, Eunice, the world will never be the same after this."

Governance

The Special Olympics guides local, area, state/provincial, and national programs internationally. A volunteer board of directors determines international policies and is composed of business and sport leaders, professional athletes, educators, and experts in intellectual disabilities from around the world. There is a senior management team composed of a chairman of the board, president and chief executive officer, chief administrative officer, chief legal officer and secretary, chief development officer, and seven regional directors.

The Mission of Special Olympics

The mission of Special Olympics is to provide (a) year-round sports training and athletic competition in a variety of Olympic-type sports for children and adults with intellectual disabilities, and (b) continuing opportunities to develop physical fitness, demonstrate courage, experience joy, and participate in a sharing of gifts, skills, and friendship with their families, other Special Olympics athletes, and the community.

Philosophy of the Special Olympics

Special Olympics is founded on the belief that people with intellectual disabilities can, with proper instruction and encouragement, learn, enjoy, and benefit from participation in individual and team sports. Special Olympics believes that consistent training is essential to the development of sports skills and that competition among those of equal abilities is the most appropriate means of testing these skills, measuring progress, and providing incentives for personal growth. Finally, it believes that through sports training and competition, people with intellectual disabilities benefit physically, mentally, socially, and spiritually, families are strengthened, and the community at large, both through participation and observation, is united in understanding people with intellectual disabilities in an environment of equality, respect, and acceptance.

Principles of the Special Olympics

To provide the most enjoyable, beneficial, and challenging activities for athletes with intellectual disabilities, Special Olympics operates worldwide in accordance with the following principles and beliefs:

- "That the goal of Special Olympics is to help bring all persons with intellectual disabilities into the larger society under conditions whereby they are accepted, respected, and given a chance to become productive citizens.
- That as a means of achieving this goal, Special Olympics encourages its more

capable athletes to move from Special Olympics training and competition into school and community programs where they can compete in regular sports activities. The decision to leave or to continue involvement in Special Olympics is the athlete's choice.
- That all Special Olympics activities — at the local, state/provincial, national, and international levels — reflect the values, standards, traditions, ceremonies, and events embodied in the modern Olympic movement. These Olympic-type activities have been broadened and enriched to celebrate the moral and spiritual qualities of persons with intellectual disabilities so as to enhance their dignity and self-esteem.
- That participation in Special Olympics training programs and competitive events is open to all people with intellectual disabilities who are at least eight years old, regardless of the degree of their disability.
- That comprehensive, year-round sports training is available to every Special Olympics athlete, conducted by well-qualified coaches in accordance with the standardized Sports Rules formulated and adopted by Special Olympics, and that every athlete who participates in a Special Olympics sport will be trained in that sport.
- That every Special Olympics Program includes sports events and activities that are appropriate to the age and ability level of each athlete, from motor activities to the most advanced competition.
- That Special Olympics provides full participation for every athlete regardless of economic circumstance and conducts training and competition under the most favorable conditions possible, including facilities, administration, training, coaching, officiating, and events.

- That at every awards ceremony, in addition to the traditional medals for first, second and third places, athletes finishing from fourth to last place are presented a suitable place ribbon with appropriate ceremony.
- That to the greatest extent possible, Special Olympics activities will be run by and involve local volunteers, from school and college-age individuals to senior citizens, in order to create greater opportunities for public understanding of intellectual disabilities.
- That although Special Olympics is primarily a program of sports training and competition, efforts are made to offer athletes a full range of artistic, social, and cultural experiences through activities such as dances, art exhibits, concerts, visits to historic sites, clinics, theatrical performances, and similar activities.
- That the "Spirit of Special Olympics" — skill, courage, sharing and joy — incorporates universal values which transcend all boundaries of geography, nationality, political philosophy, gender, age, race, or religion" (http://www.specialolympics.org).

The Special Olympics movement aims to achieve quality growth by creating innovative opportunities to bring the Special Olympics experience to more of the world's 190 million people with intellectual disabilities. At the same time, Special Olympics will work to create positive public attitudes toward a population that is often rejected or forgotten.

Within the last five years, Special Olympics has made great strides toward active worldwide growth in the number of athletes — between 2000 and 2005, participation in Special Olympics grew at a 129-percent rate, with Special Olympics Programs reaching out to 1,270,760 new athletes. The quest is far from complete; the new Special Olympics 2006-2010 Strategic Plan calls for reaching three million athletes by the end of 2010, all the while maintaining the quality of the program (http://www.specialolympics.org).

The Special Olympics will (a) promote global athlete leadership and dedicate the movement to empowerment and dignity, not charity, and (b) change negative attitudes and misperceptions about people with intellectual disabilities, replacing stigma and rejection with an emphasis on potential, ability, and acceptance.

Special Olympics Funding

The Special Olympics is a nonprofit tax-exempt corporation. It receives its funding through the following sources:

- Individual donations (e.g., direct-mail solicitation, telephone solicitation, planned giving, online donations)
- Corporate donations (e.g., direct gift, matching gifts for employees)
- Corporate sponsorships (e.g., CARQUEST auto parts, Coca-Cola, Mattel, McDonalds, Michelin, Midwest Trophy Manufacturing, Procter & Gamble)
- Grants from state and federal governments, corporations (e.g., Mattel), and foundations (e.g., Joseph P. Kennedy, Jr. Foundation)
- Federal legislations (Special Olympics Sport and Empowerment Act of 2004)
- Sale of licensed merchandise

Special Olympics Sports

Special Olympics offer year-round sports training and athletic competition in 26 Olympic-type sports (individual and team) to children and adults with intellectual disabilities. Participation is open to anyone ages eight and older and programs are designed to serve all ability levels. There is no charge to participate in Special Olympics.

Special Olympics Unified Sports®

Special Olympics Unified Sports® is an initiative that combines approximately equal numbers of Special Olympics athletes and athletes without intellectual disabilities (called Partners) on sports teams for training and competition. Age and ability matching of athletes and Partners is defined on a sport-by-sport basis.

Throughout the year, in a variety of sports ranging from basketball to golf to figure skating, Unified Sports athletes improve their physical fitness, sharpen their skills, challenge the competition, and have fun, too.

The concept of combining athletes with intellectual disabilities and those without was first introduced in the mid-1980s to provide another level of challenge for higher ability athletes and to promote equality and inclusion. Today, the initiative includes virtually all Special Olympics sports and Unified Sports competitions are an important part of Special Olympics World Games, as well as local, state/provincial, and National Games.

Unified Sports enables Special Olympics athletes to: learn new sports, develop higher-level sports skills, have new competition experiences, experience meaningful inclusion (each athlete is ensured of playing a valued role on the team), socialize with peers and form friendships (the initiative provides a forum for positive social interaction between teammates and often leads to long-lasting friendships), while participating in their communities and selecting choices outside of Special Olympics. Unified Sports programs often are initiated by community partners, including parks and recreation departments, schools, Boys and Girls Clubs of America, and community sports organizations. These partnerships help further include these athletes in their community.

Special Olympics Special Programs

There are two special programs offered by the Special Olympics. These programs are Special Olympics Young Athletes and Special Olympics Motor Activities Training Program (MATP). Each of these programs will be discussed below briefly.

Special Olympics Young Athletes

Young Athletes™ is an innovative sports play program for children with intellectual disabilities designed to introduce them to the world of sports prior to Special Olympics eligibility at age eight. The pilot has

Table 15.1
Special Olympics Sports

Alpine Skiing	Aquatics	Athletics	Badminton
Basketball	Bocce	Bowling	Cross Country Skiing
Cycling	Equestrian	Figure Skating	Floor Hockey
Football (Soccer)	Golf	Gymnastics	Power Lifting
Roller Skating	Sailing	Snowboarding	Snowshoeing
Softball	Speedskating	Table Tennis	Team Handball
Tennis	Volleyball		

been implemented thanks to the generous support of the Mattel Children's Foundation.

The Young Athletes program strengthens physical development and self-esteem for children ages two through seven by building skills for future sports participation and socialization. Family members and caregivers also are encouraged to become involved as the child learns success through physical activity.

Young Athletes is designed to address two specific levels of play:

+ *Level 1* includes physical activities focused on developing fundamental motor tracking and eye-hand coordination play.
+ *Level 2* concentrates on the application of Level 1 physical activities through a sports skills activity program. Level 2 also focuses on developing skills consistent with **Special Olympics official sports.**

Young Athletes Resource

The Young Athletes program will consist of:

• Play Activities Guide
• Play Activities Training DVD
• Young Athletes Equipment Kit

"The support of the **Mattel Children's Foundation** and Mattel employees globally will not only help grow the Special Olympics movement to reach more of the 180 million people with intellectual disabilities worldwide, but also help us create a world of acceptance for Special Olympics athletes," said Timothy Shriver, Special Olympics Chairman (http://www.specialolympics.org).

Special Olympics Motor Activities Training Program (MATP)

Special Olympics Motor Activities Training Program (MATP) is designed for persons with severe limitations who do not yet possess the physical and/or behavioral skills necessary to participate in official Special Olympics sports. The program provides a comprehensive motor activity and recreation training curriculum for these participants. MATP emphasizes training and participation rather than competition. In addition, the program provides the means for people with severe limitations to participate in appropriate recreation activities geared to their ability levels.

When MATP participants reach the necessary readiness and skill levels, every Special Olympics sport provides an appropriate transition into that sport at an introductory level. Specific events are identified in most sports for athletes with low ability levels; examples of MATP activities include: Bean bag lift, ball kick, wide beam and bench, ball lift (small), ball lift (large), ball push, and log roll. Individuals who participate in MATP activities work as hard as other Special Olympics athletes and they are recognized for their efforts.

Special Olympics Partners

As the largest amateur sports organization in the world, Special Olympics has established relationships with many of the leading sports organizations, as well as other nonprofit organizations. These relationships are crucial in the success of the Special Olympic Movement. As Special Olympics continues to grow the number of partners will also expand.

The International Olympic Committee (IOC)

In February, 1988, the IOC, the umbrella organization of the Olympic movement, officially recognized Special Olympics and agreed to cooperate with Special Olympics as a representative of the interests of athletes with intellectual disabilities.

Special Olympics is the only organization authorized by the IOC to use the word "Olympics" worldwide.

National Olympic Committees

Within the United States, Special Olympics has been designated by the United States Olympic Committee as the National Governing Body/Disabled Sports Organization for athletes with intellectual disabilities. Special Olympics also maintain active relationships with the National Olympic Committees of other nations.

International Sports Federations and National Sports Governing Bodies

International Sports Federations are recognized by the IOC as the world governing bodies for their respective sports. National Sports Governing Bodies govern and oversee particular sports within their respective countries. All games or competitions held by Special Olympics Programs must comply with the sports rules issued by the National Sports Governing Bodies in their respective countries except where those rules conflict with the Special Olympics Sports Rules (which then take precedence).

World Olympians Association (WOA)

In April 2002, Special Olympics and WOA agreed to work closely together to provide opportunities for Olympians to become more involved with Special Olympics athletes, programs, and events. WOA was created by International Olympic Committee President Juan Antonio Samaranch in 1994 to encourage and assist the approximately 100,000 Olympians around the world to be active participants in the Olympic movement beyond their Olympic competition. The initiative with Special Olympics is designed to provide Olympians with opportunities to be role models for Special Olympics athletes while increasing awareness of their many skills and achievements.

Joseph P. Kennedy, Jr. Foundation

The Kennedy Foundation is a private foundation that shares Special Olympics' goal of providing people with intellectual disabilities the opportunity to reach their fullest potential. The foundation provided critical funding necessary for the establishment of Special Olympics. Although the foundation no longer provides funding to Special Olympics, it continues to provide technical assistance, guidance, and professional consultation, as well as other forms of support and assistance in expanding the Special Olympics movement.

The United Nations

Special Olympics is a registered nongovernmental organization (NGO) of the United Nations. As an NGO, Special Olympics has the responsibility of working with nations throughout the world to help develop sports training and competition programs for persons with intellectual disabilities.

Special Olympics Sport and Empowerment Act (2004)

U.S. President George W. Bush signed legislation on October 30, 2004, marking the first time ever that support for Special Olympics has been secured through authorizing legislation. "The President signed into law, H.R. 5131, the 'Special Olympics Sport and Empowerment Act of 2004, which authorizes appropriations through FY 2009 for grants, contracts, or cooperative agreements with Special Olympics for certain education, international, and health activities," said former White House Press Secretary Scott McClellan.

The bill passed unanimously in both

the House of Representatives and the Senate, indicating that the U.S. government — at the highest levels — values the work of Special Olympics to promote inclusion, acceptance, and understanding of people with intellectual disabilities. Special Olympics is particularly appreciative of the Members of Congress who initiated the legislation and shepherded the bill through Congress. Representatives Roy Blunt (R-MO) and Steny Hoyer (D-MD) and Senators Rick Santorum (R-PA) and Harry Reid (D-NV) were the bill's lead sponsors.

"In a year where both Houses of Congress were polarized by politics, these four men worked across the aisle to ensure HR 5131 passed as a standalone bill, which is phenomenal," said Timothy P. Shriver, chairman and CEO of Special Olympics.

> I also want to thank President Bush for making this important piece of legislation the law of the land. This statute sends a message of commitment and will positively change the lives of people with intellectual disabilities, as well as the lives of everyone who witnesses their accomplishments. (http://www.specialolympics.org)

The Special Olympics Sport and Empowerment Act authorizes $15 million per year over five years in funding for the growth of Special Olympics and initiatives that foster greater understanding and respect for people with intellectual disabilities:

- Special Olympics Healthy Athletes®: to provide critical screening for vision, dental, nutrition, and health promotion of people with intellectual disabilities by volunteer health professionals at the national, state, regional, and world games. Thus far, the Special Olympics Healthy Athletes initiative has assisted tens of thousands of persons with intellectual disabilities in communities around the world.

- Worldwide Expansion: to increase the number of athletes involved with Special Olympics, with a goal of adding one million new athletes in the next five years. Special Olympics will also seek to educate the global community about individuals with intellectual disabilities.

- Character Education: a school-based curriculum and program development tool that offers students of all abilities the chance to learn about differences, reduce the isolation experienced by children with special needs, and engage in creating local Special Olympics teams and events that unite the community.

Special Olympics Issues

There are a number of key concerns that face the Special Olympics. They include leadership, fundraising, volunteers, and corporate sponsorships. Each of these will be discussed briefly below:

Fundraising, Leadership, and Volunteers

Almost any nonprofit (e.g., American Red Cross, American Cancer Society, Big Brothers and Big Sisters, Boys and Girls Club of American, International Olympic Committee, Paralympics, United States Olympic Committee, YMCA, YWCA, and on and on) you can think of has three key challenges—leadership, fundraising, and volunteers. The key to survival for a nonprofit is good solid dependable leadership, consistent fundraising, and many dependable volunteers.

Leadership

The leadership for a nonprofit organization is composed of paid staff and volunteers. Successful nonprofit organizations have consistent, dependable, and strong leadership. The Special Olympics organization, like other nonprofits, needs to maintain strong leadership within its paid staff and volunteers nationwide. Special Olympic organizations are found in each state in America as well as in many of the larger metropolitan areas. These organizations, as well as national, must maintain a strong leadership base. Organization boards of directors need to be concerned about the leadership qualities of the professional staff and volunteers. Further, the board needs to establish a sound in-service education programs for the various groups of employees and volunteers with an emphasis on enhancing leadership capabilities.

Fundraising

There is not one nonprofit that is not constantly concerned about fundraising. The Special Olympics organizations are also concerned about raising adequate funds to maintain and expand programming. Fundraising is not a once-a-year activity. It is a regular activity throughout the year. The sport manager needs to develop a sound fundraising strategy for the nonprofit sport organization. This should include corporate sponsorships, direct mail campaigns, grants (state and federal as well as private corporations and foundations), special events, and much more. The successful nonprofit sport organization has adequate revenue streams to meet expenses and build a sound reserve.

Volunteers

Leadership and fundraising come from strong volunteers. Nonprofit organizations will never be able to employee adequate numbers of professional staff to implement all the programs offered. Therefore, it is vital to recruit strong volunteers to assist in implementing the programs, maintaining the daily organizations operations, and raising the necessary funds for the organizations survival. The sport manager needs to carefully recruit adequate numbers of volunteers with the skills to assist the organization. These volunteers need to be educated, supervised, and evaluated on a regular basis. Finally, the volunteers need to be recognized for their value to the organization on a regular basis.

Corporate Sponsorships

Corporate sponsorships are a key to success for many sport organizations. Sport is also a great vehicle for corporation to use to get their message out to the general public. Often it is a win-win for the sport organization and the corporation.

The Special Olympics represents people with "intellectual disabilities" and their families. This market is a small segment of the American population but one that has shown its loyalty to brand names. This segment has been compared to the Motor Sports fans who are fiercely loyal to the corporate sponsors of their favorite drivers and racing teams. The Special Olympics has enjoyed support from a variety of corporations (e.g., CARQUEST auto parts, Coca-Cola, Mattel, McDonalds, Michelin, Midwest Trophy Manufacturing, Procter and Gamble, and many more) over the years. However, maintaining corporate sponsors is a major undertaking. Securing new corporate sponsors is also very challenging, since every corporation is sought after to become a corporate sponsor. The sport manager needs to develop strategies to maintain and expand corporate sponsorships for the organization. The best examples for gaining corporate sponsorship support are in the motorsport industry. For example, NASCAR drivers and cars are covered with the logos of the various corporate sponsors for that particular racing team. Without corporate sponsors, they would not be able to survive in the expensive world of motorsports.

Summary

Special Olympics is an international organization that changes lives by promoting understanding, acceptance, and inclusion between people with and without intellectual disabilities. Through year-round sports training and athletic competition and other related programming for more than 2.25 million children and adults with intellectual disabilities in more than 150 countries, Special Olympics has created a model community that celebrates people's diverse gifts. Founded in 1968 by *Eunice Kennedy Shriver,* Special Olympics provides people with intellectual disabilities continuing opportunities to realize their potential, develop physical fitness, demonstrate courage, and experience joy and friendship. There is no cost to participate in Special Olympics.

There are a number of key concerns that face the Special Olympics. They include leadership, fundraising, volunteers, and corporate sponsorships.

References

http://www.specialolympic.org. (2006).

 NOTES

CHAPTER 16

Senior Olympics/Senior Games Governance

The National Senior Games Association (NSGA) and its infrastructure of state affiliate organizations and regional and local competitions fill an important and critical role in American communities. It is well documented that the demographic shifts in the U.S. population are developing a higher proportion of older adults who are healthier, wealthier, more active, living longer, and expecting a more active retirement than previous generations (Orsega-Smith, Payne, & Godbey, 2003; Schaumleffel, 2006; U.S. Census Bureau, 2000). The increase in older adults in the United States is a result of the baby boom that took place from 1946 to 1964. It is projected that the percentage of senior citizens will be 26 percent of the U.S. population by 2010 (Michigan Senior Olympics, 2000a).

The Senior Games serves a socially relevant and significant role in the American recreation and sport delivery system. Gandee and Layfield (as cited in Gandee, Campbell, Knierim, Cosky, Leslie, Ziegler, & Snodgrass, 1989) asserted that the Senior Games improves the quality of life and well-being of senior citizens by promoting respect and acceptance of seniors, promoting regular physical activity, encouraging service providers to address the needs of older adults, providing opportunities for recognition of fitness achievement, and providing opportunities for friendly and respectful competition and socialization.

Moreover, in the next decade, it will likely prove even more critical for Senior Games to strategically impact rural communities due to the increasing median age of rural communities. As families and children move to metropolitan areas for economic opportunities, rural communities are left with smaller and older populations of citizens in need of recreation and sport services. (Schaumleffel, 2006). Parks and recreation and health clubs are the second to the home as the most popular place for senior citizens to exercise and nearly 80 percent of older adults begin a new physical activity after age 50, which reflects the trend that seniors are seeking more rigorous activity (Fontane & Hurd, 1996).

Learning Objectives

Upon completion this chapter, the reader should be able to:

• Understand the history and mission, governance structure, function, authority, requirements for membership, sanctions and appeals processes, funding, and current issues for the Senior Olympics/Senior Games.

- Discuss various impact issues, such as: funding for the national organization and member state organizations, stability of member state organizations, participation, changing demographics and the perceptions of individuals entering older adulthood, and sustainable impact on the health of seniors.

Historical Developments

In the mid-1960s, the National Recreation and Park Association (NRPA), then the National Recreation Association, developed the Lifetime Sports program, which strived to involve individuals in sporting activities and competitions across their lifespan (Ohio Senior Olympics, 2006a). As NRPA's Lifetime Sports concept matured in the mid-1970s, athletic competitions for athletes ages 55 and over started in California and spread throughout the United States (Ohio Senior Olympics, 2006a).

By 1985, senior games were being conducted in 33 states. Thus, seven individuals officially formed a national leadership team, incorporated the National Senior Olympics Organization (NSOO) as a nonprofit organization in Missouri, and hosted a meeting of state organizers to plan the first national competition that would take place in 1987 (National Senior Games Association [NSGA], 2006a). The first national competition, the U.S. National Senior Sports Classic, attracted 2,500 participants and 10,000 spectators to St. Louis (NSGA, 2006a; Ohio Senior Olympics, 2006a). In 1989, 3,500 seniors participated in the second national Games in St. Louis. (NSGA, 2006a) The second national games not only grew in participation, but also generated significant media coverage by the *New York*

Times, ESPN, and *Good Morning America* (NSGA, 2006a).

By the late 1980s, the United States Olympic Committee (USOC) objected to the NSOO's use of the term Olympic in the organization's corporate name, which caused the NSOO to change its name to the U.S. National Senior Sports Organization (NSGA, 2006a). More recently, the senior sports organization again changed the corporate name to the National Senior Games Association; however, the national competition continues to be called The Summer National Senior Games–The Senior Olympics by agreement with the United States Olympic Committee. (NSGA, 2006a) At the state level, many state organizations had already been operating for several years under the name Senior Olympics (NSGA, 2006a, 2006b). Through a grandfather clause, the USOC agreed to allow state organizations that were in existence prior to 1988 to continue identifying their organizations as Senior Olympics; however, the use of the "Olympic rings" or other official United States Olympic Committee icons is not permitted (NSGA, 2006a, 2006b).

Today, the Senior Olympics is "the largest multisport event in the world for seniors, and other national senior athletic events" (NSGA, 2006b, p. 1). Currently, every state in the U.S. has a state-level senior games provider that is affiliated with the National Senior Games Association. Most state organizations are called Senior Games or Senior Olympics; however, a handful of states also use the names Golden Olympics, Golden Age Games, and Senior Sports Classic. Approximately, 330 local senior games take place each year across the United States.

Governance

Organizational Structure

The Senior Olympics/Senior Games is a confederation of national, state, regional, and local organizations and competitions for older adults. All events typically include official ceremonies, athletic events, awards, and social functions (Gandee, et al., 1989).

National

The NSGA is a 501(c)iii, nonprofit member of the United States Olympic Committee and governs the Summer National Senior Games–The Senior Olympics (NSGA, 2006b: NSGA "serves as an umbrella for member state organizations across the United States that host State Senior Games or Senior Olympics" (NSGA, 2006b: p. 1). "The NSGA supports and sanctions these member state organizations so that adults can participate in their state in events year-round that will keep them moti-

vated to achieve greater value and quality in their lives by staying healthy, active and fit" (NSGA, 2006b: p. 1). The NSGA supports state organizations by providing a national newsletter, calendar of events, national conference, standard rules for competition, and software to maintain performance records from competitive events. The NSGA also provides some marketing materials and staff review and support when called upon by a state organization.

State

State level Senior Olympics/Senior Games are planned, implemented, and evaluated in two significantly different ways: (a) through member organizations which are separate 501(c)iii, tax-exempt nonprofit

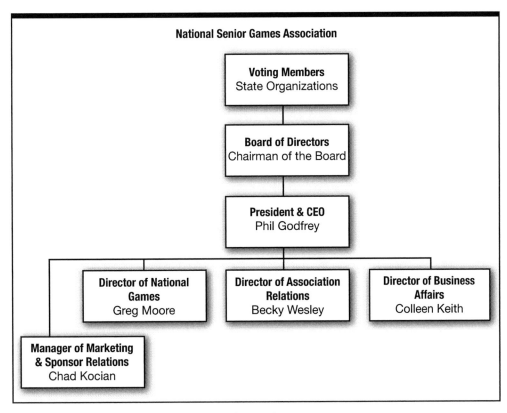

Figure 16.1
Organizational Chart
National Senior Games Association

organizations from the national association (e.g., Utah Huntsman State Games, California Senior Games, Delaware Senior Olympics), and (b) through existing government or nonprofit organizations such as metropolitan parks and recreation departments or state agencies on aging (e.g., Indiana).

> It is important to note the simple yet significant difference between a Member Organization and a State Games. A Member Organization is the nonprofit entity whose sole purpose is to establish and maintain Association related events and programs in its state. A Member Organization may either (a) Establish and conduct events and programs using its own resources and staff , or (b) Establish and then delegate, to a separate entity, the conduct of its events (e.g., a State Games) and programs. (National Senior Games Association [NSGA], 2003: p. 1)

Each state member organization is a separate nonprofit corporation from the national organization and is governed by a voluntary board of directors. A State Games is simply the state-level competition that is administered by the member organization or by another agency that is delegated the task of administering the state level competition by the member organization.

Typically, state level Senior Games/Senior Olympics administered by a separate nonprofit organization tend to be more successful because event managers' and coordinators' focus is on event planning, implementation, and evaluation throughout the year. Although events managed by a member organization tend to be more successful, the events are often administered by individuals who work from home offices or in other non-traditional office environments.

Conversely, in states where the state games are administered by existing government or nonprofit organizations, the events tend to not be administered as well due to the event managers or coordinators having multiple job responsibilities within their agencies and planning and implementing the Senior Olympics/Senior Games is just a small component of their annual workload. However, the office environment is usually more professional and business hours tend to be kept on a regular basis.

Regional

In a few states, it is necessary for participants to compete in a regional competition to qualify for the state level games (e.g., Tennessee, Florida). However, most states do not have a regional qualifier requirement and, therefore, do not conduct regional games. Currently, in most states, it is not necessary to competitively qualify in a local or regional competition to compete in the state level games. Furthermore, most states do not offer regional competitions. As participation decreases in local and state games, the need for regional competitions has decreased.

Local

Local Senior Games/Senior Olympics events are often administered by branch offices of the existing government or nonprofit organizations that administer the state games. For example, in Indiana, the state agency on aging administers the state and local games. Indiana is broken into 16 area agencies on aging. Fourteen of the 16 area agencies on aging conduct local Senior Olympics/Senior Games; while one of the area agencies on aging, the Southwestern Indiana Regional Council on Aging (SWIRCA), conducts a local competition, the River City Senior Games, and hosts the Indiana Senior Olympics, the state level competition. One of the 14 area agencies on aging, Area 8, in Indiana that offers a local competition contracts with the Indianapolis Parks and Recreation Department to administer the local games.

In North Carolina, 50 – 53 local competitions are administered each year on average, serve approximately 60,000 older adults, and are structured in basically two ways. In contrast to Indiana's model of predominantly administering local competitions through area agencies on aging, about half of North Carolina's local competitions tend to be conducted by city and county parks and recreation departments and the other 50 percent tend to be administered by the aging network (i.e., senior centers, agencies on aging).

In contrast to the heavily populated states of Indiana and North Carolina, Wyoming does not conduct local or regional competitions due to the lack of a significant population base in the state. Wyoming has approximately 500,000 residents, which makes it feasible to only conduct a state-level competition due to potentially low participation rates. In other states, state and local agencies responsible for planning and implementing local competitions often contract with hospitals and fitness centers to administer the events.

Mission

The National Senior Games Association (http://www.nsga.com/) is "dedicated to motivating senior men and women to lead a healthy lifestyle through the senior games movement" (NSGA, 2006b). The Senior Olympics/Senior Games are open to any individual who has attained the age of 50 years old or older; however, the majority of participants are over the age of 65. The national organization has two key functions: (a) plan, implement, and evaluate the annual summer and winter national competitions and (b) support the development of stable member state organizations.

Programming

Opportunities for older adults to participate in the games exist at the local, regional, state, and national levels. The level of competition, the commitment to the individual events by participants, and the number of seniors seeking a serious leisure experience increases from the local competition to the national competition. When programming Senior Olympic events, professionals should encourage participants to participate in the planning and implementations phases of the event (Fontane & Hurd, 1996). Moreover, events should be flexibly scheduled to increase the satisfaction of all participants and spectators, by including recreational and social events, as well as sporting competitions.

The documentation of winners in senior games and masters competitions in Ohio, Illinois, Florida, California, Maryland, Missouri, and many other sites across the country benchmark the success of older adults in tennis, table tennis, swimming, golf, shuffleboard, horseshoes, bowling, and track and field events. The senior games concept provides opportunities for older adults to challenge themselves and to experience the exhilaration of actual participation. The enthusiasm with which the games are received by older adults is evidence that athletic achievements has no age barrier and contrasts sharply with societal expectations regarding aging, such as inactivity, weight gain and loss of previous skills (Gandee, et al., 1989: p. 72).

Each competition (i.e., local, regional, state, or national games) has an event manager or coordinator and a cadre of trained volunteers to assist with the logistics and programmatic aspects of the event. Examples of volunteer positions utilized during the Games are: registrars, assistants, finish line personnel, judges, referees, retrievers, scorers, office clerks, award presenters, equipment managers, results managers, medics, and water/fruit distributors. Event managers recruit volunteers from the military, universities, high schools, senior citizens groups, service organizations, retirement communities, and corporate sponsors. Furthermore, at all levels of competition, participants receive medals for first through third place by age division in each competitive event. Seniors also receive cloth fitness patches and personalized achievement certificates at the state and national levels for completing various levels of fitness activity. Not only do seniors have opportunities for physical activity but they also have a number of opportunities for socializing and maintaining friendships at all levels of the Senior Olympics/Senior Games.

National

The Summer National Senior Games–Senior Olympics, which began in 1987, is held during odd-numbered years and offers competition in 18 sports such as archery, badminton, basketball, bowling, cycling, golf, horseshoes, race walk, racquetball, shuffleboard, softball, swimming, table tennis, tennis, and track and field (Fontane & Hurd, 1996; Senior Something, 2006). The summer games typically take place in June or July of each year. The Winter National Senior Games–Senior Olympics was added to NSGA's offering to seniors in 2000 and it is held during even-numbered years (Senior Something, 2006). "The Winter National Senior Games offers competition in seven sports: alpine skiing, cross-country skiing, curling, figure skating, ice hockey, snowshoeing, and speedskating" (Senior Something, 2006: p. 1). For both the national summer and winter games, participants must be at least 50 years old and are presently not required to qualify at the state-level games (Senior Something, 2006).

State

Participants are not required to participate or qualify at the local or regional level to participate in most state competitions (e.g., Florida and Tennessee require regional competitions). However, many states have a closed state games format meaning that only individuals from that particular state can compete in the state games. Many state organizations have extended their services beyond hosting an annual competition by offering year-round fitness programs (e.g., Walk Delaware, Torch Run Celebration), training information, and healthy lifestyle literature (Delaware Senior Olympics, 2006; Michigan Senior Olympics, 2000b).

Regional

Regional competitions typically take place on an annual basis, usually between September and October, at sites around each state, and are sponsored by a variety of organizations. The schedule of activities at regional sites usually includes many of the competitive activities that take place at the national competitions along with a variety of other activities and events. However, each regional sponsoring organization determines, plans, and implements the activities causing a variety of events being offered at different regional sites within a state.

Local

At the local and regional games, participants not only compete in the national competition activities, but they also participate in other activities that include physical and non-physical activities such as billiards, cooking and nutrition classes, frisbee, softball, meteorology seminars, bingo, healthy living, tai-chi, bocci, dancing, and walking. Many times, local games even include activities such as water balloon tosses and water gun shoots. Local-level Senior Games/Senior Olympics competitions tend to focus on fun and socialization and include dances and meals as part of the event. Many local games essentially function like non-competitive, recreational, social clubs with an extremely low level of interest in winning or qualifying for higher level competition. Most local games are open for participation from inside or outside the locality; but some local games are closed games. Local competitions are typically in the summer so that participants who wish to compete at regional competitions and that qualify for state and national competitions can do so.

Authority

The rules used for Senior Olympics/Senior Games competitions are those established by the NSGA, the national governing body (Ohio Senior Olympics, 2006b). For most events, the rules used by NSGA mirror those in use by the official national governing body for that sport. For example, the rules for track and field are those used by U.S. Track and Field (Ohio Senior Olympics, 2006b). A copy of the rules is provided to each participant in advance of the games so that each participant may read and familiarize themselves with the rules prior to competing (Ohio Senior Olympics, 2006b).

Requirements for Membership

State Organizations

Membership in the Senior Olympics/Senior Games infrastructure is unique. State affiliate organizations join the national association as an organizational member, however, individual participants do not join the Senior Olympics/Senior Games as a member at the local, state, regional, or national levels. "Eligibility for membership in the national association, conditions, obligations and class of membership are established by the Board of Directors and rati-

fied by the members" (NSGA, 2006b: p. 1). State affiliates join the national association as a provisional member for a three-year period where they are accorded all of the rights of an active member except that they may not vote in years one and two (NSGA, 2006b). Within the three-years, provisional member organizations must improve their programs, so that they satisfy all national by-laws, policies, and procedures. (NSGA, 2006b). Furthermore, within three years of applying for membership in NSGA, the state affiliate is required to incorporate as a nonprofit corporation. Currently, all 50 states have a state organization that is a member of the National Senior Games Association.

In cases where a state affiliate fails to comply with the minimum requirements of NSGA, the organization is placed on restricted membership for one year and loses its right to vote. Failure to pay dues or to comply with NSGA requirements while on restricted membership results in the state affiliate yet again being reclassified to corresponding membership (NSGA, 2006b). An organization can only be placed on restricted membership once in any five-year period. (NSGA, 2006b)

NSGA imposes other requirements on state affiliate organizations that include: reporting new sponsors, creating marketing and public relation materials, publishing an annual newsletter to participants and membership, and producing a strategic plan every three years (NSGA, 2006b).

Athletes

As previously mentioned, individual athletes do not join the Senior Olympics/Senior Games as a member at the local, state, regional, or national levels. However, to participate in a Senior Olympics/Senior Games competition, athletes must be 50 years of age or older and, in most states, pay an entry fee. All athletes may be required to show proof of age during the Games. Any athlete unable to provide proof of age or who was not of the minimum age for which they competed will be disqualified. Any team with a rostered individual who is not of minimum age will be disqualified (San Antonio Senior Games, 2006).

Sanctions and Appeals Process

For a state organization to gain certification as a state senior games organization, the organization must file an initial application that is reviewed by the NSGA staff, a committee, and the board of directors. The board votes to approve or disapprove all initial applications in terms of compliance with NSGA national policy. All state organizations must renew their certification every five years. It is possible for certified state organizations to be decertified and expelled if the agency is not in compliance. However, if a non-compliance issue is out of the control of the certified state organization, then a waiver can be filed by the state organization and approved by a two-thirds majority vote of the board of directors. State organizations may appeal their disapproved application or their decertification and expulsion by submitting a written notice of appeal to the president and CEO of the NSGA. Reinstatement of an expelled member can take place by a two-thirds majority vote of the Board of Directors.

Funding

As 501(c)iii, tax-exempt nonprofit organizations at the national and state levels, Senior Olympics/Senior Games organizations and local agencies that sponsor local competitions raise money by relying on grants, donations, corporate sponsorships, participant memberships, and/or entry fees for events. Furthermore, the NSGA has developed a fundraising arm, the National Senior Games Association Foundation. The Foundation is a tax-exempt corporation established for the purposes of encouraging, supporting, and promoting the educational, research, and other missions of the National Senior Games Association and its 50 member state organizations (National Senior Games Association [NSGA], 2006c). The NSGA Foundation also serves as a vehicle for the receipt, management, protection, and grant distribution of bequests, contributions, donations, and other charitable gifts (NSGA, 2006c).

Senior Olympic/Senior Game Issues

Funding

As with almost all human service related nonprofit organizations, the most pressing issue for Senior Olympics/Senior Games is continued funding for the national organization, member state organizations, and local competitions. Currently, each level of the Senior Olympics/Senior Games confederation is essentially independently responsible for raising funds to operate their organizations and administer each competition.

Moreover, state games administered by existing government and nonprofit agencies tend to be not growing but simply maintaining participation. This problem is embedded within the larger issue of the need to strengthen state member organizations and to move struggling state games administered by existing government and nonprofit organizations to be administered by a strong and independent state organization that funds full-time staff positions. The key component to strong member state organizations is sustainable funding, which in turn would fund full-time staff that would afford individuals the time to increase participation through marketing and to solicit sponsorships and donations to increase sustainable funding. Currently, the NSGA is searching for strategies to strengthen the national organization financially and to support struggling or stagnant state organizations by assisting with fundraising and financial stability. A result of the national association's efforts to strengthen state organizations should be to position state organizations to more directly assist in the administration (i.e., funding, marketing) of local games. The national organization partially funds itself and its activities through sponsorship; however, the national organization cannot guarantee sponsorship dollars to the state organizations. Ultimately, state organizations must be financially sustainable.

Considering the movement to promote active living, to address the American obesity epidemic, and the demographic of an increasingly larger proportion of the U.S. population being older adults, senior citizens are a key market for private corporations to invest in through marketing strategies that include sponsorship of local, state, and national competitions. Senior Olympics/Senior Games administrators need to work to secure sustainable funding from private corporations that provide goods and services to older adults.

Furthermore, to increase not only financial capital, but also social capital, local, state, and national event planners and managers need to partner with allied public and non-profit agencies to increase the probability of achieving the NSGA mission by reducing the waste of precious resources through service duplication and competition with similar agencies, programs, and events.

Expectations and Perceptions

A second important issue is participation and the changing expectations and perceptions of new senior citizens. Participation tends to be marginal at local compe-

titions (i.e., 30-40 participants). The Senior Games/Senior Olympics has lowered the age requirement to participate from 65 to 50 years of age over the last decade; however, participation has not significantly increased. If the Senior Olympics/Senior Games plans to increase participation, the organization will have to consider current demographic trends and the expectations of individuals entering older adulthood.

As previously mentioned, the Baby Boomer generation is entering older adulthood; however, most Baby Boomers do not view themselves as senior citizens and they have expectations of physically, mentally, and emotionally challenging activities as part of their leisure, sport, and physical activity regimens. Individuals entering older adulthood do not view the Senior Olympics/Senior Games as something that they would like to participate in because they do not perceive a senior sport competition as an outlet that provides the type of rewarding experiences that they are seeking. Today's senior citizens expect recreation programmers to provide opportunities beyond bingo and shuffleboard. Event managers need to offer physically challenging activities such as weightlifting and adventure/outdoor recreation events (e.g., hiking, biking, kayaking). In many cases, today's older adults are in better physical shape than the younger professionals who plan the events.

Health and Well-Being Impact

Another issue facing the Senior Olympics/Senior Games is whether or not the organization, at all levels, has any significantly measurable effect on the long-term health and wellbeing of senior citizens. Some could argue that an annual two-day event does little to improve the overall health and wellness of older adults. If the Senior Olympics/Senior Games continues to establish strong, independent state organizations, the Senior Olympics/Senior Games will need to find ways to interact with seniors at all levels on a regular basis. More regular interaction between seniors and the Senior Olympics/Senior Games could be achieved through regular paper-based communication (i.e., newsletters), practices, walking clubs, and one-event competitions throughout the year.

Moreover, as previously discussed in regard to funding, Senior Olympics/Senior Games providers need to continue to develop strategic partnerships with other agencies to increase the amount of contact that Senior Olympics/Senior Games has with individual participants. To achieve the NSGA mission, older adults need to hear the NSGA message of healthy and active older adulthood on a week-to-week basis throughout the year, as opposed to competing at a local competition two days a year.

Senior Citizens with Disabilities

All Senior Games are conducted under able-bodied rules of the various national governing bodies of each sport. Although most local competitions do not have enough resources to offer divisions of competition for individual with disabilities, Senior Olympics/Senior Games competitions typically take place at fully accessible facilities. Furthermore, reasonable accommodations are made for participants who need assistance to participate. Often times, individuals with disabilities will have a health care provider assist in an event. Higher levels of accommodation are made at local competitions since the emphases of the events is on fun, leisure, and recreation, however, at many state and national events less accommodation is made for individuals with disabilities. The NSGA refers individuals with disabilities to participate in other organizations and organization's events who specialize in recreation and sport programming for individuals with specific disabilities.

Senior Citizens Who Are Institutionalized

At the local level of competition, it is common for local providers to offer a separate Senior Games/Senior Olympics competition for individuals who are institutionalized in nursing homes and other assisted-living facilities.

Future of Senior Olympics/Senior Games

The future of the Senior Olympics/Senior Games rests on the success of the national organization being able to functionally strengthen member state organizations by providing adequate support and assistance with fundraising to operate the competitions and the organizations. The Senior Olympics/Senior Games, from the national level to the local competitions, will need to continue to re-identify with a changing demographic of older adults who have significantly different leisure expectations and perceptions of their physical abilities. To achieve the NSGA mission, the Senior Olympic/Senior Games, at all levels, must find ways to not only increase participation, but also to develop a program model that will have a sustainable effect on individual senior citizen's overall health.

Summary

By participating in senior games competitions, older adults can experience competition, flow, leisure, and positive social relationships (Gandee, et al., 1989, p. 72). The Senior Games provides opportunities for seniors to improve societal attitudes and behaviors toward older adults by demonstrating their physical abilities (Gandee, et al., 1989). Senior Olympics/Senior Games are administered and organized in a variety of organizational structures from state to state, region to region, and locality to locality. Every state, regional, and locality has its commonalities and administrative idio-syncrasies when planning, implementing, and evaluation of Senior Olympics/Senior Games competitions.

Although creating strong, independent state organizations to administer the Senior Olympics/State Games is critical for administering high-quality annual competitions, the Senior Olympics/Senior Games organization must continue to seek partnerships with other state and local organizations that serve older adults to increase the year-round presence of Senior Olympics/Senior Games events and activities so that the organization has a better chance of making significant headway toward achieving its mission to motivate senior men and women to lead a healthy lifestyle through the senior games movement.

References

Delaware Senior Olympics. (2006). *What is Delaware senior games?* Retrieved September 16, 2006, from http://www.delawareseniorolympics.org/

Fontane, P. E., & Hurd, P. D. (1996). Leisure activities of national senior Olympians. *Journal of Physical Education, Recreation, and Dance, 67* (6), 61.

Gandee, R. N., Campbell, T. A., Knierim, H., Cosky, A. C., Leslie, D. K., Ziegler, R. G., & Snodgrass, J. E. (1989). Senior Olympic games: Opportunities for older adults. *Journal of Physical Education, Recreation, and Dance, 60* (3), 72-76.

Michigan Senior Olympics. (2000a). *About MSO: Philosophy.* Retrieved September 16, 2006, from http://michiganseniorolympics.com/about_MSO_philosophy.html

Michigan Senior Olympics. (2000b). *Summer games: Registration information.* Retrieved September

16, 2006, from http://michiganseniorolympics.com/sg_reg_info.html

National Senior Games Association [NSGA]. (2003). *Association membership criteria.* Baton Rouge, LA: National Senior Games Association.

National Senior Games Association [NSGA]. (2006a). *History of the NSGA.* Retrieved November 3, 2006, from http://www.nsga.com/history.html.

National Senior Games Association [NSGA]. (2006b). *National Senior Games Association.* Retrieved November 3, 2006, from http://www.nsga.com/about.html

National Senior Games Association [NSGA]. (2006c). *NSGA foundation.* Retrieved November 3, 2006, from http://www.nsga.com/found.html

Ohio Senior Olympics. (2006a). *How Senior Olympics began.* Retrieved September 16, 2006, from http://www.ohioseniorolympics.org/senior_olympics_in_ohio.htm

Ohio Senior Olympics. (2006b). *Our state games.* Retrieved September 16, 2006, from http://www.ohioseniorolympics.org/the_state_games.htm

Orsega-Smith, E., Payne, L., & Godbey, G. (2003). Outcomes associated with participation in a community parks and recreation based wellness program for older adults. *Journal of Aging and Physical Activity, 11*(4) 516-531.

San Antonio Senior Games. (2006). *General information.* Retrieved September 16, 2006, from http://www.seniorolympicssa.com/GenInfo.htm

Schaumleffel, N. A. (2006, January). *Rural recreation development: Helping communities help themselves across Indiana.* Presentation conducted at the annual meeting of the Indiana Park and Recreation Association, Indianapolis, IN.

Senior Something. (2006). *Senior Olympics/Senior Games qualification requirements.* Retrieved November 3, 2006, from http://www.seniorsomething.com/srolymqualify.html

U.S. Census Bureau (2000). *Population trends.* Retrieved December 21, 2006, from http://www.census.gov/

NOTES

CHAPTER 17

Community Sport Support Structures

Many cities, counties, and states in the United States have established a community or state sport support structures. These support structures have been designed to promote sport or sporting events within the community or state. Further, these structures are either quasi-governmental or nonprofit tax deductible organizations used to raise funds for a specific sport, sporting event, or sport facilities. Generally, these structures are known as sport authorities, sport commissions, sport corporations, sport councils, or sport foundations. Finally, there is one sport support structure known as a sport congress that brings together sport leaders and academics to talk about sport issues, conduct research, and make recommendations regarding sports issues discussed.

Learning Objectives

Upon completion this chapter, the reader should be able to:

- Identify and describe the various community sport support structures.

- Discuss the governance of these sport support structures.
- Identify and discuss the various revenue streams that support these community sport support structures.

What are Community Sport Support Structures?

Sport has become a multibillion-dollar industry in the United States and a great deal more when sport is viewed globally. Every medium to large city in the United States wants to attract a major sporting event or professional team. These events or teams bring prosperity to the community.

The 41st NFL Super Bowl generated over $8.5 billion in sales in 2007. The city of Miami was grateful to be able to host the Super Bowl in 2007 and again in 2011. However, it took a great deal of work and money to prepare the bid for the Super Bowl. Often, this type of work is too great for the local city government. In these cases a local community sport support organization, such as a sport authority, sport commission, sport corporation, sport council, or sport foundation, prepares the necessary documents, gains the necessary approvals and permits, raises the necessary funding, gathers the necessary personnel, secures the appropriate sport venue or has one constructed, and submits the necessary bid documents to the organization seeking a host for a major sporting event.

Another example where a community sport support entity was used to prepare for a major sporting event is the Olympic Organizing Committees formed in Los Angeles, Lake Placid, Atlanta, Salt Lake, Chicago, and New York. These committees were responsible for preparing the Olympic bid and later managing the Olympic Games in those cities if they won the bid from the International Olympic Committee to host the games.

In the next few pages, community sport support structures will be highlighted with examples of each provided. These are important structures for the continuation and expansion of sport in America and worldwide. These structures are not just in the United States, they are worldwide.

Sport Authorities

Sports authorities are generally formed to serve as a financing mechanism, landlord for pro-sport venues and other public assembly areas such as convention centers, and a promoter of economic development through sports. Many sports authorities are established by statute and many others are nonprofit organizations. The quasi-governmental authorities are commonly granted:

- Administrative and operational authority for sports complexes, stadiums, arenas, and other public assembly facilities.
- Condemnation authority.
- Special financing authority.
- The ability to implement a ticket surcharge.

- The ability to collect state and local sales tax generated by ticket, concession, parking, or merchandise sales.
- The ability to plan, promote, finance, construct, acquire, renovate, equip, and enlarge buildings.
- The authority to promote economic development, increase use of existing spectator facilities and sports venues, promote civic pride, and diversify the variety of events available to sports enthusiasts.

There are approximately 190 nonprofit organizations nationally doing similar whose functions and missions are to:

- Promote economic development,
- Increase use of existing spectator facilities and sports venues,
- Promote civic pride,
- Diversify the variety of events available to sports enthusiasts, and
- Raise funds to support the sport project(s).

The revenues generated by quasi-governmental sport authorities and nonprofit organizations are used to pay the bond obligations on sport and other public assembly facilities that have been built or are being built such as Maryland Stadium Authority and the Camden Yards project in Baltimore for the Baltimore Orioles, and the operating costs for the authority.

Board members of quasi-governmental sports authorities are appointed by the government officials (e.g., mayor or governor) for terms of four to six years, which are renewable. The board members for nonprofit authorities are elected by the members of the organization.

The following are five examples of quasi-governmental nonprofit authorities:

Maryland Stadium Authority
Lubbock Sports Authority

Oregon Sports Authority
San Jose Sports Authority
Nashville Metropolitan Sports
Authority

Quasi-Governmental Sport Authorities

Maryland Sports Authority

In 1987, legislation was enacted approving Camden Yards as the site for the new stadium complex and granting to the Stadium Authority administrative and operational powers, including condemnation authority and a special financing mechanism. In 1988, a memorandum of agreement was negotiated between the team and the Maryland Stadium Authority (MSA); property acquisition, design, and construction began on what would become Oriole Park at Camden Yards. The ballpark opened on April 6, 1992. The opening resulted in the first significant increase in the size of MSA's staff with the addition of facilities management personnel (http://www.msa.com).

The original mission of the MSA evolved and expanded and the reputation built with the Camden Yards ballpark resulted in the Maryland. The Maryland General Assembly later charged MSA with the oversight role in facilities other than baseball and football stadiums. The next MSA projects were the refurbishment and expansion of the Baltimore and Ocean City Convention Centers.

In November, 1996, more than a dozen years after the Colts' departure, the design and construction process for Ravens Stadium began. It necessitated more than $2 million in improvements to Memorial Stadium which became the home of the Baltimore Ravens for the 1996 and 1997 seasons. Ravens Stadium opened in August, 1998 (http://www.msa.com).

MSA's responsibilities continued to expand as new projects began and were completed. These projects included the design and construction of University Commons at the University of Maryland, Baltimore County. demolition of Memorial Stadium, the Sports Complex at Towson University, the University of Maryland College Park Parking Garage, the Comcast Center at the University of Maryland College Park (the replacement for Cole Field House), Ripken Stadium, the Veterans' Memorial, and the Hippodrome Theater (http://www.msa.com). Projects on which the MSA currently is working include improvements to the interior of Camden Stadium and oversight of construction on the Montgomery County Conference Center.

Nashville Metropolitan Sports Authority

The Sports Authority of the Metropolitan Government of Nashville and Davidson County was formed January 8, 1996, to serve as a financing mechanism and landlord for Nashville's two pro-sport venues, the Gaylord Entertainment Center and Adelphia Coliseum. The Sports Authority Act gives the Authority the ability to implement a ticket surcharge and collect state and local sales tax generated by ticket, concession, and merchandise sales in the two facilities. These revenues are used to pay Metro and the Sports Authority bond obligations on the two facilities. Board Members of the Sports Authority are appointed by the Mayor for terms of four to six years. (http://www.msfc.com)

The Metropolitan Sports Authority serves to:

- Plan, promote, finance, construct, acquire, renovate, equip, and enlarge buildings,
- Operate sports complexes, stadiums, arenas, structures, and facilities for public,
- Participation and enjoyment of pro-

fessional and amateur sports, fitness, health, and recreational activities, and

- Conduct itself to do what is reasonable and necessary to attract professional sports franchises to Nashville.

Nonprofit Sport Authorities

Lubbock Sports Authority

The Lubbock Sports Authority (LSA) is a nonprofit entity operating under the auspices of Market Lubbock, Inc. created to attract major sporting events and sports groups to the Lubbock area. Established in 1996, the expressed mission of the Lubbock Sports Authority is "to establish Lubbock as the Sports Capital of West Texas and Eastern New Mexico." It is the goal of the Lubbock Sports Authority to use sports events and sports-related meetings as an economic development tool by promoting and marketing Lubbock as a premier destination to host first class events of a sports related nature. At the current time, the Lubbock Sports Authority is subsidized entirely with Room Occupancy Tax dollars (http://www.lubbocksports.org).

The Lubbock Sports Authority is one of rapidly growing number (approximately 190) organizations of its kind nationwide. A small full-time staff handles the logistics and marketing of sporting events and a tremendous team of volunteers assists with actual event operations. In order to achieve its goals and fulfill this mission, the ultimate job of the Lubbock Sports Authority is twofold:

- To establish on-going relationships with National Governing Bodies of Sport, organized sports groups, and local sports entities in order to market Lubbock as a desirable destination to attract and hold first class major sporting events.
- To ensure that appropriate marketing, organizational, administrative, and vol-

unteer support systems are in place to enhance the ultimate success of these events (http://www.lubbocksports.org).

Sports have always been an integral part of American life. Organized Games have been in existence for centuries. This competitive spirit and the pursuit of excellence embodied by sports are an important part of what made this country and West Texas great. Sports also unite a citizenry and fill them with pride. Sports can cut across all economic, ethnic, and racial barriers to help create a sense of community and enhance the quality of life for the residents of a city where sporting events are held. More importantly, cities that host sporting events realize tremendous positive economic benefits. Participants and spectators who come to town to attend sporting events create a very positive economic impact for the community. They stay in hotel rooms, eat in restaurants, visit local tourist attractions, rent cars, purchase groceries, fuel, and souvenirs.

San Jose Sports Authority

The San Jose Sports Authority is a non-for-profit organization that serves as the sports marketing agency for the City of San Jose. The authority was formed in 1991. It has brought more than 150 premier events and programs to the San Jose area. The following is just a sample of our premier events:

- 2001 & 2002 Siebel Classic in Silicon Valley (Senior PGA event)
- 2001 Major League Soccer All-Star Game
- 2002 NCAA Men's West Regional Basketball Championships
- 2003 USOC Titan Games: The Road to Athens
- 2003-2008 Pac-10 Women's Basketball Championships
- 2004 U.S. Olympic Team Trials in

Rhythmic Gymnastics and Trampoline
- 2004 U.S. Olympic Team Trials in Judo and Taekwondo
- 2005 Taylor Woodrow Grand Prix of San Jose
- 2007 NCAA Division I Men's Basketball Championships San Jose Regional
- 2007 USA Gymnastics Visa Championships (http://www.sjsa.org)

Just as important as the high-profile events listed above is the dedication of the San Jose Sports Authority to youth and amateur athletics. The REACH Youth Scholarship program was started in 1996 by the Sports Authority to recognize the role that sports play in helping kids develop self-confidence and the strength to persevere in the face of adversity.

The First Tee of San Jose is a youth golf program, a youth golf program started by the Sports Authority and designed to expose economically disadvantaged youths to the game of golf. The program offers 32 hours of PGA and LPGA instruction, equipment, and transportation, all free of charge. Alongside the instruction, the participants learn life skills such as integrity, responsibility, and self-confidence.

Co-founded by the Sports Authority and community activists in the mid-1990s, the Greater San Jose After-School All-Stars provides educational, cultural, and community enrichment activities for youngsters from the ages of seven to 17. Chaired nationally by Arnold Schwarzenegger, the organization currently serves approximately 7,000 youngsters through 15 national chapters. The San Jose Sports Authority enriches the community through sports (http://www.sjsa.org).

Sport Commissions

The mission of a sport commissions is to recruit, retain, and grow professional, collegiate, and amateur sporting events for a community. The commission staff works with organizers to locate appropriate venues and vendors, to secure sponsorships, and to help increase participation and attendance at the events. The commission is a nonprofit amateur sports advocacy entity that promotes economic development of communities by assisting to identify, pursue, and facilitate athletic events. The commission is very similar to the nonprofit sport authority. The commission generally has the following objectives:

- To assist local sports organizations in their pursuit of sports events that provide economic benefits to the area.
- To assist in identifying, recruiting, and promoting those events and meetings that bring out-of-town visitors to enhance the area economy.
- To promote the community and its assets.
- To educate the public on the economic, public relations, health, fitness, and recreational value of sports events and activities.
- To provide a sports information center for groups seeking help and advice.
- To advise and facilitate local organizations of the economic potential for the proposed construction or remodeling of sports facilities.

The following are examples of sport commissions:

National Association of Sports Commissions
Greater Louisville Sports Commission
Sacramento Sports Commission

National Association of Sports Commissions

The National Association of Sports Commissions (NASC) is the sports event industry's leading networking organization. Founded in 1992, the NASC represents over 400 organizations within the sports event travel industry (http://www.sportscommission.org).

Members include organizations that attract sporting events to their community (i.e., sports commissions and convention and visitors bureaus), event owners and vendors, and suppliers to the sports event industry. The NASC is the primary network for communication and information sharing on all topics relating to the sports event industry.

Examples of Sport Commissions

Greater Louisville Sports Commission

The Greater Louisville Sports Commission is dedicated to attracting, producing, and supporting the best sporting events available. It supports a wide range of events that offer opportunities for a diverse demographic mix of athletes from all age groups and all sports.

The Greater Louisville Sports Commission is a nonprofit entity established in 1999. Its mission is attracting, creating, and hosting sports-related events and opportunities that:

- Have a positive economic impact on greater Louisville.
- Enhance the image of the greater Louisville area as a premier destination for sporting events.
- Improve the quality of life for area residents and sports enthusiasts.

It is the goal of the Greater Louisville Sports Commission to put Louisville on the map as a nationally recognized "player" for hosting top quality sports activities (http://www.louisvillesports.org).

Sacramento Sports Commission

The Sacramento Sports Commission is a joint city-county advisory board created in the 1980s to attract and develop major professional and amateur sporting events in the capital region. In 1998, the Sports Commission formed a non-profit organization – the Sacramento Region Sports Education Foundation – to administer SSC events. Since its inception in 1988, the Sports Commission has been responsible for bringing a number of high profile events to Sacramento, including the 1994, 1998, and 2002 NCAA Men's Basketball Tournament, the 1995 U.S. Outdoor Track and Field Championships, the 1999 John Hancock U.S. Gymnastics Championships, the 2000 U.S. Olympic Team Trials for Track and Field, and the 2001 National Junior Olympic Track and Field Championships (http://www.sacsports.com).

Sport Congress

A sport congress is a gathering of sport professionals and academics/scholars (e.g., sport business executives, sport biomechanists, sport exercise physiologists, sport psychologists, sport sociologists, or sport managers) on an irregular basis. The Congress is organized by professional educators, sport managers, or sporting organizations (e.g., International Olympic Committee) to discuss issues (e.g., athletic injuries, youth sports, sport law, women in sport, etc.) or research findings regarding a broad array of topics. The role of the Congress is consultative in nature. It also provides an opportunity to share information through presentations by practitioners and researchers about specific issues within the sport world globally.

The participants of a congress pay a registration fee as well as the cost of transportation, room, and board. The organizations or groups that sponsor a congress are generally nonprofit organizations (e.g., colleges or universities, sport organizations, or a government agencies). Many congresses are held annually (e.g., third annual sport law congress, seventh annual international congress on youth sports, first annual international congress on athletic injuries, etc.).

The following are some examples of a sport congress:

Olympic Congress

The Olympic Congress is a vast gathering of the Olympic Movement which happens on an irregular basis, but generally, every ten years or so during the last few decades. The Congress is organized by the International Olympic Committee (IOC). Olympic Congresses bring together representatives of all the parties that make up the Olympic Movement, namely the IOC, the National Olympic Committees, the International Sports Federations, the Olympic Games Organizing Committees, the athletes, coaches, judges, and the media, as well as other participants and observers. The role of the Congress is consultative. Table 17.1 summarizes past and present Olympic Congress topics.

IMG World Sport Congress

The initial IMG World Sport Congress focused on the Intersection of Sports and Entertainment. The second IMG annual World Sport Congress had a focus on The Changing Face of Consumers and Sports Consumption. The third annual IMG World Sport Congress focused on Sport Media and the Global Market. It is planned for the IMG World Congress to continue on an annual basis.

Table 17.1
Summary of Olympic Congresses

	Year	City	Themes
I	1894	Paris	Re-establishment of the Olympic Games
II	1897	Le Havre	Sports hygiene and pedagogy
III	1905	Brussels	Sport and physical education
IV	1906	Paris	Art, literature, and sport
V	1913	Lausanne	Sports psychology and physiology
VI	1914	Paris	Olympic regulations
VII	1921	Lausanne	Olympic regulations
VIII	1925	Prague	Sports pedagogy – Olympic regulations
IX	1930	Berlin	Olympic regulations
X	1973	Varna	Sport for a world of peace – The Olympic Movement and its future
XI	1981	Baden-Baden	United by and for sport The future of the Olympic Games – International cooperation – The future Olympic Movement
XII	1994	Paris	Centennial Olympic Congress, Congress of Unity The Olympic Movement's contribution to modern society – The contemporary athlete – Sport in its social context – Sport and the mass media
XIII	2009	Copenhagen	(http://www.ioc.org)

International Youth Sports Congress

The Congress represents a special opportunity to gain valuable insight from some of the world's top experts on important and complex subjects that impact all youth sports programs. More than 500 delegates are scheduled to attend including Certified Youth Sports Administrators, Police Athletic League administrators, park and recreation professionals, military youth sports directors, private league administrators, key officials of international sports organizations, and representatives from the YMCA, YWCA, and JCC.

Sport Corporations

A sports corporation is generally a nonprofit organization that serves as a catalyst for engaging the community in enhancing its sports economy. The sport corporation has a board of directors and a paid professional staff. Further, the sport corporation generally enlists a large number of volunteers in fundraising and operations for the various events supported by the entity. Finally, the sport corporations are supported most often by corporate donations or sponsorships, local, state, and federal grants, and foundation grants. Often, the sports corporation enlists its many volunteers in organizing specials events to raise funds for the various sporting events.

The following are examples of a sports corporation:

Indiana Sports Corporation

The Indiana Sports Corporation (ISC) is a nonprofit organization which serves as the catalyst for Indianapolis' thriving sports economy making the city and surrounding communities the envy of other cities throughout the U.S. The ISC was founded in 1981. It was responsible for bringing the 1987 Pan American Games to the city, the NCAA Final Four for men and women,

professional tennis, international swimming and diving competitions, and, most recently, the 2005 Solheim Cup to the Indianapolis area.

Fort Wayne Sports Corporation

In 1990, the Chamber of Commerce in Fort Wayne, In incorporated its "sports task force" into the Fort Wayne Sports Corporation. The mission of the Fort Wayne Sports Corporation is to promote the development of the Fort Wayne area through sports as well as to further the quality of life of its citizens through the promotion and awareness of sports. The corporation has established four key strategic objectives including stimulating the Fort Wayne economy by attracting sporting events and organizations, enhancing and increasing youth programs that teach valuable life lessons through sports, researching, reviewing, and determining the feasibility of new or remodeled sports facilities, and providing assistance to existing sports activities and organizations (http://www.fwsportscorp.org).

The Fort Wayne Sports Corporation has a volunteer Board of Directors and one staff person. It relies heavily on volunteers to implement its mission. Its main revenue streams are through corporate, club, and individual membership revenue and charitable grants.

The Fort Wayne Sports Corporation has accomplished many projects, including Champions Grant program which is geared to increase collegiate scholarship opportunities or reaching an Olympic potential for select local youth, development of an aquatics and ice/recreational sports facility, the Fort Wayne Sports Hall of Fame, development of the Allen County Memorial Baseball Stadium, Lifetime Sports Academy, Rod Woodson/Jason Fabini Football Camp, Eric Wedge Baseball Camp, Activate Fort Wayne, and a variety of national and regional sporting events.

The Colorado Springs Sports Corporation

The Colorado Springs Sports Corporation was created in 1978. It plays a vital role in assisting the United States Olympic Committee and the 48 other national and international sports organizations which call Colorado Springs home.

The mission of the Colorado Springs Sports Corporation is to: attract, retain, and support sport organizations and businesses, support youth sports through the recognition of athletes and coaches and provide financial assistance to enable disadvantaged youngsters to participate in sports programs, create and attract sporting events that contribute to the quality of life for citizens of the Pikes Peak region, and support the economy of Colorado Sports by promoting the region as a destination for sports business, competition, and meetings (http://www.thesportscorp.org).

Sport Councils

Sport Councils are groups of sport and recreation leaders, and others interested in the development of sport and recreation within a community, who meet and work together to build sport in a community or region. They serve as a forum for information exchange and coordination among sport clubs and associations and they also create independent, collective projects to support their community.

Sport Councils can have a diverse volunteer membership. They are nonprofit tax-exempted corporations and rely upon corporate donations or sponsorships, individual donations, and government and foundation grants.

Although sport organizations and clubs dominate, there are other stakeholder groups including:

- Schools, School Boards

- Businesses
- Health Agencies
- Social Service Agencies
- Service Clubs
- Tourism Associations
- Colleges/Universities.

The following are examples of a sport council:

Sport Councils in the United Kingdom (Great Britain)

Sport in the UK takes its direction from a wide range of organizations including national and local government, Sports Councils, national governing bodies of sport, and specialist organizations, not to mention the many schools and clubs at a local level, across all corners of the United Kingdom. The system for administering sport has evolved over many years. Many of the world's sports have their roots in Britain and the structures in place today have developed over time as both participation and competition in sport grew ever more popular.

At Government level, policy direction is provided through the Department for Culture, Media, and Sport and the administrations through:

- The Department for Environment, Sport, and Culture in Scotland
- The Department of Education and Culture in Wales
- The Department of Culture, Arts, and Leisure in Northern Ireland

These Departments oversee the work of their respective Home Country Sports Councils - the bodies responsible for coordinating sport at all levels including performance and development as well as facilities.

The Home Country Sports Councils are:
- Sport England

- Sport Scotland
- Sports Council for Wales
- Sports Council for Northern Ireland

UK Sport co-ordinates overall policy, the support of elite sport at the UK level as well as UK-wide programs such as anti-doping and major events. In addition, it manages the international relationships of the UK and coordinates a UK-wide approach to any international issues. UK Sport is funded by, and responsible to, the Department for Culture, Media, and Sport.

The Sports Councils form an important link between Government policy-makers, at both a national and local authority level, and the numerous sports organizations serving a diverse range of sports and specialist interests. The enormous network of sports clubs throughout the UK are administered through their own national governing bodies (NGBs) of sport. These NGBs form the focal point for their sport providing the link between recreation and development, training and competition, as well as facility and policy development. The NGBs are responsible for representing their members' interests to their sport's international federation as well as implementing and overseeing new policies.

San Diego International Sports Council

The mission of the San Diego International Sports Council (SDISC) is to promote San Diego/Tijuana as the preferred region for sporting events and activities that benefit our community both socially and economically. Founded as the Greater San Diego Sports Association (GSDSA) with ten members in 1960, this organization was one of the first civic sports associations in America. However, to meet the challenges of a growing and changing sports industry, the GSDSA reorganized as the San Diego International Sports Council in 1995 (http://www.sdisc.com).

The SDISC has delivered more than $1 billion in economic impact by staging many of the world's best sporting events including: Foot Locker Cross Country Championships, NAIA Volleyball Championships, NCAA Basketball Championships, ESPN X Games, America's Cup, Major League Soccer All-Star Game, Major League Baseball All-Star Game, and NFL Super Bowls XXII, XXXII and XXXVII, to name just a few (http://www.sdisc.com).

Further, the SDISC seeks to attract sporting events of national and/or international significance. The staff reviews bid opportunities that are appropriate for San Diego's venues, climate, economy, and community interests. By utilizing San Diego's venues for these events, SDISC can further promote activity at these facilities. Some events are specifically bid so that we may further utilize a facility to increase its use and make it more financially sound. It also creates an effect of attracting more San Diegans to these venues for local events.

The SDISC also works with our local professional and collegiate programs to ensure their future success. This support comes in the area of public relations, sponsorship, ticket promotion, special functions, and securing events that will lead to their long-term success. By further involving the local community with these organizations, San Diego's sports organizations will continue to thrive.

Oakville Sports Council

The Oakville Sports Council is a partnership of community sport organizations that work cooperatively to provide a collective voice for sport in Oakville. We do this through:

- Fostering and promoting good sportsmanship through training and education,
- Providing leadership and a voice for collective sport initiatives, and

- Facilitating and developing networking, communication, and cooperation in the sport community (http://www.eteamz.active.com/oakvillesportscouncil/index.cfm?).

We promote the benefits of sport within the Town of Oakville by:

- Liaising between amateur sport, the Department of Recreation and Culture, and the Parks and Recreation Advisory Committee,
- Providing funding assistance on behalf of the Town of Oakville to member sport groups through the Development Grant Fund, and
- Promoting the values of commitment, fair play, and teamwork to create a unified sport community (http://www.eteamz.active.com/oakvillesportscouncil/index.cfm?).

Sport Foundations

Sport foundations are private nonprofit tax-exempted foundations that raise and distribute funds for sporting activities. The foundation is managed by its own trustees and directors. It is established to further sport activities by making grants available. The foundation receives its funds from, and is subject to control of, an individual family, corporation, or other group of limited number (http://www.yscf.org/glossary.html).

The following are examples of sport foundations.

Florida Sports Foundation

The Florida Sports Foundation, Inc. is the official sports promotion and development organization for the State of Florida. The Foundation is a private, nonprofit tax-exempted corporation operating under contract with the Office of Tourism, Trade, and Economic Development under the Ex-

ecutive Office of the Governor. The Foundation functions as a private entity and is overseen by a board of directors appointed by the governor and fifteen board of directors appointed from the private sector.

With an endless list of sporting ventures, the Florida Sports Foundation strives to globally promote Florida's unique sports industry. Located in Tallahassee, the Foundation's staff is dedicated to serving the needs and interests of Florida's sports community and remains available to assist with any questions concerning Florida sporting activities (http://www.flasports.com).

Women's Sports Foundation

The Women's Sports Foundation is an educational not-for profit tax-exempted corporation founded in 1974 by tennis legend Billie Jean King so that girls following in her footsteps would not have to face the barriers she faced playing sports. The foundation's mission is to advance the lives of girls and women through sports and physical activity.

The Foundation's advocacy efforts have directly affected the amount of scholarship dollars supporting educational opportunities for female student-athletes in the United States. In 1972, women received only $100,000 but now receive more than $372 million a year. Further, the Foundation's support of national laws prohibiting sex discrimination has resulted in an increase in high school girls' varsity sports participation from one in 27 in 1972 to one in 2.5 girls in 2002 (http://www.womensportfoundation.org).

It is one of the top five public grant-giving women's funds in the USA; the Foundation distributes $10-20,000 dollars per week to girls' and women's sports programs, researchers, student-athletes, and leaders in women's sports. In the 2000, 2002, and 2004 Olympic Games, 58 of the female athletes competing received Travel and Training grants from the Foundation and 15 medals were earned by the grantees (http://www.womensportfoundation.org).

Joy of Sports Foundation

The Joy of Sports Foundation (JSF), a nonprofit tax-exempted corporation founded in 1989. It has since served over 30,000 children. The JSF mission is to inspire at-risk children to grow healthy in body, mind, and spirit by teaching them critical life success skills through sports. Utilizing a variety of sport-based educational programs, we currently serve children in the Washington, D.C., San Francisco, and San Diego metropolitan areas (http://www.joyofsports.org).

JSF programs have been recognized as models by the President's Council on Physical Fitness and Sports, the U.S. Department of Health and Human Services Head Start Bureau, the Boys & Girls Clubs of America, and the United States Tennis Association. The White House has also recognized JSF as a Point of Light in appreciation of our service to at-risk children. Generous support from foundations, government, corporations, and private individuals has fueled our continued growth over the past sixteen years—enabling JSF to make a significant and lasting positive impact in the lives of thousands of disadvantaged children in the communities we serve.

JSF has a 16-year track record of developing and implementing programs which effectively help children develop key life skills through sports. Through our tennis, soccer, basketball, and multi-sport programs, including our award-winning Healthy Kids Program, JSF teaches children critical life success skills proven to positively enhance their school performance and ability to attain personal goals. In addition, we address the alarming childhood obesity epidemic by teaching healthy lifestyle choices, including nutritional awareness and the value of an active lifestyle.

Progress of all JSF program participants is evaluated by an outside consultant to ensure the quality and success of our efforts. Formal evaluations by a professor at Harvard Medical School show that our programs are working. For instance, our Healthy Kids program in San Diego achieved a virtually unprecedented 22 percent reduction in obesity. Children participating in our programs consistently:

- Increase their self-confidence and fitness,
- Build key life skills such as concentration, cooperation, and relaxation, and
- Adopt healthier lifestyles and diets. (http://www.joyofsports.org).

JSF programs focus on teaching life skills development and healthy behaviors to at-risk children ages three to 13. Our "Seeing the Star In Every Child" approach helps kids discover the joy of physical activity without pressure to perform or compete. Children who had previously been inactive and had low self-esteem are instilled with a love of sports and a new belief in themselves. We are proud to have such a strong track record of delivering high impact sports-based educational programs (http://www.joyofsports.org).

Greater New Orleans Sports Foundation

Organized in August 1988, the Greater New Orleans Sports Foundation (GNOSF) is a nonprofit tax-exempted corporation. The GNOSF mission is to attract and manage sporting events that have a positive economic impact on the Greater New Orleans area. Since 1988, the GNOSF has turned a $25 Million investment, from public and private sources, into a $1 Billion Economic impact (http://www.gnosf.org).

Sacramento Sports Education Foundation

The Sacramento Sports Education Foundation (SRSEF) is a non-profit, charitable organization funded through private and corporate donations and formed to foster, support, and develop amateur sports within the Sacramento region. SRSEF provides necessary administrative and logistical support to sporting events held in Sacramento and encourages youth interest and participation in sports by displaying educational exhibits and providing instructive clinics for community youth (http://www.srsef.org).

Challenges for State or Community Sport Support Structures

There are two major challenges that face state and community sport support structures nationally. These challenges are donor fatigue and the decline of volunteerism. These can be critical to the success of these structures because without adequate revenue streams or numbers of loyal volunteers they cannot survive in the future.

Donor Fatigue

In the last decade, the number of nonprofit organizations has increased dramatically nationwide. The increase of these new organizations and the impact of 9-11 and major natural disasters (e.g., Tsunami, Florida hurricanes, and Hurricane Katrina) have caused an alarming amount of donor fatigue. The corporate and particularly individual donors are beginning to prioritize their giving, which causes a decline to the donation revenue stream for all nonprofit organizations.

For example, one of the most successful fundraising nonprofits in the United States is the American Red Cross. It has successfully raised billions of dollars for major disasters in Florida, the Gulf Coast region, California, and many other locations but its 775-chapter network is struggling to keep its head above water to keep the doors open. In 2007, the chapter network will suffer a $25 million loss and some chapters will

either close their doors or be merged into a healthier chapter nearby. In the past 20 years, the chapter network has gone from nearly 3,000 chapters to the current 775, which will most likely drop to 737 before the end of fiscal year 2008.

Another example is the challenge that the United Way of America is experiencing. A very small percentage of United Ways are achieving their fundraising goals. Many United Ways are merging into bigger and healthier United Ways to better position themselves for the continuing fundraising challenges of the future.

The nonprofit fundraisers of the future are going to need to become much more focused and creative to combat donor fatigue. The number of nonprofits competing for the finite amount of donors will continue to increase. The donor base will also need to dramatically increase to meet the challenge. Two questions must be asked: (a) How can the donor base be increased? (b) How can the amount of each donors contribution be increased on an annual basis?

Declining Volunteer Ethic

The World War II generation has been called by many as the founding generation for volunteerism. They gave birth to the largest generation this country has yet to see, the "Baby Boomers." The "baby boomers" continued their parents' love for volunteerism but failed miserably to pass on the volunteer ethic to their children. Their children have become the generation who asks "What is in it for me" rather than "How can I help?" The volunteer movement has lost at least one if not two generations to this negative view of volunteerism. It is easy and alarming to see when you belong to a nonprofit board or organization. The number of young folks is very small. The gray or white heads out number the young folks easily by 4:1. Today's environment is not healthy for generating volunteerism. As long as the attitude prevails of "What is in it for me?" and they expect to be reimbursed for all expenses and more, recruiting volunteers will be very difficult.

Within the next 10 to 20 years, the number of available volunteers will be dropping rapidly. The crisis is very near and the nonprofit must begin preparing themselves for the massive short-fall of volunteers. They must answer at least four very key questions: What is the value of being a volunteer? Why should I volunteer? How should volunteers be recruited? How can volunteers be retained?

Summary

Many communities and states in the United States have established a community or state sport support structure. These support structures have been designed to promote sport within the community or state. Further, a number of these structures are nonprofit tax deductible organizations to raise funds for specific sports or youth. Generally, these structures are known as sport authorities, commissions, corporations, councils, or foundations. Finally, there is one sport support structure known as a congress that brings together leaders to talk about specific sport issues and make recommendations.

There are two major challenges that face state and community sport support structures nationally. These challenges are donor fatigue and the decline of volunteerism. These can be critical to the success of these structures because without adequate revenue streams or numbers of loyal volunteers they cannot survive in the future.

References

http://www.commonwealthgames.com. (2006).
http://www.eteamz.active.com/oakvillesportcouncil/index.cfm
http://www.flasports.com. (2006).
http://www.fwsportscopr.org. (2007).
http://www.gnosf.org. (2007).
http://www.ico.org.
http://www.joyofsports.org. (2006).
http://louisvillesports.org.
http://www.lubbocksports.org. (2006).
http://www.msa.com. (2006).
http://www.msfc.com. (2006).
http://www.oregonsports.org. (2006).
http://www.sacsports.com. (2006).
http://www.srsef.org.
http://www.sdisc.com. (2006).
http://www.sjsa.org. (2006).
http://www.sportscommission.org. (2006).
http://www.sportsbusinessconferences.com (2007).
http://www/thecgf.com (2006).
http://www.thesportscorp.org (2007).
www.yscf.org/glossary.html (2006).
http://www.womensportfoundation.org (2006).

 NOTES

INDEX

501(c)3 corporations, 11

A

AAA (American Automobile Association), 227
AAPAR (American Association for Physical
    Activity and Recreation), 154–155
AAU (Amateur Athletic Union), 112, 113, 115–116
ACA (American Corrections Association), 153, 155
academic eligibility
    in intercollegiate sports,184–186
    in interscholastic sports, 137–138
    NCAA policy, 57
accessibility issues in recreational sports, 158–159
accountability and leadership, 15
    of policies, 50–51
ADA (Americans with Disabilities Act), 100,158–159
administrative function of governing bodies, 47
adult intrusion into youth sports, 117
AFL (American Football League), 219
AFL (Arena Football League), 204
age eligibility in interscholastic sports, 138
agenda setting in policy development, 54
agents
    in intercollegiate sports, 192–193
    Uniform Athlete Agent Act, 94
AIAW (Intercollegiate Athletics for Women),
    186–187
air racing, 233, 236
ALA (American Logistics Association), 153–154, 156
alcohol
    in intercollegiate sports, 191
    selling, ethical considerations, 74–75
AMA (American Motorcyclist Association),
    235–236
Amateur Athletic Union (AAU), 112, 113
amateur sports categories (fig.), 6
Amateur Sports Act (1978), 94–95, 96, 100, 254

Amateur Sports Act of 1973 (USOC), 246
amateurism
    in intercollegiate sports, 192
    in interscholastic sports, 135
    and Olympic Games, 254–256
American Association for Physical Activity and
    Recreation (AAPAR), 154–155
American Automobile Association (AAA), 227
American Civil Liberties Union, 98
American Corrections Association (ACA), 153, 155
American Football League (AFL), 219
American Logistics Association (ALA), 153–154, 156
American Motorcyclist Association (AMA), 235–236
Americans with Disabilities Act (1990), 100, 158–159
amphetamine drug use, 189
analysis
    policy, 43
    situational, 31–32
androstenedione, 217–218
antitrust legislation, 95, 208
appeals
    to intercollegiate sport organizations, 181–183
    process, Olympic Games, 254–256
    Senior Olympics/Senior Games, 304
    by youth sport organizations, 115–116
appraisals of existing facilities, programs, 24
arena financing issues, 105–106
Arena Football League (AFL), 204
Association for Intercollegiate Athletics for Women
    (A.I.A.W.), 167
associations
    See also specific association
    governing bodies for recreational sport, 153–154
    international sport federations (table), 244–246
athletic associations, impacts of government on,
    93–105

audits, social, 84–85
authorities, sports, 310–313
authority
    See also governing bodies
    of intercollegiate sport organizations, 178
    of organizations (legal), 10–11
    Olympic Games, 252–253
    for recreational sport, 153, 154
    Senior Olympics/Senior Games, 303
    of youth sport organizations, 113–114
autoracing
    See also motorsports
    categories of, 226–230
    sanctioning bodies, 234–236

B

Baade, Richard, 212
Baade, Robert, 211
banned substances
    conflicts between governing bodies on, 43
    doping, 255, 263–264, 283
    drug testing. See drug testing
    in intercollegiate sports, 188–191
    interscholastic sport issues, 145–146
    IOC's testing policy, 48–49
    NCAA's policy, 57–58
    in Paralympics sports, 283
    in professional sports, 217–218
    testing, and constitutional issues, 98
bargaining and decision making, 56
baseball
    history of professional, 200
    women's, 201
    basketball
    "basketbrawl," 78
    and the NCAA, 166–167
    women's, 201
behavioral theories of leadership, 18
Beijing 2008 Olympic Games, 258
beliefs, and ethics, 64–65
benefits, as policy instrument, 50
Birkland, T.A., 48
blackouts, 210
boards of directors in organizations, 11
boccia, 281–282
Bodey, Kimberly J., xiii
book, organization of this, vii–viii
Bowl Championship Series, 167
brainstorming, 21–22
Brand, Myles, 47, 192

broadcasting rights
    legal issues, and athletic associations, 103–104
    NCAA's policy, 49–50
    of Olympic Games, 256–257
    professional sports issues, 198, 209–210
Brundage, Avery, 249, 254
Buckley Amendment, 98
budgets, 29
Burke, Anne, 287
burnout in youth sports, 117–118
Bush, George W., 292–293
business law, and athletic associations, 96–98
Byer, Walter, 167
bylaws of athletic associations, 114

C

Cable Television Consumer Protection and
    Competition Act (1992), 210
caffeine, 189
Canadian Interuniversity Sport (CIS), 167–168
CART (Championship Auto Racing Teams), 227
    228, 235–236
CAS (Court of Arbitration for Sport), 255–256
Cavanaugh's model of ethical decision making,
    74–75
CBA (Collective Bargaining Agreement) and NBA
    Salary Cap, 99
Champ Car, 228
Championship Auto Racing Teams (CART), 227
    228, 235–236
cheating in interscholastic sports, 135–136
children
    See also youth sport
    educational disruption from sport, 120–121
Christian colleges, 169
churches and recreational sport, 153, 154
CIS (Canadian Interuniversity Sport), 167–168
civil rights
    See also women
    and Buckley Amendment, 98
    discrimination issues, enforcement, 100–101
Clayton Act (1914), 96
coaches
    intrusion into youth sports, 117–118
    training in youth sport, 118
codes of ethics, conduct
    described, examples of, 86–88
    in intercollegiate sports, 194
collective bargaining in professional sports, 210
Collective Bargaining Agreement (CBA) and NBA
    Salary Cap, 99

collective decision making, 56

college sports. See intercollegiate sports

Colorado Springs Sports Corporation, 317

commercial recreational sport businesses, 152–153, 161

commissions, sport, 313–314

communication and ethics, 68

community, social responsibility and, 83

community sport support structures, 309–322

conduct, codes of, 86–87

congresses, sport, 314–316

constitutional issues, impact on athletic associations, 98

constitutions of organizations, 114

contingency-situational leadership theories, 18

contract law, and athletic associations, 99

Copyright Act (1976), 208

copyright law, and athletic associations, 104

corporate social responsibility, 83–84

corporate sponsorships of Special Olympics, 294

corporations
    described, 10–11
    recreational sport in, 152
    sport, 316–317

corrections, and recreational sport, 151

costs. See funding

councils, sport, 317–319

Court of Arbitration for Sport (CAS), 255–256

cultural diversity, and ethics, 71

curriculum, NASPE/NASSM standards, vii

Curtin, Phil, 143

D

Daley, Mayor Richard, 287

data collection for needs assessment surveys, 23

Deaflympics, 274–276

decision making
    ethical, in organizations, 67
    and organizational ethics, 78–79
    and policy adoption, 55–57
    and policy development, 42–43

decisions analysis, 10

delegation in planning process, 33–34

demographic data for needs assessment surveys, 23

departmentalization in organizations, 9

developing
    objectives, 31
    policies. See policy development
    programs, 29–30
    teams, 34–35

deviance in interscholastic sports, 136

directive power as policy instrument, 50

disabilities
    See also Paralympic sports, Special Olympics
    accessibility issues in recreational sport, 158–159
    legal issues, and athletic associations, 99–100
    senior citizens with, 306
    Stevens Amendment, Amateur Sports Act, 95
    University of New Hampshire, Northeast Passage Program, 119–120
    and youth sport, 118, 120

Disabled Sports USA, 276

discrimination
    See also women
    in athletic associations, 100–101
    equity in interscholastic sports, 139–141

distributive policy, 45–46

documentation
    needs assessment reports, 25
    situational analysis, 31–32
    strategic plans, 30–31
    writing strategic plans, 33

Donaldson, T., 82

donor fatigue, 321

doping, 255, 263–264, 283

drag boat racing, 232

drag (car) racing, 226–227

drug testing
    See also banned substances
    doping, 255, 263–264, 283
    in intercollegiate sports, 189–191
    in interscholastic sports, 145–146
    legal issues, and athletic associations, 101–102
    at Olympics, 262–264

Dye, Richard, 211

E

economics
    professional sports team revenues, 207–208
    and social responsibility, 84

education. See high school athletics, intercollegiate sports
    academic eligibility in interscholastic sports,137–138
    youth coaching, 118

Education for all Handicapped Children Act (1975), 100

effectiveness of policies, 50–51

eligibility
    issues in intercollegiate sports, 184–186
    issues in interscholastic sports, 136–139
    NCAA Initial-Eligibility Clearinghouse, 192

Paralympics sports, 280–281
elite youth athletes, 120–121
Employee Services Management Association
    (ESM), 154, 156
employment diversity in professional sports,
    210–211
enforcement of rules in intercollegiate sports,
    191–192
environments, organizational, 10
equity in interscholastic sports, 139–141
ESM (Employee Services Management
    Association), 154, 156
Esman, R.G., Jr., 22
ethics, ethical issues
    See also organizational ethics
    codes of ethics, conduct, 85–88
    and decision making in organizations, 67
    defined, 66, 79
    dilemmas and conflicts, 66–67
    foundations of ethical conduct, 68–69
    in framework of organizational ethics, 80–81
    guidelines to ethical behavior, 72–75
    key terms, definitions, 64–67
    principles of ethical leadership, 69–72
evaluating policies, 58–59
event management in recreational sports, 161–162

F

F1 Powerboat Racing, 232–233
FA Premier League (soccer), 205
facilities
    appraisals of existing, 24
    competition for recreational sport, 160–161
    conducting needs assessment surveys, 22–25
    financing of professional sport, 211–212
    maintenance of, 9
    public funding of sports, 105–106
Family Educational Rights and Privacy Act of 1974,
    98
fantasy sports, and intellectual property rights, 103
federations, international sport (table), 244–246
Ferrell, O.C., 80, 88
FILOP method for guiding ethical behavior, 73–74
financing
    See also funding
    of Olympic Games, 256–257
    stadium and arena, 105–106, 211–212
Florida Sports Foundation, 319
football and the NCAA, 166, 167
for-profit companies, 11
forests, and recreational sport, 152

formal vs. informal policy, 44–45
formalization in organizations, 8
Formula One air racing, 233
Formula One auto racing, 228
Fort Wayne Sports Commission, 316
foundations, sport, 319–321
franchises, locating professional, 213–214
free choice, organizational ethics and, 79–80
Freeberg, Dr. William, 287
funding
    college athletics, 187–188
    donor fatigue, 321
    intercollegiate sport organizations, 183–184
    interscholastic sports, 141–143
    motorsports, 236
    professional sports team revenues, 207–208
    recreational sport, 159–160
    recreational sport programs, 153
    Senior Olympics/Senior Games, 304–305
    Special Olympics, 289, 293–294
    stadium and arena, 105–106
    youth sport programs, 116

G

gambling
    athletic associations' issues, 102
    policies in intercollegiate sports, 188
    in professional sports, 214, 216
Gatlin, Justin, 264
gender discrimination, 100–101
gender equity
    in intercollegiate sport organizations, 186–187
    in interscholastic sports, 140
    women in professional sports, 200–202
George, Tony, 229
Global Compact, 82
goals
    and objectives of organizations, 27
    policy, 48–49
    in situational analysis, 32
golf associations, 203
governance, 11–13
    described, good governance
    intercollegiate sports, 169–184
    motorsports, 233–234
    Olympic Games, 242–243, 246, 248–250
    Paralympics sports, 270
    of professional sports, 205–207
    recreational sport, 150–153
    Senior Olympics/Senior Games, 298–301
    Special Olympics, 287–289

youth sport, 112–116
governing bodies
    See also specific governing body
    and governance, 11–13
    intercollegiate sport governance, 166–169
    interscholastic sport, 129–131
    introduction to, 3–4, 19
    motorsports, 224–226, 234–236
    National Federation of State High School
        Associations (NFHS), 7
    NGBs (National Governing Bodies), 243–244
    Olympic Games, 242–256
    open wheel racing, 227–229
    and organizational context, 5
    policy development. See policy development
    promotion vs. regulation of sport, 12
    recreational sport, 153–158
    USOC sport (table), 247–248
    youth sport, identification of, 109–112
government
    impact on athletic associations, 93–105, 93–94
    local, and recreational sport governance, 150–151
grades. See academic eligibility
Grand American Road Racing Association, 229
Grand Prix racing, 228–229
Grand Prix Truck Racing, 231
Greater Louisville Sports Commission, 314
Greater New Orleans Sports Foundation, 320
Green, T., 65
guidelines to ethical behavior, 72–75

H
Hagiwara, Mikiko, 201
high school athletics
    eligibility in interscholastic sports, 137–138
    funding, 141–143
    and interscholastic sport governance, 127–128
higher education and college sports, 165
Holder, Marc, 260
home schoolers, and interscholastic sports equity,
    140–141
home taping sports broadcasts, 209–210
honesty, and ethics, 68
Hunt and Vitell model of ethical decision making, 67
Hunt, Lamar, 217
hydroplane racing, 232

I
IAAF (International Association of Athletics
    Federation), 243
IAAUS (Intercollegiate Athletic Association of the
    United States), 166

ICAS (International Council of Arbitration for
    Sport), 255
IHRSA (International Health, Racquet, and
    Sportsclub Association), 154, 157
IMG World Sport Congress, 315
Independent League Baseball, 202
Indiana Sports Corporation (ISC), 316
Indiana State University, workers' compensation
    issue, 105
Individuals with Disabilities Education Act (IDEA)
    (1990), 100
industries
    described, 4
    sport. *See* sport industry
Indy Racing League (IRL), 228–229
informal vs. formal policy, 44–45
injuries
    in recreational sports, 162
    risk, in youth sports, 122
instruments, policy, 50–51
intellectual disabilities, 285, 294
intellectual property rights, legal issues, 102–103,
    208–209
Intercollegiate Athletic Association of the United
    States (IAAUS). See IAAUS
Intercollegiate Athletics for Women. See AIAW
intercollegiate sports
    governance and organizational structure, 169–
    184
    governing bodies generally, 166–169
issues in, 184–194
    overview of, 165
interest groups and policy development, 48
International Association of Athletics Federation
    (IAAF), 243
International Council of Arbitration for Sport
    (ICAS), 255
International Federations, 243
International Health, Racquet, and Sportsclub
    Association (IHRSA), 154, 157
International Olympic Committee. See IOC
International Paralympic Committee (IPC), 268–
    273, 282
International Speedway Corporation (ISC), 224
international sport federations (table), 244–246
International Sports Federations, 292
International Youth Sports Congress, 316
Internet broadcast rights, 209
interscholastic sport governance
    athletic issues, 135–146
    high school athletics, 127–128
    policy areas, 134–135

structures, functions, authority, funding, 131–134
value of programs, 128–129
IOC (International Olympic Committee)
    See also Olympic Games
    corporate sponsorship policy, 41
    governance function, 249–254
    organizational chart (fig.), 250
    overview of, 242–243, 256–264
    and Paralympics, 279–280
    Salt Lake City scandal, 52
    as Special Olympics partner, 291–292
IPC (International Paralympic Committee), 268–273, 282
IRL (Indy Racing League), 228–229
ISC (Indiana Sports Corporation), 316
ISC (International Speedway Corporation), 225–226

J

jet sprint boat racing, 232
Johnson, Dave, 259, 260
Johnson, Robert, 211
Jordan, Michael, 48, 199
JSF (Joy of Sports Foundation), 320
Judge, Lawrence W., xiv
judicial function of governing bodies, 47
junior colleges, 168–169
Junior Olympics Sports Program, 111
jurisdiction of governing bodies, 12
justice, and ethical leadership, 70

K

Kennedy Foundation, 286–287
Kennedy, John F., 16
Kennedy, Mrs. and Mrs. Joseph P., 286
Kerns, C.D., 71
King, Billie Jean, 199
Kohlberg, L., 80

L

labor law
    collective bargaining, 210
legal issues, and athletic associations, 103
    and professional sports, 208
lacrosse associations, 203
Ladies League Baseball, 201
Ladies Professional Bowlers Tour (LPBT), 200
Ladies Professional Golf Association (LPGA), 200
Lanham Act of 1964 (trademark law), 102–103, 208

Las Vegas, and major leagues, 214
law
    See also legislation, and specific law
    impact of government on athletic associations, 93–105
    organizational ethics and, 79–80
Le Mans road racing series, 229
leadership
    defined, 13–15
    ethical, 85–86
    facility and event manager qualities, 15–17
    principles of ethical, 69–72
    Special Olympics issue, 293–294
    types and theories of, 17–19
legal
    See also law
    authority of organizations, 10–11
legislation
    See also specific law
    impacting professional sports, 208–209
legislative function of governing bodies, 47
Lewis, Carl, 263
licensing, 50
life-cycle leadership theory, 18
limited liability corporations (LLCs), 113–114
Little League baseball, 111
Lombardi, Vince, 217–218
long-range plans, 28
longevity rules (age eligibility), 138–139
LPBT (Ladies Professional Bowlers Tour), 200
LPGA (Ladies Professional Golf Association), 200
LSA (Lubbock Sports Authority), 312
Lubbock Sports Authority (LSA), 312

M

Machiavelli, Niccolo, 41
Major League Baseball, 200, 202
management
    See also sports managers
    in organizations, 11
    summary of functions, 19
    vs. governance, 13, 13–14
    vs. leadership, 17
Martin, Casey, 99–100
Maryland Sports Authority (MSA), 311
Master Settlement Agreement (MSA), tobacco industry, 237–238
material policy vs. symbolic policy, 45
Mattel Children's Foundation, 291

McGwire, Mark, 217
media
    See also broadcasting rights
    and policy development, 48, 54
    revenues to professional sports, 207
membership
    intercollegiate sport organizations, 178–181
    IOC, USOC, 253–254
    Olympic sports, 252–253
    Senior Olympics/Senior Games, 303–304
    youth sport organizations, 115
military
    ALA (American Logistics Association), 156
    authority for recreational sports entities, 154
    Morale, Welfare, and Recreation (MWR) Services, 151
Minor League Baseball, 200, 202
minor league systems governance, 206–207
mission statements in situational analysis, 31–32
MLB (Major League Baseball)
    franchise and league issues, 218–219
    governance, 206
    intellectual property rights over baseball statistics, 103
    Pete Rose ban, 214, 216
    player salaries, 216
models
    causal, for policy response, 49
    decision making, 67
    of ethical decision making, 67
    leadership, 18–19
    stage, of policy development, 51–59
moral agents, 66
    Morale, Welfare, and Recreation (MWR) Services in military, 151
morals and ethics, 65–66
motocross (motorcycle racing), 230, 235–236
motorboat racing, 231–233
motorcycle racing, 230
motorsports
    autoracing categories, 226–230
    governing bodies, 224–226
    issues in, 236–238
    NASCAR. See NASCAR
    overview of, 223–224
    sanctioning bodies, 234–236
    types of, 230–234
MSA (Maryland Sports Authority), 311
MWR (Morale, Welfare, and Recreation) Services in military, 151
MX racing, 230

N
NAIA (National Association of Intercollegiate Athletics), 168
    function of, 175–176
    funding of, 183–184
    membership requirements, 180–181
    organizational structure, 171–173
    sanctions, appeal process, 182
NAIB (National Association of Intercollegiate Basketball), 168
naming rights, 207
NASC (National Association of Sports Commissioners), 313–314
NASCAR (National Association for Stock Car Auto Racing)
    growth of, 238–240
    organizational culture, 10
    Paris to Rouen 1894, 223
    sanctioning motorsport body, 234–235
    stock car racing, 230
Nashville Metropolitan Sports Authority, 311–312
NASPE/NASSM curriculum standards, vii
NASPE (National Association for Sport and Physical Education), 154, 157
National Alliance for Youth Sports (NAYS), 121–122
National Association for Sport and Physical Education (NASPE), 154, 157
National Association for Stock Car Auto Racing. *See* NASCAR
National Association of Intercollegiate Athletics (NAIA). *See* NAIA
National Association of Intercollegiate Basketball (NAIB), 168
National Association of Sports Commissioners (NASC), 313–314
National Basketball Association. See NBA
National Center for Drug Free Sport, 190
National Christian College Athletic Association. *See* NCCAA
National Disability Sports Alliance (NDSA), 276
National Federation of State High School Associations (NFHS), 7, 146
National Football League. See NFL
National Governing Bodies (NGBs), 243–244
National Hockey League. See NHL
National Hot Rod Association (NHRA), 226, 235
National Intramural-Recreational Sport Association (NIRSA), 154, 157–158
National Junior College Athletic Association. *See* NJCAA

National Olympic Committees (NOCs), 242, 243, 257–258

National Pro Fastpitch, 204

National Recreation and Park Association (NRPA), 154, 158, 298

National Senior Games Association (NSGA), 299–306

NAYS (National Alliance for Youth Sports), 121–122

NBA (National Basketball Association), 197
    and drafting high school players, 206
    franchise and league issues, 219
    history of, 202–203
    player salaries, 216
    Salary Cap, 99

NBA v. Motorola, Inc., 210

NCAA (National College Athletics Association)
    academic eligibility issue, 185–186
    banned substances, 189
    broadcasting rights, 104
    Division I conferences (table), 180
    drug testing, 190
    function of, 175–177
    membership requirements, 178–180
    organizational structure, 11, 170–171
    overview of, 166–167
    and policy implementation, 57
    and policy parameters, 43
    public policy of, 43–44
    rules enforcement, 191–192
    sanctions, appeals process, 181–182
    Youth Leadership Program, 194

NCAA Clearinghouse, 47

NCCAA (National Christian College Athletic Association), 169
    function of, 178
    funding of, 184
    membership requirements, 181
    organizational structure, 174–175
    sanctions, appeal process, 182

NDSA (National Disability Sports Alliance), 276

needs assessment surveys, reports, 22–25

NFHS (National Federation of State High School Associations)
    organizational structure and, 7
    proactive drug prevention, 146

NFL (National Football League), 197
    and antitrust legislation, 97
    franchise and league issues, 219
    history of, 202
    ownership restrictions, 217
    player salaries, 216
    team issues, 211–214

NFL Europe League, 202

NGBs (National Governing Bodies), 243–244

NHL (National Hockey League), 197, 199, 200, 204–205
    and drafting high school players, 206–207
    franchise and league issues, 219–220
    history of, 203
    player salaries, 216
    team issues, 213–214
    2004-2005 player lockout, 104

NHRA (National Hot Rod Association), 226, 235

NIRSA (National Intramural-Recreational Sport Association), 154, 157–158

NJCAA (National Junior College Athletic Association), 168–169
    function of, 176
    funding of, 184
    membership requirements, 181
    organizational structure, 173–174
    sanctions, appeal process, 182–183

NOCs (National Olympic Committees), 242, 243, 257–258

nonprofit companies, 11, 151–152, 300

nonprofit sport authorities, 312–313

Northeast Passage (NEP) program, Univ. of New Jersey, 119–120

NRPA (National Recreation and Park Association), 154, 158, 298

NSCA Code of Ethics (fig.), 86

NSGA (National Senior Games Association), 297–306

nutritional supplements, 188–191

O

Oakville Sports Council, 318–319

objectives, planning, 26, 31

officers
    ethics, 88
    in organizations, 11

offshore powerboat racing, 232

Olympic Congresses, 315

Olympic Games
    financing of, 256–257
    function, authority, membership, 251–253
    governance, 242–243, 246, 248–250
    host city selection, 257–258
    issues in, 256–264

overview of, 241
    policy jurisdiction and conflicts, 41–42

sanctions, appeal process, 254–256
security at, 260
substance abuse issue, 262–264
USOC sport governing bodies (table), 247–248
Olympic Partner (TOP) program, 41, 262
open wheel racing, 227–229
organizational culture, design, 8–10
organizational ethics
    introduction to, 77–82
    social responsibility, 83–85
organizations
    See also specific organization or association
    described, 4, 5, 13
    ethical, 85–86
    and framework of organizational ethics, 81
    governance, 11–12
    impacting, organizing youth sport (table), 111
    leader types, theories, 17–19
    leadership skill mastery, 14–17
    legal authority and jurisdiction, 10–11
    need for management, 13–14
organizational behavior and culture, 5–8
organizational structure of AAU (chart), 113
    planning function, 21–36
    sports authorities, commissions, etc., 105–106
    structural elements of organizational design, 8–10
    youth sport (table), 110
Osborn, Alexander F., 21
ownership restrictions, professional sports, 216–217

P

Paralympics sports
    affiliated sports (fig.), 277–278
    Deaflympics, 274–276
    disability categories, governance, 270, 272–273
    Disabled Sports USA, NDSA, 276
    history of, 268
    IPC, governance, 268–270
    issues in, 279–283
    military program, 274
    overview of, 267
    United States Paralympics, 273–274
parents, youth sport issues with, 123–124
Paris to Rouen 1894, 223
participation
    data collection for needs assessment surveys, 23
    in interscholastic sports, 137–139
    in youth sports, 109–110
partnerships, as organization type, 10
pay-to-play interscholastic sports, 142–143

performance
    enhancement in intercollegiate sports, 188–191
    teams, 34
performance-enhancers. See banned substances
Person-Situation Interactionist Model of decision making, 67
persuasion as policy instrument, 56–57
PGA (Professional Golf Association), 99–100
piracy, 210
plane racing, 233
planning
    function described, 13, 21–22, 36
    needs assessment surveys, reports, 22–25
    objectives and pitfalls, 31–34
    plan classification, 27–30
    steps in process, 25–27
    strategic, 30–31
    teams, 34–36
player salaries in professional sports, 216
policies, 39
    See also policy development
    drug-testing, in intercollegiate sports, 189–191
    evaluating, implementing, 57–59
    examples of (table), 29
    policy development, 43
    adoption, 55–57
    interscholastic sports, 134–135
    key terms, definitions, 42–44
    overview, 39–42
policy design elements, 48–51
policy types, 44–48
    stage model of, 40, 51–59
policy formation, 54–55
powerboat racing, 236
prayer, 98–99, 144
preventing drug abuse, 146
pricing, decision making about, 69
prisons, and recreational sport, 153, 155
private clubs, 151
privatization of youth sports, 121–122
problem-solving
    and stages in policy cycle, 40–41
    teams, 34–35
problems
    identifying for policy development, 51–53
    in situational analysis, 32
    solutions for common team (chart), 35
procedural policy vs. substantive policy, 45
profanity, 65
Professional and Amateur Sports Protection Act (1992), 209, 216

professional sports
    in America (table), 204
    categories of (fig.), 6
    development of, 199–200, 220
    governing bodies and governance in, 202–207
    history of women in, 200–202
    issues in, 209–220
    legislation impacting, 208–209
    overview of industry, 197–199
    team revenues, 207–208
programming, recreational sport, 149
programs
    See also specific program
    appraisals of existing, 24
    described, 29
    drug prevention, 146
    interscholastic sport, 128–129
    Senior Olympics/Senior Games, 301–303
    Special Olympics, 290–291
    youth sport, 109, 122
projects described, 29–30
public
    funding of sports facilities, 105–106, 211–212
    interest and public policy, 41
    lands, and recreational sport, 152
    youth sport programs, 122
public policy
    See also policy development
    described, 39–41, 43–44

R

rally racing, 229
recreational sport
    accessibility, funding, 158–160
    competition for facilities, 160–161
    event, injury, and risk management, 161–162
    governance, 150–153
    national governing bodies, 153–158
    overview of, 149–150
red shirting in interscholastic sports, 138–139
redistributive policy, 46
regulations, governing bodies' authority, 12
regulatory policy, 46
Rehabilitation Act (1973), 99–100
relations analysis, 10
reliability in data collection, 24
responsibility and leadership, 15
Rest. J.R., 67
return on investment (ROI), 14

revenues
    See also funding
    of Olympic Games, 256–257
    of professional sport teams, 207–208
Riggs, Bobby, 199
risk management in recreational sports, 162
road racing, 229–230
Robinson, Jackie, 199
Rogge, Jaques, 249, 262
ROI (return on investment), 14
Rokeach, M., 65
Roosevelt, Theodore, 166
Rose, Pete, 214
rules
    eligibility, 136–139
    enforcement, in intercollegiate sports, 191–194
    in organizations, 28–29

S

Sacramento Sports Commission, 314
Sacramento Sports Education Foundation, 320–321
safety
    injury and risk management in recreational
    sports, 162
    Olympic Game security, 260
    youth sport injuries, 122
salary caps, 99, 210
Salt Lake City Olympics scandal, 253, 259–260
San Diego International Sports Council (SDISC),
    318
San Jose Sports Authority, 312–313
sanctioning bodies
    See also governing bodies
    motorsports, 234–236
sanctions
    described, 50
    by intercollegiate sport organizations, 181–182
    Olympic Games, 254–256
Senior Olympics/Senior Games, 304
    by youth sport organizations, 115–116
Santa Fe Independent School District v. Jane Doe,
    98
satellite broadcast distribution, 210
Sawyer, Thomas H., xii
schools
    prayer, 144
    and recreational sport funding, 159–160
Schultz, David, 260
SDISC (San Diego International Sports Council),
    318

Senior Olympics/Senior Games
    authority, membership, funding, 303–304
    governance, 298–301
    issues in, 304–307
    mission, programming, 301–303
    overview, history, 297–298
servant leaders, 18
services, as policy instrument, 50
settings, recreational sport (chart), 150
sexual harassment, 140
Sherman Act (1890), 96
short-term plans, 28
Shriver, Eunice Kennedy, 286, 287
Shriver, Timothy P., 293
Siegfried, John J., 211
single-use plans, 29, 30
siphoning broadcasts, 209
situational analysis, 31–32
SMI (Speedway Motorsports, Inc.), 224–225
smoking, 58, 237–238
snowmobile (snocross) racing, 233, 236
soccer
    associations, 203
    popularity of, 205
    and sport specialization, 122
    women's, 201–202
social audits, 84–85
social responsibility
    managing ethics and, 85–88
organizational ethics and, 83–85
softball, women's, 201–202
sole proprietorships, 10
Special Olympics, 120, 279
    funding, sports, programs, 289–291
    issues in, 293–294
    legislation about, 292–293
    overview and history, 285–286
    partners, 291–292
Special Olympics Sport and Empowerment Act
    (2004), 292–293
Special Olympics Unified Sports, 290
specialization
    in interscholastic sports, 144–145
    sport, 122–123
    of work in organizations, 9
spectator violence, 136
Speedway Motorsports, Inc. (SMI), 224–225
sponsorship of Olympic Games, 262
sport commissions, 313–314
sport congresses, 314–316
sport corporations, 316–317

sport councils, 317–319
Sport Councils in the United Kingdom (Great
    Britain), 317–318
sport foundations, 319–321
sport governance
    See also governance
    and sport policy, 46
sport industry
    See also specific sport
    categories of (fig.), 6
    organizational types in, 10–11
segments of, 4
sport managers
    guidelines to ethical behavior, 72–75
    and policy development, 39–42
    principles of ethical leadership, 69–72
sport organizations
    See also specific organization
    governance, 3–19
    organizational ethics in, 78–82
sport services categories of (fig.), 6
sports
    agents, 94, 192–193
    amateur. See amateur sports
    authorities, commissions, congresses,
        corporations, etc., 106, 310–321
    community support structures, 309–322
    evaluation, decertification for Olympic Games,
        259–262
    international federations (table), 244–246
    Paralympics affiliates (fig.), 277–278
    professional. See professional sports
    recreational. See recreational sport
    services, 6
    as social force, 199, 220
Sports Broadcasting Act (1961), 104, 209
sports delivery sectors, 94
sports facilities. See facilities
sportsmanship
    in intercollegiate sports, 193–194
    in interscholastic sports, 145
scholarship programs for, 136
    youth sport issues with, 123–124
stadium financing issues, 105–106
stage model of policy development, 51–59
Stage Model of policy development, 51–59
standing plans, 28, 30
Stanley Cup, 214
stare decisis (let the decision stand), 56
State of New Jersey Model of Athletic Code of
    Conduct, 87

steroids
    See also banned substances, substance abuse
    in Paralympics sports, 283
Stevens, Justice John Paul, 98
Stevens, Sen. Ted, 95
stock car racing, 230
Stotlar, David K., ix
strategic planning, 30–34
substance abuse
    in interscholastic sports, 145–146
    at Olympics, 262–264
    in professional sports, 217–218
substantive policy vs. procedural policy, 45
Super Bowl, 309
Supermoto racing, 230
surveys, needs assessment, 24–25
SWOT charts, 21–22, 26
symbolic policy vs. material policy, 45

T

targets, policy, 49–50
tax exemptions for organizations, 11
teams, planning, 34–36
Ted Stevens Olympic and Amateur Sports Act
    (1998), 242, 252-254
television
    contracts with major sports, 218
    broadcasting rights, 103–104
    and NASCAR growth, 238–239
    and professional sports growth, 198
tennis
    associations, 203
    in Olympics, 254
Theories X, Y, Z (of leadership), 18
Thorpe, Jim, 254
Title IX, Educational Amendments of 1972, 100
    101, 140, 187, 282
tobacco
    sponsorship, auto and truck racing, 237–238
    use, NCAA's policy, 58
TOP (Olympic Partner) program, 41, 262
track and field, and the NCAA, 166
trademark law, 102–103
training
    ethics, 88
    for young athletes, 144–145
transfer rules, and eligibility in interscholastic sports,
    139
truck racing, 231, 234–235

U

Uniform Athlete Agent Act (2000), 94
United Kingdom, sport councils, 317–318
United Nations, and Special Olympics, 292
United States Anti-doping Agency (USADA), 256
United States Automobile Club (USAC), 235
United States Football League (USFL), 97
United States Olympic Committee. See USOC
United Way of America, 321
University of New Hampshire, Northeast Passage
    (NEP) Program, 119–120
U.S. National Olympic Committee, 242
U.S. Olympic Committee. See USOC
USA Track and Field (USATF), 243
USAC (United States Automobile Club), 235
USADA (United States Anti-doping Agency), 256,
    263–264
USATF (USA Track and Field), 243, 246
USFL (United States Football League), 97
USOC (U.S. Olympic Committee)
    and Amateur Sports Act (1978), 94
    congressional authority over, 42
    governance and function, 249–254
    Olympic sport issues, 256–264
    sanctions, appeal process, 254–256
USP (United States Paralympics), 273–274
Utah Jazz, 213

V

Van Horn, C.E., 58
Van Meter, D.S., 58
Vernonia School District v. Action, 146
Vikelas, Dimitrius, 249
violence
    in intercollegiate sports, 193–194
    in interscholastic sports, 136
    and professional sports, 218
volleyball, women's, 201
volunteer ethic, 321–322

W

WADA (World Anti-Doping Agency), 263–264
Welsh, Tom, 259, 260
Werhane, P.H., 71
WHA (World Hockey Association), 219
winning, and youth sport, 124, 143
WNBA (Women's National Basketball
    Association), 201, 202
WOA (World Olympians Association), 292
women
    discrimination issues, 100–101

employment diversity in professional sports,
210–211
gender equity, 140, 186–187
and IOC's legislative function, 47
in Paralympics sports, 282
in professional sports, historically, 200–202
sport associations, 203–204
Women's National Basketball Association
(WNBA), 201, 202
Women's Pro Fastpitch (WPF) Tour, 204
Women's Professional Fastpitch, 201
Women's Professional Volleyball Association, 201
Women's Sports Foundation, 319–320
work specialization in organizations, 9
work stoppages in major four leagues (table), 214
workers' compensation, and athletic associations,
104–105
World Anti-Doping Agency (WADA), 263–264
World Hockey Association (WHA), 219
World Olympians Association (WOA), 292
World Rally Championship (WRC), 229

X
XFL Football League, 200

Y
youth sport
governance, 112–116
identifying governing bodies, 109–112
issues, 116–123
parents and sportsmanship, 123–124

Z
Zimbalist, Andrew, 211